SHASTA & LASSEN CAMPING & HIKING

TOM STIENSTRA

At 14,162 feet, Mount Shasta rises like a

diamond in a field of coal. Its sphere of influence spans a radius of 125 miles, and its shadow is felt everywhere in the region. This area has much to offer with giant Shasta Lake, the Sacramento River above and below the lake, the McCloud River, and the wonderful Trinity Divide with its dozens of pretty backcountry lakes and several wilderness areas. This is one of the best regions anywhere for an outdoor adventure — especially hiking, fishing, powerboating, rafting, and exploring.

In this area, you can find campgrounds that are truly remote, set near quiet wilderness, and that offer the potential for unlimited adventures. Of all the regions in this book, this is the easiest one in which to find a campground in a secluded setting near great recreation opportunities. That is the main reason people visit.

There are hundreds of destinations, but the most popular are Shasta Lake, the Trinity Alps and their surrounding lakes and streams, and the Klamath Mountains, known by the locals as "Bigfoot Country."

Shasta Lake is one of America's top recreation lakes and the boating capital of the West. It is big enough to handle all who love it. The massive reservoir boasts 370 miles of shoreline; more than a dozen each of campgrounds, boat launches, and marinas; lakeshore lodging; and 400 houseboat and cabin rentals. A remarkable 22 species of fish live in the lake. Many of the campgrounds feature lake views. In addition, getting here is easy — a straight shot off I-5.

At the charmed center of this beautiful region are the Trinity Alps, where lakes are sprinkled everywhere. It's also home to the headwaters for feeder streams to the Trinity River, Klamath River, New River, Wooley Creek, and others. Trinity Lake provides outstanding boating and fishing, and just downstream, smaller Lewiston Lake offers a quiet alternative. One advantage to Lewiston Lake is that it is always full of water, even all summer long, making for a very pretty scene. Downstream of Lewiston, the Trinity River provides low-cost rafting and outstanding shoreline access along Highway 299 for fishing for salmon and steelhead.

The neighboring Klamath Mountains are well known as Bigfoot Country. If you drive up the Forest Service road at Bluff Creek, just off Highway 96 upstream of Weitchpec, you can even find the spot where the famous Bigfoot movie was shot in the 1960s. Well, I haven't seen Bigfoot, but I have discovered tons of outdoor recreation. This remote region features miles of the Klamath and Salmon Rivers, as well as the Marble Mountain Wilderness. Options include canoeing, rafting, and fishing for steelhead on the Klamath River, or hiking to your choice of more than 100 wilderness lakes.

How to Use This Book

ABOUT THE CAMPGROUND PROFILES

The campgrounds are listed in a consistent, easy-to-read format to help you choose the ideal camping spot. Here is a sample profile:

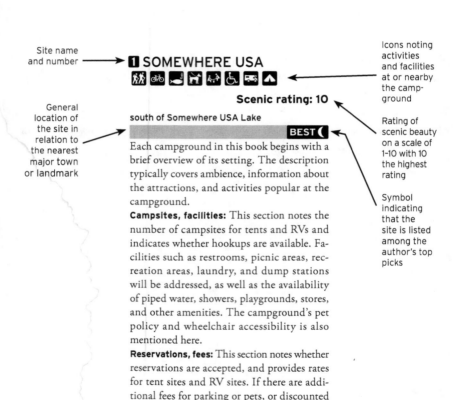

Site name and number ⟶

Icons noting activities and facilities at or nearby the camp-ground

1 SOMEWHERE USA

Scenic rating: 10

General location of the site in relation to the nearest major town or landmark ⟶

south of Somewhere USA Lake

BEST (

Rating of scenic beauty on a scale of 1-10 with 10 the highest rating

Symbol indicating that the site is listed among the author's top picks

Each campground in this book begins with a brief overview of its setting. The description typically covers ambience, information about the attractions, and activities popular at the campground.

Campsites, facilities: This section notes the number of campsites for tents and RVs and indicates whether hookups are available. Facilities such as restrooms, picnic areas, recreation areas, laundry, and dump stations will be addressed, as well as the availability of piped water, showers, playgrounds, stores, and other amenities. The campground's pet policy and wheelchair accessibility is also mentioned here.

Reservations, fees: This section notes whether reservations are accepted, and provides rates for tent sites and RV sites. If there are additional fees for parking or pets, or discounted weekly or seasonal rates, they will also be noted here.

Directions: This section provides mile-by-mile driving directions to the site from the nearest major town or highway.

Contact: This section provides an address, phone number, and website, if available, for each site.

ABOUT THE ICONS

The camping icons are designed to provide at-a-glance information on activities, facilities, and services available on-site or within walking distance of each campground.

- 🏃 Hiking trails
- 🚲 Biking trails
- 🏊 Swimming
- 🎣 Fishing
- 🚣 Boating
- 🛶 Canoeing and/or kayaking
- ❄ Winter sports

- ♨ Hot Springs
- 🐾 Pets permitted
- 🎠 Playground
- ♿ Wheelchair accessible
- 🚐 RV sites
- ⛺ Tent sites

ABOUT THE SCENIC RATING

Each campground profile employs a scenic rating on a scale of 1 to 10, with 1 being the least scenic and 10 being the most scenic. A scenic rating measures only the overall beauty of the campground and environs; it does not take into account noise level, facilities, maintenance, recreation options, or campground management. The setting of a campground with a lower scenic rating may simply not be as picturesque that of as a higher rated campground, however other factors that can influence a trip, such as noise or recreation access, can still affect or enhance your camping trip. Consider both the scenic rating and the profile description before deciding which campground is perfect for you.

ABOUT THE TRAIL PROFILES

Each hike in this book is listed in a consistent, easy-to-read format to help you choose the ideal hike. From a general overview of the setting to detailed driving directions, the profile will provide all the information you need. Here is a sample profile:

Map number and hike number →

1 SOMEWHERE USA HIKE

Round-trip mileage → **9.0 mi/5.0 hrs**

(unless otherwise noted) and the approximate amount of time needed to complete the hike (actual times can vary widely, especially on longer hikes)

Difficulty and quality ratings

at the mouth of the Somewhere River ←

General location of the trail, named by its proximity to the nearest major town or landmark

BEST (

Each hike in this book begins with a brief overview of its setting. The description typically covers what kind of terrain to expect, what might be seen, and any conditions that may make the hike difficult to navigate. Side trips, such as to waterfalls or panoramic vistas, in addition to ways to combine the trail with others nearby for a longer outing, are also noted here. In many cases, mile-by-mile trail directions are included.

Symbol indicating that the hike is listed among the author's top picks

User Groups: This section notes the types of users that are permitted on the trail, including hikers, mountain bikers, horseback riders, and dogs. Wheelchair access is also noted here.

Permits: This section notes whether a permit is required for hiking, or, if the hike spans more than one day, whether one is required for camping. Any fees, such as for parking, day use, or entrance, are also noted here.

Maps: This section provides information on how to obtain detailed trail maps of the hike and its environs. Whenever applicable, names of U.S. Geologic Survey (USGS) topographic maps and national forest maps are also included.

Directions: This section provides mile-by-mile driving directions to the trailhead from the nearest major town.

Contact: This section provides an address and phone number for each hike. The contact is usually the agency maintaining the trail but may also be a trail club or other organization.

ABOUT THE ICONS

The hiking icons are designed to provide at-a-glance information on the difficulty and quality of each hike.

The **difficulty rating** (rated **1-5** with **1** being the lowest and **5** the highest) is based on the steepness of the trail and how difficult it is to traverse

The **quality rating** (rated **1-10** with **1** being the lowest and **10** the highest) is based largely on scenic beauty, but also takes into account how crowded the trail is and whether noise of nearby civilization is audible

ABOUT THE DIFFICULTY RATINGS

Trails rated 1 are very easy and suitable for hikers of all abilities, including young children.

Trails rated 2 are easy-to-moderate and suitable for most hikers, including families with active children 6 and older.

Trails rated 3 are moderately challenging and suitable for reasonably fit adults and older children who are very active.

Trails rated 4 are very challenging and suitable for physically fit hikers who are seeking a workout.

Trails rated 5 are extremely challenging and suitable only for experienced hikers who are in top physical condition.

MAP SYMBOLS

Expressway	80	Interstate Freeway	✗	Airfield
Primary Road	101	U.S. Highway	✗	Airport
Secondary Road	21	State Highway	○	City/Town
Unpaved Road	66	County Highway	▲	Mountain
Ferry		Lake	▲	Park
National Border		Dry Lake	)(	Pass
State Border		Seasonal Lake	◉	State Capital

ABOUT THE MAPS

This book is divided into chapters based on major regions in the state; an overview map of these regions precedes the table of contents. Each chapter begins with a map of the region, which is further broken down into detail maps. Sites are noted on the detail maps by number.

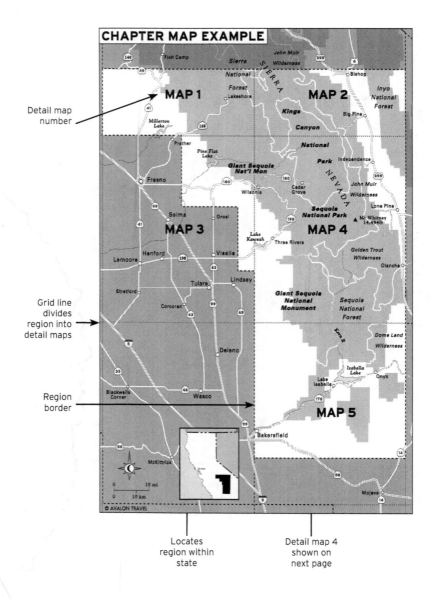

Locates detail
map within
region

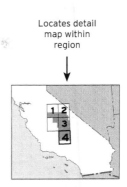

Map number ——→ **Map 4**

Sites shown ——→ **Sites 105-117**
on detail map

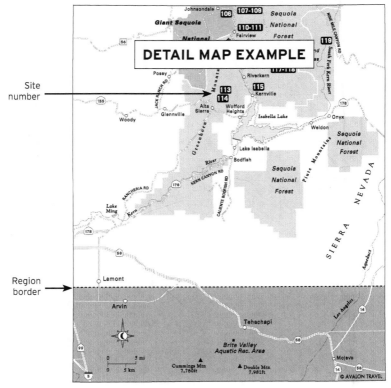

DETAIL MAP EXAMPLE

Site number

Region border

SHASTA CAMPING

© 123RF.COM/TERRANCE EMERSON

BEST CAMPGROUNDS

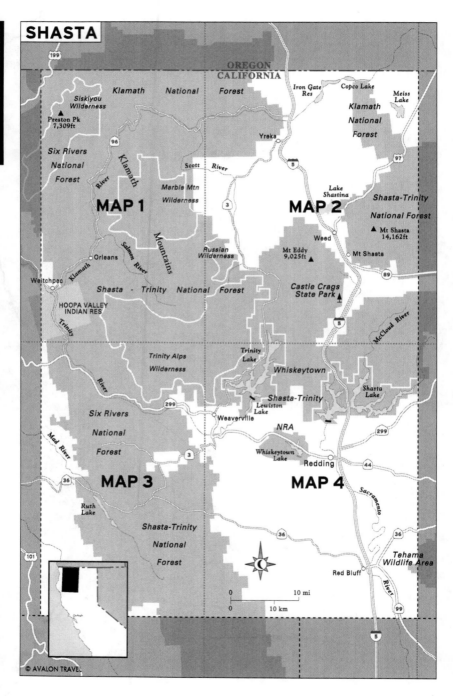

SHASTA CAMPING

SHASTA

OREGON
CALIFORNIA

Klamath National Forest

Siskiyou Wilderness

Preston Pk 7,309ft

Six Rivers National Forest

Iron Gate Res

Copco Lake

Meiss Lake

Klamath National Forest

Yreka

Scott River

Marble Mtn Wilderness

Klamath River

Salmon River

Mountains

Russian Wilderness

MAP 1

Orleans

Weitchpec

Klamath

HOOPA VALLEY INDIAN RES

Trinity

Shasta - Trinity National Forest

Lake Shastina

MAP 2

Weed

Mt Eddy 9,025ft

Mt Shasta

Shasta-Trinity National Forest

▲ Mt Shasta 14,162ft

Castle Crags State Park

McCloud River

Trinity Alps Wilderness

River

Six Rivers National Forest

Mad River

Ruth Lake

Trinity Lake

Whiskeytown

Lewiston Lake

Weaverville

Shasta-Trinity

NRA

Whiskeytown Lake

Shasta Lake

MAP 3

Shasta-Trinity National Forest

MAP 4

Redding

Sacramento

Tehama Wildlife Area

Red Bluff

River

0   10 mi
0   10 km

Map 1

Campgrounds 1-24

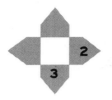

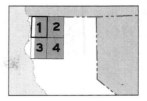

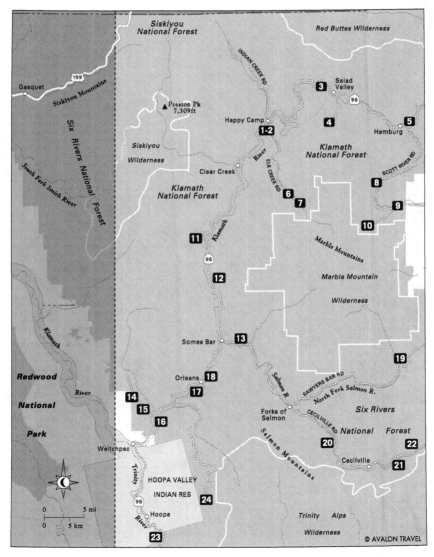

Siskiyou
National Forest

Red Buttes Wilderness

INDIAN CREEK RD

Gasquet

199

Siskiyou Mountains

Six Rivers National Forest

South Fork Smith River

▲ Preston Pk
7,309ft

Siskiyou
Wilderness

Salad
Valley

3

96

Happy Camp

1-2

4

5

Hamburg

Klamath
National Forest

River

ELK CREEK RD

SCOTT RIVER RD

Clear Creek

Klamath
National Forest

6

7

8

9

10

Klamath

11

Marble Mountains

96

Marble Mountain

12

Wilderness

Klamath

Somes Bar

13

19

Redwood

Orleans

18

SAWYERS BAR RD

River

17

Salmon R.

North Fork Salmon R.

National

14

Forks of
Salmon

CECILVILLE RD

Six Rivers

15

16

National   Forest

Park

Salmon Mountains

20

22

Weitchpec

Cecilville

21

Trinity

HOOPA VALLEY

INDIAN RES

24

Trinity   Alps

96

Hoopa

River

Wilderness

0   5 mi

0   5 km

23

© AVALON TRAVEL

Map 2

Campgrounds 25-56

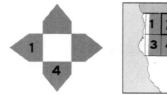

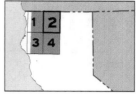

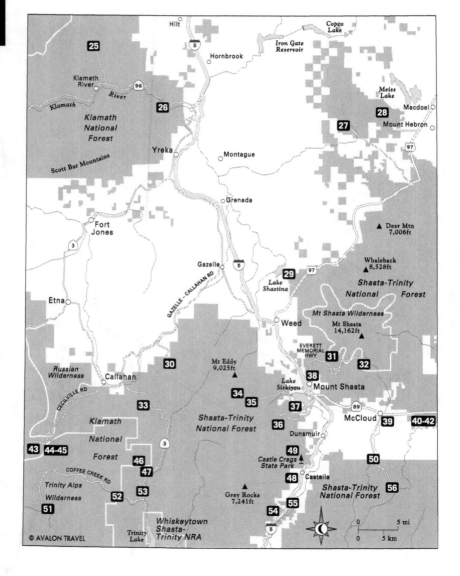

Map 3

Campgrounds 57-77

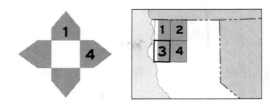

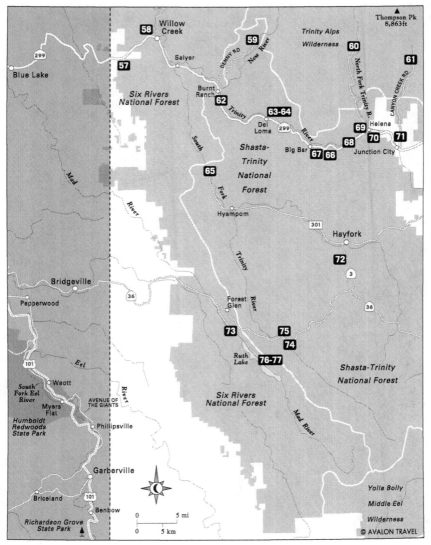

Map 4

Campgrounds 78-148

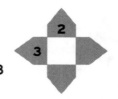

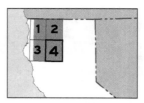

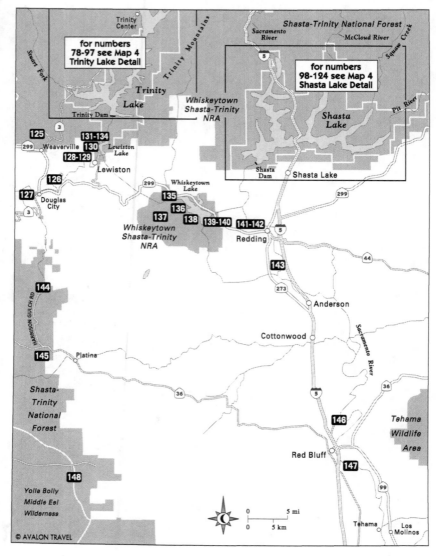

for numbers
78-97 see Map 4
Trinity Lake Detail

for numbers
98-124 see Map 4
Shasta Lake Detail

Trinity Center

Trinity Mountains

Shasta-Trinity National Forest

Sacramento River

McCloud River

Squaw Creek

Stuart Fork

Trinity Lake

Whiskeytown Shasta-Trinity NRA

Shasta Lake

Pit River

Trinity Dam

125

Weaverville

131-134

130

Lewiston Lake

128-129

Lewiston

126

127

Douglas City

Whiskeytown Lake

135

136

137

138

139-140

141-142

Redding

Whiskeytown Shasta-Trinity NRA

Shasta Dam

Shasta Lake

143

144

HARRISON GULCH RD

Anderson

Cottonwood

Sacramento River

145

Platina

Shasta-Trinity National Forest

Tehama Wildlife Area

146

Red Bluff

147

148

Yolla Bolly Middle Eel Wilderness

Tehama

Los Molinos

0   5 mi

0   5 km

© AVALON TRAVEL

TRINITY LAKE DETAIL

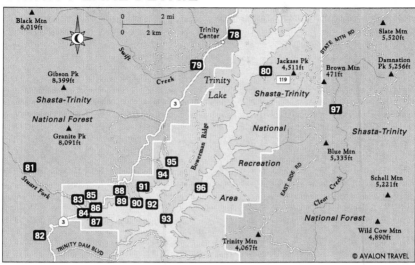

SHASTA LAKE DETAIL

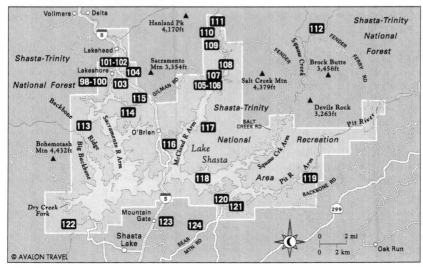

1 CURLY JACK

Scenic rating: 7

on the Klamath River in Klamath National Forest

This campground is set at 1,000 feet elevation on the Klamath River, providing opportunities for fishing, light rafting, and kayaking. What's special about Curly Jack, though, is that the water is generally warm enough through the summer for swimming.

Campsites, facilities: There are 16 sites for tents or RVs up to 22 feet, with some specially designed sites for RVs up to 45 feet, and three group sites for tents or RVs up to 22 feet that can accommodate up to 30 people each. No hookups. Fire grills and picnic tables are provided. Drinking water and vault toilets are available. Some facilities are wheelchair-accessible. Leashed pets are permitted.

Reservations, fees: Reservations are not accepted for individual sites but are required for group sites at 877/444-6777 or www.recreation.gov ($10 reservation fee). Sites are $10 per night, $30 per night for a group site. Open year-round, with limited winter facilities.

Directions: From the town of Happy Camp on Highway 96, turn south on Elk Creek Road and drive about one mile. Turn right on Curly Jack Road and drive one block to the campground entrance on the right.

Contact: Klamath National Forest, Happy Camp and Oak Knoll Ranger Districts, 530/493-2243, fax 530/493-1794.

2 ELK CREEK CAMPGROUND AND RV PARK

Scenic rating: 8

on the Klamath River

BEST (

Elk Creek Campground is a year-round RV park set where Elk Creek pours into the Kla-math River. It is a beautiful campground, with sites right on the water in a pretty, wooded setting. The section of the Klamath River nearby is perfect for inflatable kayaking and rafting. Guided trips are available, with a wide scope of white water available, rated from the easy Class I stuff all the way to the Class V to-hell-and-back rapids. In addition, the water is quite warm in the summer and flows are maintained throughout the year, making it ideal for water sports. A swimming hole gets use in summer. The park is popular with anglers and hunters.

Campsites, facilities: There are 34 sites for RVs of any length, some with full or partial hookups (30 and 50 amps); some sites are pull-through. There is a separate area for tents. Three cabins and three rental trailers are available. Picnic tables and fire grills are provided. Restrooms with showers, cable TV, Wi-Fi, recreation room with billiards and table tennis, horseshoes, beach, coin laundry, dump station, propane, and firewood are available. Leashed pets are permitted.

Reservations, fees: Reservations are recommended. RV sites are $22–25 per night, $6 per night for each additional person, $15 per night for tent sites. Weekly, monthly, and group rates are available. Some credit cards accepted. Open year-round.

Directions: From Highway 96 in the town of Happy Camp, turn south on Elk Creek Road and drive 0.75 mile to the campground on the right.

Contact: Elk Creek Campground and RV Park, 530/493-2208, www.elkcreekcampground.com.

3 FORT GOFF

Scenic rating: 7

in Klamath National Forest

This small, primitive campground is set right along the Klamath River, an ideal location for both fishing and rafting. Many of the most productive shoreline fishing spots on the Klamath River are in this area, with fair trout fishing in summer, good steelhead fishing in the fall and early winter, and a wild card for salmon in late September. There are pullouts along Highway 96 for parking, with short trails/scrambles down to the river. This is also a good spot for rafting, especially in inflatable kayaks, and commercial rafting operations have trips (Class II+ and III) available on this stretch of river. On the opposite side of Highway 96 (within walking distance, to the west) is a trailhead for a hike that is routed along Little Fort Goff Creek, an uphill tromp for five miles to Big Camp and Boundary National Recreation Trail. The creek also runs near the camp, and the elevation is 1,300 feet.

Campsites, facilities: There are five walk-in tent sites. Picnic tables and fire grills are provided. Vault toilets are available. There is no drinking water and garbage must be packed out. Supplies are available in Seiad Valley. Leashed pets are permitted.

Reservations, fees: Reservations are not accepted. There is no fee for camping. Open May through October.

Directions: From Yreka, drive north on I-5 to the junction with Highway 96. At Highway 96, turn west and drive to Seiad Valley. At Seiad Valley, continue west on Highway 96 for five miles to the campground on the left side of the road. Walk a very short distance to the campsites.

Contact: Klamath National Forest, Happy Camp and Oak Knoll Ranger Districts, 530/493-2243, fax 530/493-1794.

4 GRIDER CREEK

Scenic rating: 6

in Klamath National Forest

This obscure little camp is used primarily by hikers, since a trailhead for the Pacific Crest Trail is available, and by deer hunters in the fall. The camp is set at 1,400 feet along Grider Creek. Access to the Pacific Crest Trail is provided from a bridge across the creek. From here, the PCT is routed uphill along Grider Creek into the Marble Mountain Wilderness, about an 11-mile ripper to Huckleberry Mountain at 6,303 feet. There are no lakes along the route, only small streams and feeder creeks.

Campsites, facilities: There are 10 sites for tents or RVs up to 16 feet (no hookups). Picnic tables and fire grills are provided. Vault toilets, horse corrals, and a loading ramp are available. No drinking water is provided. Garbage must be packed out. Some facilities are wheelchair-accessible. Leashed pets are permitted.

Reservations, fees: Reservations are not accepted. There is no fee for camping. Two vehicles maximum per site. Open May through October.

Directions: From Yreka, drive north on I-5 to the junction with Highway 96. At Highway 96, turn west and drive to Walker Creek Road/Forest Road 46N64, one mile before Seiad Valley. Turn left to enter Walker Creek Road and stay to the right as it runs adjacent to the Klamath River to Grider Creek Road. At Grider Creek Road, turn left and drive south for three miles to the camp entrance.

Contact: Klamath National Forest, Happy Camp and Oak Knoll Ranger Districts, 530/493-2243, fax 530/493-1794.

5 SARAH TOTTEN

Scenic rating: 7

on the Klamath River in Klamath National Forest

This is one of the more popular Forest Service camps on the Klamath River, and it's no mystery why. In the summer, its placement is perfect for rafters (Class II+ and III), who camp here and use it as a put-in spot. In fall and winter, anglers arrive for the steelhead run.

It's in the "banana belt," or good-weather area of the Klamath, in a pretty grove of oak trees. Fishing is often good here for salmon in early October and for steelhead from November through spring, providing there are fishable water flows.

Campsites, facilities: There are eight sites for tents or RVs up to 22 feet, and two group sites for tents or RVs up to 22 feet that can accommodate up to 30 people each. No hookups. Picnic tables and fire grills are provided. Drinking water and vault toilets are available. A small grocery store is nearby. Some facilities are wheelchair-accessible. Leashed pets are permitted.

Reservations, fees: Reservations are not accepted for individual sites but are required for the group sites at 877/444-6777 or www.recreation.gov ($10 reservation fee). Sites are $10 per night, $30 per night for group sites. Open May through October.

Directions: From Yreka, drive north on I-5 to the junction with Highway 96. At Highway 96, turn west and drive to Horse Creek, continuing west for five miles to the campground on the right side of the road. If you reach the town of Hamburg, you have gone 0.5 mile too far.

Contact: Klamath National Forest, Happy Camp and Oak Knoll Ranger Districts, 530/493-2243, fax 530/493-1794.

6 SULPHUR SPRINGS

Scenic rating: 8

on Elk Creek in Klamath National Forest

This hidden spot is set along Elk Creek on the border of the Marble Mountain Wilderness. The camp is at a trailhead that provides access to miles and miles of trails that follow streams into the backcountry of the wilderness area. It is a 12-mile backpack trip one-way and largely uphill to Spirit Lake, one of the prettiest lakes in the entire wilderness.

Sulphur Springs Camp is set at 2,300 feet. The nearby hot springs (which are actually lukewarm) provide a side attraction. There are also some swimming holes nearby in Elk Creek, but these aren't hot springs, so expect the water to be cold.

Campsites, facilities: There are six walk-in tent sites. Picnic tables and fire grills are provided. Vault toilets are available. No drinking water is available. Garbage must be packed out. Leashed pets are permitted.

Reservations, fees: Reservations are not accepted. There is no fee for camping. Open late May through early October.

Directions: From Yreka, drive north on I-5 to the junction with Highway 96. At Highway 96, turn west and drive to Happy Camp. In Happy Camp, turn south on Elk Creek Road and drive 14 miles to the campground.

Contact: Klamath National Forest, Happy Camp and Oak Knoll Ranger Districts, 530/493-2243, fax 530/493-1794.

7 NORCROSS

Scenic rating: 7

near Happy Camp in Klamath National Forest

Set at 2,400 feet in elevation, this camp serves as a staging area for various trails that provide access into the Marble Mountain Wilderness. There is also access to the popular Kelsey Trail and to swimming and fishing activities.

Campsites, facilities: There are six sites for tents or RVs up to 25 feet (no hookups). Picnic tables and fire pits are provided. Vault toilets, a horse corral, stock water, and a loading ramp are available. No drinking water is available. Garbage must be packed out. Some facilities are wheelchair-accessible. Leashed pets are permitted.

Reservations, fees: Reservations are not accepted. There is no fee for camping. Open May through October.

Directions: From Yreka on I-5, drive north

on I-5 to the junction with Highway 96. Drive west on Highway 96 to the town of Happy Camp. In Happy Camp, turn south onto Elk Creek Road and drive 16 miles to the campground.

Contact: Klamath National Forest, Happy Camp and Oak Knoll Ranger Districts, 530/493-2243, fax 530/493-1794.

8 BRIDGE FLAT

Scenic rating: 7

in Klamath National Forest

This camp is set at 2,000 feet along the Scott River. Though commercial rafting trips are only rarely available here, the river is accessible during the early spring for skilled rafters and kayakers, with a good put-in and take-out spot four miles downriver; others begin their trip at the Buker bridge or the Kelsey Creek bridge (popular swimming hole here). For backpackers, a trailhead for the Kelsey Trail is nearby, leading into the Marble Mountain Wilderness. A fish-spawning area is located on Kelsey Creek, upriver from camp.

Campsites, facilities: There are four sites for tents or RVs up to 22 feet (no hookups). Picnic tables and fire grills are provided. Vault toilets are available. There is no drinking water. Garbage must be packed out. Some facilities are wheelchair-accessible. Leashed pets are permitted.

Reservations, fees: Reservations are not accepted. There is no fee for camping. Open May through September.

Directions: From Redding, drive north on I-5 to Yreka. In Yreka, turn southwest on Highway 3 and drive 16.5 miles to Fort Jones. In Fort Jones, turn right on Scott River Road and drive 21 miles to the campground on the right side of the road, just after crossing a bridge.

Contact: Klamath National Forest, Scott River and Salmon River Ranger Districts, 530/468-5351, fax 530/468-1290.

9 INDIAN SCOTTY

Scenic rating: 7

on the Scott River in Klamath National Forest

This popular camp provides direct access to the adjacent Scott River. Because it is easy to reach (no gravel roads) and shaded, it gets a lot of use. The camp is set at 2,400 feet. The levels, forces, and temperatures on the Scott River fluctuate greatly from spring to fall. In the spring, it can be a raging cauldron, but cold from snowmelt. Come summer it quiets, with some deep pools providing swimming holes. By fall, it can be reduced to a trickle. Keep your expectations flexible according to the season.

Campsites, facilities: There are 28 sites and a group site (parking lot) for tents or RVs up to 38 feet (no hookups). Picnic tables and fire grills are provided. Drinking water and vault toilets are available. There is a playground in the group-use area. Leashed pets are permitted.

Reservations, fees: Reservations are not accepted for individual sites but are required for the group site at 877/444-6777 or www.recreation.gov ($10 reservation fee). Individual sites are $10 per night, and the group site is $30 per night. Open May through October.

Directions: From Redding, drive north on I-5 to Yreka. In Yreka, turn southwest on Highway 3 and drive 16.5 miles to Fort Jones. In Fort Jones, turn right on Scott River Road and drive 14 miles to a concrete bridge and the adjacent signed campground entrance on the left.

Contact: Klamath National Forest, Scott River and Salmon River Ranger Districts, 530/468-5351, fax 530/468-1290.

SHASTA CAMPING

10 LOVERS CAMP

Scenic rating: 5

in Klamath National Forest

Lovers Camp isn't set up for lovers at all, but for horses and backpackers. This is a trailhead camp set at 4,300 feet at the edge of the Marble Mountain Wilderness, one of the best in the entire wilderness for packers with horses. The trail here is routed up along Canyon Creek to the beautiful Marble Valley at the foot of Black Marble Mountain. The most common destination is Sky High Lakes, a good one-day huff-and-puff away. Now there's a place for lovers.

Campsites, facilities: There are eight walk-in tent sites. Picnic tables and fire grills are provided. Vault toilets are available. There are also facilities for stock unloading and a corral. There is no drinking water, but water is available for stock. Garbage must be packed out. Some facilities are wheelchair-accessible. Leashed pets are permitted.

Reservations, fees: Reservations are not accepted. There is no fee for camping. Open May through October.

Directions: From Redding, drive north on I-5 to Yreka. In Yreka, turn southwest on Highway 3 and drive to Fort Jones and Scott River Road. Turn right on Scott River Road and drive 18 miles to Forest Road 43N45. Turn left (south) on Forest Road 43N45 and drive nine miles to the campground at the end of the road.

Contact: Klamath National Forest, Scott River and Salmon River Ranger Districts, 530/468-5351, fax 530/468-1290.

11 DILLON CREEK

Scenic rating: 7

on the Klamath River in Klamath National Forest

BEST (

This is a prime base camp for rafting or a steelhead fishing trip. A put-in spot for rafting is adjacent to the camp, with an excellent river run available from here on down past Presido Bar to the takeout at Ti-Bar. If you choose to go on, make absolutely certain to pull out at Green Riffle river access and take-out, or risk death at Ishi Pishi Falls. The water is warm here in the summer, and there are also many excellent swimming holes in the area. In addition, this is a good stretch of water for steelhead fishing from September to February, best in early winter from Dillon Creek to Ti-Bar, with shoreline access available at Dillon Beach. The elevation is 800 feet.

Campsites, facilities: There are 21 sites for tents or RVs up to 30 feet (no hookups). Picnic tables, food lockers, and fire grills are provided. Drinking water and vault toilets are available. There is a dump station in Happy Camp 25 miles north of the campground, and at Aikens Creek nine miles west of the town of Orleans. Some facilities are wheelchair-accessible. Leashed pets are permitted.

Reservations, fees: Reservations are not accepted. Sites are $10 per night, $5 per night for each additional vehicle. Open mid-May through early November.

Directions: From Yreka, drive north on I-5 to the junction with Highway 96. At Highway 96, turn west and drive to Happy Camp. Continue south from Happy Camp for 35 miles and look for the campground on the right side of the road.

Coming from the west, from Somes Bar, drive 15 miles northeast on Highway 96.

Contact: Six Rivers National Forest, Orleans Ranger District, 530/627-3291, fax 530/627-3401.

12 MARBLE MOUNTAIN RANCH

🏃 🚴 🏊 🛶 �!! 🛶 🏇 🚐 ⛺

Scenic rating: 6

near the Klamath River

The lodge is set just across the road from the Klamath River, an ideal location as headquarters for a rafting trip in the summer or a steelhead fishing trip in the fall. This ranch is considered a vacation destination, with most people staying for a week. The majority of people staying at the ranch are on a package deal with cabin lodging, but campers can participate in meals and organized activities if they make reservations. Commercial rafting or kayaking trips on the Klamath River and Trinity River are available here, with guided trips offered by the ranch. This piece of river is beautiful and fresh with lots of wildlife and birds, yet not dangerous. However, be absolutely certain to take out at Green Riffle boat access before reaching Ishi Pishi Falls, which cannot be run. There's a full pack station at the ranch for guided trail rides lasting from one hour to overnight. Riding lessons are available. Wilderness pack trips, salmon and steelhead drift-boat fishing, and nature walks are also available. In addition, there is a sporting clays trap course. Hiking trails and swimming holes are available on the property. This is a popular ranch for family reunions, conferences, and weddings.

Campsites, facilities: There are 30 tent sites and 10 sites with full hookups (30 amps) for RVs of any length; some sites are pull-through. Eleven housekeeping cabins and two houses are also available. Picnic tables and fire grills are provided. Restrooms with showers, drinking water, coin laundry, ice, firewood, recreation room, swimming pool, spa, fitness room, deli and gift shop, swimming and fishing pond, petting zoo, playground, horseshoe pits, and volleyball and basketball courts are available.

Reservations, fees: Reservations are recommended. RV sites are $20 per night, $5 per person per night for tent sites, $2 per person per night for more than two people. Some credit cards accepted. Open year-round, weather permitting.

Directions: From the junction of U.S. 101 and Highway 299 near Arcata, turn east on Highway 299 and drive to Willow Creek. In Willow Creek, turn north (left) on Highway 96 east and drive to Somes Bar. At Somes Bar, continue for 7.5 miles to Mile Marker 7.6 and Marble Mountain Ranch on the right.

Contact: Marble Mountain Ranch, 530/469-3322 or 800/KLAMATH (800/552-6284), www.marblemountainranch.com.

13 OAK BOTTOM

🏃 🏊 🛶 🐕 ♿ 🚐 ⛺

Scenic rating: 7

in Klamath National Forest on the Salmon River

This camp is just far enough off Highway 96 that it gets missed by zillions of out-of-towners every year. It is set across the road from the lower Salmon River, a pretty, clean, and cold stream that pours out of the surrounding wilderness high country. Swimming is very good in river holes, though the water is cold, especially when nearby Wooley Creek is full of snowmelt pouring out of the Marble Mountains to the north. In the fall, there is good shoreline fishing for steelhead, though the canyon bottom is shaded almost all day and gets very cold.

Campsites, facilities: There are 26 sites for tents or RVs up to 25 feet (no hookups). Picnic tables and fire grills are provided. Drinking water and vault toilets are available. There is a dump station at the Elk Creek Campground in Happy Camp and at Aikens Creek, 13 miles southwest of the town of Orleans. Supplies are available in Somes Bar. Some facilities are wheelchair-accessible. Leashed pets are permitted.

Reservations, fees: Reservations are not

accepted. Sites are $10 per night, $5 per night for each additional vehicle. Open April through mid-October, weather permitting.

Directions: From the junction of U.S. 101 and Highway 299 near Arcata, turn east on Highway 299 and drive to Willow Creek. In Willow Creek, turn north (left) on Highway 96 east and drive to Somes Bar-Etna Road (0.25 mile before Somes Bar). Turn right on Somes Bar-Etna Road and drive two miles to the campground on the left side of the road.

Contact: Six Rivers National Forest, Orleans Ranger District, 530/627-3291, fax 530/627-3401.

14 FISH LAKE

Scenic rating: 8

in Six Rivers National Forest

This is a pretty little lake that provides good fishing for stocked rainbow trout from the season opener on Memorial Day weekend through July. The camp gets little pressure in other months. It's in the heart of Bigfoot Country, with numerous Bigfoot sightings reported near Bluff Creek. No powerboats are permitted on the lake, but it's too small for that anyway, being better suited for a canoe, float tube, raft, or pram. The elevation is 1,800 feet. The presence here of Port-Orford-cedar root disease, spread by spores in the mud, forces closure from October through May in some years; call for current status.

Campsites, facilities: There are 24 sites for tents or RVs up to 20 feet (no hookups). Picnic tables and fire grills are provided. Drinking water and vault toilets are available. Some facilities are wheelchair-accessible. Leashed pets are permitted.

Reservations, fees: Reservations are not accepted. Sites are $10 per night, $5 per night for each additional vehicle. Open late May through early October, weather permitting.

Directions: From I-5 in Redding, turn west on

Highway 299 and drive to Willow Creek. In Willow Creek, turn north (left) on Highway 96 east and drive to Weitchpec, continuing seven miles north on Highway 96 to Fish Lake Road/Bluff Creek Road. Turn left on Fish Lake Road/Bluff Creek Road and drive five miles (stay to the right at the Y) to Fish Lake.

Contact: Six Rivers National Forest, Orleans Ranger District, 530/627-3291, fax 530/627-3401.

15 E-NE-NUCK

Scenic rating: 7

in Six Rivers National Forest

The campground gets its name from a Karuk chief who lived in the area in the late 1800s. It's a popular spot for anglers; Bluff Creek and the Klamath are within walking distance and Fish Lake is eight miles to the west. Bluff Creek is the legendary site where the Bigfoot film of the 1960s was shot. While it was finally admitted that the film was a phony, it still put Bluff Creek on the map. A unique feature at this campground is a smokehouse for lucky anglers.

Campsites, facilities: There are 11 sites for tents or RVs up to 30 feet (no hookups). Picnic tables, fire rings, and cast-iron firebox stoves are provided. Drinking water, vault toilets, and a smokehouse are available. Some facilities are wheelchair-accessible. Leashed pets are permitted.

Reservations, fees: Reservations are not accepted. Sites are $10 per night, $5 for each additional vehicle. Open late June through October.

Directions: From the junction of U.S. 101 and Highway 299 near Arcata, turn east on Highway 299 and drive to Willow Creek. In Willow Creek, turn north (left) on Highway 96 east and drive to Weitchpec, continuing on Highway 96 for about five miles to the campground. E-Ne-Nuck is just beyond Aikens Creek West campground.

Contact: Six Rivers National Forest, Orleans Ranger District, 530/627-3291, fax 530/627-3401.

16 AIKENS CREEK WEST
🚶 🏊 🛶 🎣 🐎 🚐 ⛺

Scenic rating: 7

on the Klamath River in Six Rivers National Forest

The Klamath River is warm and green here in summer, and this camp provides an ideal put-in spot for a day of easy rafting, especially for newcomers in inflatable kayaks. The camp is set at 340 feet in elevation along the Klamath. From here to Weitchpec is an easy paddle, with the take-out on the right side of the river just below the confluence with the Trinity River. The river is set in a beautiful canyon with lots of birds, and enters the Yurok Indian Reservation. The steelhead fishing can be good in this area from August through mid-November. Highway 96 is a scenic but slow cruise.

Campsites, facilities: There are dispersed sites for tents or RVs of any length (no hookups). Picnic tables and fire grills are provided. Vault toilets and a dump station are available, but there is no drinking water. There are reduced services in winter, and all garbage must be packed out. Leashed pets are permitted.

Reservations, fees: Sites are $8 per night, $5 per night for each additional vehicle; no fees during the winter. Open year-round, weather permitting.

Directions: From the junction of U.S. 101 and Highway 299 near Arcata, turn east on Highway 299 and drive to Willow Creek. In Willow Creek, turn north (left) on Highway 96 east and drive to Weitchpec, continuing on Highway 96 for five miles to the campground on the right side of the road.

Contact: Six Rivers National Forest, Orleans

Ranger District, 530/627-3291, fax 530/627-3401.

17 KLAMATH RIVERSIDE RV PARK AND CAMPGROUND
🚶 🏊 🛶 🎣 🐎 🚲 🚐 ⛺

Scenic rating: 8

on the Klamath River

Klamath Riverside RV Park and Campground is an option for RV cruisers touring Highway 96—designated the Bigfoot Scenic Byway—and looking for a place in Orleans. The camp has large grassy sites set amid pine trees, right on the river. There are spectacular views of Mount Orleans and the surrounding hills. A 12-foot Bigfoot statue is on the property. Through the years, I've seen many changes at this park. It has been transformed from a dusty fishing spot to a park more resembling a rural resort that attracts hikers, cyclists, gold panners, river enthusiasts, anglers, and hunters. One big plus is that the park offers guided fishing trips during the season.

Campsites, facilities: There are 12 tent sites and 45 sites with full hookups (30 and 50 amps) for RVs of any length; some sites are pull-through. Two cabins and six rental trailers are also available. Picnic tables and fire rings are provided. Restrooms with showers, seasonal swimming pool, a spa, group pavilion, fish-cleaning station, coin laundry, horseshoes, playground, modem access, pay phone, and RV storage are available. Guided drift-boat fishing in season is available. Leashed pets are permitted.

Reservations, fees: Reservations are accepted. Sites are $18–24 per night, $5 per person per night for more than two people. Group, weekly, and monthly rates available. Open year-round.

Directions: From the junction of U.S. 101 and Highway 299 near Arcata, drive east on Highway 299 to Willow Creek, turn north (left) on Highway 96 east and drive past Weitchpec to Orleans. This campground is at the west end of the town of Orleans on Highway 96 on the right.

Contact: Klamath Riverside RV Park and Campground, 530/627-3239 or 800/627-9779, fax 530/627-3755, www.klamathriversidervpark.com.

18 PEARCH CREEK

Scenic rating: 7

on the Klamath River in Six Rivers National Forest

This is one of the premium Forest Service camps on the Klamath River because of its easy access from the highway and easy access to the river. The camp is set on Pearch Creek, about a quarter mile from the Klamath at a deep bend in the river. Indeed, the fishing is often excellent for one- to five-pound steelhead from August through November. The elevation is 400 feet.

Campsites, facilities: There are 10 sites for tents or RVs up to 22 feet (no hookups). Picnic tables and fire grills are provided. Drinking water and vault toilets are available. A grocery store, coin laundry, and propane gas are available within one mile. Leashed pets are permitted.

Reservations, fees: Reservations are not accepted. Sites are $10 per night, $5 per night for each additional vehicle. Open late May through early November.

Directions: From I-5 in Redding, turn west on Highway 299 and drive to Willow Creek. In Willow Creek, turn north (left) on Highway 96 east, drive past Weitchpec, and continue to Orleans. In Orleans, continue for one mile and look for the campground entrance on the right side of the road.

Contact: Six Rivers National Forest, Orleans Ranger District, 530/627-3291, fax 530/627-3401.

19 IDLEWILD

Scenic rating: 8

on the North Fork of the Salmon River in Klamath National Forest

This is one of the prettiest drive-to camps in the region, set on the North Fork of the Salmon River, a beautiful, cold, clear stream and a major tributary to the Klamath River. Most campers use the camp for its nearby trailhead (two miles north on a dirt Forest Service road out of camp). The hike here is routed to the north, climbing alongside the Salmon River for miles into the Marble Mountain Wilderness (wilderness permits are required). It's a rugged 10-mile, all-day climb to Lake of the Island, with several other lakes (highlighted by Hancock Lake) to the nearby west, accessible on weeklong trips. The elevation is 2,600 feet.

Campsites, facilities: There are 18 sites for tents or RVs up to 22 feet (no hookups). Picnic tables and fire grills are provided. Drinking water and vault toilets are available, with limited winter facilities. Leashed pets are permitted.

Reservations, fees: Reservations are not accepted. Sites are $10 per night, with no fee during the winter. Open year-round.

Directions: From Yreka, turn southwest on Highway 3 and drive to Etna. In Etna, turn west on Etna-Somes Bar Road (Main Street in town) and drive about 16 miles to the campground on the right side of the road. Note: A shorter, more scenic, and more complex route is available from Gazelle (north of Weed on Old Highway 99). Take Gazelle-Callahan Road west over the summit and continue north to Etna.

Contact: Klamath National Forest, Salmon River and Scott River Ranger Districts, 530/468-5351, fax 530/468-1290.

20 MATTHEWS CREEK

🏊 🎣 🐕 🚐 ⛺

Scenic rating: 8

on the Salmon River in Klamath National
Forest

BEST (

This camp is set in a dramatic river canyon, with the beautiful South Fork of the
Salmon River nearby. Rafters call it the "Cal
Salmon," and good put-in and take-out spots
are found every few miles all the way to the
confluence with the Klamath. In early summer the water is quite cold from snowmelt,
but by midsummer it warms up significantly.
The best fishing for steelhead on the Salmon
is in December and January in the stretch of
river downstream from the town of Forks of
Salmon or upstream in the South Fork (check
regulations for closed areas). In winter the
mountain rims shield the canyon floor from
sunlight and it gets so cold you'll feel like a
human glacier. The elevation is 1,700 feet.
Campsites, facilities: There are 12 sites for
tents or RVs up to 16 feet (no hookups). Picnic
tables and fire grills are provided. Drinking
water and vault toilets are available, with limited winter facilities. Leashed or controlled
pets are permitted.
Reservations, fees: Reservations are not accepted. Sites are $10 per night. Open May
through October.
Directions: From the junction of U.S. 101
and Highway 299 near Arcata, head east on
Highway 299 and drive to Willow Creek.
In Willow Creek, turn north on Highway
96 and drive past Orleans to Somes Bar. At
Somes Bar, turn east on Salmon River Road/
Forest Road 2B01 and drive to the town of
Forks of Salmon. Turn right on Cecilville
Road/Forest Road 1002 and drive about nine
miles to the campground. Cecilville Road is
very narrow.
Contact: Klamath National Forest, Salmon
River and Scott River Ranger Districts,
530/468-5351, fax 530/468-1290.

21 EAST FORK

🏊 🎣 🐕 🚐 ⛺

Scenic rating: 6

on the Salmon River in Klamath National
Forest

This is one of the more spectacular areas
in the fall when the leaves turn different
shades of gold. It's set at 2,600 feet along
the Salmon River, just outside the town of
Cecilville. Directly adjacent to the camp is
Forest Road 37N02, which leads to a Forest Service station four miles away, and to
a trailhead for the Trinity Alps Wilderness
three miles beyond that. Note to steelhead
anglers: Check the Department of Fish and
Game regulations for closed areas on the
Salmon River.
Campsites, facilities: There are nine sites for
tents or RVs up to 16 feet (no hookups). Picnic
tables and fire grills are provided. Vault toilets
are available. No drinking water is available.
Garbage must be packed out. Leashed pets
are permitted.
Reservations, fees: Reservations are not accepted. There is no fee for camping. Open
May through October.
Directions: From Weed, drive north on I-5 to
the Edgewood exit. Take the Edgewood exit,
turn left at the stop sign, and drive a short
distance under the freeway to another stop
sign at Old Highway 99. Turn right (north)
and drive six miles to Gazelle and Gazelle-
Callahan Road. Turn left (west) on Gazelle-
Callahan Road, and drive to Callahan and
Cecilville Road. Turn left (southwest) on
Cecilville Road and drive about 30 miles to
the campground on the right side of the road.
If you reach the town of Cecilville, you have
gone two miles too far.
Contact: Klamath National Forest, Salmon
River and Scott River Ranger Districts,
530/468-5351, fax 530/468-1290.

SHASTA CAMPING

22 SHADOW CREEK

👫🏊🎣🏕🚐🛖

Scenic rating: 7

in Klamath National Forest

This tiny spot, secluded and quiet, is along little Shadow Creek where it enters the East Fork Salmon River, adjacent to a deep bend in the road. An unusual side trip is to take the Forest Service road out of camp (turn north off Cecilville Road) and follow it as it winds back and forth, finally arriving at Grouse Point, 5,409 feet elevation, for a view of the western slopes of the nearby Russian and Trinity Alps Wilderness Areas. There are three trailheads six miles to the east of the camp: Fish Creek, Long Gulch, and Trail Gulch. Note: The river adjacent to the campground is a spawning area and is closed to salmon and steelhead fishing, but you can take trout.

Campsites, facilities: There are five sites for tents or RVs up to 16 feet (no hookups). Picnic tables and fire grills are provided. Vault toilets are available. No drinking water is available. Garbage must be packed out. Leashed pets are permitted.

Reservations, fees: Reservations are not accepted. There is no fee for camping. Open May through October.

Directions: From Weed, drive north on I-5 to the Edgewood exit. Take the Edgewood exit, turn left at the stop sign, and drive a short distance under the freeway to another stop sign at Old Highway 99. Turn right (north) and drive six miles to Gazelle and Gazelle-Callahan Road. Turn left (west) and drive to Callahan and Cecilville Road. Turn left (southwest) on Cecilville Road and drive about 25 miles to the campground on the left side of the road.

Contact: Klamath National Forest, Salmon River and Scott River Ranger Districts, 530/468-5351, fax 530/468-1290.

23 TISH TANG

🏊🎣🚣🏕🚐🛖

Scenic rating: 8

in Six Rivers National Forest

This campground is adjacent to one of the best swimming holes in all of Northern California. By late July the adjacent Trinity River is warm and slow, perfect for tubing, a quick dunk, and paddling a canoe. There is a large gravel beach, and some people will bring along their shorty lawn chairs and just take a seat on the edge of the river in a few inches of water. Though Tish Tang is a good put-in spot for rafting in the late spring and early summer, the flows are too slow and quiet for most rafters to even ruffle a feather during the summer. The elevation is 300 feet.

Campsites, facilities: There are 40 sites for tents or RVs up to 22 feet (no hookups). Picnic tables and fire grills are provided. Drinking water and vault toilets are available, and there is a camp host. Leashed pets are permitted.

Reservations, fees: Reservations are accepted at 530/625-4284. Sites are $10 per night, $3 per night for each additional vehicle, $15 per night for double sites. Open late May through September.

Directions: From the junction of U.S. 101 and Highway 299 near Arcata, turn east on Highway 299 and drive to Willow Creek. In Willow Creek, turn north (left) on Highway 96 east and drive eight miles north to the campground entrance on the right side of the road.

Contact: Hoopa Valley Tribal Council, Forestry Department, 530/625-4284, fax 530/625-4230.

24 MILL CREEK LAKE HIKE-IN

👫🏊🎣🐕🛖

Scenic rating: 4

on the border of the Trinity Alps Wilderness

In 1999, a forest fire affected this area and it now is surrounded by many tree skeletons.

Recovery is occurring and in time this will again become something of a secret camp. Mill Creek Lake is a secret three-acre lake set at 5,000 feet on the edge of the Trinity Alps Wilderness. Reaching it requires a two-mile hike from the wilderness boundary, with the little lake set just north of North Trinity Mountain (6,362 feet). This is a rare chance to reach a wilderness lake with such a short walk, backpacking without having to pay the penalty of days of demanding hiking. The lake features excellent swimming, with warmer water than in higher and more remote wilderness lakes, and decent fishing for rainbow trout.

Campsites, facilities: There are three primitive tent sites at locations around the lake. Fire rings are provided. No drinking water or toilets are available. Garbage must be packed out. Leashed pets are permitted.

Reservations, fees: Reservations are not accepted. There is no fee for camping. A free wilderness permit is required from the U.S. Forest Service. Open year-round, weather permitting.

Directions: From the junction of U.S. 101 and Highway 299 near Arcata, turn east on Highway 299 and drive to Willow Creek. In Willow Creek turn north (left) on Highway 96 east and drive into the Hoopa Valley to Mill Creek Road. Turn east (right) on Mill Creek Road, and drive approximately 12 miles to the national forest boundary and Forest Road 10N02. Turn right on Forest Road 10N02 and drive about 3.5 miles, where you will reach another junction. Turn left at the signed junction to the Mill Creek Lake Trailhead and drive a short distance to the parking area. A one-hour walk is then required to reach the lake.

Contact: Six Rivers National Forest, Lower Trinity Ranger District, 530/629-2118, fax 530/629-2102.

25 BEAVER CREEK

Scenic rating: 8

in Klamath National Forest

This camp is set along Beaver Creek, a feeder stream to the nearby Klamath River, with two small creeks entering Beaver Creek on the far side of the river near the campground. It is quiet and pretty. There are several historic mining sites in the area; you'll need a map of Klamath National Forest (available for a fee at the district office) to find them. In the fall, this campground is usually taken over by deer hunters. The elevation is 2,400 feet.

Campsites, facilities: There are eight sites for tents or RVs up to 16 feet (no hookups). Picnic tables and fire grills are provided. Vault toilets are available. There is no drinking water. Garbage must be packed out. Leashed pets are permitted.

Reservations, fees: Reservations are not accepted. There is no fee for camping. Open May through October.

Directions: From Yreka, drive north on I-5 to Highway 96. Turn west on Highway 96 and drive approximately 15 miles (if you reach the town of Klamath River, you have gone 0.5 mile too far) to Beaver Creek Road. Turn right on Beaver Creek Road/Forest Road 11 and drive four miles to the campground.

Contact: Klamath National Forest, Happy Camp and Oak Knoll Ranger Districts, 530/493-2243, fax 530/493-1796.

26 TREE OF HEAVEN

Scenic rating: 7

in Klamath National Forest

BEST (

This outstanding riverside campground provides excellent access to the Klamath River for fishing, rafting, and hiking. The best deal is to put in your raft, canoe, or drift boat upstream at the ramp below Iron Gate Reservoir, then make the all-day run down to the take-out at Tree of Heaven. This section of river is an easy paddle (Class II, II+, and III) and also provides excellent steelhead fishing in the winter. A 0.25 mile paved interpretive trail is near the camp. On the drive in from the highway, you can watch the landscape turn from high chaparral to forest.

Campsites, facilities: There are 20 sites for tents or RVs up to 35 feet (no hookups). Picnic tables and fire grills are provided. Drinking water and vault toilets are available. A river access spot for put-in and take-out for rafts and drift boats is available. Some facilities are wheelchair-accessible. Leashed pets are permitted.

Reservations, fees: Reservations are accepted at 877/444-6777 or www.recreation.gov ($10 reservation fee). Sites are $10 per night. Open year-round.

Directions: From Yreka, drive north on I-5 to Highway 96. Turn west on Highway 96 and drive seven miles to the campground entrance on the left side of the road.

Contact: Klamath National Forest, Happy Camp and Oak Knoll Ranger Districts, 530/493-2243, fax 530/493-1796.

27 MARTINS DAIRY

Scenic rating: 8

on the Little Shasta River in Klamath National Forest

This camp is set at 6,000 feet, where the deer get big and the country seems wide open. A large meadow is nearby, directly across the road from this remote camp, with fantastic wildflower displays in late spring. This is one of the prettiest camps around in the fall, with dramatic color from aspens, elderberries, and willows. It also makes a good base camp for hunters in the fall. Before heading into the surrounding backcountry, obtain a map (fee)

of Klamath National Forest at the Goosenest Ranger Station on Highway 97, on your way in to camp.

Campsites, facilities: There are eight sites for tents or RVs up to 30 feet (no hookups) and a horse campsite. Picnic tables and fire grills are provided. Drinking water and vault toilets are available. Leashed pets are permitted.

Reservations, fees: Reservations are not accepted. Sites are $8 per night. Open late May through early October, weather permitting.

Directions: From Weed and I-5, turn north on U.S. 97 (Klamath Falls exit) and drive to Grass Lake. Continue about seven miles to Forest Road 70/46N10 (if you reach Hebron Summit, you have driven about a mile too far). Turn left, drive about 10 miles to a Y, take the left fork, and drive three miles (including a very sharp right turn) to the campground on the right side of the road. A map of Klamath National Forest is advised.

Contact: Klamath National Forest, Goosenest Ranger District, 530/398-4391, fax 530/398-5749.

28 JUANITA LAKE

Scenic rating: 7

in Klamath National Forest

Small and relatively unknown, this camp is set along the shore of Juanita Lake at 5,100 feet. Swimming is not recommended because the water is cold and mucky, and mosquitoes can be abundant as well. It is stocked with rainbow trout, brown trout, bass, and catfish, but a problem with golden shiners has cut into the lake's fishing productivity. It's a small lake and forested, set near the Butte Valley Wildlife Area in the plateau country just five miles to the northeast. The latter provides an opportunity to see waterfowl and, in the winter, bald eagles. Campers will discover a network of Forest Service roads in the area, providing an opportunity for mountain biking. There are designated fishing areas and a paved trail around the lake that is wheelchair-accessible and spans approximately 1.25 miles.

Campsites, facilities: There are 23 sites for tents or RVs up to 32 feet (no hookups), and a group tent site that can accommodate up to 50 people. Picnic tables and fire grills are provided. Drinking water and vault toilets are available. Boating is allowed, but no motors are permitted on the lake. Many facilities are wheelchair-accessible. Leashed pets are permitted.

Reservations, fees: Reservations are not accepted for individual sites but are required for the group site at 530/398-4391. Individual sites are $10 per night, and the group site is $30 per night. Open late May through mid-October, weather permitting.

Directions: From Weed and I-5, turn north on U.S. 97 (Klamath Falls exit) and drive approximately 37 miles to Ball Mountain Road. Turn left on Ball Mountain Road and drive 2.5 miles, veer right at the fork, and continue to the campground entrance at the lake.

Contact: Klamath National Forest, Goosenest Ranger District, 530/398-4391, fax 530/398-5749.

29 LAKE SHASTINA
🏊 🚣 🛥 🏕 🚐 ⛺

Scenic rating: 5

near Klamath National Forest and Weed

Lake Shastina is set at the northern foot of Mount Shasta at 3,000 feet in elevation. The campground is located on the access road to the boat ramp, about 0.25 mile from the lake. It offers sweeping views, good swimming on hot summer days, waterskiing, and all water sports. There is fishing for catfish and bass in the spring and summer, an occasional opportunity for crappie, and good fishing for trout in late winter and spring. One reason the views of Mount Shasta are so good is that this is largely high sagebrush country with few trees. As such, it can get very dusty, windy, and, in the winter,

nasty cold. When the lake is full, the wind is down, and the weather is good, there are few complaints. But that is only rarely the case. The lake level is often low, with the water drained for hay farmers to the north. This is one of the few lakes in Northern California that has property with lakeside housing. Lake Shastina Golf Course is nearby.

Campsites, facilities: There is a small primitive area for tents or RVs of any length (no hookups). There is one faucet, but you should bring your own water just in case. A vault toilet is available and a boat launch is nearby; the boat ramp is nonfunctional when the lake level drops below the concrete ramp. Garbage service available May to September only. There is a 14-day limit for camping. Supplies can be obtained five miles away in Weed. Leashed pets are permitted.

Reservations, fees: Reservations are not accepted. There is no fee for camping. Open May through September.

Directions: From Redding, take I-5 north to the central Weed exit and U.S. 97. Take the exit to the stop sign, turn right, drive through Weed, exiting for U.S. 97/Klamath Falls. Merge right (north) on U.S. 97 and drive about five miles to Big Springs Road. Turn left (west) on Big Springs Road and drive about two miles to Jackson Ranch Road. Turn left (west) on Jackson Ranch Road and drive about one mile to Emerald Isle Road (watch for the signed turnoff). Turn right and drive one mile to the campground.

Contact: Siskiyou County Public Works, 530/842-8250.

30 KANGAROO LAKE WALK-IN
🚶 🏊 🚣 🏕 ♿ 🚐 ⛺

Scenic rating: 9

in Klamath National Forest

A remote paved road leads to the parking area for Kangaroo Lake, set at 6,500 feet. This provides a genuine rarity: a beautiful and pristine mountain lake with a camp-ground, good fishing for brook and rainbow trout, and an excellent trailhead for hikers. The walk to the campsites is very short, 1–3 minutes, with many sites very close. Camp-sites are in a forested setting with no lake view. Reaching the lake requires another five minutes, but a paved wheelchair-accessible trail is available. In addition, a switchback ramp for wheelchairs makes it one of the best wheelchair-accessible fishing areas in Califor-nia. The lake is small, 25 acres, but deep at 100 feet. No boat motors are allowed. A hik-ing trail rises steeply out of the campground and connects to the Pacific Crest Trail, from which you turn left to gain a dramatic look-out of Northern California peaks as well as the lake below.

Campsites, facilities: There are 18 walk-in sites for tents, and RVs up to 25 feet (no hookups) are allowed in the parking lot. Picnic tables and fire grills are provided. Drinking water and vault toilets are available. Some facilities are wheelchair-accessible, including a nearby fishing pier. Leashed pets are permitted.

Reservations, fees: Reservations are not ac-cepted. Sites are $10 per night. Open June through October, weather permitting.

Directions: From Weed, drive north on I-5 and take the Edgewood exit. At the stop sign, turn left and drive a short distance under the freeway to the stop sign at Old Highway 99. Turn right (north) on Old Highway 99 and drive six miles to Gazelle and Gazelle-Cal-lahan Road. Turn left at Gazelle-Callahan Road and drive over the summit. From the summit, continue about five miles to Rail Creek Road. Turn left at Rail Creek Road and drive approximately eight miles to where the road dead-ends near the campground. Walk approximately 30–150 yards to reach the campsites.

Contact: Klamath National Forest, Scott River and Salmon River Ranger Districts, 530/468-5351, fax 530/468-1290.

31 McBRIDE SPRINGS

Scenic rating: 8

in Shasta-Trinity National Forest

This camp is set at 4,880 feet on the slopes of the awesome Mount Shasta (14,162 feet), California's most majestic mountain. Stargaz-ing is fantastic here, and during full moons, an eerie glow is cast on the adjoining high mountain slopes. A good side trip is to drive to the end of Everitt Memorial Highway, which tops out above 7,800 feet. You'll find great lookouts to the west, and a jump-off point for a Shasta expedition or day hike to Panther Meadows.

Campsites, facilities: There are nine sites for tents or RVs up to 16 feet (no hookups). Picnic tables and fire grills are provided. Drinking water (from a single well with a hand pump at the north end of the campground) and vault toilets are available. Supplies and a coin laundry are available in the town of Mount Shasta. Some facilities are wheelchair-acces-sible. Leashed pets are permitted.

Reservations, fees: Reservations are not ac-cepted. Sites are $10 per night. Open Memo-rial Day weekend through October, weather permitting.

Directions: From Redding drive north on I-5 to the town of Mount Shasta and the Central Mount Shasta exit. Take that exit and drive to the stop sign and Lake Street. Turn right and continue on Lake Street through town; once out of town, the road becomes Everitt Memo-rial Highway. Continue on Everitt Memorial Highway for four miles to the campground entrance on the left side of the road.

Contact: Shasta-Trinity National Forest, Mount Shasta Ranger District, 530/926-4511, fax 530/926-5120.

32 PANTHER MEADOWS WALK-IN

🚶 🏠 ⛺

Scenic rating: 9

in Shasta-Trinity National Forest

BEST (

This quiet site, on the slopes of Mount Shasta at 7,500 feet, features access to the pristine Panther Meadows, a high mountain meadow set just below tree line. It's a sacred place, regardless of your religious orientation. The hiking is excellent here, with a short hike out to Gray Butte (8,119 feet) for a perfect look to the south of Castle Crags, Mount Lassen, and the Sacramento River Canyon. A three-night maximum stay is enforced to minimize long-term impacts.

Campsites, facilities: There are 10 walk-in tent sites (trailers not allowed). Picnic tables and fire grills are provided. Vault toilets are available. No drinking water is available. Garbage must be packed out. Supplies are available in the town of Mount Shasta. Leashed pets are permitted.

Reservations, fees: Reservations are not accepted. There is no fee for camping. Open mid-June through mid-October, weather permitting.

Directions: From Redding, drive north on I-5 to the town of Mount Shasta and the Central Mount Shasta exit. Take that exit and drive to the stop sign and Lake Street. Turn right and continue on Lake Street through town; once out of town, Lake Street becomes Everitt Memorial Highway. Continue on Everitt Memorial Highway for about 12 miles (passing the Bunny Flat parking area) to the campground parking area on the right. Park and walk a short distance to the campsites. Note: When the gate is closed just past Bunny Flat, the walk in is 1.5 miles from the gate to the campground.

Contact: Shasta-Trinity National Forest, Mount Shasta Ranger District, 530/926-4511, fax 530/926-5120.

33 SCOTT MOUNTAIN

🚶 🏠 ⛺

Scenic rating: 7

in Shasta-Trinity National Forest

This camp is a jump-off point for hikers, with the Pacific Crest Trail passing right by here. If you hike southwest, it leads into the Scott Mountains and skirts the northern edge of the Trinity Alps Wilderness. Another option here is driving on Forest Road 40N08, which begins directly across from camp and Highway 3. On this road, it's only two miles to Big Carmen Lake, a small, largely unknown and pretty little spot. Campground elevation is 5,300 feet. A Forest Service map is advisable.

Campsites, facilities: There are five tent sites. Picnic tables and fire grills are provided. Vault toilets are available. No drinking water is available. Garbage must be packed out. Leashed pets are permitted.

Reservations, fees: Reservations are not accepted. There is no fee for camping. Open May through October, weather permitting.

Directions: From Weed, drive north on I-5 and take the Edgewood exit. At the stop sign, turn left and drive a short distance under the freeway to the stop sign at Old Highway 99. Turn right (north) and drive six miles to Gazelle and Gazelle-Callahan Road. Turn left at Gazelle-Callahan Road and drive to Callahan and Highway 3. Turn south on Highway 3 and drive to Scott Mountain Summit and look for the campground on the right side of the road.

Contact: Klamath National Forest, Shasta-Trinity National Forest, Weaverville Ranger District, 530/623-2121, fax 530/623-6010.

34 TOAD LAKE WALK-IN
🏃 🏊 🛶 🏕 5% ⛰

Scenic rating: 9

in Shasta-Trinity National Forest

Some people think this site is closed, since the Forest Service no longer lists it as an active campground. Nope. There are six primitive campsites at Toad Lake, including two with picnic tables—one on the east side of the lake and one on the west. Because it is a free site with no maintenance provided, it is off the mainstream grid. So if you want the remote beauty and splendor of an alpine lake on the Pacific Crest Trail, yet you don't want to walk far to get there, this is the place. Toad Lake is no easy trick to get to, with a bone-jarring ride for the last half hour followed by a 15-minute walk, but it's worth the effort. It's a beautiful little lake, just 23.5 acres, set at 6,900 feet in the Mount Eddy Range, with lakeside sites, excellent swimming, fair fishing for small trout, and great hiking. The best hike is a 45-minute trail out of the Toad Lake Basin to pristine Porcupine Lake. To get there, follow the trail to the head of the lake. There it rises up the slope and to the top of the ridge, intersecting with the Pacific Crest Trail. Turn left and walk a short distance to a spur trail junction on the right, which leads to Porcupine Lake.

Campsites, facilities: There are six walk-in tent sites. A vault toilet is available. No drinking water is available. Garbage must be packed out. Leashed pets are permitted.

Reservations, fees: Reservations are not accepted. There is no fee for camping. Open May through October, weather permitting.

Directions: From the town of Mount Shasta on I-5, take the Central Mount Shasta exit and drive to the stop sign. Turn west and drive less than a mile to Old Stage Road. Turn left and drive 0.25 mile to a Y intersection at W. A. Barr Road. Bear right and drive past Box Canyon Dam and the entrance to Lake Siskiyou, and continue up the mountain (the road becomes Forest Road 26). Just past a concrete bridge, turn right on Forest Road 41N53 and drive 0.2 mile to a fork and Toad Lake Road. Turn left onto Toad Lake Road (a dirt road) and continue for 11 miles to the parking area. The road is bumpy and twisty, and the final half-mile to the trailhead is rocky and rough. High-clearance or four-wheel-drive vehicles are recommended. Walk in about 0.5 mile to the lake and campsites. Note: Access roads may be closed because of flooding; call ahead for status.

Contact: Shasta-Trinity National Forest, Mount Shasta Ranger District, 530/926-4511, fax 530/926-5120.

35 GUMBOOT LAKE
🏃 🏊 🛶 🐕 ♿ 🚐 ⛰

Scenic rating: 9

in Shasta-Trinity National Forest

This pretty spot at 6,080 feet elevation provides a few small camps set beside a small yet beautiful high mountain lake, the kind of place many think you can reach only with long hikes. Not so with Gumboot. In addition, the fishing is good here, with rainbow trout in the 12-inch class. The lake is small, almost too small for even a canoe, and better suited to a pram, raft, or float tube. No motors of any kind are permitted, including electric motors. When the fishing gets good, it can get crowded, with both out-of-towners and locals making casts from the shoreline. A better bet is floating in a pram or inflatable to the far end of the lake and flyfishing with black leeches and a sink-tip line. Another option is hiking 10 minutes through forest to Upper Gumboot Lake, which is more of a pond with small trout. Another excellent hike is available here, tromping off-trail beyond Upper Gumboot Lake and up the back slope of the lake to the Pacific Crest Trail, then turning left and scrambling to a great lookout of Mount Shasta in the distance and Gumboot in the foreground.

Campsites, facilities: There are four sites for tents or RVs up to 16 feet (no hookups), and across the creek there are four walk-in tent sites. Picnic tables are provided. Vault toilets are available. No drinking water is available. Garbage must be packed out. Some facilities are wheelchair-accessible. Leashed pets are permitted.

Reservations, fees: Reservations are not accepted. There is no fee for camping. Open May through October, weather permitting.

Directions: From the town of Mount Shasta on I-5, take the Central Mount Shasta exit and drive to the stop sign. Turn west and continue less than a mile to Old Stage Road. Turn left and drive 0.25 mile to a Y intersection at W. A. Barr Road. Bear right on W. A. Barr Road and drive past Box Canyon Dam and the Lake Siskiyou Campground entrance. Continue 10 miles to a fork, signed for Gumboot Lake. Bear left and drive 0.5 mile to the lake and campsites. Note: Access roads may be closed because of flooding; call for current status.

Contact: Shasta-Trinity National Forest, Mount Shasta Ranger District, 530/926-4511, fax 530/926-5120.

36 CASTLE LAKE
🥾 🏞 🛶 ⛵ 🐕 🚐 ⛺

Scenic rating: 10

in Shasta-Trinity National Forest

Castle Lake is a beautiful spot, a deep blue lake set in a granite bowl with a spectacular wall on the far side. The views of Mount Shasta are great, fishing is decent (especially ice fishing in winter), canoeing or floating around on a raft is a lot of fun, and there is a terrific hike that loops around the left side of the lake, rising to the ridge overlooking the lake for dramatic views. Locals use this lake for ice-skating in winter. The campground is not right beside the lake, to ensure the pristine clear waters remain untouched, but is rather just a short distance downstream along Castle Lake Creek.

The lake is only 47 acres, but 120 feet deep. The elevation is 5,280 at the camp, and 5,450 feet at the lake.

Campsites, facilities: There are six sites for tents or RVs up to 16 feet (no hookups). Picnic tables and fire grills are provided. Vault toilets are available. No drinking water is available. Garbage must be packed out. Leashed pets are permitted.

Reservations, fees: Reservations are not accepted. There is no fee for camping. Open May through October, weather permitting.

Directions: From the town of Mount Shasta on I-5, take the Central Mount Shasta exit and drive to the stop sign. Turn west and drive less than a mile to Old Stage Road. Turn left and drive 0.25 mile to a Y intersection at W. A. Barr Road. Bear right on W. A. Barr Road and drive past Box Canyon Dam. Turn left at Castle Lake Road and drive seven miles to the campground access road on the left. Turn left and drive a short distance to the campground. Note: Castle Lake is another 0.25 mile up the road; there are no legal campsites along the lake's shoreline.

Contact: Shasta-Trinity National Forest, Mount Shasta Ranger District, 530/926-4511, fax 530/926-5120.

37 LAKE SISKIYOU CAMP-RESORT
🥾 🏞 🛶 🛥 🐕 🧒 ♿ 🚐 ⛺

Scenic rating: 9

near Mount Shasta

BEST (

This is a true gem of a lake, a jewel set at the foot of Mount Shasta at 3,181 feet. The lake level is almost always full (because it was built for recreation, not water storage) and offers a variety of quality recreation options, with great swimming, low-speed boating, and fishing. The campground complexes are huge, yet they are tucked into the forest so visitors don't get their styles cramped. The water in this 435-acre lake is clean and fresh.

There is an excellent beach and swimming area, the latter protected by a buoy line. In spring, the fishing is good for trout, and then as the water warms, for smallmouth bass. A good boat ramp and boat rentals are available, and a 10-mph speed limit is strictly enforced, keeping the lake pristine and quiet. The City of Mount Shasta holds its July 4 fireworks display above the lake.

Campsites, facilities: There are 150 sites with full or partial hookups (30 and 50 amps) for RVs of any length, including some pull-through sites, and 225 additional sites for tents, seven of which are group areas. There are also 20 cabins and 10 park-model cabins. Picnic tables and fire grills are provided. Drinking water, restrooms with flush toilets and showers, playground, propane, convenience store, gift shop, deli, coin laundry, and a dump station are available. There are also a marina, boat rentals (canoes, kayaks, pedal boats, motorized boats), free boat launching, fishing dock, fish-cleaning station, boat slips, swimming beach, horseshoes, volleyball, group facilities, and a recreation room. A free movie plays every night in the summer. Some facilities are wheelchair-accessible. Leashed pets are permitted at the campground only.

Reservations, fees: Reservations are accepted. RV sites are $29 per night, $3 per person per night for more than two people, $5 per night for each additional vehicle, $2 per pet per night; tent sites are $20 per night. Some credit cards accepted. Open April through October, weather permitting.

Directions: From the town of Mount Shasta on I-5, take the Central Mount Shasta exit and drive to the stop sign. Turn west and drive less than a mile to Old Stage Road. Turn left and drive 0.25 mile to a Y intersection at W. A. Barr Road. Bear right on W. A. Barr Road and drive past Box Canyon Dam. Two miles farther, turn right at the entrance road for Lake Siskiyou Campground and Marina and drive a short distance to the entrance station.

Contact: Lake Siskiyou Camp-Resort, 530/926-2618 or 888/926-2618, www.lake-sis.com.

38 KOA MOUNT SHASTA

Scenic rating: 7

in Mount Shasta City

Despite this KOA camp's relative proximity to the town of Mount Shasta, the extended driveway, wooded grounds, and view of Mount Shasta offer some feeling of seclusion. There are many excellent side trips. The best is driving up Everitt Memorial Highway, which rises up the slopes of Mount Shasta to the tree line at Bunny Flat, where you can take outstanding, short day hikes with great views to the south of the Sacramento River Canyon and Castle Crags. In the winter, you can play in the snow, including heading up to Bunny Flat for snowplay or to the Mount Shasta Board and Ski Park for developed downhill and cross-country skiing. An ice skating rink is in Mount Shasta. One of the biggest events of the year in Mount Shasta is the Fourth of July Run for Fun (billed as the largest small-town foot race anywhere) and associated parade and fireworks display at nearby Lake Siskiyou.

Campsites, facilities: There are 47 sites with full or partial hookups (20, 30, and 50 amps) for RVs of any length, 50 additional sites with partial hookups for tents or RVs, and four camping cabins. All sites are pull-through. Picnic tables are provided, and fire grills are provided at tent sites only. Restrooms with showers, a playground, propane gas, a convenience store, recreation room with arcade, horseshoe pit, shuffleboard, a seasonal swimming pool, high-speed modem access and Wi-Fi, and coin laundry are available. Leashed pets are permitted.

Reservations, fees: Reservations are accepted at 800/562-3617. Sites are $25–40 per night, $3–4 per person per night for more than two people, $3.50 for each additional vehicle, and a $5 site guarantee fee. Some credit cards accepted. Open year-round.

Directions: From Redding, drive north on I-5 to the town of Mount Shasta. Continue past the first Mount Shasta exit and take the Central Mount Shasta exit. At the stop sign, turn right (east) on Lake Street and drive 0.6 mile to Mount Shasta Boulevard. Turn left and drive 0.5 mile to East Hinckley Boulevard. Turn right (signed KOA) on East Hinckley, drive a very short distance, then turn left at the entrance to the extended driveway for KOA Mount Shasta.

Contact: KOA Mount Shasta, 530/926-4029, www.mtshastakoa.com or www.koa.com.

39 McCLOUD DANCE COUNTRY RV PARK
🏃‍♂️🚣🎿🐕♿🚐⛺

Scenic rating: 6

in McCloud

McCloud Dance Country RV Park is very popular with square dancers in the summer. The town of McCloud is the home of McCloud Dance Country Hall, a large dance hall dedicated to square and round dancing. The park used to be affiliated with the dance hall, but now it is open to the public. The park is sprinkled with old-growth pine trees and bordered by Squaw Valley Creek, a pretty stream. The RV sites are grassy and manicured, many shaded. McCloud River's three waterfalls are accessible from the McCloud River Loop, five miles south of the park on Highway 89. Mount Shasta Board and Ski Park also offers summer activities such as biking, a rock-climbing structure, and chairlift rides to great views of the surrounding forests. The ski park access road is six miles west of McCloud off Highway 89 at Snowman's Hill Summit. The McCloud River Railroad runs an excursion and a dinner train on summer weekends out of McCloud; reservations are available in town. If you're lucky you might see "Old Engine No. 25," one of the few remaining steam engines in service. (For more information, see the *Fowler's Camp* listing.)

Campsites, facilities: There are 136 sites with full or partial hookups (30 and 50 amps) for RVs of any length, a grassy area for dispersed tent camping, and seven cabins. There are a few long-term rentals. Large groups are welcome. Picnic tables are provided. Drinking water, restrooms with hot showers (heated bathhouse), a central barbecue and campfire area, cable TV, pay telephone, coin laundry, dump station, propane, horseshoes, fish-cleaning station, and two pet walks are available. Some facilities are wheelchair-accessible. Leashed pets are permitted, except in cabins.

Reservations, fees: Reservations are recommended. Sites are $14–41 per night, $7 per person per night for more than two people. Weekly rates available. Some credit cards accepted. Open year-round.

Directions: From Redding, drive north on I-5 and continue just past Dunsmuir to the junction with Highway 89. Turn east on Highway 89 and drive nine miles to McCloud and Squaw Valley Road. Turn right on Squaw Valley Road and then turn immediately left into the park entrance.

Contact: McCloud Dance Country RV Park, 530/964-2252, www.mccloudrvpark.com.

40 FOWLER'S CAMP
🏃‍♂️🚣🛶🐕♿🚐⛺

Scenic rating: 10

on the McCloud River in Shasta-Trinity National Forest

This campground is set beside the beautiful McCloud River at 3,400 feet, providing the chance for an easy hike to two waterfalls, including one of the most dramatic in Northern California. From the camp, the trail is routed upstream through forest, a near-level walk for only 15 minutes, then arrives at awesome Middle Falls, a wide-sweeping and powerful cascade best viewed in April. By summer, the flows subside and warm to the point that some people will swim in the pool at the base of the falls. The trail is also routed from camp downstream to Lower Falls, an outstanding swimming hole in midsummer. Fishing the McCloud River here is fair, with trout stocks made from Lakim Dam on downstream to the camp. If this camp is full, Cattle Camp and Algoma, described in this chapter, offer overflow areas.

Campsites, facilities: There are 38 sites and one double site for tents or RVs up to 30 feet (no hookups). Picnic tables and fire grills are provided. Drinking water and vault toilets are available. Some facilities are wheelchair-accessible. Leashed pets are permitted.

Reservations, fees: Reservations are not accepted. Sites are $12 per night. Open year-round, weather permitting.

Directions: From Redding, drive north on I-5 and continue just past Dunsmuir to the junction with Highway 89. Turn east on Highway 89 and drive 12 miles to McCloud. From McCloud, continue driving on Highway 89 for five miles to the campground entrance road on the right. Turn right and drive a short distance to a Y intersection, then turn left at the Y to the campground.

Contact: Shasta-Trinity National Forest, McCloud Ranger District, 530/964-2184, fax 530/964-2938.

41 ALGOMA

Scenic rating: 7

on the McCloud River in Shasta-Trinity National Forest

This little-known, undeveloped spot along the McCloud River at 3,800 feet elevation is quite dusty in August. It is an alternative to Fowler's Camp and Cattle Camp. (See the *Fowler's Camp* and *Cattle Camp* listings for side-trip options.) A dirt road out of Algoma (turn right at the junction) follows along the headwaters of the McCloud River, past Cattle Camp to Upper Falls. There is a parking area for a short walk to view Middle Falls and on to Fowler's Camp and Lower Falls.

Campsites, facilities: There are eight sites for tents or RVs up to 27 feet (no hookups). Picnic tables and fire grills are provided. Drinking water and vault toilets are available. Leashed pets are permitted.

Reservations, fees: Reservations are not accepted. There is no fee for camping. Open year-round, weather permitting.

Directions: From Redding, drive north on I-5 and continue just past Dunsmuir to the junction with Highway 89. Turn east on Highway 89 and drive to McCloud. From McCloud, continue driving on Highway 89 for 14 miles to the campground entrance road on the right (signed). Turn right and drive one mile to the campground by the bridge.

Contact: Shasta-Trinity National Forest, McCloud Ranger District, 530/964-2184, fax 530/964-2938.

42 CATTLE CAMP

Scenic rating: 5

on the McCloud River in Shasta-Trinity National Forest

This campground, at 3,700 feet, is ideal for RV campers who want a rustic setting, or as an overflow area if the more attractive Fowler's Camp is filled. A small swimming hole in the McCloud River is near the camp, although the water is typically cold. There are several good side trips in the area, including fishing on the nearby McCloud River, visiting the three waterfalls near Fowler's Camp, and exploring the north slopes of Mount Shasta (a map of Shasta-Trinity National Forest details the back roads).

Campsites, facilities: There are 19 individual sites and four double sites for tents or RVs up to 32 feet (no hookups). Picnic tables and fire grills are provided. Drinking water and vault toilets are available. Some facilities are wheelchair-accessible. Leashed pets are permitted.

Reservations, fees: Reservations are not accepted. Sites are $12 per night. Open year-round, weather permitting.

Directions: From Redding, drive north on I-5 and continue just past Dunsmuir to the junction with Highway 89. Turn east on Highway 89 and drive to McCloud. From McCloud, continue driving on Highway 89 for 11 miles to the campground entrance road on the right. Turn right and drive 0.5 mile to the campground on the left side of the road.

Contact: Shasta-Trinity National Forest, McCloud Ranger District, 530/964-2184, fax 530/964-2938.

43 TRAIL CREEK

Scenic rating: 7

in Klamath National Forest

This simple and quiet camp is set beside Trail Creek, a small tributary to the upper Salmon River, at an elevation of 4,700 feet. A trailhead is about a mile to the south, accessible via a Forest Service road, providing access to a two-mile trail routed along Fish Creek and leading to little Fish Lake. From Fish Lake the trail climbs steeply, switchbacking at times, for another two miles to larger Trail Gull Lake, a very pretty spot set below Deadman Peak (7,741 feet).

Campsites, facilities: There are 12 sites for tents or RVs up to 22 feet (no hookups). Picnic tables and fire grills are provided. Drinking water and vault toilets are available. Leashed pets are permitted.

Reservations, fees: Reservations are not accepted. Sites are $10 per night. Open May through October.

Directions: From Weed, drive north on I-5 to the Edgewood exit. Take the Edgewood exit, turn left at the stop sign, and drive a short distance under the freeway to another stop sign at Old Highway 99. Turn right (north) and drive

six miles to Gazelle and Gazelle-Callahan Road. Turn left (west) on Gazelle-Callahan Road and continue to Callahan and Cecilville Road. Turn left (southwest) on Cecilville Road and drive 17 miles to the campground.

Contact: Klamath National Forest, Scott River Ranger District, 530/468-5351, fax 530/468-1290.

44 HIDDEN HORSE

Scenic rating: 7

in Klamath National Forest

Hidden Horse provides an alternate horse camp to nearby Carter Meadows. The horse camps are in close proximity to the Pacific Crest Trail, which passes through the area and serves as access to the Russian Wilderness to the north and the Trinity Alps Wilderness to the south. Trail Creek and East Fork campgrounds are nearby. The elevation is 6,000 feet.

Campsites, facilities: There are six sites for tents or RVs up to 35 feet (no hookups). Picnic tables and fire grills are provided. Drinking water and vault toilets are available. A horse-mounting ramp and corrals are also available. There is no designated water for stock available, so bring a bucket. Some facilities are wheelchair-accessible. Leashed pets are permitted.

Reservations, fees: Reservations are not accepted. Sites are $10 per night. Open June through October, weather permitting.

Directions: From Weed, drive north on I-5 to the Edgewood exit. Take the Edgewood exit, turn left at the stop sign, and drive a short distance under the freeway to Old Highway 99. Turn right (north) and drive six miles to Gazelle and Gazelle-Callahan Road. Turn left (west) on Gazelle-Callahan Road, and continue to Callahan and Cecilville Road. Turn left (southwest) on Cecilville Road and drive 11 miles to Carter Meadows Horse

Camp. Continue 0.25 mile to the campground on the left.

Contact: Klamath National Forest, Scott River and Salmon River Ranger Districts, 530/468-5351, fax 530/468-1290.

45 CARTER MEADOWS GROUP HORSE CAMP

Scenic rating: 7

in Klamath National Forest

Carter Meadows offers an extensive trail network for riding and hiking. The Pacific Crest Trail passes through the area and serves as access to the Russian Wilderness to the north and the Trinity Alps Wilderness to the south. Stream fishing is another option here. Trail Creek and East Fork campgrounds are nearby.

Campsites, facilities: There is one disbursed group equestrian site for tents or RVs up to 35 feet (no hookups) that can accommodate up to 25 people and 25 horses. Group barbecues and picnic tables are provided. Drinking water, vault toilets, and 13 horse corrals are available. Leashed pets are permitted.

Reservations, fees: Reservations are required at 877/444-6777 or www.recreation.gov ($10 reservation fee). The camp is $30 per night. Open mid-May through October, weather permitting.

Directions: From Weed, drive north on I-5 to the Edgewood exit. Take the Edgewood exit, turn left at the stop sign, and drive a short distance under the freeway to Old Highway 99. Turn right (north) and drive six miles to Gazelle and Gazelle-Callahan Road. Turn left (west) on Gazelle-Callahan Road, and continue to Callahan and Cecilville Road. Turn left (southwest) on Cecilville Road and drive 11 miles to the campground.

Contact: Klamath National Forest, Scott River and Salmon River Ranger Districts, 530/468-5351, fax 530/468-1290.

46 HORSE FLAT

Scenic rating: 6

on Eagle Creek in Shasta-Trinity National Forest

This camp is used by commercial pack operations as well as horse owners preparing for trips into the Trinity Alps. A trail starts right out of camp and is routed deep into the Trinity Alps Wilderness. It starts at 3,200 feet in elevation, then climbs all the way along Eagle Creek to Eagle Peak, where it intersects with the Pacific Crest Trail, then drops over the ridge to little Telephone Lake, a nine-mile hike. Note: Horse owners should call for the conditions of the corral and trail before making the trip.

Campsites, facilities: There are 16 sites for tents or RVs up to 16 feet (no hookups). Picnic tables and fire grills are provided. Vault toilets are available. No drinking water is available. Horse corrals are available. Garbage must be packed out. Leashed pets are permitted.

Reservations, fees: Reservations are not accepted. There is no fee for camping. Open mid-May through October.

Directions: From Redding, drive west on Highway 299 to Weaverville and Highway 3. Turn right (north) on Highway 3 and drive to Trinity Center at the north end of Trinity Lake. From Trinity Center, continue north on Highway 3 for 16.5 miles to Eagle Creek Campground (on the left) and Forest Road 38N27. Turn left on Forest Road 38N27 and drive two miles to the campground.

Contact: Shasta-Trinity National Forest, Weaverville Ranger Station, 530/623-2121, fax 530/623-6010.

47 EAGLE CREEK

Scenic rating: 7

in Shasta-Trinity National Forest

This campground is set where little Eagle Creek enters the north Trinity River. Some campers use it as a base camp for a fishing trip, with the rainbow trout often abundant but predictably small in this stretch of water. The elevation is 2,800 feet.

Campsites, facilities: There are 17 sites for tents or RVs up to 35 feet (no hookups). Picnic tables and fire grills are provided. Drinking water and vault toilets are available. Leashed pets are permitted.

Reservations, fees: Reservations are not accepted. Sites are $10 per night. Open mid-May through October.

Directions: From Redding, drive west on Highway 299 to Weaverville and Highway 3. Turn right (north) on Highway 3 and drive to Trinity Center at the north end of Trinity Lake. From Trinity Center, continue north on Highway 3 for 16.5 miles to the campground on the left side of the road.

Contact: Shasta-Trinity National Forest, Weaverville Ranger Station, 530/623-2121, fax 530/623-6010.

48 RAILROAD PARK RV AND CAMPGROUND

Scenic rating: 7

south of Dunsmuir

The resort adjacent to the RV park and campground was designed in the spirit of the railroad, when steam trains ruled the rails. The property features old stage cars (available for overnight lodging) and a steam locomotive. The railroad theme does not extend to the campground, however. What you'll find at the park is a classic campground set amid tall trees. There is a swimming hole in Little Castle Creek alongside the park. Many good side trips are available in the area, including excellent hiking and sightseeing at Castle Crags State Park (where there is a series of awesome granite spires) and outstanding trout fishing on the upper Sacramento River. At night, the sound of occasional passing trains soothes some, wakes others.

Campsites, facilities: There are 21 sites with full or partial hookups (30 amps) for RVs of any length, 31 sites with no hookups for tents or RVs. Some sites are pull-through. Cabins and a motel are next door at the resort. Picnic tables and fire rings are provided. Restrooms with showers, ice, coin laundry, group barbecue pit, game room, and horseshoes are available. A restaurant and lounge are within walking distance. Some facilities are wheelchair-accessible. Leashed pets are permitted.

Reservations, fees: Reservations are accepted. Sites are $22–30 per night, $3 per person per night for more than two people, $3 per night for each additional vehicle. Some credit cards accepted. Open April through November, weather permitting.

Directions: From Redding, drive north on I-5 for 45 miles to Exit 728 for Cragview Drive/Railroad Park Road. Take that exit and drive to the stop sign and Railroad Park Road. Turn left and drive under the freeway and continue to the campground on the left.

Contact: Railroad Park RV and Campground, 530/235-0420 or 800/974-7245 (California residents only), www.rrpark.com.

49 CASTLE CRAGS STATE PARK

Scenic rating: 9

on the Sacramento River

This park is named for the awesome granite spires that tower 6,000 feet above the park. Beyond to the north is giant Mount Shasta

(14,162 feet), making for a spectacular natural setting. The campsites are set in forest, shaded, very pretty, and sprinkled along a paved access road. But not a year goes by when people don't write in complaining of the highway noise from I-5 echoing in the Sacramento River Canyon, as well as of the occasional passing freight trains in the night. Pristine and quiet, this campground is not. (In the future, its location may be moved farther up the canyon for a quieter setting.) At the end of the access road is a parking area for the two-minute walk to the Crags Lookout, a beautiful view. Nearby is the trailhead (at 2,500 feet elevation) for hikes up the Crags, featuring a 5.4-mile round-trip that rises to the base of Castle Dome at 4,800 feet, the leading spire on the crag's ridge. Again, road noise echoing up the canyon provides a background once you clear the tree line. Trout fishing is good in the nearby Sacramento River and requires driving, walking, and exploring to find the best spots. There are also some good swimming holes, but the water is cold. This is a popular state park, with reservations often required in summer, but with your choice of any campsite even in late spring.

Campsites, facilities: There are 52 sites for tents only, three sites for RVs up to 27 feet (no hookups), an overflow area with 12 sites and limited facilities, six walk-in environmental sites (100-yard walk required) with limited facilities, and a hike-in/bike-in site. Picnic tables, food lockers, and fire grills or fire rings are provided. Drinking water, restrooms with flush toilets and showers, and firewood are available. Leashed pets are permitted at campsites only.

Reservations, fees: Reservations are accepted ($7.50 reservation fee) at 800/444-PARK (800/444-7275) or www.reserveamerica.com. Sites are $13–20 per night, $9 per night for walk-in environmental sites, $6 per night for each additional vehicle. The hike-in/bike-in site is $3 per person per night. Open year-round.

Directions: From Redding, drive north on I-5

for 45 miles to the Castle Crags State Park exit. Take that exit, turn west, and drive a short distance to the well-signed park entrance on the right side of the road.

Contact: Castle Crags State Park, 530/235-2684, fax 530/235-1965, www.parks.ca.gov.

50 FRIDAY'S RV RETREAT AND MCCLOUD FLY FISHING RANCH

🏃 🛶 🏠 ♿ 🚐 ⛺

Scenic rating: 7

near McCloud

Friday's RV Retreat and McCloud Fly Fishing Ranch offers great recreation opportunities for every member of the family. The property features a small private fishing lake, two casting ponds, 1.5 miles of Squaw Valley Creek frontage, and five miles of hiking trails. The ranch specializes in fly-fishing packages, with both lodging and fly-fishing for one price. However, campers are welcome to stay here. In addition, the McCloud River's wild trout section is a 45-minute drive to the south, the beautiful McCloud Golf Course (nine holes) is within a five-minute drive, and a trailhead for the Pacific Crest Trail is also only five minutes away. Lake McCloud is three miles away and offers fishing and water-sports options. The park covers 400 wooded and grassy acres. Owner Bob Friday is quite a character, and he figured out that if he planted giant rainbow trout in the ponds for catch-and-release fishing, fly fishers would stop to catch a monster and take a photograph, and then tell people they caught the fish on the McCloud River, where they are smaller and elusive. Weeds are occasionally a problem at the ponds; call ahead if that is a concern. Also available is the dinner and excursion train that runs out of McCloud on summer weekends. (See *Ah-Di-Na* and *McCloud Dance Country RV Park* listings in this chapter for other information and side-trip options.)

Campsites, facilities: There are 30 sites with full hookups (30 and 50 amps) for RVs of any length, a large, grassy area for dispersed tent camping, and two cabins. Most RV sites are pull-through. Picnic tables and fire pits are provided. Drinking water, restrooms with showers and flush toilets, coin laundry, pay phone, propane gas, and a recreation room are available. A fly-fishing school is available by arrangement. Some facilities are wheelchair-accessible. Leashed pets are permitted.

Reservations, fees: Reservations are recommended. Sites are $16–24 per night, $3.50 per person per night for more than two people. Monthly rates available. Open early May through September.

Directions: From Redding, drive north on I-5 and continue just past Dunsmuir to the junction with Highway 89. Bear right on Highway 89 and drive nine miles to McCloud and Squaw Valley Road. Turn right at Squaw Valley Road and drive six miles to the park entrance on the right.

Contact: Friday's RV Retreat and McCloud Fly Fishing Ranch, 530/964-2878.

51 BIG FLAT

Scenic rating: 8

on Coffee Creek in Klamath National Forest

This is a great jump-off spot for a wilderness backpacking trip into the adjacent Trinity Alps. An 11-mile hike will take you into the beautiful Caribou Lakes Basin for lakeside campsites, excellent swimming, dramatic sunsets, and fair trout fishing. The trail is routed out of camp, crosses the stream, then climbs a series of switchbacks to the ridge. From here it gets easier, rounding a mountain and depositing you in the basin. Bypass Little Caribou, Lower Caribou, and Snowslide Lakes, and instead head all the way to Caribou, the

biggest and best of the lot. Big Flat is set at 5,000 feet elevation along Coffee Creek, and on the drive in, you'll see big piles of boulders along the stream, evidence of past gold mining activity.

Campsites, facilities: There are nine sites for tents or RVs up to 16 feet (no hookups). Picnic tables and fire grills are provided. Vault toilets are available. No drinking water is available. Garbage must be packed out. Leashed pets are permitted.

Reservations, fees: Reservations are not accepted. There is no fee for camping. Open May through October, weather permitting.

Directions: From Redding, turn east on Highway 299 and drive to Weaverville. In Weaverville, turn right (north) on Highway 3 and drive just past the north end of Trinity Lake to Coffee Creek Road/Forest Road 104, adjacent to a Forest Service ranger station. Turn left on Coffee Creek Road and drive 21 miles to the campground at the end of the road.

Contact: Klamath National Forest, Salmon River Ranger District, 530/468-5351, fax 530/468-1290.

52 GOLDFIELD

Scenic rating: 6

in Shasta-Trinity National Forest

For hikers, this camp makes a perfect first stop after a long drive. You wake up, get your gear organized, and then take the trailhead to the south. It is routed along Boulder Creek, and with a left turn at the junction (about four miles in), will take you to Boulder Lake (another two miles), set inside the edge of the Trinity Alps Wilderness. Former 49er coach George Seifert first told me about the beauty of this place and how perfectly this campground is situated for the hike. Campground elevation is 3,000 feet.

Campsites, facilities: There are six sites for tents or RVs up to 16 feet (no hookups). Picnic tables and fire grills are provided. Vault toilets and hitching posts for horses are available. No drinking water is available. Garbage must be packed out. Leashed pets are permitted.

Reservations, fees: Reservations are not accepted. There is no fee for camping. Open year-round.

Directions: From Redding, head east on Highway 299 and drive to Weaverville. Turn right (north) on Highway 3 and drive just past the north end of Trinity Lake to Coffee Creek Road/Forest Road 104 (a Forest Service ranger station is nearby). Turn left on Coffee Creek Road/Forest Road 104 and drive 6.5 miles to the campground on the left side of the road.

Contact: Shasta-Trinity National Forest, Weaverville Ranger Station, 530/623-2121, fax 530/623-6010.

53 TRINITY RIVER
🏃 🏊 🎣 🐕 🚐 ⛺

Scenic rating: 7

in Shasta-Trinity National Forest

This camp offers easy access off Highway 3, yet it is fairly secluded and provides streamside access to the upper Trinity River. It's a good base camp for a fishing trip when the upper Trinity is loaded with small trout. The elevation is 2,500 feet.

Campsites, facilities: There are seven sites for tents or RVs up to 35 feet (no hookups). Picnic tables and fire grills are provided. Drinking water and vault toilets are available. Leashed pets are permitted.

Reservations, fees: Reservations are not accepted. Sites are $10 per night. Open May through October.

Directions: From Redding, drive west on Highway 299 to Weaverville and Highway 3. Turn right (north) on Highway 3 and drive to Trinity Center at the north end of Trinity Lake. From Trinity Center, continue north on Highway 3 for 9.5 miles to the campground on the left side of the road.

Contact: Shasta-Trinity National Forest, Weaverville Ranger Station, 530/623-2121, fax 530/623-6010.

54 BEST IN THE WEST RESORT
🏃 🏊 🎣 🐕 🚐 ⛺

Scenic rating: 3

near Dunsmuir

This is a good layover spot for RV cruisers looking to take a break. The proximity to Castle Crags State Park, the Sacramento River, and Mount Shasta make the location a winner. Meers Creek runs through the property, and the local area has outstanding swimming holes on the Sacramento River. Trains make regular runs every night in the Sacramento River Canyon and the noise is a problem for some visitors.

Campsites, facilities: There are 12 sites with full hookups (30 and 50 amps) for RVs, a separate grassy area for dispersed tent camping, eight cabins, and a lodge. Picnic tables are provided. Coin laundry, cable TV, and restrooms with showers are available. Leashed pets are permitted.

Reservations, fees: Reservations are accepted. Sites are $15–23 per night. Monthly rates available. Open year-round.

Directions: From Redding, drive north on I-5 for about 40 miles to the Sims Road exit. Take the Sims Road exit and drive one block west on Sims Road to the resort on the left.

Contact: Best in the West Resort, 530/235-2603, www.eggerbestwest.com.

55 SIMS FLAT
🏃 🏊 🎣 🐕 ♿ 🚐 ⛺

Scenic rating: 7

on the Sacramento River

The upper Sacramento River is again becoming one of the best trout streams in the West, with easy and direct access off an interstate highway.

This camp is a good example. Sitting beside the upper Sacramento River at an elevation of 1,600 feet, it provides access to some of the better spots for trout fishing, particularly from late April through July. The trout population has recovered since the devastating spill from a train derailment that occurred in 1991, and there's good trout fishing in this area. There is a wheelchair-accessible interpretive trail. If you want to literally get away from it all, there is a trailhead about three miles east on Sims Flat Road that climbs along South Fork, including a terrible, steep, one-mile section near the top, eventually popping out at Tombstone Mountain. The noise from passing trains can be a shock for newcomers.

Campsites, facilities: There are 20 sites for tents or RVs up to 24 feet (no hookups). Picnic tables and fire grills are provided. Drinking water and flush and vault toilets are available. A nearby seasonal grocery store is open intermittently. Supplies are available to the north in Castella and Dunsmuir. Some facilities are wheelchair-accessible. Leashed pets are permitted.

Reservations, fees: Reservations are not accepted. Sites are $12 per night. Open late April through October.

Directions: From Redding, drive north on I-5 for about 40 miles to the Sims Road exit. Take the Sims Road exit (on the east side of the highway) and drive south for a mile (crossing the railroad tracks and a bridge) to the campground on the right.

Contact: Shasta-Trinity National Forest, Mount Shasta Ranger District, 530/926-4511, fax 530/926-5120.

56 AH-DI-NA

Scenic rating: 9

on the McCloud River in Shasta-Trinity National Forest

BEST (

This is the perfect base camp for trout fishing on the lower McCloud River, with camp-sites just a cast away from one of the prettiest streams in California. Downstream of the camp is a special two-mile stretch of river governed by the Nature Conservancy, where all fish must be released, no bait is permitted, single, barbless hooks are mandated, and only 10 rods are allowed on the river at any one time. Wildlife is abundant in the area, the Pacific Crest Trail passes adjacent to the camp, and an excellent nature trail is also available along the river in the McCloud Nature Conservancy.

Campsites, facilities: There are 16 sites for tents. Picnic tables and fire grills are provided. Drinking water, flush toilets, and garbage bins are available. Leashed pets are permitted.

Reservations, fees: Reservations are not accepted. Sites are $8 per night. Open late April through October, weather permitting.

Directions: From Redding, drive north on I-5 past Dunsmuir to the junction with Highway 89. Turn right and drive nine miles to McCloud and Squaw Valley Road. Turn right on Squaw Valley Road and drive to Lake McCloud. Turn right at Lake McCloud and continue along the lake to a signed turnoff on the right side of the road (at a deep cove in the lake). Turn right (the road turns to dirt) and drive four miles to the campground entrance on the left side of the road. Turn left and drive a short distance to the campground. The road in is dusty and winding—RVs and trailers are not advised.

Contact: Shasta-Trinity National Forest, Mc-Cloud Ranger District, 530/964-2184, fax 530/964-2938.

57 EAST FORK WILLOW CREEK

Scenic rating: 9

on Willow Creek

This is a beautiful spot along Willow Creek. Set at a 2,000-foot elevation, it's one of the prettiest campgrounds in the area. While you can dunk into the cold creek, it's not really a good swimming area. Fishing is prohibited here.

Campsites, facilities: There are 10 sites for tents or RVs up to 20 feet (no hookups). Picnic tables and fire rings are provided. Vault toilets are available. No drinking water is available. Leashed pets are permitted.

Reservations, fees: Reservations are not accepted. Sites are $8 per night, $5 per night for each additional vehicle. Open late May through September, weather permitting.

Directions: From the junction of U.S. 101 and Highway 299 near Arcata, turn east on Highway 299 and drive 32 miles (six miles west of Willow Creek) and look for the camp's entrance road (well signed) on the right (south) side of the road.

Contact: Six Rivers National Forest, Lower Trinity Ranger District, 530/629-2118, fax 530/629-2102.

58 BOISE CREEK

Scenic rating: 7

in Six Rivers National Forest

This camp features a 0.25-mile-long trail down to Willlow Creek and nearby access to the Trinity River. If you have ever wanted to see Bigfoot, you can do it while camping here—there's a giant wooden Bigfoot on display in nearby Willow Creek. After your Bigfoot experience, your best bet during summer is to head north on nearby Highway 96 (turn north in Willow Creek) to the campground at Tish Tang, where there is excellent river access, swimming, and rafting in the late summer's warm flows. The Trinity River also provides good salmon and steelhead fishing during fall and winter, respectively. Note that fishing is prohibited in nearby Willow Creek.

Campsites, facilities: There are 17 sites for tents or RVs up to 35 feet (no hookups). Picnic tables and fire grills are provided. No drinking

water. Vault toilets are available, and a camp host is on-site. A grocery store, gas station, restaurant, and propane gas are available nearby. Some facilities are wheelchair-accessible. Leashed pets are permitted.

Reservations, fees: Reservations accepted at 877/444-6777 or www.recreation.gov ($10 reservation fee). Sites are $10 per night, $5 per night for each additional vehicle. Open year-round.

Directions: From the intersection of U.S. 101 and Highway 299 near Arcata, drive 38 miles east on Highway 299 and look for the campground entrance on the left side of the road. If you reach the town of Willow Creek, you have gone 1.5 miles too far.

Contact: Six Rivers National Forest, Lower Trinity Ranger District, 530/629-2118, fax 530/629-2102.

59 DENNY

Scenic rating: 6

on the New River in Shasta-Trinity National Forest

This is a secluded and quiet campground along the New River, a tributary to the Trinity River and a designated Wild and Scenic River. The stream here is OK for swimming but too cold to even dip a toe in until late summer. If you drive north from the camp on Denny Road, you will find several trailheads for trips into the Trinity Alps Wilderness. The best of them is at the end of the road, where there is a good parking area, with a trail that is routed along the East Fork New River up toward Limestone Ridge. Note that the stretch of river near the camp is closed to fishing year-round. The campground is set at 1,400 feet.

Campsites, facilities: There are five sites for tents or RVs up to 22 feet (no hookups). Picnic tables and fire grills are provided. Vault toilets are available. No drinking water is available.

Garbage must be packed out. Leashed pets are permitted. Supplies are available about one hour away in Sal-yers Bar.

Reservations, fees: Reservations are not accepted. There is no fee for camping. Open year-round.

Directions: From the junction of U.S. 101 and Highway 299 near Arcata, turn east on Highway 299 and drive to Willow Creek. In Willow Creek, continue east on Highway 299 and, after reaching Salyer, continue for four miles to Denny Road/County Road 402. Turn north (left) on Denny Road and drive about 14 miles on a paved but very windy road to the campground.

Contact: Shasta-Trinity National Forest, Big Bar Ranger Station, 530/623-6106, fax 530/623-6123.

60 HOBO GULCH

Scenic rating: 7

on the North Fork of the Trinity River in Shasta-Trinity National Forest

Only the ambitious need apply. This is a trailhead camp set on the edge of the Trinity Alps Wilderness, and the reason only the ambitious show up is that it is a 20-mile uphill haul all the way to Grizzly Lake, set at the foot of the awesome Thompson Peak (8,663 feet), with no other lakes available en route. The camp is set at 2,200 feet along the North Fork of the Trinity River. The adjacent slopes of the wilderness are known for little creeks, woods, and a few pristine meadows, and are largely devoid of lakes.

Campsites, facilities: There are 10 sites for tents or RVs up to 16 feet (no hookups). Picnic tables and fire grills are provided. Vault toilets are available. No drinking water is available. Garbage must be packed out. Supplies can be obtained in Junction City, about one hour away. Leashed pets are permitted.

Reservations, fees: Reservations are not ac-

cepted. There is no fee for camping. Open year-round.

Directions: From Redding, turn on Highway 299 west and drive west past Weaverville, and continue 13 miles to Helena and County East Fork Road. Turn right on County East Fork Road and drive four miles to Hobo Gulch Road. At Hobo Gulch Road, turn left (north) and drive 16 miles (very rough road) to the end of the road at the campground.

Contact: Shasta-Trinity National Forest, Big Bar Ranger Station, 530/623-6106, fax 530/623-6123.

61 RIPSTEIN

Scenic rating: 8

on Canyon Creek in Shasta-Trinity National Forest

This is one of the great trailhead camps for the neighboring Trinity Alps. It is set at 3,000 feet on the southern edge of the wilderness and is a popular spot for a late-night arrival followed by a backpacking trip the next morning. The Canyon Creek Lakes await via a six-mile uphill hike along Canyon Creek. The destination is extremely beautiful—two alpine lakes set in high granite mountains. The route passes Canyon Creek Falls, a set of two different waterfalls, about 3.5 miles out. This is one of the most popular backpacking destinations in Northern California. Seasonal guided rafting trips on Canyon Creek are also available.

Campsites, facilities: There are 10 sites for tents or RVs up to 22 feet (no hookups). Picnic tables and fire grills are provided. Vault toilets are available. No drinking water is available. Garbage must be packed out. Supplies can be obtained 25 minutes away in Junction City. Leashed pets are permitted.

Reservations, fees: Reservations are not accepted. There is no fee for camping. Open year-round.

Directions: From Redding, turn on Highway

299 west and drive west to Junction City and Canyon Creek Road. Turn right on Canyon Creek Road and drive 15 miles to the campground on the left side of the road.

Contact: Shasta-Trinity National Forest, Big Bar Ranger Station, 530/623-6106, fax 530/623-6123; Trinity River Rafting Company, 530/623-3033.

62 BURNT RANCH

Scenic rating: 7

on the Trinity River in Shasta-Trinity National Forest

This campground is set on a bluff above the Trinity River and is one of its most compelling spots. This section of river is very pretty, with deep, dramatic canyons nearby. The elevation is 1,000 feet. Note that the trail to Burnt Ranch Falls is not maintained and is partially on private land—the landowners will not take kindly to anyone trespassing.

Campsites, facilities: There are 16 sites for tents or RVs up to 25 feet (no hookups). Picnic tables and fire grills are provided. Drinking water and vault toilets are available. Garbage must be packed out. Supplies can be obtained in Hawkins Bar about one hour away. Leashed pets are permitted.

Reservations, fees: Reservations are not accepted. Sites are $8 per night. Open year-round, weather permitting.

Directions: From Redding, take Highway 299 west and drive past Weaverville to Burnt Ranch. In Burnt Ranch, continue 0.5 mile and look for the campground entrance on the right side of the road.

Contact: Shasta-Trinity National Forest, Big Bar Ranger Station, 530/623-6106, fax 530/623-6123; Trinity River Rafting Company, 530/623-3033.

63 DEL LOMA RV PARK AND CAMPGROUND

Scenic rating: 7

on the Trinity River

RV cruisers looking for a layover spot near the Trinity River will find just that at Del Loma. Shady sites and sandy beaches are available here along the Trinity. Rafting and tubing trips are popular in this area during the summer. Salmon fishing is best in the fall, steelhead fishing in the winter. This camp is popular for family reunions and groups. Salmon fishing can be sensational on the Trinity in the fall, and some anglers will book a year in advance to make certain they get a spot. About two-thirds of the sites are rented for extended periods.

Campsites, facilities: There are 41 sites, including two pull-through, with full hookups (50 amps) for RVs and tents, five park-model cabins, and two apartments. Picnic tables and fire grills are provided. Restrooms with flush toilets and showers, dump station, convenience store, clubhouse, heated pool, deli, Wi-Fi, RV supplies, firewood, coin laundry, recreation room, volleyball, tetherball, 18-hole mini golf, and horseshoe pits are available. Leashed pets are permitted.

Reservations, fees: Reservations are accepted at 800/839-0194. Sites are $25 per night, $2 per person per night for more than two people. Group and monthly rates available. Some credit cards accepted. Open year-round.

Directions: From the junction of U.S. 101 and Highway 299 in Arcata, turn east on Highway 299 and drive to Burnt Ranch. From Burnt Ranch, continue 10 miles east on Highway 299 to the town of Del Loma and look for the campground entrance on the right.

Contact: Del Loma RV Park and Campground, 530/623-2834 or 800/839-0194, www.dellomarv.com.

64 HAYDEN FLAT GROUP

Scenic rating: 7

on the Trinity River in Shasta-Trinity National Forest

This campground is split into two pieces, with most of the sites grouped in a large, shaded area across the road from the river and a few on the river side. A beach is available along the river; it is a good spot for swimming as well as a popular put-in and take-out spot for rafters. The elevation is 1,200 feet.

Campsites, facilities: There are 36 sites for tents or RVs up to 25 feet (no hookups); it can also be used as a group camp with a three-site minimum. Picnic tables and fire grills are provided. Drinking water and vault toilets are available. Some facilities are wheelchair-accessible. Leashed pets are permitted.

Reservations, fees: Reservations are required for groups (minimum of three additional sites) at 530/623-6106. Sites are $10 per night. Open year-round.

Directions: From the junction of U.S. 101 and Highway 299 in Arcata, head east on Highway 299 and drive to Burnt Ranch. From Burnt Ranch, continue 10 miles east on Highway 299 and look for the campground entrance. If you reach the town of Del Loma, you have gone 0.5 mile too far.

Contact: Shasta-Trinity National Forest, Big Bar Ranger Station, 530/623-6106, fax 530/623-6123.

65 BIG SLIDE

Scenic rating: 7

on the South Fork of the Trinity River in Shasta-Trinity National Forest

This camp is literally out in the middle of nowhere. Free? Of course it's free. Otherwise, someone would actually have to show up now and then to collect. It's a tiny, secluded, little-visited spot set along the South Fork of the Trinity River. The elevation is 1,250 feet.

Campsites, facilities: There are eight sites for tents or RVs up to 16 feet (no hookups). Picnic tables and fire grills are provided. Vault toilets are available. No drinking water is available. Leashed pets are permitted.

Reservations, fees: Reservations are not accepted. There is no fee for camping. Open late May to early October, weather permitting.

Directions: From Redding, turn on Highway 299 west and drive west over the Buckhorn Summit to the junction with Highway 3 near Douglas City. Turn south on Highway 3 and drive to Hayfork. From Hayfork, turn right on County Road 301 and drive about 20 miles to the town of Hyampom. In Hyampom, turn right on Lower South Fork Road/County Road 311 and drive five miles on County Road 311 to the campground on the right.

Contact: Shasta-Trinity National Forest, Hayfork Ranger Station, 530/628-5227, fax 530/628-5212.

66 SKUNK POINT GROUP CAMP

Scenic rating: 7

on the Trinity River in Shasta-Trinity National Forest

This is an ideal site for groups on rafting trips. You get easy access to the nearby Trinity River with a streamside setting and privacy for the group. A beach on the river is nearby. In the spring, this section of river offers primarily Class II rapids (only more difficult during high water), but most of it is rated Class I. By late summer, the water is warm and benign, ideal for families. Guided rafting trips and inflatables are available for hire and rent in nearby Big Flat. The camp elevation is 1,200 feet.

Campsites, facilities: There are two group tent sites that can accommodate up to 30 people each. Picnic tables and fire grills are provided. Vault toilets are available. No drinking water is available. Some facilities are wheelchair-accessible. Leashed pets are permitted.

Reservations, fees: Reservations are required at 530/623-6106. The fee is $30 per night per site. Open year-round.

Directions: From Redding, turn on Highway 299 west, and drive west past Weaverville, Junction City, and Helena, and continue for about seven miles. Look for the campground entrance on the left side of the road. If you reach the town of Big Bar, you have gone two miles too far.

Contact: Shasta-Trinity National Forest, Big Bar Ranger Station, 530/623-6106, fax 530/623-6123; Trinity River Rafting Company, 530/623-3033.

67 BIG BAR

Scenic rating: 6

near the Trinity River in Shasta-Trinity National Forest

You name it, you got it—a quiet, small campground with easy access, and good fishing nearby (in the fall). In addition, there is a good put-in spot for inflatable kayaks and rafts. It is an ideal piece of water for newcomers, with Trinity River Rafting offering inflatable rentals for as low as $35. The elevation is 1,200 feet. If the shoe fits. . .

Campsites, facilities: There are three sites for tents or RVs up to 20 feet (no hookups). Picnic tables and fire grills are provided. Vault toilets are available. No drinking water is available. Garbage must be packed out. Supplies are available one mile away in Big Bar. Leashed pets are permitted.

Reservations, fees: Reservations are not accepted. There is no fee for camping. Open year-round.

Directions: From Redding, turn on Highway 299 west and drive west to Weaverville. Continue on Highway 299 for 25 miles to the ranger station one mile east of Big Bar, and look for Corral Bottom Road (across from the ranger station). Turn left on Corral Bottom Road and drive 0.25 mile to the campground on the left.

Contact: Shasta-Trinity National Forest, Big Bar Ranger Station, 530/623-6106, fax 530/623-6123; Trinity River Rafting, 530/623-3033, www.trinityriverrafting. com.

68 BIG FLAT

Scenic rating: 6

on the Trinity River in Shasta-Trinity National Forest

This level campground is set off Highway 299, just across the road from the Trinity River. The sites are close together, and it can be hot and dusty in midsummer. No problem. That is when you will be on the Trinity River, taking a rafting or kayaking trip—as low as $35 to rent an inflatable kayak from Trinity River Rafting in nearby Big Bar. It's fun, exciting, and easy (newcomers are welcome).

Campsites, facilities: There are 10 sites for tents or RVs up to 22 feet (no hookups). Picnic tables and fire grills are provided. Drinking water and vault toilets are available. Some facilities are wheelchair-accessible. Leashed pets are permitted.

Reservations, fees: Reservations are not accepted. Sites are $8 per night. Open year-round.

Directions: From Redding, turn on Highway 299 west, and drive west past Weaverville, Junction City, and Helena, and continue for about seven miles. Look for the campground entrance on the right side of the road. If you reach the town of Big Bar, you have gone three miles too far.

Contact: Shasta-Trinity National Forest,

Big Bar Ranger Station, 530/623-6106, fax 530/623-6123; Trinity River Rafting Company, 530/623-3033, www.trinityriverrafting.com.

69 PIGEON POINT AND GROUP

Scenic rating: 7

on the Trinity River in Shasta-Trinity National Forest

In the good old days, huge flocks of band-tail pigeons flew the Trinity River Canyon, swooping and diving in dramatic shows. Nowadays you don't see too many pigeons, but this camp still keeps its namesake. It is better known for its access to the Trinity River, with a large beach for swimming. The elevation is 1,100 feet.

Campsites, facilities: There are 10 sites for tents or RVs up to 22 feet, two multi-family sites, and one group site that can accommodate up to 50 people with tents or RVs up to 16 feet. No hookups. Picnic tables and fire grills are provided. Vault toilets are available. No drinking water is available. Supplies can be obtained within 10 miles in Big Bar or Junction City. Some facilities are wheelchair-accessible. Leashed pets are permitted.

Reservations, fees: Reservations are not accepted for individual sites but are required for the group site at 530/623-6106. Sites are $8 per night, $12 for multi-family sites, and $50 per night for the group site. Open year-round.

Directions: From Redding, turn on Highway 299 west and drive west to Weaverville. Continue west on Highway 299 to Helena and continue 0.5 mile to the campground on the left (south) side of the road.

Contact: Shasta-Trinity National Forest, Big Bar Ranger Station, 530/623-6106, fax 530/623-6123.

70 BIGFOOT CAMPGROUND AND RV PARK

Scenic rating: 8

on the Trinity River

This private RV park is set along the Trinity River and has become one of the most popular spots on the Trinity River. Rafting and fishing trips are a feature, along with cabin rentals. It is also a popular layover for Highway 299 cruisers but provides the option for longer stays with rafting, gold panning, and in the fall and winter, fishing for salmon and steelhead, respectively. RV sites are exceptionally large, and a bonus is that a storage area is available. A three-acre site for tent camping is set along the river.

Campsites, facilities: There are 46 sites with full or partial hookups (30 and 50 amps) for RVs of any length, a separate area for tent camping, and four cabins. Tent camping is not allowed during the winter. Picnic tables and barbecues are provided. Restrooms with flush toilets and coin showers, coin laundry, convenience store, dump station, propane gas, solar-heated swimming pool (summer only), and horseshoe pits are available. Modem hookups, television hookups, fishing licenses, and a tackle shop are also available. Some facilities are wheelchair-accessible. Leashed pets are permitted.

Reservations, fees: Reservations are recommended from June through October. Sites are $16–25.50 per night, $2 per night per person for more than two people. Some credit cards accepted. Open year-round.

Directions: From Redding, turn on Highway 299 west and drive west to Junction City. Continue west on Highway 299 for three miles to the camp on the left.

Contact: Bigfoot Campground and RV Park, 530/623-6088 or 800/422-5219, www.bigfootrvcabins.com.

71 JUNCTION CITY

Scenic rating: 7

on the Trinity River

Some of the Trinity River's best fall salmon fishing is in this area in September and early October, with steelhead following from mid-October into the winter. That makes it an ideal base camp for a fishing or camping trip.

Campsites, facilities: There are 22 sites for tents or RVs up to 40 feet (no hookups). Picnic tables, fire grills, and bearproof food lockers are provided. Drinking water and vault toilets are available. Groceries and propane gas are available within two miles in Junction City. Some facilities are wheelchair-accessible. Leashed pets are permitted.

Reservations, fees: Reservations are not accepted. Sites are $10 per night per vehicle. Open May through November.

Directions: From Redding, turn on Highway 299 west and drive west to Junction City. At Junction City, continue west on Highway 299 for 1.5 miles to the camp on the right.

Contact: Bureau of Land Management, Redding Field Office, 530/224-2100, fax 530/224-2172.

72 PHILPOT

Scenic rating: 7

on the North Fork of Salt Creek in Shasta-Trinity National Forest

It's time to join the 5 Percent Club; that is, the 5 percent of the people who know the little-used, beautiful spots in California. This is one of those places, set on the North Fork of Salt Creek on national forest land. The elevation is 2,600 feet. Remember: 95 percent of the people use just 5 percent of the available open space. Why would anyone come here? To join the 5 Percent Club, that's why. Note: The road

is too rough for many vehicles, and the sites are too small for most RVs. Trailers and RVs are not recommended.

Campsites, facilities: There are six sites for tents only. Picnic tables and fire grills are provided. Vault toilets are available. No drinking water is available. Garbage must be packed out. Leashed pets are permitted.

Reservations, fees: Reservations are not accepted. There is no fee for camping. Open late May to early November, weather permitting.

Directions: From Redding, turn on Highway 299 west and drive west over the Buckhorn Summit, and continue to the junction with Highway 3 near Douglas City. Turn left (south) on Highway 3 and drive to Hayfork. From Hayfork, continue southwest on Highway 3 for eight miles to County Road 353 (Rattlesnake Creek Road). Turn right and drive one mile to Forest Road 30N31. Turn right and drive 0.5 mile to the campground on the left. Trailers and RVs are not recommended.

Contact: Shasta-Trinity National Forest, Hayfork Ranger Station, 530/628-5227, fax 530/628-5212.

73 MAD RIVER

Scenic rating: 7

in Six Rivers National Forest

This Forest Service campground is set along an alluvial flood terrace, a unique landscape for this region, featuring a forest of manzanita and Douglas fir. It is often hot, always remote, in a relatively unknown section of Six Rivers National Forest at an elevation of 2,600 feet. The headwaters of the Mad River pour right past the campground, about two miles downstream from the Ruth Lake Dam. People making weekend trips to Ruth Lake sometimes end up at this little-used camp. Ruth Lake is a designated Watchable Wildlife Site and is the only major recreation lake within decent driving range of Eureka, offering a small marina with boat rentals and a good boat ramp for access to trout and bass fishing and waterskiing. Swimming and all water sports are allowed at Ruth Lake.

Campsites, facilities: There are 40 sites for tents or RVs up to 22 feet (no hookups). Picnic tables and fire grills are provided. Drinking water and vault toilets are available. Leashed pets are permitted.

Reservations, fees: Reservations are not accepted. Sites are $12 per night, $5 per night for each additional vehicle. Open late May through mid-September.

Directions: From Eureka, drive south on U.S. 101 to Alton. Turn east on Highway 36 and drive about 50 miles to the town of Mad River. Turn southeast on Lower Mad River Road and drive four miles to the camp on the right side of the road.

Contact: Six Rivers National Forest, Mad River Ranger District, 707/574-6233, fax 707/574-6273.

⁊⁴ HELLS GATE

Scenic rating: 7

on the South Fork of the Trinity River in Shasta-Trinity National Forest

This is a pretty spot bordering the South Fork of the Trinity River. The prime feature is for hikers. The South Fork National Recreation Trail begins at the campground and follows the river for many miles. Additional trails branch off and up into the South Fork Mountains. This area is extremely hot in summer. The elevation is 2,300 feet. It gets moderate use and may even fill on three-day weekends. Insider's note: If Hells Gate is full, there are seven primitive campsites at Scott's Flat Campground, 0.5 mile beyond Hells Gate, that can accommodate RVs up to 20 feet.

Campsites, facilities: There are 15 sites for

tents or RVs up to 16 feet (no hookups). Picnic tables and fire grills are provided. Drinking water and vault toilets are available. Some facilities are wheelchair-accessible. Leashed pets are permitted.

Reservations, fees: Reservations are not accepted. Sites are $6 per night. Open late May through early November, weather permitting.

Directions: From Red Bluff, turn west on Highway 36 (very twisty) and drive past Platina to the junction with Highway 3. Continue west on Highway 36 for 10 miles to the campground entrance on the left side of the road. If you reach Forest Glen, you have gone a mile too far.

Contact: Shasta-Trinity National Forest, Hayfork Ranger Station, 530/628-5227, fax 530/628-5212.

⁷⁵ FOREST GLEN

Scenic rating: 7

on the South Fork of the Trinity River in Shasta-Trinity National Forest

If you get stuck for a spot in this region, this camp almost always has sites open, even during three-day weekends. It is on the edge of a forest near the South Fork of the Trinity River. If you hit it wrong, during a surprise storm, a primitive shelter is available at the nearby Forest Glen Guard Station—a historic cabin that sleeps eight and rents out from the Forest Service for $35 a night.

Campsites, facilities: There are 15 sites for tents or RVs up to 15 feet (no hookups). Picnic tables and fire grills are provided. Vault toilets are available. No drinking water is available. Some facilities are wheelchair-accessible. Leashed pets are permitted.

Reservations, fees: Reservations are not accepted. Sites are $6 per night. Open late May through early November, weather permitting.

Directions: From Red Bluff, turn west on Highway 36 (very twisty) and drive past Platina to the junction with Highway 3. Continue west on Highway 36 for 11 miles to Forest Glen. The campground is at the west end of town on the right side of the road.

Contact: Shasta-Trinity National Forest, Hayfork Ranger Station, 530/628-5227, fax 530/628-5212.

76 FIR COVE CAMP

Scenic rating: 7

on Ruth Lake in Six Rivers National Forest

This spot is situated along Ruth Lake adjacent to Bailey Cove. The elevation is 2,600 feet, and the lake covers 1,200 acres. Swimming and all water sports are allowed on Ruth Lake, and there are three boat ramps. In the summer the warm water makes this an ideal place for families to spend some time swimming. Fishing is decent for rainbow trout in the spring and for bass in the summer.

Campsites, facilities: There 19 sites for tents or RVs up to 22 feet (no hookups). Picnic tables and fire grills are provided. Drinking water and vault toilets are available. Some facilities are wheelchair-accessible. Leashed pets are permitted.

Reservations, fees: Reservations are not accepted. Sites are $12 per night, $5 per night for each additional vehicle. Open late May through mid-September.

Directions: From Eureka, drive south on U.S. 101 to Alton and the junction with Highway 36. Turn east on Highway 36 and drive about 50 miles to the town of Mad River. Turn right at the sign for Ruth Lake/Lower Mad River Road and drive 12 miles to the campground on the right side of the road.

Contact: Six Rivers National Forest, Mad River Ranger District, 707/574-6233, fax 707/574-6273.

77 BAILEY CANYON

Scenic rating: 7

on Ruth Lake in Six Rivers National Forest

Ruth Lake is the only major lake within a reasonable driving distance of U.S. 101, although some people might argue with you over how reasonable this twisty drive is. Regardless, you end up at a camp along the east shore of Ruth Lake, where fishing for trout or bass and waterskiing are popular. What really wins out is that it is hot and sunny all summer, the exact opposite of the fogged-in Humboldt coast. The elevation is 2,600 feet.

Campsites, facilities: There are 25 sites for tents or RVs up to 22 feet (no hookups). Picnic tables and fire grills are provided. Drinking water and vault toilets are available. A boat ramp and small marina are available nearby. Some facilities are wheelchair-accessible. Leashed pets are permitted.

Reservations, fees: Reservations are not accepted. Sites are $12 per night, $5 per night for each additional vehicle. Open late May through mid-September.

Directions: From Eureka, drive south on U.S. 101 to Alton and the junction with Highway 36. Turn east on Highway 36 and drive about 50 miles to the town of Mad River. Turn right at the sign for Ruth Lake/Lower Mad River Road and drive 13 miles to the campground on the right side of the road.

Contact: Six Rivers National Forest, Mad River Ranger District, 707/574-6233, fax 707/574-6273.

78 TRINITY LAKE KOA

Scenic rating: 8

on Trinity Lake

This huge resort (some may remember this as the former Wyntoon Resort) is an ideal family vacation destination. Set in a wooded area covering 90 acres on the north shore of Trinity Lake, it provides opportunities for fishing, boating, swimming, and waterskiing, with access within walking distance. The lake boasts a wide variety of fish, including smallmouth bass and rainbow trout. The tent sites are spread out on 20 forested acres. The lake sits at the base of the dramatic Trinity Alps, one of the most beautiful regions in the state.

Campsites, facilities: There are 77 tent sites, 136 sites with full hookups (30 and 50 amps) for RVs of any length, and 19 cottages. Some RV sites are pull-through. Picnic tables and fire rings are provided. Drinking water, restrooms with showers, coin laundry, playground, seasonal heated pool, dump station, gasoline, convenience store, ice, snack bar, fish-cleaning area, boat rentals, and slips are available. Some facilities are wheelchair-accessible. Leashed pets are permitted, with certain restrictions.

Reservations, fees: Reservations are accepted. Sites are $30–52 per night, $3–6 per person per night for more than two people. Some credit cards accepted. Open year-round.

Directions: From Redding, drive west on Highway 299 to Weaverville and Highway 3. Turn right (north) on Highway 3 and drive approximately 30 miles to Trinity Lake. At Trinity Center, continue 0.5 mile north on Highway 3 to the resort on the right.

Contact: Trinity Lake KOA, 530/266-3337 or 800/562-7706, www.trinitylakekoa.com or www.koa.com.

79 PREACHER MEADOW
👣 🏕 🚐 ⛺

Scenic rating: 7

in Shasta-Trinity National Forest

The view of the Trinity Alps can be excellent here from the right vantage point. Otherwise, compared to all the other camps in the area so close to Trinity Lake, it has trouble matching up in the quality department. If the lakeside camps

are full, this camp provides an overflow option. The winter of 2000 was one of the strangest on record, where a localized wind storm knocked down 66 trees at this campground.

Campsites, facilities: There are 45 sites for tents or RVs up to 40 feet (no hookups). Picnic tables and fire grills are provided. Drinking water and vault toilets are available. Supplies, a coin laundry, and a small airport are available nearby. Leashed pets are permitted.

Reservations, fees: Reservations are not accepted. Sites are $12 per night. Open mid-May through October.

Directions: From Redding, drive west on Highway 299 to Weaverville at Highway 3. Turn right (north) on Highway 3 and drive to Trinity Lake. Continue toward Trinity Center and look for the campground entrance on the left side of the road (if you reach Trinity Center you have gone two miles too far).

Contact: Shasta-Trinity National Forest, Weaverville Ranger Station, 530/623-2121, fax 530/623-6010.

80 JACKASS SPRINGS
👣 ⛵ 🚣 🚐 🐕 🚗 ⛺

Scenic rating: 6

near Trinity Lake in Shasta-Trinity National Forest

If you're poking around for a more secluded campsite on this end of the lake, halt your search and pick the best spot you can find at this campground, since it's the only one in this area of Trinity Lake. The campground is 0.5 mile from Trinity Lake, but you can't see the lake from the camp. It is most popular in the fall as a base camp for deer hunters. The elevation is 2,500 feet.

Campsites, facilities: There are 21 sites for tents or RVs up to 32 feet (no hookups). Picnic tables and fire grills are provided. Vault toilets are available. No drinking water is available. Garbage must be packed out. Leashed pets are permitted.

Reservations, fees: Reservations are not accepted. There is no fee for camping. Open year-round, weather permitting.

Directions: From Redding, drive west on Highway 299 to Weaverville and the junction with Highway 3. Turn right (north) on Highway 3 and drive 29 miles to Trinity Center. Continue five miles past Trinity Center to County Road 106. Turn right on County Road 106 and drive 12 miles to the Jackass Springs/County Road 119 turnoff. Turn right on County Road 119 and drive five miles to the campground near the end of the road.

Contact: Shasta-Trinity National Forest, Weaverville Ranger Station, 530/623-2121, fax 530/623-6010.

81 BRIDGE CAMP

Scenic rating: 8

on Stuarts Fork in Shasta-Trinity National Forest

This remote spot is an ideal jump-off point for backpackers. It's at the head of Stuarts Fork Trail, about 2.5 miles from the western shore of Trinity Lake. The trail leads into the Trinity Alps Wilderness, along Stuarts Fork, past Oak Flat and Morris Meadows, and up to Emerald Lake and the Sawtooth Ridge. It is a long and grueling climb, but fishing is excellent at Emerald Lake as well as at neighboring Sapphire Lake. There's a great view of the Alps from this camp. It is set at 2,700 feet and remains open year-round, but there's no piped water in the winter and it gets mighty cold up here.

Campsites, facilities: There are 10 sites for tents or RVs up to 20 feet (no hookups). Picnic tables and fire grills are provided. Drinking water (summer season), vault toilets, and horse corrals are available. Leashed pets are permitted.

Reservations, fees: Reservations are not accepted. Sites are $12 per night in the summer, $5 per night in the winter. Open year-round.

Directions: From Redding, drive west on Highway 299 to Weaverville. In Weaverville, turn right (north) on Highway 3 and drive 17 miles to Trinity Alps Road (at Stuarts Fork of Trinity Lake). Turn left at Trinity Alps Road and drive about two miles to the campground on the right side of the road.

Contact: Shasta-Trinity National Forest, Weaverville Ranger Station, 530/623-2121, fax 530/623-6010.

82 RUSH CREEK

Scenic rating: 4

in Shasta-Trinity National Forest, north of Weaverville

This small, primitive camp provides overflow space during busy holiday weekends when the camps at Lewiston and Trinity Lakes are near capacity. It may not be much, but hey, at least if you know about Rush Creek you'll never get stuck for a spot. The camp borders Rush Creek and is secluded, but again, it's nearly five miles to the nearest access point to Trinity Lake.

Campsites, facilities: There are 10 sites for tents or RVs up to 20 feet (no hookups). Picnic tables and fire pits are provided. Vault toilets are available. No drinking water is available. Leashed pets are permitted.

Reservations, fees: Reservations are not accepted. Sites are $7 per night. Open mid-May through mid-September.

Directions: From Redding, drive west on Highway 299 to Weaverville. In Weaverville, turn right (north) on Highway 3 and drive about eight miles to the signed turnoff on the left side of the road. Turn left and drive 0.25 mile on the short spur road to the campground on the left side of the road. If you get to Forest Road 113, you've gone too far.

Contact: Shasta-Trinity National Forest, Weaverville Ranger Station, 530/623-2121, fax 530/623-6010.

83 STONEY POINT

🚶 ☀ 🛶 🚤 🐾 ⛺

Scenic rating: 7

on Trinity Lake in Shasta-Trinity National Forest

This is a popular spot at Trinity Lake, easily discovered and easily reached. Set near the outlet of Stuarts Fork, it often fills up, but two other campgrounds close by provide overflow options. The elevation is 2,400 feet.

Campsites, facilities: There are 21 sites for tents only. Picnic tables and fire grills are provided. Drinking water and flush toilets are available, with limited facilities during the winter season. Leashed pets are permitted.

Reservations, fees: Reservations are not accepted. Sites are $13 per night in summer, $6 per night in winter. Open year-round, weather permitting.

Directions: From Redding, drive west on Highway 299 to Weaverville. In Weaverville, turn right (north) on Highway 3 and drive 14 miles (about 0.25 mile past the Stuarts Fork Bridge) to the campground.

Contact: Shasta-Trinity National Forest, Weaverville Ranger Station, 530/623-2121, fax 530/623-6010.

84 PINEWOOD COVE RESORT

🚶 ☀ 🛶 🚤 🐾 ♿ 🚐 ⛺

Scenic rating: 7

on Trinity Lake

This is a privately operated camp with full boating facilities at Trinity Lake. If you don't have a boat but want to get on Trinity Lake, this can be a good starting point. A reservation is advised during the peak summer season. The elevation is 2,300 feet.

Campsites, facilities: There are 50 sites with full or partial hookups (30 and 50 amps) for RVs up to 40 feet, including 10 RV sites rented for the entire season and wait-listed, and 28 tent

sites. There are also 15 park-model cabins. Picnic tables and fire grills are provided. Restrooms with showers, coin laundry, dump station, RV supplies, seasonal heated swimming pool, playground, children's treehouse, volleyball, badminton, free movies three nights a week in summer, modem access, video rentals, recreation room with billiards and video arcade, convenience store, ice, fishing tackle, library, boat dock with 32 slips, beach, and canoe and kayak rentals are available. Some facilities are wheelchair-accessible. Leashed pets are permitted.

Reservations, fees: Reservations are recommended in the summer. Sites are $27.50–37.50 per night, $4 per person per night for more than two people, $4 per pet per night. Some credit cards accepted. Open mid-April through October.

Directions: From Redding, drive west on Highway 299 to Weaverville. In Weaverville, turn north (right) on Highway 3 and drive 14 miles to the campground entrance on the right.

Contact: Pinewood Cove Resort, 530/286-2201 or 800/988-5253, www.pinewoodcove.com.

85 STONEY CREEK GROUP CAMP

🚶 ☀ 🛶 🚤 🐾 ⛺

Scenic rating: 7

on Trinity Lake in Shasta-Trinity National Forest

A couple of camps sit on the northern shore of the Stuarts Fork arm of Trinity Lake. This is one of two designed for groups (the other is Fawn), and it is clearly the better. It is set along the Stoney Creek arm, a cove with a feeder creek, with the camp large but relatively private. A swimming beach nearby is a bonus. The elevation is 2,400 feet.

Campsites, facilities: This group tent site can accommodate up to 50 people. Picnic tables and fire grills are provided. Drinking water and flush toilets are available. Leashed pets are permitted.

Reservations, fees: Reservations are required at 877/444-6777 or www.recreation.gov ($10 reservation fee). The camp is $75 per night. Open early May through late September.

Directions: From Redding, drive west on Highway 299 to Weaverville. In Weaverville, turn right (north) on Highway 3 and drive 14.5 miles (about a mile past the Stuarts Fork Bridge) to the campground.

Contact: Shasta-Trinity National Forest, Weaverville Ranger Station, 530/623-2121, fax 530/623-6010.

86 FAWN GROUP CAMP

Scenic rating: 7

on Trinity Lake in Shasta-Trinity National Forest

If you want Trinity Lake all to yourself, one way to do it is to get a group together and then reserve this camp near the shore of Trinity Lake. The elevation is 2,500 feet.

Campsites, facilities: There are two group sites for tents or RVs up to 37 feet (no hookups) that can accommodate up to 100 people each. Picnic tables and fire grills are provided. Drinking water and flush toilets are available. A marina is nearby. Leashed pets are permitted.

Reservations, fees: Reservations are required at 877/444-6777 or www.recreation.gov ($10 reservation fee). Sites are $100 per night. Open early May through late September.

Directions: From Redding, drive west on Highway 299 to Weaverville. In Weaverville, turn right (north) on Highway 3 and drive 15 miles to the campground.

Contact: Shasta-Trinity National Forest, Weaverville Ranger Station, 530/623-2121, fax 530/623-6010.

87 TANNERY GULCH

Scenic rating: 8

on Trinity Lake in Shasta-Trinity National Forest

This is one of the more popular Forest Service camps on the southwest shore of huge Trinity Lake. There's a nice beach near the campground, provided the infamous Bureau of Reclamation hasn't drawn the lake level down too far. It can be quite low in the fall. The elevation is 2,400 feet. Side note: This campground was named by the tannery that once operated in the area; bark from local trees was used in the tanning process.

Campsites, facilities: There are 72 sites and four double sites for tents or RVs up to 40 feet (no hookups). Picnic tables and fire grills are provided. Drinking water, flush and vault toilets, and a boat ramp are available. Leashed pets are permitted.

Reservations, fees: Reservations are accepted at 877/444-6777 or www.recreation.gov ($10 reservation fee). Sites are $17–23 per night, $5 per night for each additional vehicle. Open early May through late September.

Directions: From Redding, drive west on Highway 299 to Weaverville. In Weaverville, turn right (north) on Highway 3 and drive 13.5 miles north to County Road 172. Turn right on County Road 172 and drive 1.5 miles to the campground entrance.

Contact: Shasta-Trinity National Forest, Weaverville Ranger Station, 530/623-2121, fax 530/623-6010.

88 BUSHY TAIL AND BUSH TAIL GROUP

Scenic rating: 7

on Trinity Lake in Shasta-Trinity National Forest

This is a great spot for families and water-sports enthusiasts. It's pretty here on Trinity

Lake, and the nearby boat launch is a bonus. The elevation is 2,500 feet.

Campsites, facilities: There are 11 sites with partial hookups (30 amps) for tents or RVs up to 40 feet. The sites are single, double, and triple sizes. Picnic tables and fire grills are provided. Drinking water and restrooms with flush toilets and coin showers are available. Supplies, a swimming beach, and a boat ramp are available nearby. Leashed pets are permitted.

Reservations, fees: Reservations are required at 877/444-6777 or www.recreation.gov ($10 reservation fee). Sites are $16–24 per night for single sites, $40 per night for double sites, $55 per night for triple sites, $80 per night for group camp. Open mid-May through late September.

Directions: From Redding, drive west on Highway 299 to Weaverville. In Weaverville, turn right (north) on Highway 3 and drive 16.2 miles (approximately 3.5 miles past the Stuarts Fork Bridge) to the campground entrance road on the right. Turn right and drive a short distance to the camp on the left side of the road.

Contact: Shasta-Trinity National Forest, Weaverville Ranger Station, 530/623-2121, fax 530/623-6010.

89 MINERSVILLE
🏃 ⛵ 🏊 🎣 🐕 🚐 ⛺

Scenic rating: 7

on Trinity Lake in Shasta-Trinity National Forest

The setting is near lakeside, quite beautiful when Trinity Lake is fullest in the spring and early summer. This is a good camp for boaters, with a boat ramp in the cove a short distance to the north. But note that the boat ramp is not always functional. When the lake level drops to 65 feet below full, the ramp is not usable. The elevation is 2,400 feet.

Campsites, facilities: There are 14 sites for tents or RVs up to 36 feet (no hookups).

Picnic tables and fire grills are provided. Drinking water, flush toilets, and a low-water boat ramp are provided. Leashed pets are permitted.

Reservations, fees: Reservations are not accepted. Sites are $13–24 per night, $7–12 per night during the winter season. Open year-round, with limited winter services.

Directions: From Redding, drive west on Highway 299 to Weaverville. Turn right (north) on Highway 3 and drive about 18 miles (if you reach the Mule Creek Ranger Station, you have gone 0.5 mile too far). Turn right at the signed campground access road and drive 0.5 mile to the camp.

Contact: Shasta-Trinity National Forest, Weaverville Ranger Station, 530/623-2121, fax 530/623-6010.

90 RIDGEVILLE BOAT-IN CAMP
⛵ 🏊 🚤 🐕 5% ⛺

Scenic rating: 9

on Trinity Lake in Shasta-Trinity National Forest   **BEST (**

This is one of the ways to get a camping spot to call your own—go by boat. The camp is exposed on a peninsula, providing beautiful views. Prospects for waterskiing and trout or bass fishing are often outstanding. The early part of the season is the prime time here for boaters, before the furnace heat of full summer. A great view of the Trinity Alps is a bonus. The only downer is the typical lake drawdown at the end of summer and beginning of fall, when this boat-in camp becomes a long traipse from water's edge.

Campsites, facilities: There are 21 tent sites. Picnic tables and fire grills are provided. Vault toilets are available. No drinking water is available. Garbage must be packed out. Boat ramps can be found near Clark Springs, Alpine View, or farther north at Trinity Center. Leashed pets are permitted.

Reservations, fees: Reservations are not accepted. There is no fee for camping. Open year-round.

Directions: From Redding, drive west on Highway 299 to Weaverville. In Weaverville, turn right (north) on Highway 3 and drive seven miles to the Stuarts Fork arm of Trinity Lake. You'll find boat launches at Stuarts Fork. After launching, drive your boat to the mouth of Stuarts Fork. The campground is set on the western shore at the end of a peninsula at the entrance to that part of the lake.

Contact: Shasta-Trinity National Forest, Weaverville Ranger Station, 530/623-2121, fax 530/623-6010.

91 CLARK SPRINGS

Scenic rating: 7

on Trinity Lake in Shasta-Trinity National Forest

This used to be a day-use-only picnic area, but because of popular demand, the Forest Service opened it for camping. That makes sense because people were bound to declare it a campground anyway, since it has a nearby boat ramp and a beach. The elevation is 2,400 feet.

Campsites, facilities: There are 21 sites for tents or RVs up to 25 feet (no hookups). Picnic tables and fire grills are provided. Drinking water and flush toilets are available, with limited facilities in the winter. Supplies are available in Weaverville. Leashed pets are permitted.

Reservations, fees: Reservations are not accepted. Sites are $12 per night. Open early April through October.

Directions: From Redding, drive west on Highway 299 to Weaverville. In Weaverville, turn right (north) on Highway 3 and drive 16.5 miles (about four miles past the Stuarts Fork Bridge) to the campground entrance road on the right.

Contact: Shasta-Trinity National Forest, Weaverville Ranger Station, 530/623-2121, fax 530/623-6010.

92 RIDGEVILLE ISLAND BOAT-IN CAMP

Scenic rating: 9

on Trinity Lake in Shasta-Trinity National Forest

How would you like to be on a deserted island? You'll learn the answer at this tiny, little-known island with a great view of the Trinity Alps. It is one of several boat-in camps in the Trinity Lake region. The elevation is 2,400 feet. Note that the lake level at Trinity Lake is typically dropped significantly from September through October.

Campsites, facilities: There are three tent sites. Picnic tables and fire grills are provided. Vault toilets are available. No drinking water is available. Garbage must be packed out. Several boat ramps are available at campgrounds and private resorts at Trinity Lake. Leashed pets are permitted.

Reservations, fees: Reservations are not accepted. There is no fee for camping. Open year-round.

Directions: From Redding, drive west on Highway 299 to Weaverville. In Weaverville, turn right (north) on Highway 3 and drive seven miles to the Stuarts Fork arm of Trinity Lake. You'll find boat launches at Stuarts Fork. After launching, drive your boat to the campground set on a small island near Estrelita Marina, between Minersville and Mariner's Roost.

Contact: Shasta-Trinity National Forest, Weaverville Ranger Station, 530/623-2121, fax 530/623-6010.

93 MARINERS ROOST BOAT-IN CAMP

Scenic rating: 8

on Trinity Lake in Shasta-Trinity National Forest

A perfect boat camp? This comes close at Trinity because it's positioned perfectly for boaters, with spectacular views of the Trinity Alps to the west, and it is an ideal spot for water-skiers. That is because it is on the western side of the lake's major peninsula, topped by Bowerman Ridge. Secluded and wooded, this area is set at 2,400 feet elevation.

Campsites, facilities: There are seven tent sites. Picnic tables and fire grills are provided. Vault toilets are available. No drinking water is available. Garbage must be packed out. Several boat ramps are available at campgrounds and private resorts at Trinity Lake. Leashed pets are permitted.

Reservations, fees: Reservations are not accepted. There is no fee for camping. Open year-round.

Directions: From Redding, drive west on Highway 299 to Weaverville. In Weaverville, turn right (north) on Highway 3 and drive seven miles to the Stuarts Fork arm of Trinity Lake. You'll find boat launches at Stuarts Fork. After launching, drive your boat to West Bowerman Ridge (near the point of the main arm of the lake) and look for the camp on the peninsula, just east and on the opposite shore of Ridgeville Island Boat-In Camp.

Contact: Shasta-Trinity National Forest, Weaverville Ranger Station, 530/623-2121, fax 530/623-6010.

94 HAYWARD FLAT

Scenic rating: 7

on Trinity Lake in Shasta-Trinity National Forest

When giant Trinity Lake is full of water, Hayward Flat is one of the prettiest places you could ask for. The camp has become one of the most popular Forest Service campgrounds on Trinity Lake because it sits right along the shore and offers a beach. The elevation is 2,400 feet.

Campsites, facilities: There are 98 sites for tents or RVs up to 40 feet (no hookups) and four double sites. Picnic tables and fire grills

are provided. Drinking water and flush toilets are available, and there is usually a camp host. Supplies and a boat ramp are nearby. Some facilities are wheelchair-accessible. Leashed pets are permitted.

Reservations, fees: Reservations are accepted at 877/444-6777 or www.recreation.gov ($10 reservation fee). Sites are $17–23 per night, $5 per night for each additional vehicle. Open mid-May through mid-September.

Directions: From Redding, drive west on Highway 299 to Weaverville. In Weaverville, turn right (north) on Highway 3 and drive 19.5 miles, approximately three miles past the Mule Creek Ranger Station. Turn right at the signed access road for Hayward Flat and drive about three miles to the campground at the end of the road.

Contact: Shasta-Trinity National Forest, Weaverville Ranger Station, 530/623-2121, fax 530/623-6010.

95 ALPINE VIEW

Scenic rating: 9

on Trinity Lake in Shasta-Trinity National Forest

This is an attractive area, set on the shore of Trinity Lake at a creek inlet. The boat ramp nearby provides a bonus. It's a very pretty spot, with views to the west across the lake arm and to the Trinity Alps, featuring Granite Peak. The Forest Service occasionally runs tours from the campground to historic Bowerman Barn, which was built in 1894. The elevation is 2,400 feet.

Campsites, facilities: There are 53 sites for tents or RVs up to 32 feet (no hookups). Picnic tables and fire grills are provided. Drinking water and flush toilets are available. Some facilities are wheelchair-accessible. The Bowerman boat ramp is nearby. Leashed pets are permitted.

Reservations, fees: Reservations are not accepted. Sites are $17–23 per night, $5 per night for each additional vehicle. Open mid-May through mid-September.

Directions: From Redding, drive west on Highway 299 to Weaverville. In Weaverville, turn right (north) on Highway 3 and drive 22.5 miles to Covington Mill (south of Trinity Center). Turn right (south) on Guy Covington Drive and drive three miles to the camp (one mile past Bowerman boat ramp) on the right side of the road.

Contact: Shasta-Trinity National Forest, Weaverville Ranger Station, 530/623-2121, fax 530/623-6010.

96 CAPTAIN'S POINT BOAT-IN CAMP

🏊 🚣 🎣 🐴 5% ⛺

Scenic rating: 7

on Trinity Lake in Shasta-Trinity National Forest

The Trinity River arm of Trinity Lake is a massive piece of water, stretching north from the giant Trinity Dam for nearly 20 miles. This camp is the only boat-in camp along this entire stretch of shore, and it is situated at a prominent spot, where a peninsula juts well into the main lake body. This is a perfect boat-in site for water-skiers or anglers. The fishing is often excellent for smallmouth bass in the cove adjacent to Captain's Point, using grubs. The elevation is 2,400 feet.

Campsites, facilities: There are three tent sites. Picnic tables and fire grills are provided. Vault toilets are available. No drinking water is available. Garbage must be packed out. Several boat ramps are available at campgrounds and private resorts at Trinity Lake. Leashed pets are permitted.

Reservations, fees: Reservations are not accepted. There is no fee for camping. Open year-round.

Directions: From Redding, drive west on Highway 299 to Weaverville. In Weaverville, turn right (north) on Highway 3 and drive about seven miles to the signed turnoff on the right

side of the road for the Trinity Alps Marina. Turn right and drive approximately 10 miles to the marina and boat ramp. Launch your boat and cruise north about four miles up the main Trinity River arm of the lake. Look for Captain's Point on the left side of the lake.

Contact: Shasta-Trinity National Forest, Weaverville Ranger Station, 530/623-2121, fax 530/623-6010.

97 CLEAR CREEK

🥾 🐴 5% 🚐 ⛺

Scenic rating: 6

in Shasta-Trinity National Forest

This is a primitive, little-known camp that gets little use. It is set near Clear Creek at 3,500 feet elevation. In fall hunters will occasionally turn it into a deer camp, with the adjacent slopes of Blue Mountain and Damnation Peak in the Trinity Divide country providing fair numbers of large bucks three points or better. Trinity Lake is only seven miles to the west, but it seems as if it's in a different world.

Campsites, facilities: There are eight sites for tents or RVs up to 22 feet (no hookups). Picnic tables and fire grills are provided. Vault toilets are available. No drinking water is available. Garbage must be packed out. Leashed pets are permitted.

Reservations, fees: Reservations are not accepted. There is no fee for camping. Open year-round.

Directions: From Redding, drive west on Highway 299 for 17 miles to Trinity Mountain Road. Turn right (north) on Trinity Mountain Road and continue past the town of French Gulch for about 12 miles to East Side Road/County Road 106. Turn right on the gravel road and drive north for about 11 miles to the campground access road (dirt) on right. Turn right on the access road and drive two miles to the campground.

Contact: Shasta-Trinity National Forest, Weaverville Ranger District, 530/623-2121, fax 530/623-6010.

98 LAKESHORE VILLA RV PARK

Scenic rating: 7

on Shasta Lake

This is a large campground with level, shaded sites for RVs, set near the northern Sacramento River arm of giant Shasta Lake. Most of the campers visiting here are boaters coming for the water sports—waterskiing, wakeboarding, or tubing. The sites are level and graveled.

Campsites, facilities: There are 92 sites with full or partial hookups (20, 30, and 50 amps) for RVs up to 45 feet; some sites are pull-through. There are also two RV rentals. No tents. Restrooms with showers, ice, dump station, cable TV, modem access, playground, group facilities, and a boat dock are available. Boat ramp, store, restaurant, and bar are nearby. Some facilities are wheelchair-accessible. Leashed pets are permitted.

Reservations, fees: Reservations are accepted. Sites are $25–38 per night. Some credit cards accepted. Open year-round.

Directions: From Redding, drive north on I-5 for 24 miles to Exit 702 for Lakeshore Drive/Antlers Road in Lakehead. Take that exit, turn left at the stop sign, and drive under the freeway to Lakeshore Drive. Turn left on Lakeshore Drive and drive 0.5 mile to the campground on the right.

Contact: Lakeshore Villa RV Park, 530/238-8688, www.lakeshorevillarvpark.com.

99 LAKESHORE INN AND RV

Scenic rating: 7

on Shasta Lake

Shasta Lake is a boater's paradise and an ideal spot for campers with boats. The nearest marina is 2.75 miles away. It is on the Sacramento River arm of Shasta Lake. Shasta Lake Caverns are 10 miles away, and Shasta Dam tours are available about 20 miles away.

Campsites, facilities: There are 40 sites with full or partial hookups (30 and 50 amps) for tents or RVs of any length; some sites are pull-through. Ten cabins are also available. Picnic tables are provided. Restrooms with showers, cable TV, dump station, seasonal swimming pool, playground, video arcade, coin laundry, seasonal bar and restaurant, and a small seasonal convenience store are available. Family barbecues are held on Sunday in season, 5 P.M.–9 P.M. Live music is scheduled most Friday and Saturday nights. Some facilities are wheelchair-accessible. Leashed pets are permitted in the campground only.

Reservations, fees: Reservations are recommended at 530/238-2003. Sites are $29–33 per night, $2.50 per person per night for more than two people, $1 per pet per night. Some credit cards accepted. Open year-round, with limited winter facilities.

Directions: From Redding, drive north on I-5 for 24 miles to Exit 702 for Lakeshore Drive/Antlers Road in Lakehead. Take that exit, turn left at the stop sign, and drive under the freeway to Lakeshore Drive. Turn left on Lakeshore Drive and drive one mile to the campground.

Contact: Lakeshore Inn and RV, 530/238-2003, www.shastacamping.com.

100 SHASTA LAKE RV RESORT AND CAMPGROUND

Scenic rating: 7

on Shasta Lake

Shasta Lake RV Resort and Campground is one of a series on the upper end of Shasta Lake with easy access off I-5 by car, then easy access by boat to premium trout or bass fishing as well as waterskiing and water sports.

Campsites, facilities: There are 53 sites with

full hookups (30 amps) for RVs up to 40 feet, 21 tent sites, one trailer rental, and three cabins. Some sites are pull-through. Picnic tables, barbecues, and fire rings are provided. Restrooms with showers, seasonal convenience store, firewood, bait, coin laundry, playground, table tennis, horseshoes, trailer and boat storage, modem access, and a seasonal swimming pool are available. There is also a private dock with 36 boat slips. Leashed pets are permitted.

Reservations, fees: Reservations are accepted at 800/374-2782. Sites are $22–32 per night, $2 per pet per night. Some credit cards accepted. Open year-round.

Directions: From Redding, drive north on I-5 for 24 miles to the Lakeshore Drive/Antlers Road exit in Lakehead. Take that exit, turn left at the stop sign, and drive under the freeway to Lakeshore Drive. Turn left on Lakeshore Drive and drive 1.5 miles to the campground on the right.

Contact: Shasta Lake RV Resort and Campground, 530/238-2370, www.shastalakerv.com.

101 ANTLERS RV PARK AND CAMPGROUND

Scenic rating: 7

on Shasta Lake

Antlers Park is set along the Sacramento River arm of Shasta Lake at 1,215 feet. The park is set on 20 acres and has shady sites. This is a full-service spot for campers, boaters, and anglers, with access to the beautiful Sacramento River arm. The camp often fills in summer, including on weekdays.

Campsites, facilities: There are 70 sites with full hookups (30 and 50 amps) for RVs of any length (several are pull-through), 40 sites for tents, and several rental trailers. Picnic tables and fire rings or fire grills are provided. Tent sites also have food lockers. Restrooms with

showers, seasonal convenience store and snack bar, ice, coin laundry, Sunday pancake breakfasts, video games, playground, volleyball court, table tennis, horseshoes, basketball, and seasonal swimming pool. Boat rentals, houseboats, moorage, and a complete marina with recreation room are adjacent to the park. Some facilities are wheelchair-accessible. Leashed pets are permitted, with a limit of two.

Reservations, fees: Reservations are recommended. Sites are $22.50–33.50 per night, $4 per person per night for more than two people, $2 per pet per night. Some credit cards accepted. Open year-round.

Directions: From Redding, drive north on I-5 for 24 miles to the Lakeshore Drive/Antlers Road exit in Lakehead. Take that exit, turn right at the stop sign, and drive a short distance to Antlers Road. At Antlers Road, turn right and drive 1.5 miles south to the campground on the left.

Contact: Antlers RV Park and Campground, 530/238-2322 or 800/642-6849, www.antlersrvpark.com.

102 ANTLERS

Scenic rating: 7

on Shasta Lake in Shasta-Trinity National Forest

This spot is set on the primary Sacramento River inlet of giant Shasta Lake. Antlers is a well-known spot that attracts returning campers and boaters year after year. It is the farthest upstream marina/camp on the lake. Lake levels can fluctuate greatly from spring through fall, and the operators will move their docks to compensate. Easy access off I-5 is a big plus for boaters.

Campsites, facilities: There are 41 individual sites and 18 double sites for tents or RVs up to 30 feet (no hookups). Picnic tables, food lockers, and fire grills are provided. Drinking water and flush and vault toilets are available. A boat ramp, amphitheater with summer interpretive programs, grocery store, and coin laundry are nearby. Some facilities are wheelchair-accessible. Leashed pets are permitted.

Reservations, fees: Reservations are accepted at 877/444-6777 or www.recreation.gov ($10 reservation fee). Sites are $18 per night, $30 per night for a double site, $5 per night for each additional vehicle. Open year-round.

Directions: From Redding, drive north on I-5 for 24 miles to the Lakeshore Drive/Antlers Road exit in Lakehead. Take that exit, turn right at the stop sign, and drive a short distance to Antlers Road. At Antlers Road, turn right and drive one mile south to the campground.

Contact: Shasta-Trinity National Forest, Shasta Lake Ranger District, 530/275-1587, fax 530/275-1512; Shasta Lake Visitor Center, 530/275-1589; Shasta Recreation Company, 530/275-8113.

103 LAKESHORE EAST
🏃 🏊 🎣 🚤 🏕 ♿ 🚐 ⛺

Scenic rating: 7

on Shasta Lake in Shasta-Trinity National Forest

Lakeshore East is near the full-service community of Lakehead and is on the Sacramento arm of Shasta Lake. It's a nice spot, with a good boat ramp and marina nearby at Antlers or Sugarloaf.

Campsites, facilities: There are 20 individual sites and six double sites for tents or RVs up to 30 feet (no hookups). Picnic tables and fire grills are provided. Drinking water and flush toilets are available. A boat ramp, grocery store, and coin laundry are available nearby. Some facilities are wheelchair-accessible. Leashed pets are permitted.

Reservations, fees: Reservations are accepted at 877/444-6777 or www.recreation.gov ($10 reservation fee). Sites are $18 per night for a single site, $30 for a double site, $5 per night for each additional vehicle. Open year-round.

Directions: From Redding, drive north on I-5

for 24 miles to the Lakeshore Drive/Antlers Road exit at Lakehead. Take the Antlers exit, turn left at the stop sign, and drive under the freeway to Lakeshore Drive. Turn left on Lakeshore Drive and drive three miles. Look for the campground entrance on the left side of the road.

Contact: Shasta-Trinity National Forest, Shasta Lake Ranger District, 530/275-1587, fax 530/275-1512; Shasta Lake Visitor Center, 530/275-1589; Shasta Recreation Company, 530/275-8113.

104 GREGORY CREEK
🏊 🏕 🚐 ⛺

Scenic rating: 7

on Shasta Lake in Shasta-Trinity National Forest

This is one of the more secluded Forest Service campgrounds on Shasta Lake, and it has become extremely popular with the younger crowd. It is set just above lakeside, on the eastern shore of the northern Sacramento River arm of the lake. When the lake is fullest in the spring and early summer, this is a great spot. Note: This is a bald eagle nesting area and the campground is subject to closures for habitat protection.

Campsites, facilities: There are 18 sites for tents or RVs up to 16 feet (no hookups). Picnic tables and fire grills are provided. Drinking water and flush toilets are available. Leashed pets are permitted.

Reservations, fees: Reservations are not accepted. Sites are $14 per night, $5 per night for each additional vehicle. Open early August through September; call to verify current status.

Directions: From Redding, drive north on I-5 for 21 miles to the Salt Creek/Gilman Road exit. Take that exit and drive over the freeway to Gregory Creek Road. Turn right and drive 10 miles to the campground at the end of the road.

Contact: Shasta-Trinity National Forest,

Shasta Lake Ranger District, 530/275-1587, fax 530/275-1512; Shasta Lake Visitor Center, 530/275-1589; Shasta Recreation Company, 530/275-8113.

105 HIRZ BAY GROUP CAMP

Scenic rating: 8

on Shasta Lake in Shasta-Trinity National Forest

This is the spot for your own private party—provided you get a reservation—set on a point at the entrance of Hirz Bay on the McCloud River arm of Shasta Lake. A boat ramp is only 0.5 mile away on the camp access road, giving access to the McCloud River arm. This is an excellent spot to make a base camp for a fishing trip, with great trolling for trout in this stretch of the lake.

Campsites, facilities: There are two group sites for tents or RVs up to 30 feet (no hookups) that can accommodate 80–120 people each. Picnic tables and fire grills are provided. Drinking water, vault toilets, and a group picnic area are available. Leashed pets are permitted.

Reservations, fees: Reservations are required at 877/444-6777 or www.recreation.gov ($10 reservation fee). Sites are $80–110 per night. Open April through late September.

Directions: From Redding, drive north on I-5 for about 20 miles to the Salt Creek/Gilman exit. Turn right on Gilman Road/County Road 7H009 and drive northeast for 10 miles to the campground/boat launch access road. Turn right and drive 0.5 mile to the camp on the left side of the road. The group camp is past the family campground.

Contact: Shasta-Trinity National Forest, Shasta Lake Ranger District, 530/275-1587, fax 530/275-1512; Shasta Lake Visitor Center, 530/275-1589; Shasta Recreation Company, 530/275-8113.

106 HIRZ BAY

Scenic rating: 8

on Shasta Lake in Shasta-Trinity National Forest

BEST (

This is one of two camps in the immediate area (the other is Hirz Bay Group Camp) that provides nearby access to a boat ramp (0.5 mile down the road) and the McCloud River arm of Shasta Lake. The camp is set on a point at the entrance of Hirz Bay. This is an excellent spot to make a base camp for a fishing trip, with great trolling for trout in this stretch of the lake.

Campsites, facilities: There are 37 individual sites and 10 double sites for tents or RVs up to 40 feet (no hookups). Picnic tables and fire grills are provided. Drinking water and flush and vault toilets are available. A camp host is usually available in the summer. A boat ramp is nearby. Some facilities are wheelchair-accessible. Leashed pets are permitted.

Reservations, fees: Reservations are accepted at 877/444-6777 or www.recreation. gov ($10 reservation fee). Sites are $18 per night, $30 per night for a double site, $5 per night for each additional vehicle. Open year-round.

Directions: From Redding, drive north on I-5 for about 20 miles to the Salt Creek/Gilman exit. Turn right on Gilman Road/County Road 7H009 and drive northeast for 10 miles to the campground/boat launch access road. Turn right and drive 0.5 mile to the camp on the left side of the road.

Contact: Shasta-Trinity National Forest, Shasta Lake Ranger District, 530/275-1587, fax 530/275-1512; Shasta Lake Visitor Center, 530/275-1589; Shasta Recreation Company, 530/275-8113.

107 DEKKAS ROCK GROUP CAMP

Scenic rating: 8

on Shasta Lake in Shasta-Trinity National Forest

The few people who know about this camp love this little spot. It is an ideal group camp, set on a flat above the McCloud arm of Shasta Lake, shaded primarily by bays and oaks, with a boat ramp two miles to the south at Hirz Bay. The views are pretty here, looking across the lake at the limestone ridge that borders the McCloud arm. In late summer and fall when the lake level drops, it can be a hike from the camp down to water's edge.

Campsites, facilities: There is one group site for tents or RVs up to 16 feet (no hookups) that can accommodate up to 60 people. A central meeting area with preparation tables, picnic tables, two pedestal grills, and a large barbecue is provided. Drinking water and vault toilets are available. Leashed pets are permitted.

Reservations, fees: Reservations are required at 877/444-6777 or www.recreation. gov ($10 reservation fee). The camp is $110 per night.

Directions: From Redding, drive north on I-5 for about 20 miles to the Salt Creek/ Gilman exit. Turn right on Gilman Road/ County Road 7H009 and drive northeast for 11 miles to the campground on the right side of the road.

Contact: Shasta-Trinity National Forest, Shasta Lake Ranger District, 530/275-1587, fax 530/275-1512; Shasta Lake Visitor Center, 530/275-1589; Shasta Recreation Company, 530/275-8113.

108 MOORE CREEK GROUP AND OVERFLOW

Scenic rating: 8

on Shasta Lake in Shasta-Trinity National Forest

The McCloud arm of Shasta Lake is the most beautiful of the five arms at Shasta, with its emerald-green waters and limestone canyon towering overhead to the east. That beautiful setting is taken advantage of at this camp, with a good view of the lake and limestone, along with good trout fishing on the adjacent section of water. Moore Creek is rented as a group camp most of the summer, except during holidays when individual sites are available on a first-come, first-served basis.

Campsites, facilities: There are 12 sites for tents or RVs up to 16 feet (no hookups) that are usually rented as one group site for up to 90 people. Picnic tables and fire grills are provided. Drinking water and vault toilets are available. Leashed pets are permitted.

Reservations, fees: Reservations are required for the group site at 877/444-6777 or www. recreation.gov ($10 reservation fee). Sites are $14 per night for individual sites, $5 per night for each additional vehicle, $110 per night for group site. Open late May through early September.

Directions: From Redding, drive north on I-5 for about 20 miles to the Salt Creek/Gilman exit. Take that exit and turn right on Gilman Road/County Road 7H009 and drive northeast for 14 miles to the campground on the right side of the road.

Contact: Shasta-Trinity National Forest, Shasta Lake Ranger District, 530/275-1587, fax 530/275-1512; Shasta Lake Visitor Center, 530/275-1589; Shasta Recreation Company, 530/275-8113.

109 ELLERY CREEK

🏊 🚣 🚤 🏕 🚙 ⛰

Scenic rating: 7

on Shasta Lake in Shasta-Trinity National Forest

This camp is set at a pretty spot where Ellery Creek empties into the upper McCloud arm of Shasta Lake. Several sites are set on the pavement with an unobstructed view of the beautiful McCloud arm. This stretch of water is excellent for trout fishing in the summer, with bank-fishing access available two miles upstream at the McCloud Bridge. In the spring, there are tons of small spotted bass along the shore from the camp continuing upstream to the inlet of the McCloud River. Boat-launching facilities are available five miles south at Hirz Bay.

Campsites, facilities: There are 19 sites for tents or RVs up to 25 feet (no hookups). Picnic tables, food lockers, and fire grills are provided. Drinking water and vault toilets are available. Leashed pets are permitted.

Reservations, fees: Reservations are accepted at 877/444-6777 or www.recreation.gov ($10 reservation fee). Sites are $16 per night, $5 per night for each additional vehicle. Open early May through September.

Directions: From Redding, drive north on I-5 for about 20 miles to the Salt Creek/ Gilman exit. Turn right on Gilman Road/ County Road 7H009 and drive northeast for 15 miles to the campground on the right side of the road.

Contact: Shasta-Trinity National Forest, Shasta Lake Ranger District, 530/275-1587, fax 530/275-1512; Shasta Lake Visitor Center, 530/275-1589; Shasta Recreation Company, 530/275-8113.

110 PINE POINT AND GROUP CAMP

🏊 🚣 🚤 🏕 🚙 ⛰

Scenic rating: 7

on Shasta Lake in Shasta-Trinity National Forest

Pine Point is a pretty little camp, set on a ridge above the McCloud arm of Shasta Lake amid oak trees and scattered ponderosa pines. The view is best in spring, when lake levels are generally highest. Boat-launching facilities are available at Hirz Bay; boaters park their boats on shore below the camp while the rest of their party arrives at the camp by car. That provides a chance not only for camping, but also for boating, swimming, waterskiing, and fishing. Note: From July through September, this campground can be reserved as a group site only. It is also used as a summer overflow camping area on weekends and holidays.

Campsites, facilities: There are 14 sites for tents or RVs up to 24 feet (no hookups), which can also be used as a group camp for up to 100 people. Picnic tables, food lockers, and fire rings are provided. Drinking water and vault toilets are available. Leashed pets are permitted.

Reservations, fees: Reservations are required for group site at 877/444-6777 or www.recreation.gov ($10 reservation fee). Sites are $14 per night, $5 per night for each additional vehicle, $110 per night for a group site. Open May through early September.

Directions: From Redding, drive north on I-5 for about 20 miles to the Salt Creek/ Gilman exit. Turn right on Gilman Road/ County Road 7H009 and drive northeast for 17 miles to the campground entrance road on the right.

Contact: Shasta-Trinity National Forest, Shasta Lake Ranger District, 530/275-1587, fax 530/275-1512; Shasta Lake Visitor Center, 530/275-1589; Shasta Recreation Company, 530/275-8113.

111 McCLOUD BRIDGE

Scenic rating: 7

on Shasta Lake in Shasta-Trinity National Forest

Even though reaching this camp requires a long drive, it remains popular. That is because the best shore-fishing access at the lake is available at nearby McCloud Bridge. It is common to see 15 or 20 people shore fishing here for trout on summer weekends. In the fall, big brown trout migrate through this section of lake en route to their upstream spawning grounds.

Campsites, facilities: There are 11 individual sites and three double sites for tents or RVs up to 16 feet (no hookups). Picnic tables and fire grills are provided. Drinking water, vault toilets, and a group picnic area are available. Some facilities are wheelchair-accessible. Leashed pets are permitted.

Reservations, fees: Reservations are not accepted. Sites are $18 per night, $30 per night for double sites, $5 per night for each additional vehicle. Open early May through September.

Directions: From Redding, drive north on I-5 for about 20 miles to the Salt Creek/Gilman exit. Turn right on Gilman Road/County Road 7H009 and drive northeast for 18.5 miles. Cross the McCloud Bridge and drive one mile to the campground entrance on the right.

Contact: Shasta-Trinity National Forest, Shasta Lake Ranger District, 530/275-1587, fax 530/275-1512; Shasta Lake Visitor Center, 530/275-1589; Shasta Recreation Company, 530/275-8113.

112 MADRONE CAMP

Scenic rating: 7

on Squaw Creek in Shasta-Trinity National Forest

Tired of people? Then you've come to the right place. This remote camp is set along Squaw Creek, a feeder stream of Shasta Lake, which lies to the southwest. It's way out there, far away from anybody. Even though Shasta Lake is relatively close, about 10 miles away, it is in another world. A network of four-wheel-drive roads provides a recreation option, detailed on a map of Shasta-Trinity National Forest.

Campsites, facilities: There are 10 sites for tents or RVs up to 16 feet (no hookups). Picnic tables and fire grills are provided. Vault toilets are available. No drinking water is available. Garbage must be packed out. Leashed pets are permitted.

Reservations, fees: Reservations are not accepted. There is no fee for camping. Open year-round.

Directions: From Redding, drive 31 miles east on Highway 299 to the town of Montgomery Creek. Turn left on Fenders Ferry Road/Forest Road 27 and drive 18 miles to the camp (the road starts as gravel and then becomes dirt). Note: The access road is rough and RVs are not advised.

Contact: Shasta-Trinity National Forest, Shasta Lake Ranger District, 530/275-1587, fax 530/275-1512; Shasta Lake Visitor Center, 530/275-1589.

113 GOOSENECK COVE BOAT-IN

Scenic rating: 4

on Shasta Lake in Shasta-Trinity National Forest

You want a camp all to yourself? There's a good chance of that here at Gooseneck Cove. One reason is because it is well hidden, set back in a cove on the west side of the Sacramento River arm of giant Shasta Lake. The other reason is that there was fire damage here in 1999, and some burned oaks and manzanita will take years to grow out. So there you have it, a chance any day of the year to have a campground all to yourself. The fishing on the Sacramento River arm of Shasta Lake is very good, both trolling for trout all summer, especially at the headwaters in midsummer, and for bass in the spring on plastic worms. Waterskiing is also excellent here, with water temperatures in the high 70s for most of summer.

Campsites, facilities: There are eight boat-in sites for tents. Picnic tables and fire grills are provided. Vault toilets are available. No drinking water is available. Garbage must be packed out. Small stores with supplies are available at Antlers. Leashed pets are permitted.

Reservations, fees: Reservations are not accepted. There is no fee for camping. An $8 fee is charged for boat launching. Open year-round.

Directions: From Redding, drive north on I-5 for 24 miles to the Lakeshore Drive/Antlers Road exit in Lakehead. Take that exit, turn left at the stop sign, and drive a short distance to Antlers Road. At Antlers Road, turn right and drive one mile south to the campground and nearby boat launch. Launch your boat and cruise seven miles south to the boat-in campground.

Contact: Shasta-Trinity National Forest, Shasta Lake Ranger District, 530/275-1587, fax 530/275-1512; Shasta Lake Visitor Center, 530/275-1589.

114 TRAIL IN RV PARK AND CAMPGROUND

Scenic rating: 7

near Shasta Lake

This is a privately operated campground near the Salt Creek arm of giant Shasta Lake. Open, level sites are available. Many of the sites are filled with long-term renters. The nearest boat launch is one mile away and the lake offers fishing, boating, and swimming. Its proximity to I-5 makes this a popular spot, fast and easy to reach, which is extremely attractive for drivers of RVs and trailers who

want to avoid the many twisty roads surrounding Shasta Lake.

Campsites, facilities: There are 39 sites with full hookups (30 and 50 amps) for RVs of any length and four tent sites; some sites are pull-through. Picnic tables and fire grills are provided. Restrooms with showers, satellite TV hookups, seasonal heated swimming pool, playground, convenience store, ice, firewood, Wi-Fi, full-service deli, Saturday night barbecue, and coin laundry are available. Leashed pets are permitted.

Reservations, fees: Reservations are accepted. Sites are $28 per night for RV camping, $17 per night for tent camping, $2 per person per night for more than two people, $1 per pet per night. Monthly rates available. Some credit cards accepted. Open year-round.

Directions: From Redding, drive 22 miles north on I-5 to Exit 698/Gilman Road/Salt Creek Road exit. Take that exit and turn left on Salt Creek Road and drive a short distance to Gregory Creek Road. Turn right and drive 0.25 mile to the campground on the right.

Contact: Trail In RV Park and Campground, tel./fax 530/238-8533.

115 NELSON POINT AND GROUP CAMP

Scenic rating: 7

on Shasta Lake in Shasta-Trinity National Forest

This is an easy-to-reach campground, only a few minutes from I-5. It's set beside the Salt Creek inlet of Shasta Lake, deep in a cove. In low-water years, or when the lake level is low in the fall and early winter, this camp can seem quite distant from water's edge. This campground can be reserved as a group camp July through September.

Campsites, facilities: There are eight sites for tents or RVs up to 16 feet, and a group site for tents or RVs up to 16 feet that can accommodate up to 60 people. No hookups. Vault toilets, picnic tables, and fire grills are provided. No drinking water is available. A grocery store and coin laundry are nearby in Lakehead. Leashed pets are permitted.

Reservations, fees: Reservations are required for group sites only at 877/444-6777 or www. recreation.gov ($10 reservation fee). Sites are $10 per night, $5 per night for each additional vehicle, and $80 per night for a group site. Open May through early September.

Directions: From Redding, drive north on I-5 for about 20 miles to the Salt Creek Road/ Gilman Road exit. Take that exit, turn left and drive 0.25 mile to Gregory Creek Road. Turn right and drive one mile to Conflict Point Road. Turn left and drive one mile to the campground on the left.

Contact: Shasta-Trinity National Forest, Shasta Lake Ranger District, 530/275-1587, fax 530/275-1512; Shasta Lake Visitor Center, 530/275-1589; Shasta Recreation Company, 530/275-8113.

116 HOLIDAY HARBOR RESORT

Scenic rating: 7

on Shasta Lake   BEST (

This camp is one of the more popular family-oriented, all-service resorts on Shasta Lake, which has the second-largest dam in the United States. It is set on the lower Mc-Cloud arm of the lake, which is extremely beautiful, with a limestone mountain ridge off to the east. It is an ideal jump-off point for all water sports, especially waterskiing, houseboating and boating, and fishing. A good boat ramp, boat rentals, and store with all the goodies are bonuses. The place is full service and even offers boat-launching service. Campers staying here also get a 15 percent discount on boat rentals. Another plus is the nearby side trip to Shasta Caverns,

a privately guided adventure (fee charged) into limestone caves. This camp often fills in summer, even on weekdays.

Campsites, facilities: There are 28 sites with full hookups (50 amps) for RVs up to 40 feet, with tents allowed in several sites. Picnic tables and barbecues are provided. Restrooms with showers, general store, seasonal café, gift shop, coin laundry, marina, marine repair service, boat moorage, swim area, playground, propane gas, and houseboat and boat and personal watercraft rentals are available. Some facilities are wheelchair-accessible. Leashed pets are permitted.

Reservations, fees: Reservations are recommended. Sites are $22.75–36 per night, $6 per person per night for more than two people, $4.50–6 per night for each additional vehicle, and $7.75–12.50 per night for boat moorage. Some credit cards accepted. Open April through October.

Directions: From Redding, drive 18 miles north on I-5 to Exit 695 and the O'Brien Road/Shasta Caverns Road exit. Turn right (east) at Shasta Caverns Road and drive one mile to the resort entrance on the right; check in at the store (20061 Shasta Caverns Road).

Contact: Holiday Harbor Resort, 530/238-2383 or 800/776-2628, www.lakeshasta. com.

117 GREENS CREEK BOAT-IN

Scenic rating: 10

on Shasta Lake in Shasta-Trinity National Forest   BEST (

This is one of my favorite spots on the planet on a warm spring day, maybe mid-April, but it is always special. This boat-in campsite provides an exceptional base camp and boat-in headquarters for a recreation paradise. The camp is set at the foot of dramatic limestone formations on the McCloud arm of Shasta Lake. By boat, this is one of the best fishing spots. The campsites are in a region well wooded and little traveled, with good opportunities in the evening to see wildlife.

Campsites, facilities: There are nine boat-in sites for tents. Picnic tables, bear lockers, and fire grills are provided. Vault toilets are available. No drinking water is available. Garbage must be packed out. Small stores with supplies are available at Holiday Harbor. Leashed pets are permitted.

Reservations, fees: Reservations are not accepted. There is no fee for camping. An $8 fee is charged for boat launching. Open year-round.

Directions: From Redding, drive north on I-5 over the Pit River Bridge at Shasta Lake to the O'Brien Road/Shasta Caverns Road exit. Turn east (right) on Shasta Caverns Road and drive 0.25 mile to a signed turnoff for Bailey Cove. Turn right and drive one mile to Bailey Cove boat ramp. Launch your boat and cruise four miles northeast up the McCloud Arm. Land your boat and pick your campsite. Note: The Bailey Cove boat ramp is not usable when the lake level drops more than 50 feet.

Contact: Shasta-Trinity National Forest, Shasta Lake Ranger District, 530/275-1587, fax 530/275-1512; Shasta Lake Visitor Center, 530/275-1589.

118 SKI ISLAND BOAT-IN

Scenic rating: 8

on Shasta Lake in Shasta-Trinity National Forest

Could there be any secrets left about Shasta Lake? You bet, with boat-in campsites providing the best of all worlds for people willing to rough it just a little. Ski Island is an outstanding place to set up camp and then boat, fish, ski, or explore this giant lake. It is on the Pit River arm of the lake about three miles upstream from the Pit River (I-5) bridge. The closest boat ramp to Ski Island is at Silverthorn

Resort, which is in a cove on the Pit River arm of the lake. The closest public boat ramp is at Jones Valley, also on the Pit River arm. Here you will find this three-acre island with a boat-in campground and several little trails. It is well out of sight, and out of mind for most campers as well. One note: In wet weather, the reddish, iron-based soil on the island will turn the bottom of your boat rust-colored with even a minimum of tracking in.

Campsites, facilities: There are 23 boat-in sites for tents. Picnic tables and fire grills are provided. Vault toilets are available. No drinking water is available. Garbage must be packed out. Small stores with supplies are available at Silverthorn Resort and Jones Valley Resort. Leashed pets are permitted.

Reservations, fees: Reservations are not accepted. There is no fee for camping. An $8 fee is charged for boat launching. Open year-round.

Directions: From Redding, drive north on I-5 for three miles to Exit 682 for Oasis Road. Take that exit and drive to Oasis Road. Turn right on Oasis Road and drive 3.5 miles to Bear Mountain Road. Turn right and drive to Dry Creek Road. Turn left on Dry Creek Road and drive seven miles to a fork in the road. Bear right at the fork and drive to Jones Valley Boat Ramp (a left at the fork takes you to Silverthorn Resort). Launch your boat and head west (to the left) for four miles to Ski Island. Land and pick your campsite.

Contact: Shasta-Trinity National Forest, Shasta Lake Ranger District, 530/275-1587, fax 530/275-1512; Shasta Lake Visitor Center, 530/275-1589.

119 ARBUCKLE FLAT BOAT-IN

Scenic rating: 8

on Shasta Lake in Shasta-Trinity National Forest

How could anything be secluded on Northern California's most popular recreation lake?

Well, here is your answer. Arbuckle Flat is a truly secluded boat-in campground well up the Pit River arm of the lake, set far back in a deep cove. You will feel a million miles away from all the fast traffic back at the main lake body. Specifically, it is five miles east of the Jones Valley Boat Ramp, set on the right (south) side of a deep cove. You pay a small price for this seclusion. After landing your boat, you must then carry your gear up a hill to the campsites. When the lake is low, this is like a march up Cardiac Hill. The landscape surrounding the campsites is peppered with oak. The fishing in the area is often good for bass and, where you find submerged trees, for crappie as well.

Campsites, facilities: There are 11 boat-in sites for tents. Picnic tables and fire grills are provided. Vault toilets are available. No drinking water is available. Garbage must be packed out. Small stores with supplies are available at Silverthorn Resort and Jones Valley Resort. Leashed pets are permitted.

Reservations, fees: Reservations are not accepted. There is no fee for camping. An $8 fee is charged for boat launching. Open year-round.

Directions: From Redding, drive north on I-5 for three miles to Exit 682 for Oasis Road. Take that exit and drive to Oasis Road. Turn right on Oasis Road and drive 3.5 miles to Bear Mountain Road. Turn right and drive to Dry Creek Road. Turn left on Dry Creek Road and drive seven miles to a fork in the road. Bear right at the fork and drive to Jones Valley Boat Ramp (a left at the fork takes you to Silverthorn Resort). Launch your boat and head east (to the right) for five miles. The last major arm off to your right hides the campground at the back of the cove, in the oaks above the shore. Land and pick your campsite.

Contact: Shasta-Trinity National Forest, Shasta Lake Ranger District, 530/275-1587, fax 530/275-1512; Shasta Lake Visitor Center, 530/275-1589.

120 JONES VALLEY INLET

Scenic rating: 4

on Shasta Lake in Shasta-Trinity National Forest

This is one of the few primitive camp areas on Shasta Lake, set on the distant Pit River arm of the lake. It is an ideal camp for hiking and biking, with nearby Clickapudi Trail routed for miles along the lake's shore, in and out of coves, and then entering the surrounding foothills and oak/bay woodlands. The camp is pretty, if a bit exposed, with two nearby resorts, Jones Valley and Silverthorn, providing boat rentals and supplies.

Campsites, facilities: There is an area for dispersed, primitive camping for tents or RVs up to 40 feet (no hookups). Portable toilets are available. No drinking water is available. Garbage must be packed out. A boat ramp at Jones Valley is two miles from camp. Groceries are available nearby. Leashed pets are permitted.

Reservations, fees: Reservations are not accepted. Sites are $8 per vehicle per night. Open year-round.

Directions: From Redding, turn east on Highway 299 and drive 7.5 miles just past the town of Bella Vista. At Dry Creek Road turn left and drive nine miles to a Y intersection. Bear right at the Y (left will take you to Silverthorn Resort) and drive a short distance to the campground entrance on the left side of the road.

Contact: Shasta-Trinity National Forest, Shasta Lake Ranger District, 530/275-1587, fax 530/275-1512; Shasta Lake Visitor Center, 530/275-1589; Shasta Recreation Company, 530/275-8113.

SHASTA CAMPING

121 UPPER AND LOWER JONES VALLEY CAMPS

Scenic rating: 3

on Shasta Lake in Shasta-Trinity National Forest

Lower Jones is a small camp set along a deep cove in the remote Pit River arm of Shasta Lake. The advantage of Lower Jones Valley is that it is closer to the lake than Upper Jones Valley. Unfortunately, the Bear Fire of 2004 burned the trees and vegetation around these campgrounds. There is a trailhead at the camp that provides access to Clickapudi Trail, a great hiking and biking trail that traces the lake's shore, routed through woodlands. Two nearby resorts, Jones Valley and Silverthorn, provide boat rentals and supplies.

Campsites, facilities: There are 18 sites and three double sites for tents or RVs up to 16 feet (no hookups) in two adjacent campgrounds. Picnic tables and fire grills are provided. Drinking water, food lockers, and vault toilets are available. Some facilities are wheelchair-accessible. A boat ramp at Jones Valley is two miles from camp. Leashed pets are permitted.

Reservations, fees: Reservations are not accepted. Upper Jones sites are $18 per night, Lower Jones sites are $18 per night and $30 per night for a double site, $5 per night for each additional vehicle. Lower Jones is open year-round. Upper Jones is open May through September.

Directions: From Redding, turn east on Highway 299 and drive 7.5 miles just past the town of Bella Vista. At Dry Creek Road, turn left and drive nine miles to a Y intersection. Bear right at the Y (left will take you to Silverthorn Resort) and drive a short distance to the campground entrances, on the left side for Lower Jones and the right side for Upper Jones.

Contact: Shasta-Trinity National Forest, Shasta Lake Ranger District, 530/275-1587, fax 530/275-1512; Shasta Lake Visitor Center, 530/275-1589; Shasta Recreation Company, 530/275-8113.

122 SHASTA

Scenic rating: 6

on the Sacramento River in Shasta-Trinity National Forest

Because campers must drive across Shasta Dam to reach this campground, general access was closed in 2002 for national security reasons. Call at least one week in advance (Bureau of Reclamation, Security Office, 530/275-4253) to get approval to cross the dam and make arrangements before planning a visit. The closed road also provides access to an adjacent OHV area, one of the few in the north state. Thus when open this place is for quads and dirt bikes—loud and wild and hey, it's a perfect spot for them. Because of past mining in the area, it's barren with almost no shade, but the views of the river and Shasta Dam are incredible. Nearby dam tours are unique and memorable.

Campsites, facilities: There are 22 sites for tents or RVs up to 30 feet (no hookups). Picnic tables and fire rings are provided. Drinking water and vault toilets are available. A boat ramp is nearby. Groceries and bait are available in Shasta Lake City. Leashed pets are permitted.

Reservations, fees: Reservations are not accepted. Sites are $10 per night, $5 per night for each additional vehicle. Open year-round.

Directions: From I-5 in Redding, drive north for three miles to the exit for the town of Shasta Lake City and Shasta Dam Boulevard. Take that exit and bear west on Shasta Dam Boulevard and drive three miles to Lake Boulevard. Turn right on Lake Boulevard and drive two miles. Cross Shasta Dam and continue four miles to the signed campground.

Contact: Bureau of Reclamation, Shasta Dam Visitor Center, 530/275-4463; Shasta-Trinity National Forest, Shasta Lake Ranger District, 530/275-1587, fax 530/275-1512; Shasta Lake Visitor Center, 530/275-1589.

123 FAWNDALE OAKS RV PARK

Scenic rating: 5

near Shasta Lake

This park is midway between Shasta Lake and Redding, so it's close to many recreational activities. Toward Redding, the options include Turtle Bay Exploration Park, WaterWorks Park, public golf courses, and Sacramento River trails, which are paved, making them accessible for wheelchairs and bicycles. Toward Shasta Lake, there are tours of Shasta Caverns, via a short drive to Holiday Harbor. The RV park is on 40 acres and has shaded sites.

Campsites, facilities: There are 10 tent sites and 15 sites with full hookups (30 and 50 amps) and cable TV for RVs up to 45 feet. Some sites are pull-through. A cabin and trailer are also available for rent. Picnic tables are provided and some sites have barbecues. Phone/modem hookups, coin laundry, boat and RV storage, a general store, picnic area, playground, seasonal swimming pool, club room, game room, propane, and group facilities are available. Some facilities are wheelchair-accessible. Leashed pets are permitted.

Reservations, fees: Reservations are accepted by telephone or website. RV sites are $25–27.50 per night for two people, tent sites are $19 per night for a family of four, $2 per person per night for any additional people, $1 per pet per night, $1 per night for each additional vehicle. Weekly and monthly rates are available. Some credit cards accepted. Open year-round.

Directions: From Redding, drive north on I-5 for nine miles to the Fawndale Road exit (Exit 689). Take that exit and turn right (east) on Fawndale Road. Drive 0.5 mile to the second RV park at the end of the road at 15015 Fawndale Road.

Contact: Fawndale Oaks RV Park, 530/275-0764 or 888/838-2159, www.fawndaleoaks. com.

124 BEAR MOUNTAIN RV RESORT AND CAMPGROUND

Scenic rating: 5

near Shasta Lake

This is a privately operated park in the remote Jones Valley area five miles from Shasta Lake. It is set on 52 acres. A hiking trail leaves from the campground, rises up a hill, and provides a great view of Redding. The resort emphasizes that there is no train noise here, as there often is at campgrounds closer to Shasta Lake.

Campsites, facilities: There are 70 sites with full or partial hookups (30 amps) for RVs up to 40 feet, 24 tent sites, and four park-model cabins. Some RV sites are pull-through. Picnic tables and fire rings are provided. Drinking water, restrooms with flush toilets and coin showers, coin laundry, modem access, convenience store, dump station, a seasonal swimming pool, recreation hall, arcade, table tennis, two playgrounds, volleyball, and horseshoe pit are available. Some facilities are wheelchair-accessible. A boat ramp is within three miles. Leashed pets are permitted.

Reservations, fees: Reservations are accepted at 800/952-0551. Tent sites are $14 per night, RV sites are $16–20 per night, $2 per person per night for more than two people, $2 per night for each additional vehicle. Weekly and monthly rates available. Some credit cards accepted. Open year-round.

Directions: From Redding, drive north on I-5 for three miles to Exit 682 for Oasis Road. Take that exit and drive to Oasis Road. Turn right on Oasis Road and drive 3.5 miles to Bear Mountain Road. Turn right on Bear Mountain Road and drive 3.5 miles to the campground on the left.

Contact: Bear Mountain RV Resort and Campground, 530/275-4728, www.campshasta.com.

125 EAST WEAVER

Scenic rating: 6

on the east branch of Weaver Creek in
Shasta-Trinity National Forest

This camp is set along East Weaver Creek. Another mile to the west on East Weaver Road, the road dead-ends at a trailhead, a good side trip. From here, the hiking trail is routed four miles, a significant climb, to tiny East Weaver Lake, set to the southwest of Monument Peak (7,771 feet elevation). The elevation at East Weaver is 2,700 feet.

Campsites, facilities: There are 11 sites for tents or RVs up to 25 feet (no hookups). Picnic tables and fire grills are provided. Drinking water and vault toilets are available. Supplies and a coin laundry are available in Weaverville. Leashed pets are permitted.

Reservations, fees: Reservations are not accepted. Sites are $11 per night, $5 per night in the winter. Open year-round.

Directions: From Redding, drive west on Highway 299 to Weaverville. In Weaverville, turn right (north) on Highway 3 and drive about two miles to East Weaver Road. Turn left on East Weaver Road and drive 3.5 miles to the campground.

Contact: Shasta-Trinity National Forest, Weaverville Ranger Station, 530/623-2121, fax 530/623-6010.

126 STEELBRIDGE

Scenic rating: 7

on the Trinity River

Very few people know of this spot, yet it can be a prime spot for anglers and campers. It's one of the better stretches of water in the area for steelhead, with good shore-fishing access. The prime time is from October through December. In the summer, the shade of conifers will keep you cool. Don't forget to bring your own water. The elevation is 1,700 feet.

Campsites, facilities: There are nine sites for tents or RVs up to 20 feet (no hookups). Picnic tables and fire grills are provided. Vault toilets are available. No drinking water is available. Supplies are available within three miles in Douglas City. Some facilities are wheelchair-accessible. Leashed pets are permitted.

Reservations, fees: Reservations are not accepted. Sites are $5 per night. Open year-round, weather permitting.

Directions: From Redding, turn west on Highway 299 and drive over Buckhorn Summit. Continue toward Douglas City to Steel Bridge Road (if you reach Douglas City, you have gone 2.3 miles too far). At Steel Bridge Road, turn right and drive about four miles to the campground at the end of the road.

Contact: Bureau of Land Management, Redding Field Office, 530/224-2100, fax 530/224-2172.

127 DOUGLAS CITY AND STEINER FLAT

Scenic rating: 7

on the Trinity River

If you want to camp along this stretch of the main Trinity River, these camps are your best bet (they're along the river about two miles from each other). They are set off the main road, near the river, with good bank fishing access (the prime season is from mid-August through winter for salmon and steelhead). There's paved parking and two beaches at Douglas City Campground. Steiner Flat, a more primitive camp, provides better access for fishing. This can be a good base camp for an off-season fishing trip on the Trinity River or a lounging spot during the summer. The elevation is 1,700 feet.

Campsites, facilities: There are 20 sites for tents or RVs up to 28 feet at Douglas City, and dispersed camping for tents and small RVs at Steiner Flat. No hookups. At Douglas City, picnic tables and fire grills are provided. Drinking water and restrooms with sinks and flush toilets are available. At Steiner Flat, no drinking water or toilets are available. Supplies are available within one mile in the town of Douglas City. Leashed pets are permitted.

Reservations, fees: Reservations are not accepted. Sites are $10 per night at Douglas City; no fee at Steiner Flat. Open mid-May through November.

Directions: From Redding, turn on Highway 299 west and drive west (toward Weaverville). Continue over the bridge at the Trinity River near Douglas City to Steiner Flat Road. Turn left on Steiner Flat Road and drive 0.5 mile to Douglas City campground on the left. To reach Steiner Flat, continue two more miles and look for the campground on the left.

Contact: Bureau of Land Management, Redding Field Office, 530/224-2100, fax 530/224-2172.

128 OLD LEWISTON BRIDGE RV RESORT

Scenic rating: 7

on the Trinity River

This is a popular spot for calm-water kayaking, rafting, and fishing. Though much of the water from Trinity and Lewiston Lakes is diverted via tunnel to Whiskeytown Lake (en route to the valley and points south), enough escapes downstream to provide a viable stream here near the town of Lewiston. This upstream section below Lewiston Lake is prime in the early summer for trout, particularly the chance for a huge brown trout (special regulations in effect). A fishing shuttle service is available. The campground is in a hilly area but has level sites, with nearby Lewiston Lake also a major attraction. Some sites are occupied by long-term renters.

Campsites, facilities: There are 52 sites with full hookups (30 amps) for RVs up to 45 feet, a separate area for tents, and five rental trailers. Picnic tables are provided. Restrooms with showers, coin laundry, grocery store, modem access, ice, bait and tackle, and propane gas refills are available. A group picnic area is available by reservation. A restaurant is within 0.5 mile. Leashed pets are permitted.

Reservations, fees: Reservations are accepted by phone or website. Sites are $26 per night for RVs, $14 per night per vehicle for tent campers, $2 per person per night for more than two people. Monthly rates available. Some credit cards accepted. Open year-round.

Directions: From Redding, turn on Highway 299 and drive west over Buckhorn Summit, and continue for five miles to Trinity Dam Boulevard. Turn right on Trinity Dam Boulevard and drive four miles to Lewiston, and continue north to Rush Creek Road. Turn left (west) on Rush Creek Road and drive 0.25 mile to the resort on the left.

Contact: Old Lewiston Bridge RV Resort, 800/922-1924 or tel./fax 530/778-3894, www. lewistonbridgerv.com.

129 TRINITY RIVER LODGE RV RESORT

Scenic rating: 7

on the Trinity River

For many, this privately operated park has an ideal location. You get level, grassy sites with shade trees along the Trinity River, yet it is just a short drive north to Lewiston Lake or a bit farther to giant Trinity Lake. Lake or river, take your pick. The resort covers nearly 14 acres, and about half the sites are rented for the entire summer.

Campsites, facilities: There are 60 sites with full hookups (30 and 50 amps) for RVs up to 40 feet, five tent sites, and one cottage. Restrooms with showers, a coin laundry, cable

TV, modem access, recreation room, lending library, clubhouse, athletic field, propane gas, camp store, ice, firewood, boat and trailer storage, horseshoes, and picnic area are available. Some facilities are wheelchair-accessible. Leashed pets are permitted.

Reservations, fees: Reservations are recommended. Tent sites are $15.75 per night, and RV sites are $28.35 per night. Some credit cards accepted. Open year-round.

Directions: From Redding, turn on Highway 299 west and drive west over Buckhorn Summit. Continue for five miles to Trinity Dam Boulevard. Turn right on Trinity Dam Boulevard and drive four miles to Lewiston. Continue on Trinity Dam Boulevard to Rush Creek Road. Turn left on Rush Creek Road and drive 2.3 miles to the campground on the left.

Contact: Trinity River Lodge RV Resort, 530/778-3791, www.trinityriverresort.com.

130 MARY SMITH

Scenic rating: 10

on Lewiston Lake in Shasta-Trinity National Forest

BEST (

This is one of the prettiest spots you'll ever see, set along the southwestern shore of Lewiston Lake. When you wake up and peek out of your sleeping bag, the natural beauty of this serene lake can take your breath away. Hand-launched boats, such as canoes, are ideal here, and the lake speed limit is 10 mph. The lake has 15 miles of shoreline. Although swimming is allowed, the water is too cold for most people. Bird-watching is good in this area. The best fishing is from Lakeview Terrace and the tules upstream to just below Trinity Dam. The elevation is 2,000 feet.

Campsites, facilities: There are 18 sites for tents only, some requiring a very short walk. Picnic tables and fire grills are provided. Drinking water and flush and vault toilets

are available. Boat launching and rentals are available nearby at Pine Cove Marina. Supplies and a coin laundry are available in Lewiston. Leashed pets are permitted.

Reservations, fees: Reservations are not accepted. Sites are $11 per night. Open early May through mid-September.

Directions: From Redding, turn on Highway 299 west and drive west over Buckhorn Summit. Continue for five miles to Trinity Dam Boulevard. Turn right on Trinity Dam Boulevard and drive four miles to Lewiston, and then continue on Trinity Dam Boulevard for 2.5 miles to the campground.

Contact: Shasta-Trinity National Forest, Weaverville Ranger Station, 530/623-2121, fax 530/623-6010; Pine Cove Marina, 530/778-3770.

131 COOPER GULCH

Scenic rating: 8

on Lewiston Lake in Shasta-Trinity National Forest

Here is a nice spot along a beautiful lake, featuring a short trail to Baker Gulch, where a pretty creek enters Lewiston Lake. The trout fishing is good on the upper end of the lake (where the current starts) and upstream. The lake speed limit is 10 mph. Swimming is allowed, although the water is cold because it flows in from the bottom of Trinity Lake. The lake is designated a wildlife-viewing area, with large numbers of waterfowl and other birds often spotted near the tules off the shore of Lakeview Terrace. Bring all of your own supplies and plan on hunkering down here for a while.

Campsites, facilities: There are five sites for tents or RVs up to 16 feet (no hookups). Picnic tables and fire grills are provided. Vault toilets and drinking water are available. Boat launching and rentals are nearby at Pine Cove Marina. Supplies and a coin laundry are available in Lewiston. Some facilities are wheelchair-accessible. Leashed pets are permitted.

Reservations, fees: Reservations are not accepted. Sites are $13 per night. Open early April through late October.

Directions: From Redding, turn on Highway 299 west and drive west over Buckhorn Summit. Continue for five miles to Trinity Dam Boulevard. Turn right on Trinity Dam Boulevard, drive four miles to Lewiston, and then continue on Trinity Dam Boulevard another four miles north to the campground.

Contact: Shasta-Trinity National Forest, Weaverville Ranger Station, 530/623-2121, fax 530/623-6010; Pine Cove Marina, 530/778-3770.

132 LAKEVIEW TERRACE RESORT

Scenic rating: 8

on Lewiston Lake

This might be your Golden Pond. It's a terraced RV park—with cabin rentals also available—that overlooks Lewiston Lake, one of the prettiest drive-to lakes in the region. Fishing for trout is excellent from Lakeview Terrace continuing upstream toward the dam. Lewiston Lake is perfect for fishing, with a 10-mph speed limit in effect (all the hot boats go to nearby Trinity Lake), along with excellent prospects for rainbow and brown trout. Other fish species include brook trout and kokanee salmon. The topper is that Lewiston Lake is always full to the brim, just the opposite of the up-and-down nightmare of its neighboring big brother, Trinity.

Campsites, facilities: There are 40 sites with full hookups (50 amps) for RVs up to 40 feet; some sites are pull-through. No tents. Cabins are also available. Picnic tables and barbecues are provided. Restrooms with showers, coin laundry, seasonal heated pool, propane gas, ice, horseshoes, playground, bait, and boat

and patio-boat rentals are available. Supplies are available within five miles. Leashed pets are permitted.

Reservations, fees: Reservations are recommended. Sites are $26 per night, $3 per person per night for more than two people, $2 per additional vehicle per night. Weekly and monthly rates available. Some credit cards accepted. Open year-round.

Directions: From Redding, turn on Highway 299 west and drive west over Buckhorn Summit. Continue for five miles to Trinity Dam Boulevard. Turn right on Trinity Dam Boulevard and drive 10 miles (five miles past Lewiston) to the resort on the left side of the road.

Contact: Lakeview Terrace Resort, 530/778-3803, fax 530/778-3960, www.lakeviewterraceresort.com.

133 TUNNEL ROCK

Scenic rating: 7

on Lewiston Lake in Shasta-Trinity National Forest

This is a very small, primitive alternative to Ackerman, which is more developed and another mile up the road to the north. The proximity to the Pine Cove boat ramp and fish-cleaning station, less than two miles to the south, is a primary attraction. Pine Cove Marina is full service and rents fishing boats. The elevation is 1,700 feet.

Campsites, facilities: There are six sites for tents or RVs up to 15 feet (no hookups). Picnic tables and fire grills are provided. Vault toilets are available. No drinking water is available. Leashed pets are permitted.

Reservations, fees: Reservations are not accepted. Sites are $7 per night. Open year-round.

Directions: From Redding, turn on Highway 299 west and drive over Buckhorn Summit. Continue for five miles to County Road 105/

Trinity Dam Road. Turn right on Trinity Dam Road and drive four miles to Lewiston, and then continue another seven miles north on Trinity Dam Boulevard to the campground. **Contact:** Shasta-Trinity National Forest, Weaverville Ranger Station, 530/623-2121, fax 530/623-6010.

134 ACKERMAN

Scenic rating: 7

on Lewiston Lake in Shasta-Trinity National Forest

Of the camps and parks at Lewiston Lake, Ackerman is closest to the lake's headwaters. This stretch of water below Trinity Dam is the best area for trout fishing on Lewiston Lake. Nearby Pine Cove boat ramp, two miles south of the camp, offers the only boat launch on Lewiston Lake with docks and a fish-cleaning station—a popular spot for anglers. When the Trinity powerhouse is running, trout fishing is excellent in this area. The elevation is 2,000 feet.

Campsites, facilities: There are 66 sites for tents or RVs up to 40 feet (no hookups). Picnic tables and fire grills are provided. Drinking water, flush toilets, and a dump station are available. Leashed pets are permitted.

Reservations, fees: Reservations are not accepted. Sites are $13 per night, and $7 per night during the winter. Open year-round.

Directions: From Redding, turn on Highway 299 west and drive west over Buckhorn Summit. Continue for five miles to Trinity Dam Boulevard. Turn right on Trinity Dam Boulevard and drive four miles to Lewiston. Continue north on Trinity Dam Boulevard for eight miles to the campground.

Contact: Shasta-Trinity National Forest, Weaverville Ranger Station, 530/623-2121, fax 530/623-6010.

135 OAK BOTTOM

Scenic rating: 7

on Whiskeytown Lake

The prettiest hiking trails at Whiskeytown Lake are at the far western end of the reservoir, and this camp provides excellent access to them. One hiking and biking trail skirts the north shoreline of the lake and is routed to the lake's inlet at the Judge Carr Powerhouse. The other, with the trailhead just a short drive to the west, is routed along Mill Creek, a pristine, clear-running stream with the trail jumping over the water many times. The campground sites seem a little close, but the camp is next to a beach area. There are junior ranger programs, and evening ranger programs at the Oak Bottom Amphitheater are available several nights per week from mid-June through Labor Day. A self-guided nature trail is five miles away at the visitors center.

Campsites, facilities: There are 100 walk-in tent sites with picnic tables and fire grills. There are 22 sites for RVs up to 32 feet (no hookups) in the large parking area near the launch ramp. Drinking water, restrooms with flush toilets and coin showers, storage lockers, convenience store, ice, firewood, dump station, boat ramp, and boat rentals are available. Some facilities are wheelchair-accessible. Leashed pets are permitted.

Reservations, fees: Reservations accepted during summer at 877/444-6777 or www.recreation.gov ($10 reservation fee). Sites are $16–18 per night, plus a park-use permit of $5 per day, $10 per week, or $25 per year. Open year-round.

Directions: From Redding, turn on Highway 299 west and drive west for 15 miles (past the visitors center) to the campground entrance road on the left. Turn left and drive a short distance to the campground.

Contact: Whiskeytown National Recreation Area, 530/242-3400 or 530/242-3412, fax 530/246-5154; Whiskeytown

Visitor Center, 530/246-1225, www.nps.gov/whis; Oak Bottom Campground Store, 530/359-2269; Forever Resorts, www.whiskeytownmarinas.com.

136 DRY CREEK GROUP CAMP

Scenic rating: 7

on Whiskeytown Lake

If you're in a group and take the time to reserve this spot, you'll be rewarded with some room and the quiet that goes along with it. This is the most remote drive-to camp at Whiskeytown Lake. A boat ramp is about two miles away (to the east) at Brandy Creek. You'll pass it on the way in. Note: Reservations are an absolute must, and can be made five months in advance.

Campsites, facilities: There are two tents-only group sites that can accommodate 50 people each. Picnic tables and fire grills are provided. Drinking water, storage lockers, and vault toilets are available. Leashed pets are permitted.

Reservations, fees: Reservations accepted during summer at 877/444-6777 or www.recreation.gov ($10 reservation fee). Sites are $75 per night, plus a park-use permit of $5 per day, $10 per week, or $25 per year. Open early April through October.

Directions: From Redding, drive west on Highway 299 for 10 miles to the visitors center and Kennedy Memorial Drive. Turn left and drive six miles to the campground on the right side of the road.

Contact: Whiskeytown National Recreation Area, 530/242-3400 or 530/242-3412, fax 530/246-5154; Whiskeytown Visitor Center, 530/246-1225, www.nps.gov/whis.

137 SHEEP CAMP

Scenic rating: 8

in Whiskeytown National Recreation Area

Sheep Camp is a tiny, primitive camp often overlooked in Whiskeytown National Recreation Area. It is set near a cliff with great views; you will likely have it to yourself. One of the highlights here is the nearby hike to Brandy Creek Falls, a series of pool-and-drops that pours into a big pool. From the trailhead, it's a 1.5-mile one-way trip.

Campsites, facilities: There are four sites for tents only. Picnic tables, food lockers, and fire pits are provided. Vault toilets are available, but there is no drinking water except at the Whiskeytown Visitor Center. Garbage must be packed out.

Reservations, fees: Reservations are not accepted. The fee is $10 per night, plus a Whiskeytown permit available for $5 daily, $10 weekly or $25 annually. A Backcountry Use Permit is required and may be obtained from the visitor center. Open seasonally, weather permitting.

Directions: From Redding, turn west on Highway 299 and drive west for 10 miles to the visitor center on the left and get your permits. From the visitor center, continue south on Kennedy Memorial Drive to a fork. Bear right at the fork, cross over the dam, and continue pass the Brandy Creek campground area to Shasta Bally Road. Turn left and drive about eight miles to the campground.

Contact: Whiskeytown National Recreation Area, 530/242-3412, fax 530/246-5154; Whiskeytown Visitor Center, 530/246-1225, www.nps.gov/whis.

138 BRANDY CREEK

Scenic rating: 7

on Whiskeytown Lake

For campers with boats, this is the best place to stay at Whiskeytown Lake, with a boat ramp less than a quarter mile away. Whiskeytown is popular for sailing and sailboarding, as it gets a lot more wind than other lakes in the region. Personal watercraft have been banned from this lake. Fishing for kokanee salmon is good in the early morning before the wind comes up; trout fishing is pretty good as well. The lake has 36 miles of shoreline.

Campsites, facilities: There are 37 sites for RVs up to 35 feet (no hookups). No tents. Drinking water and a dump station are available. Leashed pets are permitted.

Reservations, fees: Reservations are not accepted. Sites are $14 per night, $7 per night during off-season, plus a park-use permit of $5 per day, $10 per week, or $25 per year. Open year-round.

Directions: From Redding, drive west on Highway 299 for eight miles to the visitors center and Kennedy Memorial Drive. Turn left at the visitors center (Kennedy Memorial Drive) and drive five miles to the campground entrance road on the right. Turn right and drive a short distance to the camp.

Contact: Whiskeytown National Recreation Area, 530/242-3400 or 530/242-3412, fax 530/246-5154; Whiskeytown Visitor Center, 530/246-1225, www.nps.gov/whis.

139 PELTIER BRIDGE

Scenic rating: 7

below the dam on Clear Creek

This is a small, pretty, and virtually secret campground located on Clear Creek in Whiskeytown National Recreation Area. Secret? That's right—rangers requested its exact location not be revealed. Only when you get your permit at the visitor center overlooking Whiskeytown Lake will they provide specific directions. The camp is set in the woods and requires a short hike to get there. I can tell you that Clear Creek is stocked with rainbow trout in the 6- to 8-inch class.

Campsites, facilities: There are seven sites for tents only. Picnic tables, food lockers, and fire pits are provided. Vault toilets are available, but there is no drinking water except at the Whiskeytown Visitor Center. Garbage must be packed out.

Reservations, fees: Reservations are not accepted. The fee is $10 per night, plus a Whiskeytown permit available for $5 daily, $10 weekly or $25 annually. A Backcountry Use Permit is required and may be obtained from the visitor center. Open seasonally, weather permitting.

Directions: From Redding, turn on Highway 299 west and drive west for 10 miles to the visitor center. Rangers will provide specific directions to the campground at that time.

Contact: Whiskeytown National Recreation Area, 530/242-3412, fax 530/246-5154; Whiskeytown Visitor Center, 530/246-1225, www.nps.gov/whis.

140 HORSE CAMP

Scenic rating: 6

in Whiskeytown National Recreation Area

Horse Camp is located on a well-maintained dirt road and is accessible to vehicles pulling horse trailers. This is the only campground in Whiskeytown National Recreation Area where horse camping is allowed.

Campsites, facilities: There are two sites for tents only. Picnic tables, food lockers, and fire pits are provided. Vault toilets and drinking water (summer only) are available. Garbage must be packed out.

Reservations, fees: Reservations are required at 530/242-3412. The fee is $10 per night, plus a Whiskeytown permit available for $5 daily, $10 weekly or $25 annually. A Backcountry Use Permit is required and may be obtained from the visitor center. Open seasonally, weather permitting.

Directions: From Redding, turn west on Highway 299 and drive west for 10 miles to the visitor center. Note that campers with horses must register at the visitor center to get permits and directions to the horse camp.

Contact: Whiskeytown National Recreation Area, 530/242-3412, fax 530/246-5154; Whiskeytown Visitor Center, 530/246-1225, www.nps.gov/whis.

141 PREMIER RV RESORT

Scenic rating: 2

in Redding

If you're stuck with no place to go, this large park could be your savior. Nearby recreation options include a waterslide park and the Turtle Bay Museum and Exploration Park on the Sacramento River. The newest attraction is Sundial Bridge, with its glass walkway that allows users to look down into the river, a stunning feat of architecture—where the experience simulates walking on air. In addition, Whiskeytown Lake is nearby to the west, and Shasta Lake to the north. A casino and several golf courses are nearby.

Campsites, facilities: There are 111 sites with full or partial hookups (30 and 50 amps) for RVs of any length, and two yurts. A flat cutout area on a hillside provides space for dispersed tent sites. Picnic tables and fire grills are provided. Drinking water, restrooms with flush toilets and showers, playground, seasonal swimming pool, coin laundry, dump station, satellite TV hookups, modem access, a convenience store, propane gas, and recreation room are available. Some facilities

are wheelchair accessible. Leashed pets are permitted.

Reservations, fees: Reservations are accepted. RV sites are $47.50 per night, $3 per person per night for more than two people; tent sites are $37 per night. Some credit cards accepted. Open year-round.

Directions: In Redding, drive north on I-5 to the Lake Boulevard/Burney-Alturas exit. Turn west (left) on Lake Boulevard and drive 0.25 mile to North Boulder Drive. Turn right (north) on North Boulder Drive and drive one block to the resort on the left.

Contact: Premier RV Resort, 530/246-0101 or 888/710-8450, fax 530/246-0123, www.premierrvresorts.com.

142 MARINA RV PARK

Scenic rating: 6

on the Sacramento River

The riverside setting is a highlight here, with the Sacramento River providing relief from the dog days of summer. An easy, paved walking and bike trail is available nearby at the Sacramento River Parkway, providing river views and sometimes a needed breeze on hot summer evenings. It is also two miles away from the Turtle Bay Museum, and close to a movie theater. A golf driving range is nearby. This park includes an area with long-term RV renters.

Campsites, facilities: There are 42 sites with full or partial hookups (30 amps) for RVs up to 40 feet. Picnic tables, restrooms with showers, a coin laundry, small store, modem access, seasonal swimming pool, spa, boat ramp, and a dump station are available. Leashed pets are permitted.

Reservations, fees: Reservations are accepted. Sites are $31.90 per night, $2 per person per night for more than two people. Weekly and monthly rates available. Open year-round.

Directions: In Redding, turn west on Highway

44 and drive 1.5 miles to the exit for Convention Center/Marina Park Drive. Take that exit, turn left, and drive over the highway to a stoplight and Marina Park Drive. Turn left (south) on Marina Park Drive and drive 0.8 mile to the park on the left.

Contact: Marina RV Park, 530/241-4396, www.marinapark.com.

143 SACRAMENTO RIVER RV RESORT

🏊 🚣 �- 🏕 🐕 🚴 ♿ 🚐 ⛺

Scenic rating: 7

south of Redding

This makes a good headquarters for a fall fishing trip on the Sacramento River, where the salmon come big from August through October. In the summer, trout fishing is very good from this area as well, but a boat is a must. No problem; there's a boat ramp at the park. In addition, you can hire fishing guides who launch from here daily. The park is open year-round, and if you want to stay close to home, a three-acre pond with bass, bluegill, and perch is also available at the resort. You also get great long-distance views of Mount Shasta and Mount Lassen.

Campsites, facilities: There are 140 sites with full hookups (30 and 50 amps) for RVs of any length and 10 sites for tents in a shaded grassy area. Some RV sites are pull-through. Picnic tables, restrooms with showers, coin laundry, dump station, cable TV, Wi-Fi, modem access, bait, boat launch, playground, two tennis courts, horseshoes, golf driving range, and a large seasonal swimming pool are available. A clubhouse is available by reservation. Some facilities are wheelchair-accessible. Leashed pets are permitted.

Reservations, fees: Reservations are accepted. Sites are $16.50–28 per night. Some credit cards accepted. Open year-round.

Directions: From Redding, drive south on I-5 for five miles to the Knighton Road exit.

Turn west (right) and drive a short distance to Riverland Drive. Turn left on Riverland Drive and drive two miles to the park at the end of the road.

Contact: Sacramento River RV Resort, 530/365-6402, fax 530/365-2601, www.sacramentoriverrvresort.com.

144 DEERLICK SPRINGS

🚶 🚣 🏕 5% 🚐 ⛺

Scenic rating: 8

on Browns Creek in Shasta-Trinity National Forest

It's a long, twisty drive to this remote and primitive camp set on the edge of the Chanchelulla Wilderness in the transition zone where the valley's oak grasslands give way to conifers. This quiet little spot is set along Browns Creek. A trailhead just north of camp provides a streamside walk. The elevation is 3,100 feet.

Campsites, facilities: There are 13 sites for tents or RVs up to 20 feet (no hookups). Picnic tables and fire grills are provided. Vault toilets are available. No drinking water is available. Garbage must be packed out. Leashed pets are permitted.

Reservations, fees: Reservations are not accepted. There is no fee for camping. Open May through October.

Directions: From Red Bluff, turn west on Highway 36 (very twisty) and drive to the Forest Service ranger station in Platina. In Platina, turn right (north) on Harrison Gulch Road and drive 10 miles to the campground on the left.

Contact: Shasta-Trinity National Forest, Yolla Bolly Ranger Station, 530/352-4211, fax 530/352-4312.

145 BASIN GULCH

Scenic rating: 5

in Shasta-Trinity National Forest

This is one of two little-known campgrounds in the vicinity that rarely gets much use. A trail out of this camp climbs Noble Ridge, eventually rising to a good lookout at 3,933 feet, providing sweeping views of the north valley. Of course, you could also just drive there, taking a dirt road out of Platina. There are many backcountry Forest Service roads in the area, so your best bet is to get a Shasta-Trinity National Forest map, which details the roads. The elevation is 2,600 feet. There is evidence in the area of a wildfire that occurred in 2001.

Campsites, facilities: There are 13 sites for tents or RVs up to 20 feet (no hookups). Picnic tables and fire grills are provided. Vault toilets are available. No drinking water is available. Leashed pets are permitted.

Reservations, fees: Reservations are not accepted. Sites are $6 per night. Open May through October.

Directions: From Red Bluff, drive about 45 miles west on Highway 36 to the Yolla Bolly District Ranger Station. From the ranger station, turn south on Stuart Gap Road and drive two miles to the campground on the left.

Contact: Shasta-Trinity National Forest, Yolla Bolly Ranger Station, 530/352-4211, fax 530/352-4312.

146 BEND RV PARK AND FISHING RESORT

Scenic rating: 7

on the Sacramento River

Here's a spot for RV cruisers to rest their rigs for a while. Bend RV Park and Fishing Resort is open year-round and is set beside

the Sacramento River. The salmon average 15–25 pounds in this area, and anglers typically have the best results from mid-August through October. In recent years, the gates of the Red Bluff Diversion Dam have been raised in early September. When that occurs, huge numbers of salmon charge upstream from Red Bluff to Anderson, holding in each deep river hole. Expect very hot weather in July and August.

Campsites, facilities: There are 14 sites with full or partial hookups (30 amps) for RVs up to 40 feet. In addition, there is a separate area for tents only. Picnic tables are provided. Drinking water, restrooms with showers and flush toilets, convenience store, bait and tackle, boat ramp, boat dock, coin laundry, and a dump station are available. Leashed pets are permitted.

Reservations, fees: Reservations are accepted. Sites are $21.50–24 per night, $3.50 per person per night for more than two people. Open year-round.

Directions: From I-5 in Red Bluff, drive four miles north on I-5 to the Jelly's Ferry Road exit. Take that exit and turn northeast on Jelly's Ferry Road and drive 2.5 miles to the resort at 21795 Bend Ferry Road.

Contact: Bend RV Park and Fishing Resort, 530/527-6289.

147 LAKE RED BLUFF

Scenic rating: 6

on the Sacramento River near Red Bluff

Lake Red Bluff is created by the Red Bluff Diversion Dam on the Sacramento River, and waterskiing, bird-watching, hiking, and fishing are the most popular activities. A three-mile-long paved trail parallels the river, and cycling and skating are allowed on the trail. It has become a backyard swimming hole for local residents in the summer when the temperatures reach the high 90s and low 100s

SHASTA CAMPING

almost every day. In early September, the Bureau of Reclamation raises the gates at the diversion dam to allow migrating salmon an easier course on the upstream journey, and in the process, Lake Red Bluff reverts to its former self as the Sacramento River.

Campsites, facilities: At Sycamore Camp, there are 30 sites for tents or RVs up to 35 feet (no hookups). There is also a tent-only group camp (Camp Discovery) that has 11 screened cabins and can accommodate up to 100 people. Drinking water, restrooms with coin showers and flush toilets, vault toilets, picnic areas, visitors center, two boat ramps, and a fish-viewing plaza are available. There are two large barbecues, electrical outlets, lockable storage, five large picnic tables, restroom with showers and sinks, and an amphitheater in the group camp area. Some facilities are wheelchair-accessible. Leashed pets are permitted.

Reservations, fees: Reservations are not accepted for individual sites but are required for the group camp at 530/527-1196. Sites are $12–24 per night for individual sites; the group camp is $150 per night. Open April through October.

Directions: From I-5 at Red Bluff, turn east on Highway 36 and drive 100 yards to the first turnoff at Sale Lane. Turn right (south) on Sale Lane and drive 2.5 miles to the campground at the end of the road.

Contact: Mendocino National Forest, Red Bluff Recreation Area, 530/527-2813, fax 530/527-1312; Discovery Center, 530/527-1196.

148 TOMHEAD SADDLE

Scenic rating: 4

in Shasta-Trinity National Forest

This one is way out there in remote wildlands. Little known and rarely visited, it's primarily a jump-off point for ambitious backpackers. The camp is on the edge of the Yolla Bolly-Middle Eel Wilderness. A trailhead here is routed to the South Fork of Cottonwood Creek, a trek that entails hiking eight miles in dry, hot terrain. The elevation is 5,700 feet.

Campsites, facilities: There are five sites for tents or RVs up to 16 feet (no hookups). Picnic tables and fire grills are provided. Vault toilets are available. No drinking water is available. Garbage must be packed out. Leashed pets are permitted.

Reservations, fees: Reservations are not accepted. There is no fee for camping. Open late June through mid-September, weather permitting.

Directions: From I-5 in Red Bluff, turn west on Highway 36 and drive about 13 miles to Cannon Road. Turn left on Cannon Road and drive about five miles to Pettyjohn Road. Turn west on Pettyjohn Road, drive to Saddle Camp and Forest Road 27N06. Turn south on Forest Road 27N06 and drive three miles to the campground on the left. It is advisable to obtain a map of Shasta-Trinity National Forest.

Contact: Shasta-Trinity National Forest, Yolla Bolly Ranger Station, 530/352-4211, fax 530/352-4312.

LASSEN CAMPING

COURTESY OF THE NATIONAL PARK SERVICE

BEST CAMPGROUNDS

◖ **Hikes with Views**
Summit Lake: North, South, and Equestrian,
page 119

◖ **Family Destinations**
Summit Lake: North, South, and Equestrian,
page 119

Mount Lassen and its awesome volcanic past

seem to cast a shadow everywhere you go in this region. At 10,457 feet, the mountain's domed summit is visible for more than 100 miles in all directions. It blew its top in 1914, with continuing eruptions through 1918. Although now dormant, the volcanic-based geology dominates the landscape everywhere you look.

Of all the areas covered in this book, this region has the least number of romantic getaway spots. Instead it caters primarily to outdoors enthusiasts. And Lassen Volcanic National Park is one of the best places to lace up the hiking boots or spool new line on the reel. It's often off the radar of vacationers, making it one of the few national parks where you can enjoy the wilderness in relative solitude.

The national park is easily explored along the main route, the Lassen Park Highway. Along the way, you can pick a few trails for adventure. The best hikes are the Summit Climb (moderate to challenging), best done first thing in the morning, and Bumpass Hell (easy and great for kids) to see the sulfur vents and boiling mud pots. Another favorite for classic alpine beauty is the Shadow Lake Trail.

Unique features of the region include its pumice boulders, volcanic rock, and spring-fed streams from underground lava tubes. Highlights include the best still-water canoeing and fly-fishing at Fall River, Big Lake, and Ahjumawi State Park. Ahjumawi is reached by canoe or powerboat only – a great boat-in campground with access to a matrix of clear, cold waters with giant trout.

Nearby is Burney Falls State Park, along with the Pit River and Lake Britton, which together make up one of Northern California's best recreation destinations for families. This is also one of the best areas for fly-fishing, especially at Hat Creek, Pit River, Burney Creek, and Manzanita Lake. For more beautiful settings, you can visit Lake Almanor and Eagle Lake, both of which provide lakeside campgrounds and excellent fishing and boating recreation.

And there's more. In remote Modoc County, you'll find Lava Beds National Monument and the South Warner Wilderness. Lava Beds is a stark, pretty, and often lonely place. It's sprinkled with small lakes full of trout, is home to large-antlered deer that migrate in after the first snow (and after the hunting season has closed), and features a unique volcanic habitat with huge flows of obsidian (dark, smooth, natural glass formed by the cooling of molten lava) and dacite (gray, craggy, volcanic flow). Lava Beds National Monument boasts about 500 caves and lava tubes, including the 6,000-foot Catacomb Tunnel. Nearby is pretty Medicine Lake, formed in a caldera, which provides good trout fishing, hiking, and exploring.

There are so many campgrounds that, no matter where you go, it seems you can always find a match for what you desire.

LASSEN CAMPING

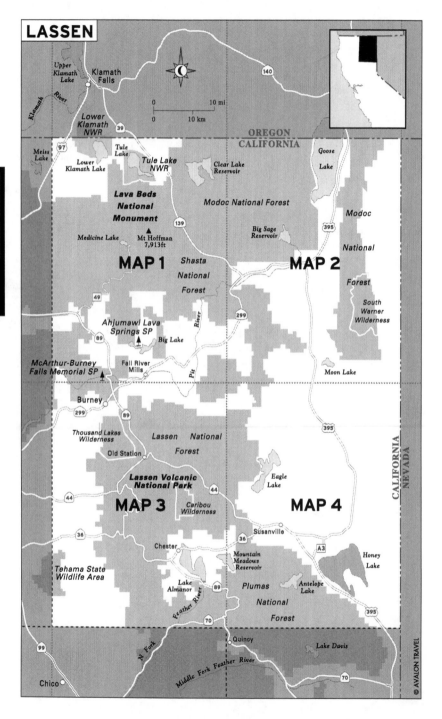

Map 1

Campgrounds 1-16

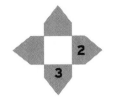

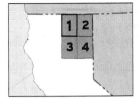

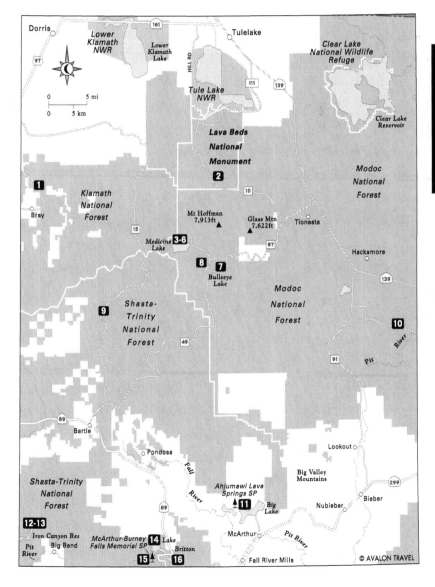

Dorris

Lower
Klamath
NWR

Lower
Klamath
Lake

Tulelake

Clear Lake
National Wildlife
Refuge

161

97

HILL RD

111

139

Tule Lake
NWR

Clear Lake
Reservoir

Lava Beds

National

Monument

2

10

Modoc
National
Forest

1

Klamath
National
Forest

Bray

Mt Hoffman
7,913ft ▲

Glass Mtn
7,622ft ▲

Tionesta

15

Medicine
Lake

3-6

97

Hackamore

8 **7**

Bullseye
Lake

139

Shasta-
Trinity
National
Forest

9

Modoc

National

Forest

10

49

River

91

Pit

89

Bartle

Pondosa

Lookout

Big Valley
Mountains

299

Shasta-Trinity
National
Forest

Fall

River

Ahjumawi Lava
Springs SP

▲ **11**

Big
Lake

Nubieber

Bieber

89

12-13

Iron Canyon Res

Pit
River

Big Bend

McArthur-Burney
Falls Memorial SP

14 Lake

15 ▲ **16**

Britton

McArthur

Pit River

Fall River Mills

© AVALON TRAVEL

0   5 mi
0   5 km

Map 2

Campgrounds 17-33

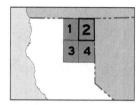

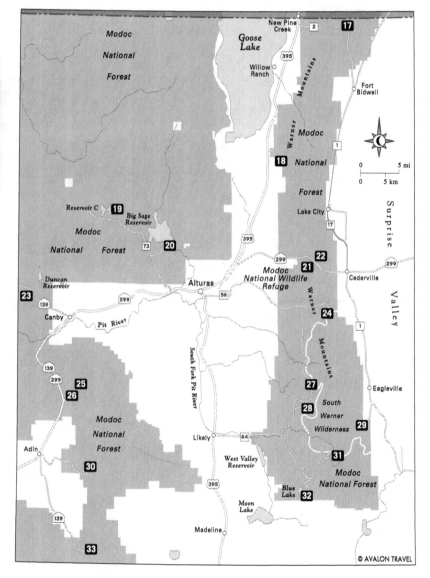

Map 3

Campgrounds 34-86

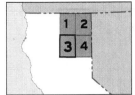

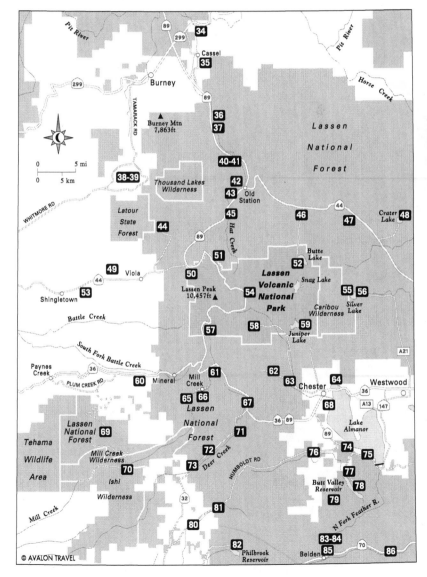

Map 4

Campgrounds 87-103

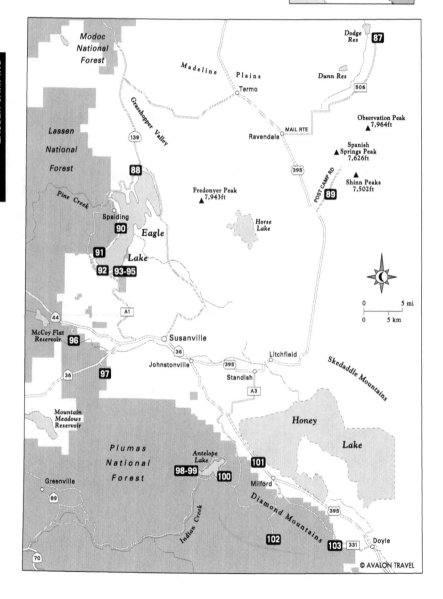

1 SHAFTER

🏃 🏊 🚣 🐴 5% 🚐 ⛺

Scenic rating: 4

in Klamath National Forest

This is a little-used camp, with trout fishing at nearby Butte Creek for small rainbows, primarily six- to eight-inchers. Little Orr Lake, about a 10-minute drive away on the southwest flank of Orr Mountain, provides fishing for bass and larger rainbow trout, 10- to 12-inchers, as well as a sprinkling of smaller brook trout. This camp is primitive and not well known, set in a juniper- and sage-filled landscape. The elevation is 4,300 feet. A great side trip is to the nearby Orr Mountain Lookout, where there are spectacular views of Mount Shasta. The road adjacent to the campground is paved, keeping the dust down—a Forest Service touch that is like gold in the summer.

Campsites, facilities: There are 10 sites for tents or RVs up to 28 feet (no hookups). Picnic tables and fire grills are provided. Drinking water and vault toilets are available. A boat ramp is available at Orr Lake. Garbage must be packed out. Leashed pets are permitted.

Reservations, fees: Reservations are not accepted. Sites are $6 per night. Open year-round, with limited services in winter.

Directions: From Redding, drive north on I-5 to Weed and the exit for Central Weed/Highway 97. Take that exit, turn right at the stop sign, drive through Weed and bear right (north) on Highway 97 and drive 40 miles to Ball Mountain Road. Turn right at Ball Mountain Road and drive 2.5 miles to a T with Old State Highway 97. Turn right and drive 4.25 miles (crossing railroad tracks) to the campground on the right side of the road.

Contact: Klamath National Forest, Goose-nest Ranger District, 530/398-4391, fax 530/398-5749.

2 INDIAN WELL

🏃 🐴 ♿ 🚐 ⛺

Scenic rating: 9

in Lava Beds National Monument

Lava Beds National Monument is a one-in-a-million spot, with more than 500 lava-tube caves, Schonchin Butte (a cinder cone with a hiking trail), Mammoth Crater, Native American petroglyphs and pictographs, battlefields and campsites from the Modoc War, and wildlife overlooks of Tule Lake. After winter's first snow, this is one of the best places in the West to photograph deer. Nearby is Klamath National Wildlife Refuge, the largest bald eagle wintering area in the lower 48. If you are new to the outdoors, an interpretive center is available to explain it all to you through informative displays. A visitors center is open year-round.

Campsites, facilities: There are 43 sites for tents or RVs up to 30 feet (no hookups). Picnic tables, fire rings, and cooking grills are provided. Drinking water and flush toilets are available. Some facilities are wheelchair-accessible. The town of Tulelake (30 miles north) is the nearest supply station. Leashed pets are permitted in the campground and roads only.

Reservations, fees: Reservations are not accepted. Sites are $10 per night plus $10 per vehicle park entrance fee. Maximum of eight campers per site. Open year-round.

Directions: From Redding, drive north on I-5 to the Central Weed/Highway 97 exit. Take that exit, turn right and continue for one mile to U.S. 97. Drive north on U.S. 97 for 54 miles to Highway 161. Turn east on Highway 161 and drive 20 miles to Hill Road. Turn right (south) and drive 18 miles to the visitors center and the campground entrance on the left. Turn left and drive 0.25 mile to the campground.

Contact: Lava Beds National Monument Visitor Center, 530/667-8113, www.nps.gov/labe.

LASSEN CAMPING

₃ MEDICINE

Scenic rating: 7

on Medicine Lake in Modoc National Forest

Lakeside campsites tucked away in conifers make this camp a winner. Medicine Lake, at 640 acres, was formed in the crater of an old volcano and is surrounded by lodgepole pine and fir trees. The lake is stocked with rainbow and brook trout in the summer, gets quite cold in the fall, and freezes over in winter. All water sports are permitted. Many side trips are possible, including nearby Bullseye and Blanche Lakes and Ice Caves (both signed and off the access road) and Lava Beds National Monument just 15 miles north. At 6,700 feet, temperatures can drop in summer and the season is short.

Campsites, facilities: There are 22 sites for tents or RVs up to 30 feet (no hookups). Picnic tables and fire grills are provided. Drinking water and vault toilets are available. Ranger-guided cave tours, walks, and talks are available during the summer. A boat ramp is nearby. A café and bar are in Bartle; otherwise, no supplies are available within an hour's drive. Some facilities are wheelchair-accessible. Leashed pets are permitted.

Reservations, fees: Reservations are not accepted. Sites are $7 per vehicle per night. Open late May through early October, weather permitting.

Directions: From Redding, drive north on I-5 past Dunsmuir to Highway 89. Turn east on Highway 89 and drive 28 miles (just past Bartle) to Forest Road 15/Harris Springs Road. Turn left on Forest Road 15 and drive approximately five miles to the Y intersection with Forest Road 49/Medicine Lake Road. Turn right on Forest Road 49 and drive approximately 26 miles to the lake and campground access road.

Contact: Modoc National Forest, Doublehead Ranger District, 530/667-2246, fax 530/667-8609.

₄ A. H. HOGUE

Scenic rating: 7

on Medicine Lake in Modoc National Forest

This camp was created in 1990 when the original Medicine Lake Campground was divided in half. (For more information, see the *Medicine* listing.)

Campsites, facilities: There are 24 sites for tents or RVs up to 30 feet (no hookups). Picnic tables and fire grills are provided. Drinking water and vault toilets are available. A boat ramp is nearby. Some facilities are wheelchair-accessible. Leashed pets are permitted. A café and bar are in Bartle; otherwise, no supplies are available within an hour's drive.

Reservations, fees: Reservations are not accepted. Sites are $7 per vehicle per night. Open late May through early October, weather permitting.

Directions: From Redding, drive north on I-5 past Dunsmuir to Highway 89. Turn east on Highway 89 and drive 28 miles (just past Bartle) to Forest Road 15/Harris Springs Road. Turn left on Forest Road 15 and drive approximately five miles to the Y intersection with Forest Road 49/Medicine Lake Road. Turn right on Forest Road 49 and drive approximately 26 miles to the lake and campground access road.

Contact: Modoc National Forest, Doublehead Ranger District, 530/667-2246, fax 530/667-8609.

₅ HEMLOCK

Scenic rating: 7

on Medicine Lake in Modoc National Forest

This is one in a series of campgrounds on Medicine Lake operated by the Forest Service. A special attraction at Hemlock is the natural sand beach. (For more information, see the *Medicine* listing in this chapter.)

Campsites, facilities: There are 19 sites for tents or RVs up to 22 feet (no hookups). Picnic tables and fire grills are provided. Drinking water and vault toilets are available. A boat ramp is available nearby. Some facilities are wheelchair-accessible. Leashed pets are permitted. A café and bar are in Bartle; otherwise, no supplies are available within an hour's drive.

Reservations, fees: Reservations are not accepted. Sites are $7 per vehicle per night. Open late May through early October, weather permitting.

Directions: From Redding, drive north on I-5 past Dunsmuir to Highway 89. Turn east on Highway 89 and drive 28 miles (just past Bartle) to Forest Road 15/Harris Springs Road. Turn left on Forest Road 15 and drive approximately five miles to the Y intersection with Forest Road 49/Medicine Lake Road. Turn right on Forest Road 49 and drive approximately 26 miles to the lake and campground access road.

Contact: Modoc National Forest, Doublehead Ranger District, 530/667-2246, fax 530/667-8609.

6 HEADQUARTERS
Scenic rating: 7

on Medicine Lake in Modoc National Forest

This is one of four campgrounds set beside Medicine Lake. There is no lake access from this camp because of private property between the lake and campground. The elevation is 6,700 feet. (For more information, see the *Medicine* listing in this chapter.)

Campsites, facilities: There are 10 sites for tents or RVs up to 16 feet (no hookups). Picnic tables and fire grills are provided. Drinking water and vault toilets are available. A boat ramp is nearby. A café and bar are in Bartle; otherwise, no supplies are available within an hour's drive. Leashed pets are permitted.

Reservations, fees: Reservations are not accepted. Sites are $7 per vehicle per night. Open late May through early October, weather permitting.

Directions: From Redding, drive north on I-5 past Dunsmuir to Highway 89. Turn east on Highway 89 and drive 28 miles (just past Bartle) to Forest Road 15/Harris Springs Road. Turn left on Forest Road 15 and drive approximately five miles to the Y intersection with Forest Road 49/Medicine Lake Road. Turn right on Forest Road 49 and drive approximately 26 miles to the lake and campground access road.

Contact: Modoc National Forest, Doublehead Ranger District, 530/667-2246, fax 530/667-8609.

7 BULLSEYE LAKE
Scenic rating: 7

near Medicine Lake in Modoc National Forest

This tiny lake gets overlooked every year, mainly because of its proximity to nearby Medicine Lake. Bullseye Lake is shallow, but because snow keeps it locked up until late May or early June, the water stays plenty cold for small trout through July. It is stocked with just 750 six- to eight-inch rainbow trout, not much to crow about—or to catch, for that matter. No boat motors are allowed. Nearby are some ice caves, created by ancient volcanic action. The place is small, quiet, and pretty, but most of all, small. This camp is set at an elevation of 6,500 feet.

Campsites, facilities: There are six sites for tents or RVs up to 22 feet (no hookups). Picnic tables and fire grills are provided. A vault toilet is available. No drinking water is available. Garbage must be packed out. Supplies are available in McCloud. A café and bar are in Bartle; otherwise, no supplies are available within an hour's drive. Leashed pets are permitted.

Reservations, fees: Reservations are not accepted. There is no fee for camping. Open late May through October, weather permitting.

Directions: From Redding, drive north on I-5 past Dunsmuir to Highway 89. Turn east on Highway 89 and drive 28 miles (just past Bartle) to Forest Road 15/Harris Springs Road. Turn left on Forest Road 15 and drive approximately five miles to the Y intersection with Forest Road 49/Medicine Lake Road. Turn right on Forest Road 49 and drive approximately 24 miles to the Bullseye Lake access road (if you reach Medicine Lake, you have gone about two miles too far). Turn right at the Bullseye Lake access road and drive a short distance past Blanche Lake, then turn right and drive a short distance to the lake.

Contact: Modoc National Forest, Doublehead Ranger District, 530/667-2246, fax 530/667-8609.

8 PAYNE SPRINGS

Scenic rating: 8

near Medicine Lake in Modoc National Forest

This camp is set by a small spring in a very pretty riparian area. It's small, but it is special.

Campsites, facilities: There are six dispersed sites for tents or RVs up to 20 feet (no hookups). Picnic tables and fire grills are provided. A vault toilet is available. No drinking water is available. Garbage must be packed out. A café and bar are in Bartle. Supplies are available in Tionesta, a 30-minute drive, or McCloud. Leashed pets are permitted.

Reservations, fees: Reservations are not accepted. There is no fee for camping. Open late May through October, weather permitting.

Directions: From Redding, drive north on I-5 drive past Dunsmuir to Highway 89. Turn east on Highway 89 and drive 28 miles (just past Bartle) to Forest Road 15/Harris Springs Road. Turn left on Forest Road 15 and drive approximately five miles to the Y intersection with Forest Road 49/Medicine Lake Road. Turn right on Forest Road 49 and drive 30

miles (0.2 mile past the Bullseye Lake access road) to the Payne Springs access road (if you reach Medicine Lake, you have gone too far). Turn left on the Payne Springs access road and drive a short distance to the campground.

Contact: Modoc National Forest, Doublehead Ranger District, 530/667-2246, fax 530/667-8609.

9 HARRIS SPRINGS

Scenic rating: 3

in Shasta-Trinity National Forest

This camp is a hidden spot in remote Shasta-Trinity National Forest, nestled in the long, mountainous ridge that runs east from Mount Shasta to Lava Beds National Monument. The camp is set at 4,800 feet, with a part-time fire station within a quarter mile on the opposite side of the access road. The area is best explored by four-wheel drive, venturing to a series of small buttes, mountaintops, and lookouts in the immediate area. A map of Shasta-Trinity National Forest is a must.

Campsites, facilities: There are 15 sites for tents or RVs up to 32 feet (no hookups). Picnic tables and fire grills are provided. There is no drinking water. Vault toilets are available. Garbage must be packed out. Leashed pets are permitted.

Reservations, fees: Reservations are not accepted. There is no fee for camping. Open late May through early October, weather permitting.

Directions: From Redding, drive north on I-5 past Dunsmuir to the junction with Highway 89. Turn east on Highway 89 and drive 28 miles (just past Bartle) to Forest Road 15/Harris Springs Road. Bear left on Forest Road 15 and drive five miles to the Y intersection with Harris Springs Road and Medicine Lake Road/Forest Road 49. Bear left at the Y, staying on Harris Springs Road/Forest Road 15, and drive 12 miles to a junction with a forest road signed for the Harris Springs Ranger Station. Turn right and drive a short distance, and look for the campground entrance on the right side of the road.

Contact: Shasta-Trinity National Forest, McCloud Ranger District, 530/964-2184, fax 530/964-2938.

🔟 COTTONWOOD FLAT
🏕 🐕 🚐 ⛰

Scenic rating: 6

in Modoc National Forest

The camp is wooded and shady, set at 4,700 feet elevation in the rugged and remote Devil's Garden area of Modoc National Forest. The region is known for large mule deer, and Cottonwood Flat is well situated as a base camp for a hunting trip in the fall. The weather can get extremely cold early and late in the season.

Campsites, facilities: There are 10 sites for tents or RVs up to 16 feet (no hookups). Picnic tables and fire grills are provided. There is no drinking water. Vault toilets are available. Garbage must be packed out. Supplies are available within 10 miles in Canby. Leashed pets are permitted.

Reservations, fees: Reservations are not accepted. There is no fee for camping. Open May through October, weather permitting.

Directions: From Redding, drive east on Highway 299 for about 100 miles to Adin. Continue on Highway 299 for about 20 miles to the Canby Bridge at the Pit River and the junction with Forest Road 84. Turn left on Forest Road 84 and drive about eight miles to Forest Road 42N95. Turn right and drive 0.5 mile to the campground entrance on the left side of the road. Note: The access road is not recommended for RVs longer than 16 feet.

Contact: Modoc National Forest, Devil's Garden Ranger District, 530/233-5811, fax 530/233-8709.

🔟🔟 AHJUMAWI LAVA SPRINGS BOAT-IN
🏕 🛶 🚤 🏊 🐴 ⛰

Scenic rating: 8

at Big Lake

This is a one-of-a-kind boat-in camp set on Big Lake and connecting Horr Pond in the Fall River matrix of streams. Ahjumawi means "where the waters come together," named by the Pit River Native Americans who inhabit the area near the confluence of Big Lake, Tule River, Ja She Creek, Lava Creek, and Fall River. Together the waters form one of the largest freshwater springs in the world. Springs flowing from the lava are prominent along the shoreline. This is a place of exceptional and primeval scenery. Much of the land is covered by lava flows, including vast areas of jagged black basalt, along with lava tubes and spattercone and conic depressions. There are brilliant aqua bays and, for campers, peace and quiet. However, you may be joined on land by armies of mosquitoes in the spring; they're not so bad while you're on the water.

Access is by boat only, ideal for canoes, and, in addition, the lake is not well known outside of the region. Expert fly fishers try for giant but elusive rainbow trout, best in the early morning at the springs. Because of high water clarity, long leaders and perfect casts are essential. There are also nesting areas around the lake for bald eagles, ospreys, and blue herons, and this park is considered a stellar habitat for bird-watching. A series of connecting trails are accessible from camp. The park is a wilderness area, covering 6,000 acres, and most of it is extremely rugged lava rock. There are many signs of this area's ancient past, with bedrock mortars, ceremonial sites, and prehistoric fish traps. There are also great herds of mule deer that forage through much of the park. Bears also roam this area. Finally, there are magnificent views of Mount Shasta, Mount Lassen, and other peaks.

Campsites, facilities: There are nine boat-in

sites. Picnic tables, food lockers, and fire pits are provided. Vault toilets are available. No drinking water is available. Garbage must be packed out. Leashed pets are permitted.

Reservations, fees: Reservations are not accepted. Sites are $9 per night. Open year-round, weather permitting.

Directions: From Redding, drive east on Highway 299 for 73 miles to McArthur. Turn left on Main Street and drive 3.5 miles (becomes a dirt road) to the Rat Farm boat launch at Big Lake. Launch boat and proceed by boat one to three miles to one of the nine boat-in campsites.

Contact: McArthur-Burney Falls Memorial State Park, 530/335-2777, www.parks.ca.gov.

12 DEADLUN

🚶 🏊 🎣 🛶 🏕 🚐 ⛺

Scenic rating: 7

on Iron Canyon Reservoir in Shasta-Trinity National Forest

Deadlun is a pretty campground set in the forest, shaded and quiet, with a five-minute walk or one-minute drive to the Deadlun Creek arm of Iron Canyon Reservoir. Drive. If you have a canoe to launch or fishing equipment to carry, driving is the choice. Trout fishing is good here, both in April and May, then again in October and early November. One downer is that the shoreline is often very muddy here in March and early April. Because of an engineering error with the dam, the lake never fills completely, causing the lakeshore to be strewn with stumps and quite muddy after spring rains and snowmelt.

Campsites, facilities: There are 25 sites for tents or RVs up to 24 feet (no hookups). Picnic tables and fire grills are provided. Vault toilets are available. No drinking water is available. A small boat ramp is available one mile from the camp. Garbage must be packed out. Leashed pets are permitted.

Reservations, fees: Reservations are not accepted. There is no fee for camping. Open year-round.

Directions: From Redding, drive east on Highway 299 for 37 miles to Big Bend Road/County Road 7M01. Turn left and drive 17 miles to the town of Big Bend. Continue for five miles to the lake, bearing right at the T intersection, and continue for two miles (past the boat-launch turnoff) to the campground turnoff on the left side of the road. Turn left and drive one mile to the campground.

Contact: Shasta-Trinity National Forest, Shasta Lake Ranger District, 530/275-1587, fax 530/275-1512; Shasta Lake Visitor Center, 530/275-1589.

13 HAWKINS LANDING

🚶 🏊 🎣 🛶 🏕 🚐 ⛺

Scenic rating: 7

on Iron Canyon Reservoir

The adjacent boat ramp makes Hawkins Landing the better of the two camps at Iron Canyon Reservoir for campers with trailered boats (though Deadlun is far more secluded). Iron Canyon, with 15 miles of shoreline, provides good fishing for trout, has a resident bald eagle or two. One problem with this lake is the annual drawdown in late fall, which causes the shoreline to be extremely muddy in the spring. The lake usually rises high enough to make the boat ramp functional by mid-April. The best spot for swimming is near the earth dam, which is also a good put-in area for kayaks and canoes. This camp is set at an elevation of 2,700 feet.

Campsites, facilities: There are 10 sites for tents or RVs up to 30 feet (no hookups). Picnic tables and fire grills are provided. Drinking water, vault toilets, and a small boat ramp are available. Supplies can be obtained in Big Bend. Leashed pets are permitted.

Reservations, fees: Reservations are not accepted. Sites are $10 per night, $1 per pet per night, $3 per night for each additional vehicle, $7 per night for additional RV. Open mid-May through Labor Day weekend, weather permitting.

Directions: From Redding, drive east on Highway 299 for 37 miles to Big Bend Road. At Big Bend Road turn left and drive 15.2 miles to the town of Big Bend. Continue for 2.1 miles to Forest Road 38N11. Turn left and drive 3.3 miles to the Iron Canyon Reservoir Spillway. Turn right and drive 1.1 miles to a dirt road. Turn left and drive 0.3 mile to the campground.

Contact: PG&E Land Projects, 916/386-5164, www.pge.com/recreation.

14 NORTHSHORE

Scenic rating: 8

on Lake Britton

This peaceful campground is set among the woodlands near the shore of Lake Britton, directly across the lake from McArthur-Burney Falls Memorial State Park. Boating and fishing are popular here, and once the water warms up in midsummer, swimming is also a winner. Boat rentals are available near the boat ramp. The lake has fair prospects for trout and is sometimes excellent for crappie. For side trips, the best trout fishing in the area is on the Pit River near Powerhouse Number Three. A hot spring is available in Big Bend, about a 30-minute drive from camp. The elevation is 2,800 feet. Note: This is a bald eagle nesting area, and some areas are closed in spring when an active nest is verified.

Campsites, facilities: There are 30 sites for tents or RVs up to 30 feet (no hookups). Picnic tables and fire grills are provided. Drinking water and vault toilets are available. An unimproved boat ramp is available near the camp and an improved boat ramp is available in McArthur-Burney Falls State Park (about four miles away). Supplies can be obtained

in Fall River Mills or Burney. Leashed pets are permitted.

Reservations, fees: Reservations are not accepted. Sites are $16 per night, $3 per night for each additional car, $7 per night per additional RV, $1 per pet per night. Open mid-May through mid-September, weather permitting.

Directions: From Redding, drive east on Highway 299 to Burney and then continue for five miles to Highway 89. Turn left (north) and drive 9.7 miles (past the state park entrance and over the Lake Britton Bridge) to Clark Creek Road. Turn left (west) and drive about a mile to the camp access road. Turn left and drive one mile to the camp.

Contact: PG&E Land Projects, 916/386-5164, www.pge.com/recreation.

15 McARTHUR-BURNEY FALLS MEMORIAL STATE PARK AND HORSE CAMP

Scenic rating: 9

in McArthur-Burney Falls Memorial State Park

McArthur-Burney Falls Memorial State Park was originally formed by volcanic activity and features 910 acres of forest and five miles of stream and lake shore. The Headwaters horse camp is three miles from the main campground. (Non-equestrian campers may stay at the horse camp, but only tents are allowed.) The campground is pretty and set amid large ponderosa pines. Camping-style cabins were installed in 2008 and have been a hit here.

Burney Falls is a 129-foot waterfall, a beautiful cascade split at the top by a little grove of trees, with small trickles oozing and falling out of the adjacent moss-lined wall. Since it is fed primarily by a spring, it runs strong and glorious most of the year, producing 100 million gallons of water every day. The Headwaters Trail provides an outstanding hike, both to see the waterfall and Burney Creek, as well as for an easy adventure and fishing access to the stream. An excellent fly-fishing section of the Pit River is available below the dam. There are other stellar recreation options at this state park. At the end of the campground access road is a boat ramp for Lake Britton, with rentals available for canoes and paddleboats. This is a beautiful lake, with pretty canyon walls on its upper end, and good smallmouth bass (at rock piles) and crappie fishing (near the train trestle). There is also a good swimming beach. The Pacific Crest Trail is routed right through the park and provides an additional opportunity for a day hike, best explored downstream from the dam. Reservations for sites are essential during the summer.

Campsites, facilities: There are 128 sites for tents or RVs up to 32 feet (no hookups), six horse-camp sites, one hike-in/bike-in site, and a small group of wood cabins. Picnic tables, food lockers, and fire grills are provided. Drinking water, restrooms with flush toilets and showers, and a dump station are available. Vault toilets and a small horse corral are available at the horse camp. Some facilities are wheelchair-accessible. A grocery/gift store and boat rentals are available in the summer. Leashed pets are permitted, except on the trails and the beach.

Reservations, fees: Reservations are accepted for RV and tent sites and cabins at 800/444-PARK (800/444-7275) or www.reserveamerica.com ($7.50 reservation fee). No reservations for equestrian sites. Sites are $15–20 per night, $6 per night for each additional vehicle, $3 per person per night for hike-in/bike-in site. Horse camp is $9 per night and $2 per night per horse. Boat launching is $8 per day. Open year-round.

Directions: From Redding, drive east on Highway 299 to Burney and then continue for five miles to the junction with Highway 89. At Highway 89, turn north (left) and drive six miles to the campground entrance on the left side of the road.

Contact: McArthur-Burney Falls State Park, 530/335-2777, www.parks.ca.gov.

16 DUSTY CAMPGROUND

Scenic rating: 8

on Lake Britton

This is one in a series of campgrounds near the north shore of Lake Britton. The lake has 18 miles of shoreline. (See *Northshore* listing in this chapter for more information.) The camp is set at an elevation of 2,800 feet. It provides an alternative to nearby McArthur-Burney Falls Memorial State Park, which is far more popular.

Campsites, facilities: There are seven sites for tents or RVs up to 30 feet (no hookups); two of the sites can accommodate groups of up to 25 people each. Fire rings are provided. Vault toilets are available. Drinking water is not available. Garbage must be packed out in winter. Some facilities are wheelchair-accessible. Leashed pets are permitted.

Reservations, fees: Reservations are not accepted. Sites are $6 per night, $3 per night for each additional vehicle, $7 per night per additional RV, $1 per pet per night, and $12 per night for double sites. Open year-round.

Directions: From Redding, drive east on Highway 299 to Burney and continue for five miles to the junction with Highway 89. Turn left (north) and drive 7.5 miles (past the state park entrance and over the Lake Britton Bridge) to the campground access road on the right (it will be confusing because the campground is on the left). Turn right and drive 0.75 mile (in the process crossing the highway) to the campground.

Contact: PG&E Land Projects, 916/386-5164, www.pge.com/recreation.

17 CAVE LAKE

Scenic rating: 8

in Modoc National Forest

A pair of lakes can be discovered out here in the middle of nowhere, with Cave Lake on one end and Lily Lake on the other. Together they make a nice set, very quiet, extremely remote, with good fishing for rainbow trout and brook trout. A canoe, pram, or float tube can be ideal. No motors are permitted. Of the two lakes, it is nearby Lily Lake that is prettier and provides the better fishing. Cave Lake is set at 6,600 feet. By camping here, you become a member of the 5 Percent Club; that is, the 5 percent of campers who know of secret, isolated little spots such as this one.

Campsites, facilities: There are six sites for tents or RVs up to 15 feet (no hookups); trailers are not advised because of the steep access road. Picnic tables and fire grills are provided. There is no drinking water. Vault toilets are available. Garbage must be packed out. Motors (including electric) are prohibited on the lake. Supplies are available in New Pine Creek and Davis Creek. Leashed pets are permitted.

Reservations, fees: Reservations are not accepted. There is no fee for camping. Open July through October, weather permitting.

Directions: From Redding, drive east on Highway 299 for 146 miles to Alturas and U.S. 395. Turn north on U.S. 395 and drive 40 miles to Forest Road 2 (if you reach the town of New Pine Creek on the Oregon/California border, you have driven a mile too far). Turn right on Forest Road 2 (a steep dirt road—trailers are not recommended) and drive six miles to the campground entrance on the left side of the road, just beyond the Lily Lake picnic area.

Contact: Modoc National Forest, Warner Mountain Ranger District, 530/279-6116, fax 530/279-8309.

18 PLUM VALLEY

Scenic rating: 7

near the South Fork of Davis Creek in Modoc National Forest

This secluded and primitive camp is set near the South Fork of Davis Creek, at 5,600 feet

elevation. Davis Creek offers catch-and-release, barbless hook, no-bait fishing. You can, however, keep the brown trout. There are no other campgrounds within 15 miles.

Campsites, facilities: There are 15 sites for tents or RVs up to 15 feet (no hookups). Picnic tables and fire grills are provided. Vault toilets are available. No drinking water is available. Garbage must be packed out. Supplies are available in Davis Creek, about 3.5 miles away. Leashed pets are permitted.

Reservations, fees: Reservations are not accepted. There is no fee for camping. Open May through September.

Directions: From Alturas drive north on U.S. 395 for 18 miles to the town of Davis Creek and County Road 11. Turn right on County Road 11 and drive two miles to a Y. Bear right on Forest Road 45N35 and drive one mile to the signed entrance to the campground on the left side of the road.

Contact: Modoc National Forest, Warner Mountain Ranger District, 530/279-6116, fax 530/279-8309; Department of Fish and Game fishing information, 530/225-2146.

19 RESERVOIR C

Scenic rating: 6

near Alturas in Modoc National Forest

It is one great adventure to explore the "alphabet lakes" in the remote Devil's Garden area of Modoc County. Reservoir C and Reservoir F provide the best of the lot, but the success can go up and down like a yo-yo, just like the water levels in the lakes. Reservoir C is stocked with both Eagle Lake trout and brown trout. A sidelight to this area is the number of primitive roads that are routed through Modoc National Forest, perfect for four-wheel-drivers. The elevation is 4,900 feet.

Campsites, facilities: There are six sites for tents or RVs up to 22 feet (no hookups). Picnic tables and fire grills are provided. Vault toilets and a primitive boat ramp are available. No drinking water is available. Garbage must be packed out. Some facilities are wheelchair-accessible. Leashed pets are permitted.

Reservations, fees: Reservations are not accepted. There is no fee for camping. Open May through September.

Directions: From Alturas drive west on Highway 299 for three miles to Crowder Flat Road/ County Road 73. Turn right on Crowder Flat Road and drive 9.5 miles to Triangle Ranch Road/Forest Road 43N18. Turn left on Triangle Ranch Road and drive seven miles to Forest Road 44N32. Turn right on Forest Road 44N32, drive 0.5 mile, turn right on the access road for the lake and campground, and drive 0.5 mile to the camp at the end of the road.

Contact: Modoc National Forest, Doublehead Ranger District, 530/667-2246, fax 530/667-8309.

20 BIG SAGE RESERVOIR

Scenic rating: 5

in Modoc National Forest

This is a do-it-yourself camp; that is, pick your own spot, bring your own water, and don't expect to see anybody else. This camp is set along Big Sage Reservoir—that's right, sagebrush country at 5,100 feet elevation. It is a big lake, covering 5,000 surface acres, and a boat ramp is adjacent to the campground. This is one of the better bass lakes in Modoc County. Catfish and crappie are also here. Water sports are allowed, except for personal watercraft. Swimming is not recommended because of algae growth in midsummer, murky water, and muddy shoreline. Water levels can fluctuate greatly.

Campsites, facilities: There are six sites for tents or RVs up to 22 feet (no hookups). Picnic tables and fire grills are provided. Vault toilets are available. There is no drinking water. Some facilities are wheelchair-accessible. Garbage must be packed out. A boat ramp is available nearby.

Leashed pets are permitted. Supplies can be obtained in Alturas, about eight miles away.

Reservations, fees: Reservations are not accepted. There is no fee for camping. Open May through September.

Directions: From Alturas, drive west on Highway 299 for three miles to Crowder Flat Road/ County Road 73. Turn right on Crowder Flat Road and drive about five miles to County Road 180. Turn right on County Road 180 and drive four miles. Turn left at the access road for the campground and boat ramp and drive a short distance to the camp on the left side of the road.

Contact: Modoc National Forest, Doublehead Ranger District, 530/667-2246, fax 530/667-8309.

21 CEDAR PASS

Scenic rating: 5

on Cedar Pass in Modoc National Forest

Cedar Pass is at 5,600 feet, set on the ridge between Cedar Mountain (8,152 feet) to the north and Payne Peak (7,618) to the south, high in the north Warner Mountains. Bear Creek enters Thomas Creek adjacent to the camp; both are small streams, but it's a pretty spot.

Campsites, facilities: There are 17 sites for tents or RVs up to 16 feet (no hookups). Picnic tables and fire grills are provided. Vault toilets are available. No drinking water is available. Garbage must be packed out. Supplies can be obtained in Cedarville or Alturas. Leashed pets are permitted.

Reservations, fees: Reservations are not accepted. There is no fee for camping. Open late May through October, weather permitting.

Directions: From Redding drive east on Highway 299 to Alturas. In Alturas continue north on Highway 299/U.S. 395 for five miles to the split for Highway 299. Turn right on Highway 299 and drive about nine miles. Look for the signed entrance road on the right side of the road.

Contact: Modoc National Forest, Warner Mountain Ranger District, 530/279-6116, fax 530/279-8309.

22 STOUGH RESERVOIR
🚶 🏊 🛶 🎣 🐴 🚐 ⛺

Scenic rating: 8

in Modoc National Forest

Stough Reservoir looks like a large country pond where cattle might drink. You know why? Because it once actually was a cattle pond on a family ranch that has since been converted to Forest Service property. It is in the north Warner Mountains (not to be confused with the South Warner Wilderness), which features many back roads and remote four-wheel-drive routes. The camp is set at an elevation of 6,200 feet. Note that you may find this campground named "Stowe Reservoir" on some maps and in previous editions of this book. The name is now officially spelled "Stough Reservoir," after the family that originally owned the property.

Campsites, facilities: There are 14 sites for tents or RVs up to 22 feet (no hookups). Picnic tables and fire grills are provided. Drinking water and vault toilets are available. Garbage must be packed out. Leashed pets are permitted. Supplies can be obtained in Cedarville, six miles away.

Reservations, fees: Reservations are not accepted. There is no fee for camping. Open late May through early October, weather permitting.

Directions: From Redding, drive east on Highway 299 to Alturas. In Alturas, continue north on Highway 299/U.S. 395 for five miles to the split-off for Highway 299. Turn right on Highway 299 and drive about 12 miles (just past Cedar Pass). Look for the signed entrance road on the left side of the road. Turn left and drive one mile to the campground on the left side of the road.

Contact: Modoc National Forest, Warner Mountain Ranger District, 530/279-6116, fax 530/279-8309.

23 HOWARD'S GULCH
🚶 🛶 🎣 🐴 ♿ 🚐 ⛺

Scenic rating: 6

near Duncan Reservoir in Modoc National Forest

This is the nearest campground to Duncan Reservoir, three miles to the north and stocked with trout each year by the Department of Fish and Game. The camp is set in the typically sparse woods of Modoc National Forest, but a beautiful grove of aspen is three miles to the west on Highway 139, on the left side of the road. By the way, Highway 139 isn't much of a highway at all, but it is paved and will get you there. The elevation is 4,700 feet.

Campsites, facilities: There are 11 sites for tents or RVs up to 22 feet (no hookups). Picnic tables and fire grills are provided. Drinking water and vault toilets are available. Some facilities are wheelchair-accessible. Supplies are available within five miles in Canby. Leashed pets are permitted.

Reservations, fees: Reservations are not accepted. Sites are $6 per night. Open May through October, weather permitting.

Directions: From Redding, drive east on Highway 299 for about 100 miles to Adin. Continue on Highway 299 for about 25 miles to Highway 139. Turn left (northwest) on Highway 139 and drive six miles to the campground on the left side of the road.

Contact: Modoc National Forest, Devil's Garden Ranger District, 530/233-5811, fax 530/233-8709.

24 PEPPERDINE
🚶 🐴 5% 🚐 ⛺

Scenic rating: 5

in Modoc National Forest

This camp is outstanding for hikers planning a backpacking trip into the adjacent South Warner Wilderness. The camp is at 6,680 feet, set

LASSEN CAMPING

along the south side of tiny Porter Reservoir, with a horse corral within walking distance. A trailhead out of camp provides direct access to the Summit Trail, the best hike in the South Warner Wilderness.

Campsites, facilities: There are five sites for tents or RVs up to 16 feet (no hookups). Picnic tables and fire grills are provided. Drinking water and vault toilets are available. Corrals are available with water for stock. Garbage must be packed out. Supplies are available in Cedarville or Alturas. Leashed pets are permitted.

Reservations, fees: Reservations are not accepted. There is no fee for camping. Open July through October, weather permitting.

Directions: In Alturas, drive south on U.S. 395 to the southern end of town and County Road 56. Turn left on County Road 56 and drive 13 miles to the Modoc Forest boundary and the junction with Parker Creek Road. Bear left on Parker Creek Road and continue for six miles to the signed campground access road on the right. Turn right and drive 0.5 mile to the campground on the left side of the road.

Contact: Modoc National Forest, Warner Mountain Ranger District, 530/279-6116, fax 530/279-8309.

25 UPPER RUSH CREEK
🏃 🏊 🐕 🚗 🏕

Scenic rating: 8

in Modoc National Forest

Upper Rush Creek is a pretty campground, set along Rush Creek, a quiet, wooded spot that gets little use. It sits in the shadow of nearby Manzanita Mountain (7,036 feet elevation) to the east, where there is a Forest Service lookout for a great view. To reach the lookout, drive back toward Highway 299 and when you reach the paved road, County Road 198, turn left and drive 0.5 mile to Forest Road 22. Turn left on Forest Road 22 and head up the hill. One mile from the summit, turn left at a four-way

junction and drive to the top. You get dramatic views of the Warm Springs Valley to the north and the Likely Flats to the east, looking across miles and miles of open country.

Campsites, facilities: There are 13 sites for tents or RVs up to 22 feet (no hookups), but Lower Rush Creek is better for trailers. Picnic tables and fire grills are provided. Vault toilets are available. There is no drinking water. Supplies can be obtained about nine miles away in Adin or Canby. Leashed pets are permitted.

Reservations, fees: Reservations are not accepted. There is no camping fee. Open May through October, weather permitting.

Directions: From Redding, turn east on Highway 299 and drive to Adin. Continue east on Highway 299 for about seven miles to a signed campground turnoff on the right side of the road. Turn right and drive to the junction with Forest Road 40N05. Turn left and drive 2.5 miles to the campground at the end of the road.

Contact: Modoc National Forest, Big Valley Ranger District, 530/299-3215, fax 530/299-8409.

26 LOWER RUSH CREEK
🏊 🐕 🚗 🏕

Scenic rating: 6

on Rush Creek in Modoc National Forest

This is one of two obscure campgrounds set a short distance from Highway 299 on Rush Creek in southern Modoc County. Lower Rush Creek is the first camp you will come to, with flat campsites surrounded by an outer fence and set along Rush Creek. This camp is better suited for trailers than the one at Upper Rush Creek. It is little known and little used. It's set at 4,400 feet elevation.

Campsites, facilities: There are 10 sites for tents or RVs up to 22 feet (no hookups). Picnic tables and fire grills are provided. Vault toilets are available. There is no drinking water. Supplies are available in Adin or Canby. Leashed pets are permitted.

Reservations, fees: Reservations are not accepted. There is no camping fee. Open May through October, weather permitting.

Directions: From Redding, turn east on Highway 299 and drive to Adin. Continue east on Highway 299 for about seven miles to a signed campground turnoff on the right side of the road. Turn right and drive to the junction with Forest Road 40N05. Turn left and drive one mile to the campground on the right.

Contact: Modoc National Forest, Big Valley Ranger District, 530/299-3215, fax 530/299-8409.

27 SOUP SPRINGS

Scenic rating: 8

in Modoc National Forest

This is a beautiful, quiet, wooded campground at a trailhead into the South Warner Wilderness. Soup Creek originates at Soup Springs in the meadow adjacent to the campground. The trailhead here is routed two miles into the wilderness, where it junctions with the Mill Creek Trail. From here, turn left for a beautiful walk along Mill Creek and into Mill Creek Meadow, an easy yet pristine stroll that can provide a serene experience. The elevation is 6,800 feet.

Campsites, facilities: There are 14 sites for tents or RVs up to 22 feet (no hookups). Picnic tables and fire grills are provided. Drinking water and vault toilets are available. Corrals are also available. Supplies can be obtained in Likely. Leashed pets are permitted.

Reservations, fees: Reservations are not accepted. Sites are $6 per night. Open June through October, weather permitting.

Directions: From Alturas, drive south on U.S. 395 for 17 miles to the town of Likely, where you'll come to Jess Valley Road. Turn left on Jess Valley Road/County Road 64 and drive nine miles to the fork. Bear left on West Warner Road/Forest Road 5 and go 4.5 miles to

Soup Loop Road. Turn right on Soup Loop Road/Forest Road 40N24 and continue on that gravel road for six miles to the campground entrance on the right.

Contact: Modoc National Forest, Warner Mountain Ranger District, 530/279-6116, fax 530/279-8309.

28 MILL CREEK FALLS

Scenic rating: 9

in Modoc National Forest

This nice, wooded campground is a good base camp for a backpacking trip into the South Warner Wilderness. The camp is set on Mill Creek at 5,700 feet elevation. To see Mill Creek Falls, take the trail out of camp and bear left at the Y. To enter the interior of the South Warner Wilderness, bear right at the Y, after which the trail passes Clear Lake, heads to Poison Flat and Poison Creek, and then reaches a junction. Left will take you to the Mill Creek Trail; right will take you up to the Summit Trail. Take your pick. You can't go wrong.

Campsites, facilities: There are 19 sites for tents or RVs up to 22 feet (no hookups). Picnic tables and fire grills are provided. Drinking water and vault toilets are available. Supplies are available in Likely. Leashed pets are permitted.

Reservations, fees: Reservations are not accepted. Sites are $6 per night. Open June through October, weather permitting.

Directions: From Alturas drive 17 miles south on U.S. 395 to the town of Likely, where you'll come to Jess Valley Road. Turn left on Jess Valley Road/County Road 64 and drive nine miles to the fork. Bear left on West Warner Road/Forest Road 5 and drive 2.5 miles to Forest Road 40N46. Turn right on Forest Road 40N46 and drive two miles to the campground entrance at the end of the road.

Contact: Modoc National Forest, Warner Mountain Ranger District, 530/279-6116, fax 530/279-8309.

29 EMERSON

Scenic rating: 6

in Modoc National Forest

This tiny camp is virtually unknown, nestled at 6,000 feet on the eastern boundary of the South Warner Wilderness. Big alkali lakes and miles of the Nevada flats can be seen on the other side of the highway as you drive along the entrance road to the campground. A trailhead at this primitive setting is used by hikers and backpackers. Note that hitting the trail is a steep, sometimes wrenching climb for 4.5 miles to North Emerson Lake (poor to fair fishing). For many, this hike is a true butt-kicker.

Campsites, facilities: There are four sites for tents or RVs up to 16 feet (no hookups). Picnic tables and fire grills are provided. Vault toilets are available. No drinking water is available. Garbage must be packed out. Supplies can be obtained in Eagleville. Leashed pets are permitted.

Reservations, fees: Reservations are not accepted. There is no fee for camping. Open July through October, weather permitting.

Directions: From Alturas, drive north on U.S. 395/Highway 299 for about five miles to the junction with Highway 299. Turn right on Highway 299 and drive to Cedarville and County Road 1. Turn south on County Road 1 and drive to Eagleville. From Eagleville, continue south on County Road 1 for 1.5 miles to Forest Road 40N43/County Road 40. Turn right and drive three miles to the campground at the end of the road. The access road is steep, narrow, and very slick in wet weather. Trailers are not recommended.

Contact: Modoc National Forest, Warner Mountain Ranger District, 530/279-6116, fax 530/279-8309.

30 ASH CREEK

Scenic rating: 7

in Modoc National Forest

This remote camp has stark beauty and is set at 4,800 feet along Ash Creek, a stream with small trout. This region of Modoc National Forest has an extensive network of backcountry roads, popular with deer hunters in the fall. The Ash Creek Wildlife Area is about 10 miles west of camp. Summer comes relatively late out here, and it can be cold and wet even in early June. Stash some extra clothes, just in case. That will probably guarantee nice weather.

Campsites, facilities: There are seven sites for tents or RVs up to 22 feet (no hookups). Picnic tables and fire grills are provided. Vault toilets are available. No drinking water is available. Garbage must be packed out. Supplies can be obtained in Adin. Leashed pets are permitted.

Reservations, fees: Reservations are not accepted. There is no fee for camping. Open May through October, weather permitting.

Directions: From Redding, turn east on Highway 299 and drive to Adin and Ash Valley Road. Turn right on Ash Valley Road/County Road 88/527 and drive eight miles. Turn left at the signed campground turnoff and drive a mile to the campground on the right side of the road.

Contact: Modoc National Forest, Big Valley Ranger District, 530/299-3215, fax 530/299-8409; Ash Creek Wildlife Area, 530/294-5824.

31 PATTERSON

Scenic rating: 4

in Modoc National Forest

Patterson is set across the road from Patterson Meadow at 7,200 feet elevation. This beautiful landscape was burned by the Blue Fire of 2001, which enveloped 35,000 acres in the South Warners. During the past several years vegetation growth has improved the area's scenic beauty and it is now recovering.

There are both positives and negatives to the burn. The positives are a chance for much wider and longer views previously impossible, as well as the opportunity to watch the evolution of the landscape in a post-fire setting, as has been the case in Yellowstone for years. The negatives are the tree skeletons. The most affected area is to the east, especially on East Creek Trail, which rises through the burned area to a high, barren mountain rim.

Campsites, facilities: There are five sites for tents or RVs up to 20 feet (no hookups). Picnic tables and fire grills are provided. Drinking water and vault toilets are available. Garbage must be packed out. Supplies are available in Likely or Cedarville. Leashed pets are permitted.

Reservations, fees: Reservations are not accepted. There is no fee for camping. Open late July through October, weather permitting.

Directions: From Alturas drive 17 miles south on U.S. 395 to the town of Likely. Turn left on Jess Valley Road/County Road 64 and drive nine miles to the fork. Bear right on Forest Road 64 and drive for 16 miles to the campground on the left.

Contact: Modoc National Forest, Warner Mountain Ranger District, 530/279-6116, fax 530/279-8309.

level campsites) near the shore of Blue Lake. The lake covers 160 acres and provides fishing for large brown trout and rainbow trout. A 5-mph speed limit assures quiet water for small boats and canoes. A trail circles the lake and takes less than an hour to hike. The elevation is 6,000 feet. Bald eagles have been spotted here. While their presence negates year-round use of six campsites otherwise available, the trade-off is an unprecedented opportunity to view the national bird.

Campsites, facilities: There are 48 sites for tents or RVs up to 22 feet (no hookups). Picnic tables and fire grills are provided. Drinking water and vault toilets are available. Some facilities are wheelchair-accessible, including a paved boat launch and fishing pier. Supplies are available in Likely. Leashed pets are permitted.

Reservations, fees: Reservations are not accepted. Sites are $7 per night. Open June through October, weather permitting.

Directions: From Alturas, drive south on U.S. 395 for seven miles to the town of Likely, where you'll come to Jess Valley Road. Turn left on Jess Valley Road/County Road 64 and drive nine miles to the fork. At the fork, bear right on Forest Road 64 and drive seven miles to Forest Road 38N30. Turn right on Forest Road 38N30 and drive two miles to the campground.

Contact: Modoc National Forest, Warner Mountain Ranger District, 530/279-6116, fax 530/279-8309.

32 BLUE LAKE

Scenic rating: 6

in Modoc National Forest

The Blue Fire of 2001 burned 35,000 acres in this area, including the east and west slopes adjoining Blue Lake. Yet get this: The campground was untouched. It is a strange scene, a somewhat wooded campground (with some

33 WILLOW CREEK

Scenic rating: 7

in Modoc National Forest

This remote camp and picnic area is set at 5,200 feet along little Willow Creek amid pine, aspen, and willows. On the north side of the campground is Lower McBride Springs.

Campsites, facilities: There are eight sites for

tents or RVs up to 22 feet (no hookups). Picnic tables and fire grills are provided. Drinking water and vault toilets are available. A wheelchair-accessible toilet is at the picnic area next to the campground. Leashed pets are permitted.

Reservations, fees: Reservations are not accepted. Sites are $7 per night. Open May through October, weather permitting.

Directions: From Redding, drive east on Highway 299 to Adin and Highway 139. Turn right on Highway 139 and drive 14 miles to the campground on the left side of the road.

Contact: Modoc National Forest, Big Valley Ranger District, 530/299-3215, fax 530/299-8409.

34 PIT RIVER

Scenic rating: 6

on the Pit River

Very few out-of-towners know about this hidden campground set along the Pit River. It can provide a good base camp for a fishing trip adventure. The best stretch of trout water on the Pit is near Powerhouse Number Three. In addition to fishing there are many other recreation options. A parking area and trail along Hat Creek are available where the Highway 299 bridge crosses Hat Creek. Baum Lake, Crystal Lake, and the Cassel section of Hat Creek are all within five miles of this camp.

Campsites, facilities: There are seven sites for tents or RVs up to 40 feet (no hookups), and one double site for up to eight people. Picnic tables and fire rings are provided. Vault toilets, wheelchair-accessible fishing pier, and small-craft launch ramp are available. No drinking water is available. Garbage must be packed out. There are supplies and a coin laundry in Fall River Mills. Some facilities are wheelchair-accessible. Leashed pets are permitted.

Reservations, fees: Reservations are not accepted. Sites are $8 per night, and $12 per night for the double site. Open mid-April through mid-November.

Directions: From Redding, drive east on Highway 299 to Burney and continue for five miles to the junction with Highway 89. At the junction, continue straight on Highway 299, cross the Pit River Bridge, and drive about three miles to Pit One Powerhouse Road. Turn right and drive down the hill to the Pit River Lodge. Turn right and drive 0.5 mile to the campground.

Contact: Bureau of Land Management, Alturas Field Office, 530/233-4666, fax 530/233-5696.

35 CASSEL

Scenic rating: 8

on Hat Creek

This camp is set at 3,200 feet in the beautiful Hat Creek Valley. It is an outstanding location for a fishing trip base camp, with nearby Crystal Lake, Baum Lake, and Hat Creek (all set in the Hat Creek Valley) providing trout fishing. This section of Hat Creek is well known for its challenging fly-fishing. A good source of fishing information is Vaughn's Sporting Goods in Burney. Baum Lake is ideal for car-top boats with electric motors.

Campsites, facilities: There are 27 sites for tents or RVs up to 30 feet (no hookups). Picnic tables and fire grills are provided. Drinking water and vault toilets are available. Some facilities are wheelchair-accessible. Leashed pets are permitted.

Reservations, fees: Reservations are not accepted. Sites are $16 per night, $3 per night for each additional vehicle, $7 per night per additional RV, $1 per pet per night. Open mid-April through mid-November, weather permitting.

Directions: From Redding, drive east on

Highway 299 to Burney and continue for five miles to the junction with Highway 89. At the junction, continue straight on Highway 299 for two miles to Cassel Road. At Cassel Road, turn right and drive 3.6 miles to the campground entrance on the left.

Contact: PG&E Land Projects, 916/386-5164, www.pge.com/recreation.

36 HAT CREEK HEREFORD RANCH RV PARK AND CAMPGROUND

Scenic rating: 8

near Hat Creek

This privately operated campground is set in a working cattle ranch. Campers are not allowed near the cattle pasture or cattle. Fishing is available in Hat Creek or in the nearby stocked trout pond. Swimming is also allowed in the pond. Sightseeing is excellent with Burney Falls, Lassen Volcanic National Park, and Subway Caves all within 30 miles.

Campsites, facilities: There are 40 tent sites and 40 RV sites with full or partial hookups (30 amps); some sites are pull-through. Picnic tables and fireplaces are provided. Restrooms with showers, a dump station, coin laundry, playground, modem hookups, wireless Internet access, and a convenience store are available. Some facilities are wheelchair-accessible. Leashed pets are permitted.

Reservations, fees: Reservations are recommended and can be made by telephone or website. RV sites are $24.75–27.50 per night, tent sites are $19.50–25.50 per night, $2 per night for more than two people, $1 per night per pet. Some credit cards accepted. Open April through October.

Directions: From Redding, drive east on Highway 299 to Burney and continue for five miles to the junction with Highway 89. Turn right

(south) on Highway 89 and drive 12 miles to the second Doty Road Loop exit. Turn left and drive 0.5 mile to the park entrance on the right.

Contact: Hat Creek Hereford Ranch RV Park and Campground, 530/335-7171 or 877/459-9532, www.hatcreekrv.com.

37 HONN

Scenic rating: 7

on Hat Creek in Lassen National Forest

This primitive, tiny campground is set near the point where Honn Creek enters Hat Creek, at 3,400 feet elevation in Lassen National Forest. The creek is extremely pretty here, shaded by trees and flowing emerald green. The camp provides streamside access for trout fishing, though this stretch of creek is sometimes overlooked by the Department of Fish and Game in favor of stocking the creek at the more popular Cave and Bridge Campgrounds. (See listings in this chapter for more information.)

Campsites, facilities: There are six tent sites. Picnic tables and fire grills are provided. Vault toilets are available. Drinking water is not available. A grocery store, coin laundry, and propane gas are nearby. Leashed pets are permitted.

Reservations, fees: Reservations are not accepted. Sites are $10 per night, $5 per night for each additional vehicle. Open late April through October, weather permitting.

Directions: From Redding, drive east on Highway 299 to Burney and continue for five miles to the junction with Highway 89. Turn right (south) on Highway 89 and drive 15 miles to the campground entrance on the left side of the road.

Contact: Lassen National Forest, Hat Creek Ranger District, 530/336-5521, fax 530/336-5758; Department of Fish and Game fishing information, 530/225-2146.

LASSEN CAMPING

38 OLD COW MEADOWS

Scenic rating: 7

in Latour Demonstration State Forest

Nobody finds this campground without this book. You want quiet? You don't want to be bugged by anybody? This tiny camp, virtually unknown, is set at 5,900 feet in a wooded area along Old Cow Creek. Recreation options include all-terrain-vehicle use on existing roads and walking the dirt roads that crisscross the area.

Campsites, facilities: There are three sites for tents or RVs up to 25 feet (no hookups). Picnic tables and fire grills are provided. Vault toilets and drinking water are available. Garbage must be packed out. Some facilities are wheelchair-accessible. Leashed pets are permitted.

Reservations, fees: Reservations are not accepted. There is no fee for camping. Open June through October, weather permitting.

Directions: In Redding, turn east on Highway 44 and drive about 9.5 miles to Millville Road. Turn left on Millville Road and drive 0.5 mile to the intersection of Millville Road and Whitmore Road. Turn right on Whitmore Road and drive 13 miles, through Whitmore, until Whitmore Road becomes Tamarac Road. Continue for one mile to a fork at Bateman Road. Take the right fork on Bateman Road, drive 3.5 miles (where the road turns to gravel), and then continue 10 miles to Huckleberry Road. Turn right on Huckleberry Road and drive two miles to the campground.

Contact: Latour Demonstration State Forest, 530/225-2438, fax 530/225-2514.

39 SOUTH COW CREEK MEADOWS

Scenic rating: 6

in Latour Demonstration State Forest

This camp is set in a pretty, wooded area next to a small meadow along South Cow Creek.

It's used mostly in the fall for hunting, with off-highway-vehicle use on the surrounding roads in the summer. The camp is set at 5,600 feet. If you want to get away from it all without leaving your vehicle, this is one way to do it. The creek is a reliable water source, providing you use a water filtration pump.

Campsites, facilities: There are four sites for tents or RVs up to 30 feet (no hookups). Picnic tables and fire grills are provided. Vault toilets and drinking water are available. Garbage must be packed out. Some facilities are wheelchair-accessible. Leashed pets are permitted.

Reservations, fees: Reservations are not accepted. There is no fee for camping. Open June through October, weather permitting.

Directions: In Redding, turn east on Highway 44 and drive about 9.5 miles to Millville Road. Turn left on Millville Road and drive 0.5 mile to the intersection of Millville Road and Whitmore Road. Turn right on Whitmore Road and drive 13 miles, through Whitmore, until Whitmore Road becomes Tamarac Road. Continue for one mile to the fork at Bateman Road. Take the right fork on Bateman Road, drive 3.5 miles (where the road turns to gravel), and then continue for 11 miles to South Cow Creek Road. Turn right (east) and drive one mile to the campground.

Contact: Latour Demonstration State Forest, 530/225-2438, fax 530/225-2514.

40 BRIDGE CAMP

Scenic rating: 7

on Hat Creek in Lassen National Forest

This camp is one of four along Highway 89 in the area along Hat Creek. It is set at 4,000 feet elevation, with shaded sites and the stream within very short walking distance. Trout are stocked on this stretch of the creek, with fishing access available out of camp, as well as at Rocky and Cave Camps to the south and

Honn to the north. In one weekend, anglers might hit all four.

Campsites, facilities: There are 25 sites for tents or RVs up to 22 feet (no hookups). Picnic tables and fire grills are provided. There is no drinking water. Vault toilets are available. A grocery store and propane gas are nearby. Leashed pets are permitted.

Reservations, fees: Reservations are not accepted. Sites are $10 per night, $5 per night for each additional vehicle. Open late April through October, weather permitting.

Directions: From Redding, drive east on Highway 299 to Burney and continue for five miles to the junction with Highway 89. Turn right (south) on Highway 89 and drive 19 miles to the campground entrance on the right side of the road. If you reach Old Station, you have gone five miles too far.

Contact: Lassen National Forest, Hat Creek Ranger District, 530/336-5521, fax 530/336-5758; Department of Fish and Game fishing information, 530/225-2146.

41 ROCKY CAMP

Scenic rating: 7

on Hat Creek in Lassen National Forest

This is a small, primitive camp along Hat Creek on Highway 89. It's usually a second choice for campers if nearby Cave and Bridge Camps are full. Streamside fishing access is a plus here, with this section of stream stocked with rainbow trout. The elevation is 4,000 feet. (See the *Cave Camp* listing for more information.)

Campsites, facilities: There are eight tent sites. Picnic tables and fire grills are provided. Vault toilets are available. No drinking water is available. A grocery store and propane gas are nearby. Leashed pets are permitted.

Reservations, fees: Reservations are not accepted. Sites are $10 per night, $5 per night for each additional vehicle. Open late April through October, weather permitting.

Directions: From Redding, drive east on Highway 299 to Burney and continue for five miles to the junction with Highway 89. Turn right (south) on Highway 89 and drive 20 miles to the campground entrance on the right side of the road. If you reach Old Station, you have gone four miles too far.

Contact: Lassen National Forest, Hat Creek Ranger District, 530/336-5521, fax 530/336-5758; Department of Fish and Game fishing information, 530/225-2146.

42 CAVE CAMP

Scenic rating: 7

on Hat Creek in Lassen National Forest

Cave Camp is set right along Hat Creek, with easy access off Highway 89 and an anglers' trail available along the stream. This stretch of Hat Creek is planted with rainbow trout twice per month by the Department of Fish and Game, starting with the opening of trout season on the last Saturday of April. Nearby side trips include Lassen Volcanic National Park, about a 15-minute drive to the south on Highway 89, and Subway Caves (turn left at the junction just across the road from the campground). A rare bonus at this camp is that wheelchair-accessible fishing is available.

Campsites, facilities: There are 46 sites for tents or RVs up to 22 feet (no hookups). Picnic tables and fire grills are provided. Drinking water and flush and vault toilets are available. Some facilities are wheelchair-accessible. Supplies can be obtained in Old Station. Leashed pets are permitted.

Reservations, fees: Reservations are not accepted. Sites are $16 per night, $5 per night for each additional vehicle. Open late April through October, weather permitting.

Directions: From Redding, drive east on Highway 299 to Burney and continue for five miles to the junction with Highway 89. Turn right (south) on Highway 89 and drive 23 miles to the campground entrance on the right side of the road. If you reach Old Station, you have gone one mile too far.

Contact: Lassen National Forest, Hat Creek Ranger District, 530/336-5521, fax 530/336-5758; Department of Fish and Game fishing information, 530/225-2146.

43 HAT CREEK

Scenic rating: 7

on Hat Creek in Lassen National Forest

This is one in a series of Forest Service camps set beside beautiful Hat Creek, a good trout stream stocked regularly by the Department of Fish and Game. The elevation is 4,300 feet. The proximity to Lassen Volcanic National Park to the south is a big plus. Supplies are available in the little town of Old Station one mile to the north.

Campsites, facilities: There are 75 sites for tents or RVs up to 30 feet, and three group camps for tents or RVs up to 30 feet that can accommodate up to 50 people each. No hookups. Picnic tables and fire grills are provided. Drinking water and vault toilets are available. A grocery store, dump station, coin laundry, and propane gas are nearby. There is an accessible fishing platform. Leashed pets are permitted.

Reservations, fees: Tent and RV sites are first-come, first-served. Reservations are required for group sites at 877/444-6777 or www.recreation.gov ($10 reservation fee). Tent and RV sites are $16 per night, $5 per night for each additional vehicle, $85 per night for group camps. Open late April through October, weather permitting.

Directions: From Redding, drive east on Highway 44 to the junction with Highway 89 (near the entrance to Lassen Volcanic National Park). Turn left (north) on Highway 89 and drive about 12 miles to the campground entrance on the left side of the road.

Turn left and drive a short distance to the campground.

Contact: Lassen National Forest, Hat Creek Ranger District, 530/336-5521, fax 530/336-5758; Department of Fish and Game fishing information, 530/225-2146.

44 NORTH BATTLE CREEK RESERVOIR

Scenic rating: 7

on Battle Creek Reservoir

This little-known lake is at 5,600 feet in elevation, largely surrounded by Lassen National Forest. No gas engines are permitted on the lake, making it ideal for canoes, rafts, and car-top aluminum boats equipped with electric motors. When the lake level is up in early summer, it is a pretty setting with good trout fishing.

Campsites, facilities: There are 10 sites for tents or RVs up to 30 feet (no hookups) and five walk-in tent sites. Picnic tables and fire grills are provided. Drinking water and vault toilets are available. A car-top boat launch is available nearby. Leashed pets are permitted.

Reservations, fees: Reservations are not accepted. Sites are $13 per night, $3 per night for each additional vehicle, $7 per additional RV per night, $1 per pet per night. Open mid-May through mid-September, weather permitting.

Directions: From Redding, drive east on Highway 44 to Viola. From Viola, continue east for 3.5 miles to Forest Road 32N17. Turn left on Forest Road 32N17 and drive five miles to Forest Road 32N31. Turn left and drive four miles to Forest Road 32N18. Turn right and drive 0.5 mile to the reservoir and the campground on the right side of the road.

Contact: PG&E Land Projects, 916/386-5164, www.pge.com/recreation.

45 BIG PINE CAMP

Scenic rating: 7

on Hat Creek in Lassen National Forest

This campground is set on the headwaters of Hat Creek, a pretty spot amid ponderosa pines. The elevation is 4,500 feet. A dirt road out of camp parallels Hat Creek, providing access for trout fishing. A great vista point is set on the highway, a mile south of the campground entrance road. It is only a 10-minute drive south to the Highway 44 entrance station for Lassen Volcanic National Park.

Campsites, facilities: There are 19 sites for tents or RVs up to 22 feet (no hookups). Picnic tables and fire grills are provided. Drinking water (at two hand pumps) and vault toilets are available. A dump station, grocery store, and propane gas are nearby. Leashed pets are permitted.

Reservations, fees: Reservations are not accepted. Sites are $12 per night, $5 per night for each additional vehicle. Open late April through October, weather permitting.

Directions: From Redding, drive east on Highway 44 to the junction with Highway 89 (near the entrance to Lassen Volcanic National Park). Turn left (north) on Highway 89 and drive about eight miles (one mile past the vista point) to the campground entrance on the right side of the road. Turn right and drive 0.5 mile to the campground.

Contact: Lassen National Forest, Hat Creek Ranger District, 530/336-5521, fax 530/336-5758; Department of Fish and Game fishing information, 530/225-2146.

46 BUTTE CREEK

Scenic rating: 6

in Lassen National Forest

This primitive, little-known spot is just three miles from the northern boundary of Lassen Volcanic National Park, set on little Butte Creek. The elevation is 5,600 feet. It is a four-mile drive south out of camp on Forest Road 18 to Butte Lake in Lassen Park and to the trailhead for a great hike up to the Cinder Cone (6,907 feet), with dramatic views of the Lassen wilderness.

Campsites, facilities: There are 20 sites for tents or RVs up to 22 feet (no hookups). Vault toilets are available. No drinking water is available. Garbage must be packed out. Leashed pets are permitted.

Reservations, fees: Reservations are not accepted. There is no fee for camping. Open May through October, weather permitting.

Directions: From Redding, drive east on Highway 44 to the junction with Highway 89 (near the entrance to Lassen Volcanic National Park). Turn north on Highway 89 and drive to Highway 44. Turn east (right) on Highway 44 and drive 11 miles to Forest Road 18. Turn right at Forest Road 18 and drive three miles to the campground on the left side of the road.

Contact: Lassen National Forest, Eagle Lake Ranger District, 530/257-4188, fax 530/252-5803.

47 BOGARD

Scenic rating: 6

in Lassen National Forest

This little camp is set along Pine Creek, which flows through Pine Creek Valley at the foot of the Bogard Buttes. It is a relatively obscure camp that gets missed by many travelers. A bonus here are the beautiful aspens, breathtaking in fall. To the nearby west is a network of Forest Service roads, and beyond is the Caribou Wilderness.

Campsites, facilities: There are 11 sites for tents or RVs up to 25 feet (no hookups). Picnic tables and fire grills are provided. Drinking water and vault toilets are available. Leashed pets are permitted.

Reservations, fees: Reservations are not accepted. Sites are $13 per night. Open May through October, weather permitting.

Directions: From Redding, drive east on Highway 44 to the junction with Highway 89 (near the entrance to Lassen Volcanic National Park). Turn north on Highway 89 and drive to Highway 44. Turn east on Highway 44 and drive to the Bogard Work Center (about seven miles past Poison Lake) and the adjacent rest stop. Continue east on Highway 44 for two miles to a gravel road on the right side of the road (Forest Road 31N26). Turn right on Forest Road 31N26 and drive two miles. Turn right on Forest Road 31N21 and drive 0.5 mile to the campground at the end of the road.

Contact: Lassen National Forest, Eagle Lake Ranger District, 530/257-4188, fax 530/252-5803.

48 CRATER LAKE
🏃 ⛵ 🛶 🏊 🐾 5% ⛺

Scenic rating: 8

in Lassen National Forest

This hideaway is set near Crater Lake at 6,800 feet elevation in remote Lassen National Forest, just below Crater Mountain (that's it up there to the northeast at 7,420 feet). This 27-acre lake provides trout fishing, boating, and, if you can stand the ice-cold water, a quick dunk on warm summer days.

Campsites, facilities: There are 17 sites for tents. Picnic tables and fire grills are provided. Drinking water and vault toilets are available. No gas motors are allowed on the lake. Leashed pets are permitted.

Reservations, fees: Reservations are not accepted. Sites are $13 per night. Open June through October, weather permitting.

Directions: From Redding, drive east on Highway 44 to the junction with Highway 89 (near the entrance to Lassen Volcanic National Park). Turn north on Highway 89 and drive to Highway 44. Turn east on Highway 44

(right) and drive to the Bogard Work Center and adjacent rest stop. Turn left at Forest Road 32N08 (signed Crater Lake) and drive one mile to a T intersection. Bear right and continue on Forest Road 32N08 for six miles (including two hairpin left turns) to the campground on the left side of the road. Note: Forest Road 32N08 is a rough washboard road.

Contact: Lassen National Forest, Eagle Lake Ranger District, 530/257-4188, fax 530/252-5803.

49 MacCUMBER RESERVOIR
⛰ ⛵ 🛶 🏊 🐾 🚐 ⛺

Scenic rating: 7

on MacCumber Reservoir

Here's a small lake, easy to reach from Redding, that is little known and rarely visited. MacCumber Reservoir is set at 3,500 feet and is stocked with rainbow trout each year, providing fair fishing. No gas motors are permitted here. That's fine—it guarantees quiet, calm water, ideal for car-top boats: prams, canoes, rafts, and small aluminum boats.

Campsites, facilities: There are seven sites for tents or RVs up to 30 feet (no hookups) and five walk-in tent sites. Picnic tables and fire grills are provided. Drinking water and vault toilets are available. Leashed pets are permitted.

Reservations, fees: Reservations are not accepted. Sites are $13 per night, $3 per night for each additional vehicle, $7 per night per additional RV, $1 per pet per night. Open mid-April through mid-September, weather permitting.

Directions: In Redding, turn east on Highway 44 and drive toward Viola to Lake MacCumber Road (if you reach Viola, you have gone four miles too far). Turn left at Lake MacCumber Road and drive two miles to the reservoir and campground.

Contact: PG&E Land Projects, 916/386-5164, fax 916/923-7044, www.pge.com/recreation.

50 MANZANITA LAKE

Scenic rating: 9

in Lassen Volcanic National Park

Manzanita Lake, set at 5,890 feet, is one of the prettiest lakes in Lassen Volcanic National Park, and evening walks around the lake are beautiful. The campground, set among towering Ponderosa pines, is often crowded due to this great natural beauty.

Manzanita Lake provides good catch-and-release trout fishing for experienced fly fishers in prams and other nonpowered boats. Fishing regulations prohibit bait and lures with barbs. This is no place for a dad, mom, and a youngster to fish from shore with Power Bait; you'll end up with a citation. Swimming is permitted, but there are few takers.

Note: Small park model cabins are scheduled to be installed in 2009 and will likely be an instant hit.

Campsites, facilities: There are 179 sites for tents or RVs up to 35 feet (no hookups). Picnic tables, fire grills, and bear-proof food lockers are provided. Drinking water and flush toilets are available. A museum, visitors center, and small store, as well as propane gas, groceries, coin showers, dump station, and coin laundry are nearby. Ranger programs are offered in the summer. A boat launch is also nearby (no motors are permitted on boats at Manzanita Lake). Some facilities are wheelchair-accessible. Leashed pets are permitted at campsites only.

Reservations, fees: Reservations are accepted at 877/444-6777 or www.ReserveUSA.com ($10 reservation fee). Sites are $18 per night, $10 per vehicle park entrance fee. Some credit cards accepted. Open late May through late September, weather permitting (during the fall, it's open without drinking water until the camp is closed by snow).

Directions: From Redding, drive east on Highway 44 to the junction with Highway 89. Turn right (south) on Highway 89 and drive one mile to the entrance station to Lassen Volcanic National Park (the state highway becomes Lassen Park Highway/Main Park Road). Continue a short distance on Lassen Park Highway/Main Park Road to the campground entrance road. Turn right and drive 0.5 mile to the campground.

Contact: Lassen Volcanic National Park, 530/595-4444, fax 530/595-3262, www.nps.gov/lavo.

51 CRAGS

Scenic rating: 8

in Lassen Volcanic National Park

Crags is sometimes overlooked as a prime spot at Lassen Volcanic National Park because there is no lake nearby. No problem, because even though this campground is small compared to the giant complex at Manzanita Lake, the campsites are more spacious, do not fill up as quickly, and many are backed by forest. In addition, Emigrant Trail runs out of camp, routing east and meeting pretty Lost Creek after a little more than a mile, a great short hike. Directly across from Crags are the towering Chaos Crags, topping out at 8,503 feet. The elevation here is 5,720 feet.

Campsites, facilities: There are 45 sites for tents or RVs up to 35 feet (no hookups). Picnic tables, fire rings, and bearproof food lockers are provided. Drinking water and vault toilets are available. Wheelchair access is limited. Leashed pets are permitted in the campground and on paved roads only.

Reservations, fees: Reservations are not accepted. Sites are $12 per night, $10 per vehicle park entrance fee. Open late June through early September.

Directions: From Redding, drive east on Highway 44 for 42 miles to the junction with Highway 89. Turn right and drive one mile to the entrance station at Lassen Volcanic National Park (the state highway becomes Lassen Park

Highway/Main Park Road). Continue on Lassen Park Highway/Main Park Road for about five miles to the campground on the left side of the road.

Contact: Lassen Volcanic National Park, 530/595-4444, fax 530/595-3262, www.nps.gov/lavo.

52 BUTTE LAKE

Scenic rating: 9

in Lassen Volcanic National Park

Butte Lake campground is situated in an open, volcanic setting with a sprinkling of lodgepole pine. The contrast of the volcanics against the emerald greens of the lake is beautiful and memorable. Cinder Cone Trail can provide an even better look. The trailhead is near the boat launch area, and it's a strenuous hike involving a climb of 800 feet over the course of two miles to the top of the Cinder Cone. The footing is often loose because of volcanic pebbles. At the rim, you can peer inside the Cinder Cone, as well as be rewarded with lake views and a long-distance vista. Trout fishing is poor at Butte Lake, as at nearly all the lakes at this national park, because trout have not been planted for years. The elevation is 6,100 feet, and the lake covers 212 acres.

Campsites, facilities: There are 101 sites for tents or RVs up to 35 feet (no hookups), one equestrian site, and six group tent sites that can accommodate 10–25 people each. Some sites are pull-through. Picnic tables, fire rings, and bearproof food lockers are provided. Drinking water and flush and vault toilets are available. A boat ramp is nearby. No motors are permitted on the lake. Some facilities are wheelchair-accessible. Leashed pets are permitted at campsites only.

Reservations, fees: Reservations are accepted for individual sites and are required for group sites at 877/444-6777 or www.recreation.gov ($10 reservation fee). Reservations are also

required for equestrian sites at 530/335-7029. Tent and RV sites are $14 per night; equestrian sites are $14 per night plus $4 per horse per night; group sites are $50 per night, plus $10 park entrance fee per vehicle. Open mid-June through mid-September, weather permitting.

Directions: From Redding, drive east on Highway 44 to the junction with Highway 89. Bear north on Highway 89/44 and drive 13 miles to Old Station. Just past Old Station, turn right (east) on Highway 44 and drive 10 miles to Forest Road 32N21/Butte Lake Road. Turn right and drive six miles to the campground.

Contact: Lassen Volcanic National Park, 530/595-4444, fax 530/595-3262, www.nps.gov/lavo.

53 MOUNT LASSEN/ SHINGLETOWN KOA

Scenic rating: 6

near Lassen Volcanic National Park

This popular KOA camp is 14 miles from the entrance of Lassen Volcanic National Park and has pretty, wooded sites. Location is always the critical factor on vacations, and this park is set up perfectly for launching trips into Lassen Volcanic National Park. Hat Creek provides trout fishing along Highway 89, and just inside the Highway 44 entrance station at Lassen is Manzanita Lake, providing good fishing and hiking.

Campsites, facilities: There are 46 sites with full or partial hookups (30 and 50 amps) for tents or RVs up to 40 feet, including some pull-through sites, and five cabins. Picnic tables and fire grills are provided. Restroom with flush toilets and showers, playground, heated pool (summer only), dump station, convenience store, ice, firewood, coin laundry, video arcade and recreation room, dog run, and propane gas are available. Leashed pets are permitted.

Reservations, fees: Reservations are accepted

with a deposit at 800/562-3403. Sites are $28–45 per night, $3–5 per person per night for more than two people. Some credit cards accepted. Open mid-March through November.

Directions: From Redding, turn east on Highway 44 and drive to Shingletown. In Shingletown, continue east for four miles and look for the park entrance on the right (signed KOA).

Contact: Mount Lassen/Shingletown KOA, 530/474-3133, www.koa.com.

54 SUMMIT LAKE: NORTH, SOUTH, AND EQUESTRIAN

🚶 🏊 🛶 ⛵ 🐴 ♿ 🚐 ⛺

Scenic rating: 9

in Lassen Volcanic National Park

BEST (

Summit Lake is a beautiful spot where deer often visit in the evening on the adjacent meadow just east of the campground. The lake is small, just 15 acres, and since trout plants were suspended it has been just about fished out. Summit Lake is the most popular lake for swimming in the park. Evening walks around the lake are perfect for families. A more ambitious trail is routed out of camp and leads past lavish wildflower displays in early summer to a series of wilderness lakes. The campgrounds are set at an elevation of 6,695 feet.

Campsites, facilities: There are 46 sites for tents or RVs up to 35 feet at North Summit, 48 sites for tents or RVs up to 30 feet at South Summit, and one equestrian site for tents or RVs up to 35 feet that can accommodate up to 10 people and eight horses. No hookups. Picnic tables, fire rings, and bearproof food lockers are provided. Drinking water and toilets (flush toilets on the north side, pit toilets on the south side, and vault toilets at the equestrian site) are available. Some facilities are wheelchair-accessible. Ranger programs are sometimes offered in summer. Leashed pets are permitted at campsites only.

Reservations, fees: Reservations are accepted for individual sites at 877/444-6777 or www.recreation.gov ($10 reservation fee). Reservations are required for equestrian sites at 530/335-7029. Sites are $16 (South) to $18 (North) per night, $14 per night plus $4 per horse per night at the equestrian site, plus $10 park entrance fee per vehicle. Some credit cards accepted. Open late June through mid-September, weather permitting.

Directions: From Redding, drive east on Highway 44 to the junction with Highway 89. Turn south on Highway 89 and drive one mile to the entrance station to Lassen Volcanic National Park (where the state highway becomes Lassen Park Highway/Main Park Road). Continue on Lassen Park Highway/Main Park Road for 12 miles to the campground entrance on the left side of the road. The horse camp is located across the street from the other campsites.

Contact: Lassen Volcanic National Park, 530/595-4444, fax 530/595-3262, www.nps.gov/lavo.

55 SILVER BOWL

🚶 🛶 ⛵ 🐴 🚐 ⛺

Scenic rating: 7

on Silver Lake in Lassen National Forest

Silver Lake is a pretty lake set at 6,400 feet elevation at the edge of the Caribou Wilderness. There is an unimproved boat ramp at the southern end of the lake. It is occasionally planted by the Department of Fish and Game with Eagle Lake trout and brown trout, which provide a summer fishery for campers. A trailhead from adjacent Caribou Lake is routed west into the wilderness, with routes available both to Emerald Lake to the northwest, and Betty, Trail, and Shotoverin Lakes nearby to the southeast.

Campsites, facilities: There are 18 sites for tents or RVs up to 25 feet (no hookups). Picnic tables and fire grills are provided. Drinking water and vault toilets are available. Leashed pets are permitted.

Reservations, fees: Reservations are not accepted. Sites are $12 per night, $3 per night for each additional vehicle. Open late May through October, weather permitting.

Directions: From Red Bluff, drive east on Highway 36 to the junction with Highway 89. Continue east on Highway 36 past Lake Almanor to Westwood. In Westwood, turn left on County Road A21 and drive 12.5 miles to Silver Lake Road. Turn left on Silver Lake Road/County Road 110 and drive 8.5 miles north to Silver Lake. At Silver Lake, turn right and drive 0.75 mile to the campground.

Contact: Lassen National Forest, Almanor Ranger District, 530/258-2141, fax 530/258-5194.

56 ROCKY KNOLL

Scenic rating: 7

on Silver Lake in Lassen National Forest

This is one of two camps at pretty Silver Lake, set at 6,400 feet elevation at the edge of the Caribou Wilderness. The other camp is Silver Bowl to the nearby north, which is larger and provides better access for hikers. This camp, however, is closer to the boat ramp, which is set at the south end of the lake. Silver Lake provides a good summer fishery for campers.

Campsites, facilities: There are 18 sites for tents or RVs up to 27 feet (no hookups). Picnic tables and fire grills are provided. Drinking water and vault toilets are available. Leashed pets are permitted.

Reservations, fees: Reservations are not accepted. Sites are $12 per night, $3 per night for each additional vehicle. Open late May through early November, weather permitting.

Directions: From Red Bluff, drive east on Highway 36 to the junction with Highway 89. Continue east on Highway 36 past Lake Almanor to Westwood. In Westwood, turn

left on County Road A21 and drive 12.5 miles to Silver Lake Road. Turn left (west) on Silver Lake Road/County Road 110 and drive 8.5 miles to Silver Lake. At Silver Lake, turn left and drive 300 yards to the campground.

Contact: Lassen National Forest, Almanor Ranger District, 530/258-2141, fax 530/258-5194.

57 SOUTHWEST WALK-IN

Scenic rating: 8

in Lassen Volcanic National Park

This pretty campground at 6,700 feet elevation re-opened in late fall 2008 after the new visitors center near the southwest entrance station was built. Well, both are stellar. So is the hiking. Just taking the short walk required to reach the camp will launch you into an orbit beyond most of the highway cruisers visiting Lassen. The 4.6-mile hike to Mill Creek Falls, the park's highest waterfall, begins at the campground. The Sulphur Works and Brokeoff Mountain trailheads are nearby, as is the new visitors center.

One must-see is Bumpass Hell. The trail is about seven miles north of the campground on the right side of the Lassen Park Highway/Main Park Road. This easy hike takes you past steam vents and boiling mud pots, all set in prehistoric-looking volcanic rock. Ranger-led programs are sometimes offered.

Campsites, facilities: There are 21 walk-in tent sites, and a large parking lot available for RVs of any length (no hookups). Picnic tables, fire rings, and bearproof food lockers are provided. Drinking water and restrooms with flush toilets are available in summer. Leashed pets are permitted in campground only.

Reservations, fees: Reservations are not accepted. Sites are $14 per night for tent campers, $10 per night for RV parking, plus $10 per vehicle park entrance fee. Open year-round, weather permitting.

Directions: From Red Bluff, take Highway 36 east for 48 miles to the junction with Highway 89. Turn left on Highway 89 (becomes Lassen Park Highway/Main Park Road) and drive to the park's entrance. Just after passing through the park entrance gate, look for the camp parking area on the right side of the road.

Contact: Lassen Volcanic National Park, 530/595-4444, fax 530/595-3262, www.nps.gov/lavo.

58 WARNER VALLEY

Scenic rating: 9

on Hot Springs Creek in Lassen Volcanic National Park

Lassen is one of the great national parks of the West, yet it gets surprisingly little use compared to Yosemite, Sequoia, and Kings Canyon National Parks. This campground gets overlooked because of its remote access out of Chester. The camp is set along Hot Springs Creek at 5,650 feet. The best hike here is the 2.5-mile walk out to the unique Devil's Kitchen geothermal area. Other options are a 2.5-mile hike—with an 800-foot climb—to Drake Lake, and a three-mile hike to Boiling Springs Lakes. It's also a good horseback-riding area. The Drakesbad Resort, where securing reservations is about as difficult as finding Bigfoot, is near the campground.

Campsites, facilities: There are 18 tent sites. RVs and trailers are not recommended because of road conditions. Picnic tables, food lockers, and fire rings are provided. Drinking water and pit toilets are available. Wheelchair access is limited. Leashed pets are permitted in the campground only.

Reservations, fees: Reservations are not accepted. Sites are $14 per night, $10 per vehicle park entrance fee. Open June through late September, weather permitting, with no water from mid-September to snow closure.

Directions: From Red Bluff, take Highway 36

east for 44 miles to the junction with Highway 89 (do not turn left, or north, on Highway 89 to Lassen Volcanic National Park entrance, as signed). Continue east on Highway 36/89 to Chester and Feather River Drive. Turn left (north) on Feather River Drive (Warner Valley Road) and drive 0.75 mile to County Road 312. Bear left and drive six miles to Warner Valley Road. Turn right and drive 11 miles to the campground on the right. Note: The last 3.5 miles are unpaved, and there is one steep hill that can be difficult to climb for large or underpowered RVs, or if you are towing a trailer.

Contact: Lassen Volcanic National Park, 530/595-4444, fax 530/595-3262, www.nps.gov/lavo.

59 JUNIPER LAKE

Scenic rating: 10

in Lassen Volcanic National Park

This pretty spot is on the eastern shore of Juniper Lake, at an elevation of 6,792 feet. It is far distant from the busy Lassen Park Highway/Main Park Road (Highway 89) corridor that is routed through central Lassen Volcanic National Park. From the north end of the lake, a great side trip is to make the 0.5-mile, 400-foot climb to Inspiration Point, which provides a panoramic view of the park's backcountry. A two-mile hike up Mount Harkness begins from camp. Since no drinking water is provided, it is critical to bring a water purification pump or plenty of bottled water.

Campsites, facilities: There are 18 tent sites, an equestrian site, and two group tent sites that can accommodate 10–15 people each. No hookups. Picnic tables, fire rings, and bearproof food lockers are provided. Vault toilets are available. Drinking water is not available. Leashed pets are permitted in the campground only.

Reservations, fees: Reservations are not accepted for individual sites, but are required for the group site at 877/444-6777 or www. recreation.gov ($10 reservation fee). Reservations are also required for the equestrian site at 530/335-7029. Sites are $10 per night, $30 per night for group sites, $10 per night for the equestrian site plus $4 per horse per night, $10 park entrance fee per vehicle. Open late June through late September, weather permitting.
Directions: From Red Bluff, take Highway 36 east for 44 miles to the junction with Highway 89 (do not turn left, or north, on Highway 89 to Lassen Volcanic National Park entrance, as signed). Continue east on Highway 36/89 to Chester and Feather River Drive. Turn left (north) on Feather River Drive and drive 0.75 mile to the Y and the junction for County Road 318. Bear right (marked for Juniper Lake) on County Road 318 and drive 11 miles to the campground on the right, set along the east side of the lake. Note: This is a very rough dirt road; RVs and trailers are not recommended.
Contact: Lassen Volcanic National Park, 530/595-4444, fax 530/595-3262, www. nps.gov/lavo.

60 BATTLE CREEK
🏃 🏊 🐕 🚐 ⛺

Scenic rating: 7

on Battle Creek in Lassen National Forest

This pretty spot offers easy access and streamside camping along Battle Creek. The trout fishing can be good in May, June, and early July, when the creek is stocked with trout by the Department of Fish and Game. Many people drive right by without knowing there is a stream here and that the fishing can be good. The elevation is 4,800 feet.
Campsites, facilities: There are 50 sites for tents or RVs up to 30 feet (no hookups). Picnic tables and fire grills are provided. Drinking water, flush and vault toilets, and a day-use

picnic area are available. Supplies can be obtained in the town of Mineral. Leashed pets are permitted.
Reservations, fees: Reservations are not accepted. Sites are $18 per night, $3 per night for each additional vehicle. Open late April through early November, weather permitting.
Directions: From Red Bluff, turn east on Highway 36 and drive 39 miles to the campground (if you reach Mineral, you have gone two miles too far).
Contact: Lassen National Forest, Almanor Ranger District, 530/258-2141, fax 530/258-5194; Department of Fish and Game fishing information, 530/225-2146.

61 CHILDS MEADOW RESORT
🏃 🏊 🐕 🚐 ⛺

Scenic rating: 7

near Mill Creek

Childs Meadow Resort is an 18-acre resort set at 5,000 feet elevation. It features many recreation options, including catch-and-release fishing one mile away at Mill Creek. There are also a number of trails nearby for horseback riding. The trailhead for Spencer Meadow Trail is just east of the resort along Highway 36. The trail provides a 12-mile route (oneway) to Spencer Meadow and an effervescent spring that is the source of Mill Creek.
Campsites, facilities: There are eight tent sites and 24 sites with full hookups (50 amps) for RVs of any length; most are pull-through. Cabins, park-model cabins, and a motel are also available. Picnic tables and fire rings are provided. Drinking water and restrooms with flush toilets and showers are available. A coin laundry, store, restaurant, group picnic area, meeting room, and horseshoes are on-site. Groups can be accommodated. Leashed pets are permitted.
Reservations, fees: Reservations are accepted at 888/595-3383. Sites are $18–25 per night,

$10 per pet per night. Some credit cards accepted. Open mid-May through October, weather permitting.

Directions: From Red Bluff, drive east on Highway 36 for 43 miles to the town of Mineral. Continue east on Highway 36 for 10 miles to the resort on the left.

Contact: Childs Meadow Resort, 530/595-3383, www.childsmeadowresort.com.

62 DOMINGO SPRINGS

Scenic rating: 7

in Lassen National Forest

This camp is named after a spring adjacent to the site. It is a small fountain that pours into the headwaters of the North Fork Feather River, a good trout stream. The Pacific Crest Trail is routed from this camp north for four miles to Little Willow Lake and the southern border of Lassen Volcanic National Park. The elevation is 5,060 feet.

Campsites, facilities: There are 18 sites for tents or RVs up to 27 feet (no hookups). Picnic tables and fire grills are provided. Drinking water and vault toilets are available. Leashed pets are permitted.

Reservations, fees: Reservations are not accepted. Sites are $14 per night, $3 per night for each additional vehicle. Open late May through early November, weather permitting.

Directions: From Red Bluff, take Highway 36 east to Chester and Feather River Drive. Turn left on Feather River Drive and drive 0.75 mile to County Road 312. Bear left and drive five miles to the Y with County Road 311 and County Road 312. Bear left on County Road 311 and drive two miles to the campground entrance road on the left.

Contact: Lassen National Forest, Almanor Ranger District, 530/258-2141, fax 530/258-5194.

63 HIGH BRIDGE

Scenic rating: 8

on the North Fork of the Feather River in Lassen National Forest

This camp is set at an elevation of 5,200 feet, near where the South Cascades meet the North Sierra, and is ideal for many people. The result is that it is often full in July and August. The payoff includes a pretty, adjacent trout stream, the headwaters of the North Fork Feather. Trout fishing is often good here, including some rare large brown trout, a surprise considering the relatively small size of the stream. Nearby access to the Warner Valley/Drakesbad entrance of Lassen Volcanic National Park provides a must-do side trip. The area is wooded and the road dusty.

Campsites, facilities: There are 12 sites for tents or RVs up to 27 feet (no hookups). Picnic tables and fire grills are provided. Drinking water and vault toilets are available. Groceries and propane gas are available in Chester. Leashed pets are permitted.

Reservations, fees: Reservations are not accepted. Sites are $14 per night, $3 per night for each additional vehicle. Open late May through early November, weather permitting.

Directions: From Red Bluff, take Highway 36 east to Chester and Feather River Drive. Turn left on Feather River Drive and drive 0.75 mile to County Road 312. Bear left and drive five miles to the campground entrance road on the left.

Contact: Lassen National Forest, Almanor Ranger District, 530/258-2141, fax 530/258-5194; Department of Fish and Game fishing information, 530/225-2146.

LASSEN CAMPING

64 LAST CHANCE CREEK
🏃🛶🐕🚙⛺

Scenic rating: 7

near Lake Almanor

This secluded camp is set at 4,500 feet, adjacent to where Last Chance Creek empties into the north end of Lake Almanor. It is an unpublicized PG&E camp that is known primarily by locals and gets missed almost every time by out-of-towners. The adjacent lake area is a breeding ground in the spring for white pelicans, and the beauty of these birds in large flocks can be extraordinary.

Campsites, facilities: There are 12 sites for tents or RVs up to 30 feet (no hookups), and three group camps that can accommodate up to 100 people (total). Picnic tables and fire grills are provided. Drinking water and vault toilets are available. Leashed pets are permitted.

Reservations, fees: Reservations are not accepted for individual sites but are required for the group camps at 916/386-5164. Sites are $16 per night for individual sites, $3 per night for each additional vehicle, $7 per night for each additional RV, $60–120 per night for group sites, $1 per pet per night. Group sites require a two-night minimum stay and a three-night minimum on holidays. Open mid-May through September, weather permitting.

Directions: From Red Bluff, take Highway 36 east to Chester and continue for two miles over the causeway (at the north end of Lake Almanor). About 0.25 mile after crossing the causeway, turn left on the campground access road and drive 3.5 miles to the campground.

Contact: PG&E Land Projects, 916/386-5164, www.pge.com/recreation.

65 HOLE-IN-THE-GROUND
🏃🛶🐕🚙⛺

Scenic rating: 8

on Mill Creek in Lassen National Forest

This is one of two campgrounds set along Mill Creek at 4,300 feet. Take your pick. The highlight here is a trail that follows along Mill Creek for many miles; it provides good fishing access. Rules mandate the use of artificials with a single barbless hook, and catch-and-release; check current fishing regulations. The result is a challenging but quality wild-trout fishery. Another option is to drive 0.5 mile to the end of the Forest Service road, where there is a parking area for a trail that is routed downstream along Mill Creek and into a state game refuge. To keep things easy, obtain a map of Lassen National Forest that details the recreational opportunities.

Campsites, facilities: There are 13 sites for tents or RVs up to 24 feet (no hookups). Picnic tables and fire grills are provided. Drinking water and vault toilets are available. Supplies are available in Mineral. Leashed pets are permitted.

Reservations, fees: Reservations are not accepted. Sites are $12 per night, $3 per night for each additional vehicle. Open late April through early November, weather permitting.

Directions: From Red Bluff, drive 43 miles east on Highway 36 to the town of Mineral and the junction with Highway 172. Turn right on Highway 172 and drive six miles to the town of Mill Creek. In Mill Creek, turn south onto Forest Road 28N06 (signed) and drive five miles to the campground access road. Turn left and drive 0.25 mile to the camp.

Contact: Lassen National Forest, Almanor Ranger District, 530/258-2141, fax 530/258-5194.

66 MILL CREEK RESORT
🏕🛶🐕♿️🚐⛺️

Scenic rating: 7

on Mill Creek near Lassen National Forest

This is a great area, surrounded by Lassen National Forest and within close range of the southern Highway 89 entrance to Lassen Volcanic National Park. It is set at 4,800 feet along oft-bypassed Highway 172. A highlight here is Mill Creek (to reach it, turn south on the Forest Service road in town and drive to a parking area at the end of the road along the stream), where there is a great easy walk along the stream and fair trout fishing. Note that about half the campsites are taken by long-term renters.

Campsites, facilities: There are 14 sites for tents or RVs up to 35 feet, eight with full hookups (30 amps). Nine one- and two-bedroom cabins are also available. Picnic tables and fire rings are provided. Drinking water, vault toilets, seasonal showers, coin laundry, playground, a small grocery store, and a restaurant are also available. Some facilities are wheelchair-accessible. Leashed pets are permitted.

Reservations, fees: Reservations are accepted. Sites are $16–25 per night. Campsites are open May through October. Cabins are available year-round.

Directions: From Red Bluff, drive 43 miles east on Highway 36 to the town of Mineral and the junction with Highway 172. Turn right and drive six miles to the town of Mill Creek. In Mill Creek, look for the sign for Mill Creek Resort on the right side of the road.

Contact: Mill Creek Resort, 530/595-4449 or 888/595-4449, www.millcreekresort.net.

67 GURNSEY CREEK AND GROUP CAMPS
🏕🛶🐕🚐⛺️

Scenic rating: 7

in Lassen National Forest

This camp is set at 5,000 feet elevation in Lassen National Forest, with extremely easy access off Highway 36. The camp is on the headwaters of little Gurnsey Creek, a highlight of the surrounding Lost Creek Plateau. Gurnsey Creek runs downstream and pours into Deer Creek, a good trout stream with access along narrow, winding Highway 32 to the nearby south. The group camps are ideal spots for a Scout troop.

Campsites, facilities: There are 30 sites for tents or RVs up to 30 feet (no hookups). There are two group camps that can accommodate up to 20 people with tents or RVs up to 30 feet (no hookups). Picnic tables and fire grills are provided. Drinking water and vault toilets are available. Supplies are available in Mineral. Leashed pets are permitted.

Reservations, fees: Reservations are not accepted for individual sites, but are required for the group site at 877/444-6777 or www.recreation.gov ($10 reservation fee). Tent and RV sites are $14 per night, $3 per night for each additional vehicle. Trout Group Camp is $56 per night and Rainbow Group Camp is $112 per night, with a two-night minimum stay required on weekends. Open May through October, weather permitting.

Directions: From Red Bluff, drive east on Highway 36 for 55 miles (five miles east of Childs Meadow). Turn left at the campground entrance road and drive a short distance to the campground.

Contact: Lassen National Forest, Almanor Ranger District, 530/258-2141, fax 530/258-5194.

LASSEN CAMPING

68 NORTH SHORE CAMPGROUND

Scenic rating: 7

on Lake Almanor

This is a large, privately developed park on the northern shoreline of beautiful Lake Almanor. The park has 37 acres and a mile of shoreline. The camp is set amid pine tree cover, and most of the sites are lakefront or lakeview. About half of the sites are filled with seasonal renters. The lending library here was once the original Chester jail, built in 1925. Alas, the jail itself busted out during a storm a few years ago and was found washed ashore at this campground, which converted it to its new use.

Campsites, facilities: There are 34 tent sites and 94 sites with partial hookups (30 amps) for RVs up to 40 feet; a few are pull-through. Two log cabins are also available. Picnic tables and fire rings are provided. Drinking water, restrooms with showers and flush toilets, coin laundry, general store, playground, lending library, modem access, Wi-Fi, propane, dump station, fish-cleaning station, horseshoes, boat ramp, boat dock, boat slips, and boat rentals are available. Leashed pets are permitted.

Reservations, fees: Reservations are accepted. RV sites are $36–48 per night, tent sites are $33 per night, $5 per person per night for more than two people (children under age 12 are free), $2 per pet per night. Monthly and seasonal rates available. Some credit cards accepted. Open April through October.

Directions: From Red Bluff, take Highway 36 east for 44 miles to the junction with Highway 89. Drive east on Highway 36/89; the camp is two miles past Chester on the right.

Contact: North Shore Campground, 530/258-3376, www.northshorecampground.com.

69 SOUTH ANTELOPE

Scenic rating: 6

near the eastern edge of the Ishi Wilderness

This primitive campsite is for visitors who want to explore the Ishi Wilderness without an extensive drive (compared to other camps in the wilderness here). The South Fork of Antelope Creek runs west from the camp and provides an off-trail route for the ambitious. For easier hikes, trailheads along Ponderosa Way provide access into the eastern flank of the Ishi. The best nearby trail is Lower Mill Creek Trail, with the trailhead eight miles south at Black Rock.

Campsites, facilities: There are four sites for tents only. Picnic tables and fire pits are provided. A vault toilet is available. No drinking water is available. Garbage must be packed out. Leashed pets are permitted.

Reservations, fees: Reservations are not accepted. There is no fee for camping. Open year-round.

Directions: From Red Bluff, drive east on Highway 36 for about 35 miles to the town of Paynes Creek and Plum Creek Road. Turn right (south) on Plum Creek Road and drive two miles to Ponderosa Way. Turn right (south) and continue for nine miles to the campground on the right. Note: The road is rough and only vehicles with high clearance are advised. No RVs or trailers are allowed.

Contact: Lassen National Forest, Almanor Ranger District, 530/258-2141, fax 530/258-5194.

70 BLACK ROCK

Scenic rating: 7

on the eastern edge of the Ishi Wilderness

This remote, primitive camp is set at the base of the huge, ancient Black Rock, one of the oldest geological points in Lassen National Forest. A bonus is that Mill Creek runs adjacent to the sites, providing a water source. This is the edge of the Ishi Wilderness, where remote hiking in solitude is possible without venturing to high mountain elevations; a campfire permit is required for overnight use by backpackers. A trailhead is available right out of the camp. The trail here is routed downstream along Mill Creek, extending five miles into the Ishi Wilderness, downhill all the way. Be prepared when hiking in this area because the heat can be almost intolerable at times, often passing the 100°F mark for days on end.

Campsites, facilities: There are six tent sites. Picnic tables and fire pits are provided. A vault toilet is available. No drinking water is available. Mill Creek is adjacent to the camp and is a viable water source; remember to filter stream water. Garbage must be packed out. Leashed pets are permitted.

Reservations, fees: Reservations are not accepted. There is no fee for camping. Open year-round, weather permitting.

Directions: From Red Bluff, drive east on Highway 36 for about 35 miles to the town of Paynes Creek and Plum Creek Road. Turn right (south) on Plum Creek Road and drive two miles to Ponderosa Way. Turn right (south) and continue for 16 miles to the campground on the right. Note: The road is rough and only vehicles with high clearance are advised. No RVs or trailers are allowed.

Contact: Lassen National Forest, Almanor Ranger District, 530/258-2141, fax 530/258-5194.

71 ELAM

Scenic rating: 7

on Deer Creek in Lassen National Forest

Of the campgrounds set on Deer Creek along Highway 32, Elam gets the most use. It is the first stopping point visitors arrive at while heading west on narrow, curvy Highway 32, and it has an excellent day-use picnic area available. The stream here is stocked with rainbow trout in late spring and early summer, with good access for fishing. It is a pretty area, set where Elam Creek enters Deer Creek. A Forest Service Information Center is nearby in Chester. If the camp has too many people to suit your style, consider other more distant and primitive camps downstream on Deer Creek. The elevation here is 4,600 feet.

Campsites, facilities: There are 11 sites for tents or RVs up to 30 feet (no hookups). Picnic tables and fire grills are provided. Drinking water and vault toilets are available. Leashed pets are permitted.

Reservations, fees: Reservations are not accepted. Sites are $14 per night, $3 per night for each additional vehicle. Open mid-April through October, weather permitting.

Directions: From Red Bluff, take Highway 36 east for 44 miles to the junction with Highway 89. Continue east on Highway 36/89 to the junction with Highway 32. Turn south on Highway 32 and drive three miles to the campground on the right side of the road. Trailers are not recommended.

Contact: Lassen National Forest, Almanor Ranger District, 530/258-2141, fax 530/258-5194.

72 ALDER CREEK

Scenic rating: 7

on Deer Creek in Lassen National Forest

Deer Creek is a great little trout stream that runs along Highway 32. Alder Creek is one of three camps set along Highway 32 with streamside access; this one is at 3,900 feet elevation, set near where both Alder Creek and Round Valley Creek pour into Deer Creek. The stream's best stretch of trout water is from here to Elam, upstream.

Campsites, facilities: There are five tent sites.

Trailers and RVs are not recommended. Picnic tables and fire grills are provided. Vault toilets are available. No drinking water is available. Leashed pets are permitted.

Reservations, fees: Reservations are not accepted. Sites are $10 per night, $3 for each additional vehicle. Open late March through early November, weather permitting.

Directions: From Red Bluff, take Highway 36 east for 44 miles to the junction with Highway 89. Continue east on Highway 36/89 to the junction with Highway 32. Turn south on Highway 32 and drive eight miles to the campground on the right side of the road.

Contact: Lassen National Forest, Almanor Ranger District, 530/258-2141, fax 530/258-5194.

73 POTATO PATCH

Scenic rating: 7

on Deer Creek in Lassen National Forest

You get good hiking and fishing at this camp. It is set beside Deer Creek at 3,400 feet elevation, with good access for trout fishing. This is a wild trout stream in this area, and the use of artificials with a single barbless hook and catch-and-release are required along most of the river; check DFG regulations. An excellent anglers'/swimmers' trail is available along the river.

Campsites, facilities: There are 32 sites for tents or RVs up to 27 feet (no hookups). Picnic tables and fire grills are provided. Drinking water and vault toilets are available. Leashed pets are permitted.

Reservations, fees: Reservations are not accepted. Sites are $14 per night, $3 per night for each additional vehicle. Open early April through early November, weather permitting.

Directions: From Red Bluff, take Highway 36 east for 44 miles to the junction with Highway 89. Continue east on Highway 36/89 to the

junction with Highway 32. Turn south on Highway 32 and drive 11 miles to the campground on the right side of the road.

Contact: Lassen National Forest, Almanor Ranger District, 530/258-2141, fax 530/258-5194; Department of Fish and Game, 530/225-2146.

74 ROCKY POINT CAMPGROUND

Scenic rating: 7

on Lake Almanor

What you get here is a series of four campgrounds along the southwest shore of Lake Almanor, provided by PG&E as mitigation for its hydroelectric activities on the Feather River system. The camps are set upstream from the dam, with boat ramps available on each side of the dam. This is a pretty spot, with giant Almanor ringed by lodgepole pine and firs. The lake is usually full, or close to it, well into summer, with Mount Lassen set in the distance to the north—bring your camera. The lake is 13 miles long and all water sports are permitted. The lake level remains full most of the year and much of the shoreline is wooded. Though it can take a day or two to find the fish, once that effort is made, fishing is good for large trout and salmon in the spring and fall and for smallmouth bass in the summer.

Campsites, facilities: There are 131 sites for tents or RVs up to 30 feet (no hookups). Picnic tables and fire grills are provided. Drinking water, vault toilets, and a dump station are available. Some facilities are wheelchair-accessible. Leashed pets are permitted.

Reservations, fees: Reservations are not accepted. Sites are $18 per night, $3 per night for each additional vehicle, $7 per night per additional RV, $1 per pet per night. Open May through September.

Directions: From Red Bluff, take Highway 36 east for 44 miles to the junction with Highway

89. Continue east on Highway 36/89 to Lake Almanor and the next junction with Highway 89 (two miles before reaching Chester). Turn right on Highway 89 and drive eight miles to the southwest end of Lake Almanor. Turn left at your choice of four campground entrances.

Contact: PG&E Land Projects, 916/386-5164, www.pge.com/recreation.

75 ALMANOR NORTH AND SOUTH

🖼️🚵🏊🛶🚤🐕♿🚐⛺

Scenic rating: 8

on Lake Almanor in Lassen National Forest

This is one of Lake Almanor's best-known and most popular Forest Service campgrounds. It is set along the western shore of beautiful Almanor at 4,550 feet elevation, directly across from the beautiful Almanor Peninsula. There is an excellent view of Mount Lassen to the north, along with gorgeous sunrises. A 10-mile recreation trail runs right through the campground and is excellent for biking or hiking. This section of the lake provides good fishing for smallmouth bass in the summer. Fishing in this lake is also good for rainbow trout, brown trout, and lake-raised salmon. There are two linked campgrounds, named North and South.

Campsites, facilities: There are 104 sites for tents or RVs up to 40 feet (no hookups), and a group camp for tents or RVs up to 40 feet that can accommodate up to 100 people. Picnic tables and fire grills are provided. Drinking water and vault toilets are available. A boat ramp and beach area are nearby. Some facilities are wheelchair-accessible. Leashed pets are permitted.

Reservations, fees: Reservations are accepted for individual sites and required for the group camp at 877/444-6777 or www.recreation.gov ($10 reservation fee). Sites are $18 per night, $5 per night for each additional vehicle, and $100 per night for the group camp. Open May through October, weather permitting.

Directions: From Red Bluff, take Highway 36 east for 44 miles to the junction with Highway 89. Continue east on Highway 36/89 to Lake Almanor and the next junction with Highway 89 (two miles before reaching Chester). Turn right on Highway 89 and drive six miles to County Road 310. Turn left on County Road 310 and drive 0.25 mile to the campground.

Contact: Lassen National Forest, Almanor Ranger District, 530/258-2141, fax 530/258-5194.

76 SOLDIER MEADOWS

🛶🐕🚐⛺

Scenic rating: 7

on Soldier Creek in Lassen National Forest

This camp is little known and primitive and is used primarily by anglers and hunters in season. The campsites here are shaded, set in forest on the edge of meadows, and near a stream. The latter is Soldier Creek, which is stocked with trout by the Department of Fish and Game; check fishing regulations. In the fall, early storms can drive deer through this area on their annual migration to their wintering habitat in the valley, making this a decent base camp for hunters. However, no early storms often mean no deer. The elevation is 4,890 feet.

Campsites, facilities: There are 15 sites for tents or RVs up to 25 feet (no hookups). Picnic tables and fire rings are provided. Vault toilets are available. No drinking water is available. Leashed pets are permitted.

Reservations, fees: Reservations are not accepted. Sites are $10 per night, $5 per night for each additional vehicle. Open late May through early November, weather permitting.

Directions: From Chester, drive south on Highway 89 for approximately six miles to Humboldt Road. Turn right on Humboldt Road and drive one mile, bear right at the fork, and continue five more miles to the intersection at Fanani Meadows. Turn right and drive one mile to the campground on the left.

Contact: Lassen National Forest, Almanor Ranger District, 530/258-2141, fax 530/258-5194.

77 PONDEROSA FLAT

Scenic rating: 7

on Butt Valley Reservoir

This camp is set at the north end of Butt Valley Reservoir (more commonly called Butt Lake), the little brother to nearby Lake Almanor. It is a fairly popular camp, with the boat ramp a prime attraction, allowing campers/anglers a lakeside spot with easy access. Technically, Butt is the "afterbay" for Almanor, fed by a four-mile-long pipe with water from Almanor. What occurs is that pond smelt from Almanor get ground up in the Butt Lake powerhouse, providing a large amount of feed for trout at the head of the lake; that's why the trout often get huge at Butt Lake. The one downer here is that lake drawdowns are common, exposing tree stumps.

Campsites, facilities: There are 63 sites for tents or RVs up to 30 feet (no hookups), and an overflow camping area. Picnic tables and fire grills are provided. Drinking water, vault toilets, and a boat ramp are available. Some facilities are wheelchair-accessible. Leashed pets are permitted.

Reservations, fees: Reservations are not accepted. Sites are $18 per night, $3 per night for each additional vehicle, $1 per pet per night. Open May through October, weather permitting.

Directions: From Red Bluff, take Highway 36 east for 44 miles to the junction with Highway 89. Continue east on Highway 36/89 to Lake Almanor and the next junction with Highway 89 (two miles before reaching Chester). Turn right on Highway 89 and drive about seven miles to Butt Valley Road. Turn right on Butt Valley Road and drive 3.2 miles to the campground on the right side of the road.

Contact: PG&E Land Projects, 916/386-5164, www.pge.com/recreation.

78 COOL SPRINGS

Scenic rating: 7

on Butt Valley Reservoir

One of two camps at Butt Lake (officially known as Butt Valley Reservoir), Cool Springs is set about midway down the lake on its eastern shore, 2.5 miles south of Ponderosa Flat. Cool Springs Creek enters the lake near the camp. (See the *Ponderosa Flat* listing for more information about Butt Lake.)

Campsites, facilities: There are 25 sites for tents or RVs up to 30 feet (no hookups), and five walk-in tent sites. Picnic tables and fire grills are provided. Drinking water, vault toilets, and a boat ramp are available. Some facilities are wheelchair-accessible. Leashed pets are permitted.

Reservations, fees: Reservations are not accepted. Sites are $16 per night, $3 per night for each additional vehicle, $7 per night per additional RV, $1 per pet per night. Open May through October, weather permitting.

Directions: From Red Bluff, take Highway 36 east for 44 miles to the junction with Highway 89. Continue east on Highway 36/89 to Lake Almanor and the next junction with Highway 89 (two miles before reaching Chester). Turn right on Highway 89 and drive about seven miles to Butt Valley Road. Turn right on Butt Valley Road and drive 5.7 miles to the campground on the right side of the road.

Contact: PG&E Land Projects, 916/386-5164, www.pge.com/recreation.

79 YELLOW CREEK

Scenic rating: 8

in Humbug Valley

Yellow Creek is one of Cal Trout's pet projects. It's a beautiful stream for fly fishers, demanding the best from skilled anglers. This camp is set at 4,400 feet in Humbug Valley and provides access to this stretch of water. Another option is to fish Butt Creek, much easier fishing for small, planted rainbow trout, with access along the road on the way in.

Campsites, facilities: There are 10 sites for tents or RVs up to 30 feet (no hookups). Picnic tables and fire grills are provided. Drinking water and vault toilets are available. Leashed pets are permitted.

Reservations, fees: Reservations are not accepted. Sites are $16 per night, $3 per night for each additional vehicle, $7 per night per additional RV, $1 per pet per night. Open May through September.

Directions: From Red Bluff, take Highway 36 east for 44 miles to the junction with Highway 89. Continue east on Highway 36/89 for eight miles to Humbug Road. Turn right and drive 0.6 mile and bear left to stay on Humbug Road. Continue for 1.2 miles and bear right (signed for Longville) to stay on Humbug Road. Continue for 5.4 miles to Humbug Valley and a road intersection. Turn left to stay on Humbug Road and drive 1.2 miles (passing the Soda Springs Historic Site) to a fork. Bear right to stay on Humbug Road and drive 0.3 mile to the campground.

Contact: PG&E Land Projects, 916/386-5164, www.pge.com/recreation.

80 BUTTE MEADOWS

Scenic rating: 6

on Butte Creek in Lassen National Forest

On hot summer days, when a cold stream sounds even better than a cold drink, Butte Meadows provides a hideout in the national forest east of Chico. This is a summer camp situated along Butte Creek, which is stocked with rainbow trout by the Department of Fish and Game. Nearby Doe Mill Ridge and the surrounding Lassen National Forest can provide good side-trip adventures. The camp elevation is 4,600 feet.

Campsites, facilities: There are 13 sites for tents or RVs up to 25 feet (no hookups). Fire grills and picnic tables are provided. Drinking water and vault toilets are available. Supplies are available in Butte Meadows. Leashed pets are permitted.

Reservations, fees: Reservations are not accepted. Sites are $12 per night, $3 per night for each additional vehicle. Open late April through early November, weather permitting.

Directions: From Chico, drive about 15 miles northeast on Highway 32 to the town of Forest Ranch. Continue on Highway 32 for another nine miles. Turn right on Humboldt Road and drive five miles to Butte Meadows.

Contact: Lassen National Forest, Almanor Ranger District, 530/258-2141, fax 530/258-5194; Department of Fish and Game fishing information, 530/225-2146.

81 CHERRY HILL

Scenic rating: 7

on Butte Creek in Lassen National Forest

The camp is set along little Butte Creek at the foot of Cherry Hill, just downstream from the confluence of Colby Creek and Butte Creek. It is also on the western edge of the alpine zone in Lassen National Forest. A four-mile drive to the north, much of it along Colby Creek, will take visitors to the Colby Mountain Lookout at 6,002 feet for a dramatic view of the Ishi Wilderness to the west. Nearby to the south is Philbrook Reservoir.

Campsites, facilities: There are six walk-in tent sites and 19 sites for tents or RVs up to 30 feet (no hookups). Picnic tables and fire grills are provided. Drinking water and vault toilets are available. Supplies are available in the town of Butte Meadows. Leashed pets are permitted.

Reservations, fees: Reservations are not accepted. Sites are $12 per night, $3 per night for each additional vehicle. Open late April through early November, weather permitting.

Directions: From Chico, drive northeast on Highway 32 for approximately 24 miles to the junction with Humboldt Road (well past the town of Forest Ranch). Turn right and drive five miles to Butte Meadows. Continue on Humboldt Road for three miles to the campground on the right side of the road.

Contact: Lassen National Forest, Almanor Ranger District, 530/258-2141, fax 530/258-5194.

82 PHILBROOK RESERVOIR

Scenic rating: 7

in Lassen National Forest

Philbrook Reservoir is set at 5,600 feet on the western mountain slopes above Chico, on the southwest edge of Lassen National Forest. It is a pretty lake, though subject to late-season drawdowns, with a scenic lookout a short distance from camp. Swimming beaches and a picnic area are bonuses. The lake is loaded with small trout—a dink here, a dink there, a dink everywhere.

Campsites, facilities: There are 20 sites for tents or RVs up to 30 feet (no hookups), and an overflow camping area. Picnic tables and

fire grills are provided. Drinking water and vault toilets are available. Trailer and car-top boat launches are available. Some facilities are wheelchair-accessible. Leashed pets are permitted.

Reservations, fees: Reservations are not accepted. Sites are $16 per night, $3 per night for each additional vehicle, $7 per night per additional RV, $1 per pet per night. Open May through September.

Directions: At Orland on I-5, take the Highway 32/Chico exit and drive to Chico and the junction with Highway 99. Turn south on Highway 99 and drive to Skyway Road/Paradise (in south Chico). Turn east on Skyway Road, drive through Paradise, and continue for 27 miles to Humbug Summit Road. Turn right and drive two miles to Philbrook Road. Turn right and drive 3.1 miles to the campground entrance road. Turn right and drive 0.5 mile to the campground. Note: Access roads are unpaved and often rough.

Contact: PG&E Land Projects, 916/386-5164, www.pge.com/recreation.

83 QUEEN LILY

Scenic rating: 7

on the North Fork of the Feather River in Plumas National Forest

The North Fork Feather River is a prime destination for camping and trout fishing, especially for families. This is one of three camps along the river on Caribou Road. This stretch of river is well stocked. Insider's note: The first 150 yards of river below the dam at Caribou typically have large but elusive trout.

Campsites, facilities: There are 12 sites for tents or RVs up to 30 feet (no hookups). Picnic tables and fire grills are provided. Drinking water and vault toilets are available. A grocery store and coin laundry are available within three miles. Leashed pets are permitted.

Reservations, fees: Reservations are not

accepted. Sites are $20 per night. Open May through September.

Directions: From Oroville, drive north on Highway 70 to Caribou Road (two miles past Belden). Turn left on Caribou Road and drive about three miles to the campground on the left side of the road.

Contact: Plumas National Forest, Mount Hough Ranger District, 530/283-0555, fax 530/283-1821; Northwest Park Management, 530/283-5559.

84 NORTH FORK

Scenic rating: 7

on the North Fork of the Feather River in Plumas National Forest

This camp is between Queen Lily to the nearby north and Gansner Bar camp to the nearby south, all three set on the North Fork Feather River. The elevation is 2,600 feet. Fishing access is good and trout plants are decent, making for a good fishing/camping trip. Note: All three camps are extremely popular on summer weekends.

Campsites, facilities: There are 20 sites for tents or RVs up to 32 feet (no hookups). Picnic tables and fire grills are provided. Drinking water and vault toilets are available. A grocery store and coin laundry are available within three miles. Leashed pets are permitted.

Reservations, fees: Reservations are not accepted. Sites are $20 per night. Open May through September.

Directions: From Oroville, drive north on Highway 70 to Caribou Road (two miles past Belden at Gansner Ranch Ranger Station). Turn left on Caribou Road and drive about two miles to the campground on the left side of the road.

Contact: Plumas National Forest, Mount Hough Ranger District, 530/283-0555, fax 530/283-1821; Northwest Park Management, 530/283-5559.

85 GANSNER BAR

Scenic rating: 7

on the North Fork of the Feather River in Plumas National Forest

Gansner Bar is the first of three camps along Caribou Road, which runs parallel to the North Fork Feather River. Of the three, this one receives the highest trout stocks of rainbow trout in the 10- to 12-inch class. Caribou Road runs upstream to Caribou Dam, with stream and fishing access along almost all of it. The camps often fill on summer weekends.

Campsites, facilities: There are 14 sites for tents or RVs up to 30 feet (no hookups). Picnic tables and fire grills are provided. Drinking water and vault toilets are available. A grocery store and coin laundry are available within one mile. Some facilities are wheelchair-accessible. Leashed pets are permitted.

Reservations, fees: Reservations are not accepted. Sites are $20 per night. Open April through October.

Directions: From Oroville, drive northeast on Highway 70 to Caribou Road (two miles past Belden). Turn left on Caribou Road and drive a short distance to the campground on the left side of the road.

Contact: Plumas National Forest, Mount Hough Ranger District, 530/283-0555, fax 530/283-1821; Northwest Park Management, 530/283-5559.

86 HALLSTED

Scenic rating: 7

on the North Fork of the Feather River in Plumas National Forest

Easy highway access and a pretty trout stream right alongside have made this an extremely popular campground. It typically fills on summer weekends. Hallsted is set on the East

LASSEN CAMPING

Branch North Fork Feather River at 2,800 feet elevation. The river is stocked with trout by the Department of Fish and Game.

Campsites, facilities: There are 20 sites for tents or RVs up to 30 feet (no hookups). Picnic tables and fire grills are provided. Drinking water and vault toilets are available. A grocery store is within a quarter mile. Some facilities are wheelchair-accessible. Leashed pets are permitted.

Reservations, fees: Reservations are accepted at 877/444-6777 or www.recreation.gov ($10 reservation fee). Sites are $20 per night. Open May through September.

Directions: From Oroville, drive northeast on Highway 70 to Belden. Continue past Belden for about 12 miles to the campground entrance on the right side of the road. Turn right and drive 0.25 mile to the campground.

Contact: Plumas National Forest, Mount Hough Ranger District, 530/283-0555, fax 530/283-1821; Northwest Park Management, 530/283-5559.

87 DODGE RESERVOIR

Scenic rating: 6

near Ravendale

This camp is set at 5,735 feet elevation near Dodge Reservoir, remote and little used. The lake covers 400 acres and is stocked with Eagle Lake trout. Those who know of this lake feel as if they know a secret, because the limit is two at Eagle Lake itself, but it is five here. Small boats can be launched from the shoreline, and though it can be windy, mornings are usually calm, ideal for canoes. The surrounding hillsides are sprinkled with sage and juniper. This camp is also popular with hunters who get drawn in the annual DFG lottery for tags for this zone. There is a very good chance that, along the entire length of road from the Madeline Plain into Dodge Reservoir, you'll see some wild horses. There's no sight quite

like them. They are considered to be wild, but some will stay close to the road, while others will come no closer then 300 yards.

Campsites, facilities: There are 12 sites for tents or RVs up to 35 feet (no hookups). Picnic tables and fire pits are provided. A vault toilet is available. No drinking water is available. There is no developed boat ramp, but hand-launched boats are permitted. Leashed pets are permitted.

Reservations, fees: Reservations are not accepted. There is no fee for camping, but donations are encouraged. Open year-round, weather permitting.

Directions: From Susanville, drive north on U.S. 395 for 54 miles to Ravendale and County Road 502. Turn right on County Road 502 (Mail Route) and drive four miles, then bear left to stay on County Road 502. Continue four miles, then bear right to stay on County Road 502. Drive two miles to County Road 526. Continue straight onto County Road 526 and drive 4.5 miles to County Road 504. Turn left and drive two miles to County Road 506. Turn right and drive 7.5 miles to the access road for Dodge Reservoir. Turn left on the access road and drive one mile to the lake and camp. Note: The last mile of road before the turnoff to Dodge Reservoir can become impassable with just a small amount of rain or snow.

Contact: Bureau of Land Management, Eagle Lake Field Office, 530/257-0456, fax 530/257-4831, www.blm.gov/ca.

88 NORTH EAGLE LAKE

Scenic rating: 7

on Eagle Lake

This camp provides direct access in the fall to the best fishing area of huge Eagle Lake. When the weather turns cold, the population of big Eagle Lake trout migrates to its favorite haunts just outside the tules, often in water only 5–8 feet deep. A boat ramp is about 1.5 miles to the southwest on Stone Road. In the summer this area is quite exposed and the lake can be hammered by west winds, which can howl from midday to sunset. The elevation is 5,100 feet.

Campsites, facilities: There are 20 sites for tents or RVs up to 35 feet (no hookups). Picnic tables and fire grills are provided. Drinking water and vault toilets are available. A private dump station and boat ramp are within 1.5 miles. Leashed pets are permitted.

Reservations, fees: Reservations are not accepted. Sites are $8 per night. Open Memorial Day through mid-November, weather permitting.

Directions: From Red Bluff, drive east on Highway 36 to Susanville. In Susanville, turn left (north) on Highway 139 and drive 29 miles to County Road A1. Turn left at County Road A1 and drive 0.5 mile to the campground on the right.

Contact: Bureau of Land Management, Eagle Lake Field Office, 530/257-0456, fax 530/257-4831, www.blm.gov/ca.

89 RAMHORN SPRINGS

Scenic rating: 3

south of Ravendale

This camp is not even three miles off the biggest state highway in northeastern California, yet it feels remote and is little known. It is way out in Nowhere Land, near the flank of Shinn Peak (7,562 feet). There are large numbers of antelope in the area, along with a sprinkling of large mule deer. Hunters lucky enough to get a deer tag can use this camp for their base in the fall. It is also popular for upland game hunters in search of sage grouse and chukar.

Campsites, facilities: There are 10 sites for tents or RVs up to 35 feet (no hookups). Picnic tables and fire grills are provided. Vault toilets and a horse corral are available. There is no

drinking water, although spring water, which can be filtered, is available. Leashed pets are permitted.

Reservations, fees: Reservations are not accepted. There is no fee for camping, but donations are encouraged. Open year-round, weather permitting.

Directions: From Red Bluff, drive east on Highway 36 to Susanville. In Susanville, turn north on U.S. 395 and drive 45 miles to Post Camp Road. Turn right on Post Camp Road (unmarked except for small recreation sign) and drive 2.5 miles east to the campground.

Contact: Bureau of Land Management, Eagle Lake Field Office, 530/257-0456, fax 530/257-4831, www.blm.gov/ca.

90 EAGLE LAKE RV PARK

Scenic rating: 7

near Susanville

Eagle Lake RV Park has become something of a headquarters for anglers in pursuit of Eagle Lake trout, which typically range 18–22 inches. A nearby boat ramp provides access to Pelican Point and Eagle Point, where the fishing is often best in the summer. In the fall, the north end of the lake provides better prospects (see the *North Eagle Lake* listing in this chapter). This RV park has all the amenities, including a small store. That means no special trips into town, just vacation time, lounging beside Eagle Lake, maybe catching a big trout now and then. One downer: The wind typically howls here most summer afternoons. When the whitecaps are too big to deal with and surface conditions become choppy, get off the water; it can be dangerous here. Resident deer, including bucks with spectacular racks, can be like pets here on late summer evenings.

Campsites, facilities: There are 65 RV sites with full hookups (30 amps), including some pull-through sites, a separate grassy area for tents only, and cabin and RV rentals. Picnic tables and fire grills are provided. Restrooms with showers, coin laundry, satellite TV hookups, dump station, convenience store, propane gas, diesel, bait and tackle, video rentals, RV supplies, firewood, and recreation room are available. A boat ramp, dock, and boat slips are nearby. Some facilities are wheelchair-accessible. Leashed pets are permitted.

Reservations, fees: Reservations are recommended. RV sites are $36 per night, tent sites are $25 per night, $5 per day for each additional person, $1 per pet per night. Some credit cards accepted. Open late May through early November, weather permitting.

Directions: From Red Bluff, drive east on Highway 36 toward Susanville. Just before reaching Susanville, turn left on County Road A1 and drive approximately 25 miles to County Road 518 near Spalding Tract. Turn right on County Road 518 and drive through a small neighborhood to The Strand (the lake frontage road). Turn right on The Strand and drive about eight blocks to Palmetto Way and the entrance to the store and the park entrance at 687-125 Palmetto Way. Register at the store.

Contact: Eagle Lake RV Park, 530/825-3133, www.eaglelakeandrv.com.

91 CHRISTIE

Scenic rating: 7

on Eagle Lake in Lassen National Forest

This camp is set along the southern shore of Eagle Lake at 5,100 feet. Eagle Lake, with 100 miles of shoreline, is well known for its big trout (hooray) and big winds (boo). The camp offers some protection from the north winds. Its location is also good for seeing osprey in the Osprey Management Area, which covers a six-mile stretch of shoreline just two miles to the north above Wildcat Point. A nearby resort is a bonus. The nearest boat ramp is at Gallatin Marina. A five-mile-long paved trail runs from

Christie to Aspen Grove Campground, perfect for hiking, cycling, and horseback riding.

Campsites, facilities: There are 69 individual sites and 10 double sites for tents or RVs up to 50 feet. No hookups. Picnic tables and fire grills are provided. Drinking water and flush toilets are available. Some facilities are wheelchair-accessible. A grocery store is nearby. A dump station is 2.5 miles away at Merrill Campground. Leashed pets are permitted. A campground host is on site.

Reservations, fees: Reservations are accepted at 877/444-6777 or www.recreation.gov ($10 reservation fee). Sites are $18–24 per night, $30 per night for "small group sites" (which are like double sites), $5 per night for each additional vehicle. Open May through October, weather permitting.

Directions: From Red Bluff, drive east on Highway 36 toward Susanville. Three miles before Susanville turn left on Eagle Lake Road/County Road A1 and drive 19.5 miles to the campground on the right side of the road.

Contact: Lassen National Forest, Eagle Lake Ranger District, 530/257-4188, fax 530/252-5803.

92 MERRILL

Scenic rating: 8

on Eagle Lake in Lassen National Forest

This is one of the largest, most developed Forest Service campgrounds in the entire county. It is set along the southern shore of huge Eagle Lake at 5,100 feet. The nearest boat launch is at Gallatin Marina, where there is a developed swim beach.

Campsites, facilities: There are 173 individual sites and two double sites with full or partial hookups (30 and 50 amps) for tents or RVs up to 50 feet. Picnic tables and fire rings are provided. Drinking water and flush toilets are available. A dump station is nearby. Some facilities are wheelchair-accessible. A grocery store and boat ramp are nearby. Leashed pets are permitted. A camp host is on site.

Reservations, fees: Reservations are accepted at 877/444-6777 or www.recreation.gov ($10 reservation fee). RV sites are $29–33 per night, double sites are $56 per night, tent sites are $18–19 per night. Open May through October, weather permitting.

Directions: From Red Bluff, drive east on Highway 36 toward Susanville. Three miles before Susanville, turn left on Eagle Lake Road/ County Road A1 and drive 17.5 miles to the campground on the right side of the road.

Contact: Lassen National Forest, Eagle Lake Ranger District, 530/257-4188, fax 530/252-5803, camp host, 530/825-3450.

93 ASPEN GROVE WALK-IN

Scenic rating: 8

on Eagle Lake in Lassen National Forest

Eagle Lake is one of the great trout lakes in California, producing the fast-growing and often huge Eagle Lake rainbow trout. All water sports are allowed and, with a huge lake and 100 miles of shoreline, there's plenty of room for everyone. Just be prepared for cold lake water. This camp is one of four at the south end of the lake and is a popular choice for anglers, with a boat ramp adjacent to the campground. The one problem with Eagle Lake is the wind, which can whip the huge but shallow lake into a froth in the early summer. It is imperative that anglers/boaters get on the water early, and then get back to camp early, with the fishing for the day often done by 10:30 A.M. A bonus here is a good chance to see bald eagles and osprey. A five-mile-long paved, wheelchair-accessible recreation trail runs from this campground to Christie Campground, and then continues to other campgrounds.

Campsites, facilities: There are 28 tent sites. Picnic tables and fire grills are provided.

Drinking water and flush toilets are available. A boat ramp is nearby. There are no wheelchair facilities for campers. Leashed pets are permitted.

Reservations, fees: Reservations are not accepted. Sites are $18 per night. Open May through September.

Directions: From Red Bluff, drive east on Highway 36 toward Susanville. Three miles before Susanville, turn left on Eagle Lake Road/County Road A1 and drive 15.5 miles to County Road 231. Turn right on County Road 231 and drive two miles to the campground on the left side of the road. Walk a short distance to the campsites.

Contact: Lassen National Forest, Eagle Lake Ranger District, 530/257-4188, fax 530/252-5803.

94 WEST EAGLE GROUP CAMPS

Scenic rating: 9

on Eagle Lake in Lassen National Forest

If you are coming in a big group to Eagle Lake, you'd better get on the telephone first and reserve this camp. Then you can have your own private slice of solitude along the southern shore of Eagle Lake. Bring your boat; the Gallatin Marina and a swimming beach are only about a mile away. The elevation is 5,100 feet.

Campsites, facilities: There are two group camps for tents or RVs up to 35 feet (no hookups) that can accommodate 75–100 people each. Picnic tables and fire grills are provided. Drinking water, flush toilets, and picnic areas are available. A grocery store, dump station, and boat ramp are nearby. Leashed pets are permitted.

Reservations, fees: Reservations are required at 877/444-6777 or www.recreation.gov ($10 reservation fee). The sites are $100–125 per night. Open May through October, weather permitting.

Directions: From Red Bluff, drive east on Highway 36 toward Susanville. Three miles before Susanville, turn left on Eagle Lake Road/County Road A1 and drive 15.5 miles to County Road 231. Turn right on County Road 231 and drive 0.25 mile to the campground on the left side of the road.

Contact: Lassen National Forest, Eagle Lake Ranger District, 530/257-4188, fax 530/252-5803.

95 EAGLE

Scenic rating: 8

on Eagle Lake in Lassen National Forest

Eagle is set just up the road from Aspen Grove, which is more popular because of the boat ramp nearby. The elevation is 5,100 feet. (See the *Aspen Grove Walk-In* listing in this chapter for information about Eagle Lake.)

Campsites, facilities: There are 50 individual sites and two double sites for tents or RVs up to 25 feet (no hookups). Picnic tables and fire grills are provided. Drinking water and flush toilets are available. Some facilities are wheelchair-accessible. There is a boat launch nearby at Gallatin Marina. Leashed pets are permitted.

Reservations, fees: Reservations are accepted at 877/444-6777 or www.recreation.gov ($10 reservation fee). Sites are $18 per night, "small group sites" (which are like double sites) are $30 per night, $5 per night for each additional vehicle. Open May through October, weather permitting.

Directions: From Red Bluff, drive east on Highway 36 toward Susanville. Three miles before Susanville, turn left on Eagle Lake Road/County Road A1 and drive 15.5 miles to County Road 231. Turn right and drive 0.5 mile to the campground on the left side of the road.

Contact: Lassen National Forest, Eagle Lake Ranger District, 530/257-4188, fax 530/252-5803.

96 GOUMAZ

Scenic rating: 7

on the Susan River in Lassen National Forest

This camp is set beside the Susan River, adjacent to historic Bizz Johnson Trail, a former route for a rail line that has been converted to a 25-mile trail. The trail runs from Susanville to Westwood, but this section provides access to many of its prettiest and most remote stretches as it runs in a half-circle around Pegleg Mountain (7,112 feet) to the east. It is an outstanding route for biking, hiking, and horseback riding in the summer and cross-country skiing in the winter. Equestrian campers are welcome here. The elevation is 5,200 feet.

Campsites, facilities: There are six sites for tents or RVs up to 25 feet (no hookups). Picnic tables and fire grills are provided. Drinking water and vault toilets are available. Equestrian facilities include water troughs and tie-lines. Leashed pets are permitted.

Reservations, fees: Reservations are not accepted. Sites are $13 per night, $5 per night for each additional vehicle. Open May through October, weather permitting.

Directions: From Red Bluff, drive east on Highway 36 past Lake Almanor to the junction with Highway 44. Turn west on Highway 44 and drive six miles (one mile past the Worley Ranch) to Goumaz Road/Forest Road 30N08. Turn left on Goumaz Road and drive about five miles to the campground entrance road on the right.

Contact: Lassen National Forest, Eagle Lake Ranger District, 530/257-4188, fax 530/252-5803.

97 ROXIE PECONOM WALK-IN

Scenic rating: 5

in Lassen National Forest

This small camp, at 4,800 feet elevation, is set next to Willard Creek, a seasonal stream in eastern Lassen National Forest. It's shaded and quiet. The camp requires only about a 100-foot walk from the parking area. The best nearby recreation is the Bizz Johnson Trail, with a trailhead on Highway 36 (two miles east) at a parking area on the left side of the highway. This is an outstanding biking and hiking route.

Campsites, facilities: There are 10 walk-in tent sites. Picnic tables and fire rings are provided. Drinking water and vault toilets are available. Garbage must be packed out. Leashed pets are permitted.

Reservations, fees: Reservations are not accepted. There is no fee for camping. Open May through October, weather permitting.

Directions: From Red Bluff, drive east on Highway 36 past Lake Almanor and continue past Fredonyer Pass for three miles to Forest Road 29N03 on the right. Turn right and drive two miles to the campground parking area on the right. Park and walk 100 feet to the campground.

Contact: Lassen National Forest, Eagle Lake Ranger District, 530/257-4188, fax 530/252-5803.

98 BOULDER CREEK

Scenic rating: 7

at Antelope Lake in Plumas National Forest

Antelope Lake is a pretty mountain lake circled by conifers, with nice campsites and good trout fishing. It is set at 5,000 feet elevation in remote eastern Plumas National Forest, far enough away so the marginally inclined never

make the trip. Campgrounds are at each end of the lake (this one is just north of Lone Rock at the north end), with a boat ramp at Lost Cove on the east side of the lake. All water sports are permitted, and swimming is best near the campgrounds. The lake isn't huge, but it is big enough, with 15 miles of shoreline and little islands, coves, and peninsulas to give it an intimate feel.

Campsites, facilities: There are 70 sites for tents or RVs up to 40 feet (no hookups). Picnic tables and fire grills are provided. Drinking water and vault toilets are available. A dump station, boat ramp, and grocery store are nearby. Some facilities are wheelchair-accessible. Leashed pets are permitted.

Reservations, fees: Reservations are accepted at 877/444-6777 or www.recreation.gov ($10 reservation fee). Sites are $20 per night, double sites are $35 per night, $5 per night for each additional vehicle. Open May through early September.

Directions: From Red Bluff, drive east on Highway 36 to Susanville and U.S. 395. Turn south on U.S. 395 and drive about 10 miles (one mile past Janesville) to County Road 208. Turn right on County Road 208 (signed Antelope Lake) and drive about 15 miles to a Y (one mile before Antelope Lake). Turn left at the Y and drive four miles to the campground entrance on the right side of the road (on the northwest end of the lake).

Contact: Plumas National Forest, Mount Hough Ranger District, 530/283-0555, fax 530/283-1821; Northwest Park Management, 530/283-5559.

99 LONE ROCK

Scenic rating: 9

at Antelope Lake in Plumas National Forest

This camp provides an option to nearby Boulder Creek, to the immediate north at the northwest shore of Antelope Lake. (See the *Boulder Creek* listing for more information.) The elevation is 5,000 feet. Campfire programs are offered in the summer at the on-site amphitheater.

Campsites, facilities: There are 87 sites for tents or RVs up to 40 feet (no hookups). Picnic tables and fire grills are provided. Drinking water and vault toilets are available. A dump station, boat ramp, and grocery store are nearby. Some facilities are wheelchair-accessible. Leashed pets are permitted.

Reservations, fees: Reservations are accepted at 877/444-6777 or www.recreation.gov ($10 reservation fee). Sites are $18–20 per night. Open May through October.

Directions: From Red Bluff, drive east on Highway 36 to Susanville and U.S. 395. Go south on U.S. 395 and drive about 10 miles (one mile past Janesville) to County Road 208. Turn right on County Road 208 (signed Antelope Lake) and drive about 15 miles to a Y (one mile before Antelope Lake). Turn left at the Y and drive three miles to the campground entrance on the right side of the road (on the northwest end of the lake).

Contact: Plumas National Forest, Mount Hough Ranger District, 530/283-0555, fax 530/283-1821; Northwest Park Management, 530/283-5559.

100 LONG POINT

🚶🏽‍♂️ 🏞️ 🛶 🚤 🐕 ♿ 🚐 🏕️

Scenic rating: 7

at Antelope Lake in Plumas National Forest

Long Point is a pretty camp set on a peninsula that extends well into Antelope Lake, facing Lost Cove. The lake's boat ramp is at Lost Cove, a three-mile drive around the northeast shore. Trout fishing is often good here for both rainbow and brown trout, and there is a nature trail. A group campground is set within this campground.

Campsites, facilities: There are 38 sites for tents or RVs up to 30 feet, and four group sites for tents or RVs up to 35 feet that can

accommodate up to 25 people each. No hookups. Picnic tables and fire grills are provided. Drinking water and vault toilets are available. A grocery store, boat ramp, and dump stations are nearby. Some facilities are wheelchair-accessible. Leashed pets are permitted.

Reservations, fees: Reservations are accepted for individual sites and required for the group sites at 877/444-6777 or www.recreation.gov ($10 reservation fee). Sites are $20 per night, double sites are $35 per night, $75 per night for group sites. Open May through October.

Directions: From Red Bluff, drive east on Highway 36 to Susanville and U.S. 395. Go south on U.S. 395 and drive about 10 miles (one mile past Janesville) to County Road 208. Turn right on County Road 208 (signed Antelope Lake) and drive about 15 miles to a Y (one mile before Antelope Lake). Turn right at the Y and drive one mile to the campground entrance on the left side of the road.

Contact: Plumas National Forest, Mount Hough Ranger District, 530/283-0555, fax 530/283-1821; Northwest Park Management, 530/283-5559.

101 HONEY LAKE CAMPGROUND

🛶 🏕️ 🚙 ♿ 🚐 🏕️

Scenic rating: 4

near Milford

For newcomers, Honey Lake is a strange-looking place—a vast, shallow lake set on the edge of the desert of the Great Basin. The campground is set at 4,385 feet elevation and covers 30 acres, most of it overlooking the lake. There are a few pine trees in the campground, and a waterfowl management area is along the north shore of the lake. This campground is popular with hunters. Equestrian facilities, including a corral and exercise ring, are available. Fishing for Eagle Lake trout is good here. The lake is 26 miles across, and on rare flat calm evenings, the sunsets are spectacular here.

Campsites, facilities: There are 44 pull-through sites for tents or RVs of any length, half with full or partial hookups (30 amps), plus 25 mobile homes and trailers. Picnic tables are provided. Restrooms with showers, coin laundry, dump station, propane gas, restaurant, gift and grocery store, playground, ice, video rentals, and a recreation room are available. Some facilities are wheelchair-accessible. Leashed pets are permitted.

Reservations, fees: Reservations are not accepted. Sites are $14.95–29.95 per night, $3.50 per person per night for more than two people. Long-term rentals are available. Some credit cards accepted. Open year-round.

Directions: From Susanville on U.S. 395, drive 17 miles south (if you reach Milford, you have gone two miles too far) to the campground on the west side of the highway. It is 65 miles north of Reno.

Contact: Honey Lake Campground, 530/253-2508.

102 CONKLIN PARK

Scenic rating: 4

on Willow Creek in Plumas National Forest

This camp is along little Willow Creek on the northeastern border of the Dixie Mountain State Game Refuge. Much of the area is recovering from a fire that burned during the summer of 1989. Although the area has greened up, there remains significant evidence of the fire. The campground is little known, primitive, rarely used, and is not likely to change any time soon. The elevation is 5,900 feet.

Campsites, facilities: There are nine sites for tents or RVs up to 25 feet (no hookups). Picnic tables and fire grills are provided. Vault toilets are available. No drinking water is available. Garbage must be packed out. Leashed pets are permitted.

Reservations, fees: Reservations are not accepted. There is no fee for camping. Open May through October, weather permitting.

Directions: From Susanville on U.S. 395, drive south for 24 miles to Milford. In Milford turn right (east) on County Road 336 and drive about four miles to a Y. Bear to the right on Forest Road 70/26N70 and drive three miles. Turn right at the bridge at Willow Creek, turn left on Forest Road 70 (now paved), and drive three miles to the camp entrance road on the left side.

Contact: Plumas National Forest, Beckwourth Ranger District, 530/836-2575, fax 530/836-0493.

103 MEADOW VIEW

Scenic rating: 6

near Little Last Chance Creek in Plumas National Forest

This little-known, primitive camp is set along the headwaters of Little Last Chance Creek, along the eastern border of the Dixie Mountain State Game Refuge. The access road continues along the creek and connects with primitive roads that enter the interior of the game refuge. Side-trip options include Frenchman Lake to the south and the drive up to Dixie Mountain, at 8,323 feet elevation. The camp elevation is 6,100 feet.

Campsites, facilities: There are six sites for tents or RVs up to 30 feet (no hookups). Picnic tables and fire grills are provided. Vault toilets are available. No drinking water is available. Garbage must be packed out. Leashed pets are permitted.

Reservations, fees: Reservations are not accepted. There is no fee for camping. Open May through October, weather permitting.

Directions: From Reno, drive north on U.S. 395 for 43 miles to Doyle. At Doyle, turn west on Doyle Grade Road/County Road 331 (a dirt road most of the way) and drive seven miles to the campground.

Contact: Plumas National Forest, Beckwourth Ranger District, 530/836-2575, fax 530/836-0493.

SHASTA HIKING

© ANN MARIE BROWN

BEST HIKES

SHASTA HIKING

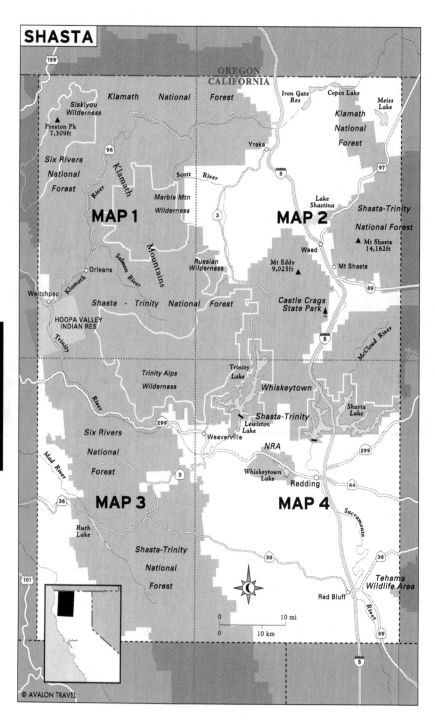

SHASTA

199

OREGON
CALIFORNIA

Klamath   National   Forest

Iron Gate
Res

Copco Lake

Meiss
Lake

Siskiyou
Wilderness

Klamath
National
Forest

▲ Preston Pk
7,309ft

96

Yreka

5

97

Six Rivers
National
Forest

Klamath

River

Scott   River

Marble Mtn

Wilderness

3

Lake
Shastina

Shasta-Trinity

National Forest

MAP 1

MAP 2

Salmon River

Orleans

Mountains

Russian
Wilderness

Weed

▲ Mt Shasta
14,162ft

Mt Eddy
9,025ft ▲

Mt Shasta

89

Weitchpec

Klamath

Shasta - Trinity National Forest

Castle Crags
State Park

5

HOOPA VALLEY
INDIAN RES

Trinity

McCloud River

Trinity Alps

Wilderness

Trinity
Lake

Whiskeytown

Shasta
Lake

River

299

Shasta-Trinity

Lewiston
Lake

Weaverville

NRA

299

3

Six Rivers

National

Whiskeytown
Lake

Redding

44

Forest

Mad River

36

MAP 3

MAP 4

Sacramento

Ruth
Lake

Shasta-Trinity

36

36

National

Forest

101

Tehama
Wildlife Area

Red Bluff

River

0   10 mi

0   10 km

99

5

© AVALON TRAVEL

Map 1

Hikes 1-22

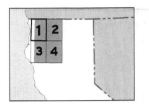

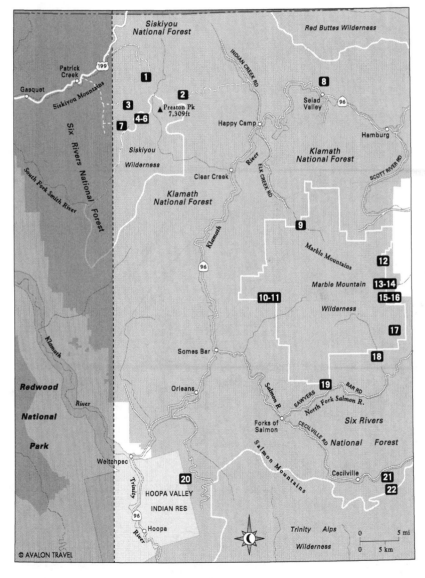

Siskiyou
National Forest

Red Buttes Wilderness

INDIAN CREEK RD

Patrick
Creek

Gasquet

Siskiyou Mountains

1

2

▲ Preston Pk
7,309ft

Happy Camp

3

4-6

7

Siskiyou

Wilderness

River

ELK CREEK RD

Clear Creek

Klamath
National Forest

8

Seiad
Valley

96

Hamburg

Klamath
National Forest

SCOTT RIVER RD

Six Rivers National Forest

South Fork Smith River

Klamath

96

Klamath

9

Marble Mountains

12

Marble Mountain

13-14

15-16

Wilderness

17

Somes Bar

18

Redwood

River

National

Orleans

Salmon R.

SAWYERS

North Fork Salmon R.

BAR RD

19

Park

CECILVILLE RD

Six Rivers

Forks of
Salmon

National   Forest

Salmon Mountains

Cecilville

21

22

Weitchpec

Trinity

20

HOOPA VALLEY

INDIAN RES

96

Hoopa

River

Trinity   Alps

0   5 mi

Wilderness

0   5 km

© AVALON TRAVEL

SHASTA HIKING

Map 2

Hikes 23-59

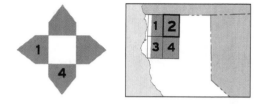

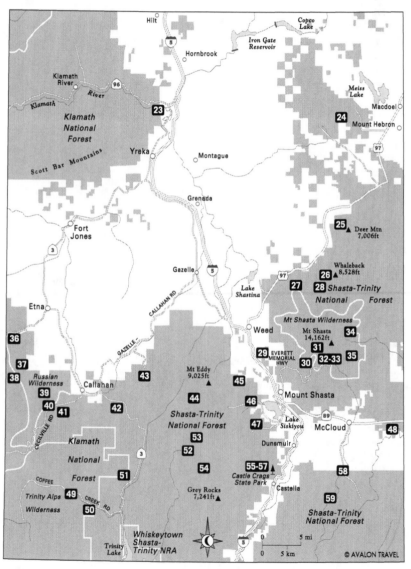

© AVALON TRAVEL

Map 3

Hikes 60-66

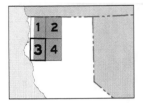

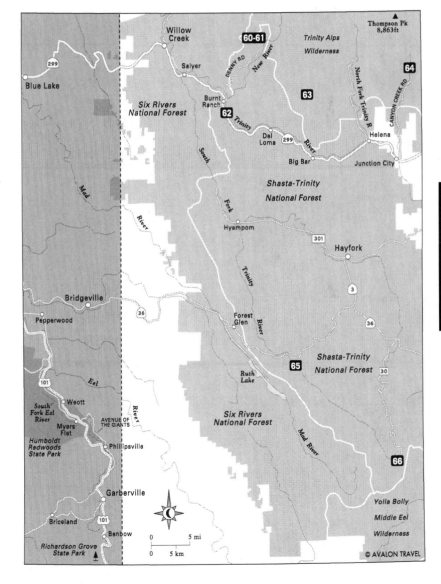

Map 4

Hikes 67-78

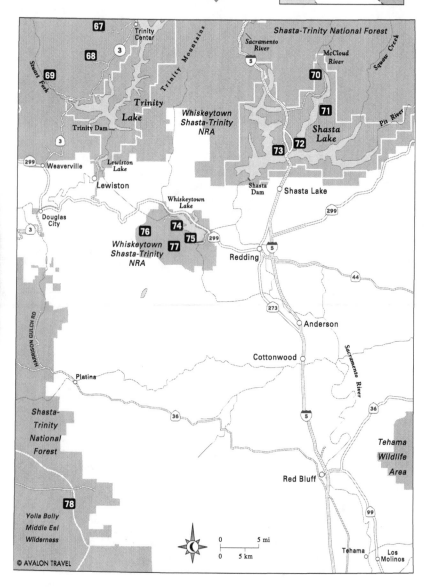

◼ YOUNGS VALLEY TRAIL

13.0 mi / 1.0 day   🏃🏃2 ⛰8

**in the Siskiyou Wilderness east of
Crescent City**

The 6.5-mile trip from Youngs Valley down
Clear Creek to Youngs Meadow is a beautiful
and rewarding trip. Youngs Meadow, set at an
elevation of 4,500 feet on the western slope
of Preston Peak, is very pretty and makes an
excellent picnic area and campsite.

The drive to the trailhead is long and circuitous. It's long just to get to U.S. 199, and
from there, you're facing more than an hour
on forest roads. The trailhead is located near
Sanger Lake and some camp there the first
night in. You start the trip by hiking on a
decommissioned Forest Service road. It turns
to trail then you start dropping down into
Youngs Valley and Clear Creek. The hike
features a 600-foot descent into the canyon
and to Clear Creek.

From here the ambitious can take this trip
farther—much farther. The Youngs Valley
Trail is a great first leg of a multiday trip,
ultimately heading either farther down Clear
Creek to Wilderness Falls, which is an awe-
some setting (see the following hike), or to
Rattlesnake Meadows, on the slopes of Preston
Peak—a short but rugged climb.

User Groups: Hikers, dogs, and horses. No
mountain bikes. No wheelchair facilities.

Permits: No permits are required. A campfire permit (free) is required for overnight use.
Parking and access are free.

Maps: For a map, ask the U.S. Forest Service for Klamath National Forest. For a
topographic map, ask the USGS for Devils
Punchbowl.

Directions: From Crescent City, drive north
on U.S. 101 for three miles to U.S. 199. Bear
right (east) on U.S. 199 and drive 32 miles
to Forest Road 18N07. Turn right and drive
five miles to a signed junction for Forest Road
18N07. Continue on Forest Road 18N07 for
10 miles (twisty) toward Sanger Lake. Just
before Sanger Lake, bear right on Forest
Road 4803 (signed Youngs Valley Trail) and
drive one mile to the end of the road and the
trailhead.

Contact: Smith River National Recreation
Area, P.O. Box 228, Gasquet, CA 95543,
707/457-3131, www.fs.fed.us/r5—click on
Forest Offices; Klamath National Forest,
Happy Camp Ranger District, P.O. Box 377,
63822 Highway 96, Happy Camp, CA 96039-
0377, 530/493-2243, fax 530/493-1796, www
.fs.fed.us/r5—click on Forest Offices.

◼ PRESTON PEAK

19.0 mi / 2.0 days   🏃🏃5 ⛰10

**in the Siskiyou Wilderness east of
Crescent City**

BEST (

Only mountaineers need sign up for this trip.
The last mile to reach the summit of Preston Peak is steep, rough, and primitive; it
can be scary and dangerous for newcomers
to mountaineering. With no marked trail on
top, hikers must have the ability to scramble
cross-country and recognize any dangerous
spots—and then avoid them. That done, you'll
gain the top—7,309 feet and by far the highest
spot in the region, with fantastic surrounding views. Even Mount Shasta, way off to
the southeast, comes clearly into view, along
with the famous peaks in the Trinity Alps and
Marble Mountain Wilderness.

The best route to climb Preston Peak is to
hike Youngs Valley Trail (see details about
Youngs Valley Trail in this chapter) to Youngs
Meadow (an easy five miles). Then head down
the Clear Creek Trail (another easy mile) to
a somewhat faint junction with the Rattlesnake Meadow Trail. Turn left on Rattlesnake
Meadow Trail, where you start to climb, including two very steep, rough, and primitive miles to the flank of Preston Peak. At
the end of Rattlesnake Meadow Trail, hikers

must go cross-country for another mile or so to the Preston Peak Summit. The last mile is a scramble. Pick your route very carefully and make no climbing mistakes. Although this is a nontechnical climb, there is one difficult spot that can be dangerous. You will see it: a mix of shale, loose gravel, and boulders, with no discernible trail. Take your time and pick your way up one step at a time.

Special note: Always stay off this mountain in wet weather, because the route near the top is very slippery. Always avoid routes that cross through loose shale, which can be extremely dangerous. A fall here can kill you.

User Groups: Hikers only. Dogs are permitted but are strongly not recommended above tree line at Preston Peak. No horses or mountain bikes. No wheelchair facilities.

Permits: A campfire permit is required for overnight use. Parking and access are free.

Maps: For maps, ask the U.S. Forest Service for Six Rivers and Klamath National Forest. For a topographic map, ask the USGS for Devils Punchbowl.

Directions: From Crescent City, drive north on U.S. 101 for three miles to U.S. 199. Bear right (east) on U.S. 199 and drive 32 miles to Forest Road 18N07. Turn right and drive five miles to Forest Road 18N07. Continue on Forest Road 18N07 for 10 miles (twisty) toward Sanger Lake. Just before Sanger Lake, bear right on Forest Road 4803 (signed Youngs Valley Trail) and drive one mile to the trailhead, at the end of the road.

Contact: Klamath National Forest, Happy Camp Ranger District, P.O. Box 377, 63822 Highway 96, Happy Camp, CA 96039-0377, 530/493-2243, www.fs.fed.us/r5—click on Forest Offices; Smith River National Recreation Area, P.O. Box 228, Gasquet, CA 95543, 707/457-3131, www.fs.fed.us/r5—click on Forest Offices.

🖪 DOE FLAT TRAIL
3.0 mi / 1.5 hr

in Smith River National Recreation Area east of Crescent City

Doe Flat is the best backpacking jump-off point for the Siskiyou Wilderness. As long as you know that, you'll have all the motivation you need for the trip. There are several excellent destinations from Doe Flat. The best are Buck Lake, nearby Devils Punchbowl, along with Bear Mountain, Clear Creek, and Wilderness Falls.

It is 1.5 miles from the parking area to the intersection of the Buck Lake Trail. The first 0.75 mile of this easy hike is on a closed forest service road. After that, a trail is routed through forest and then intersects with Buck Lake Trail. To reach Buck Lake, turn right (it's only 0.1 mile to the lake). To reach Doe Flat and its campsite, turn left and continue 0.25 mile. The area is well wooded, with some huge Jeffrey pines and cedars. For late arrivals, a bonus at the trailhead is a small, primitive camping area with three sites and a vault toilet.

User Groups: Hikers, dogs, and horses. No mountain bikes. No wheelchair facilities.

Permits: No permits are required. A campfire permit (free) is required for overnight use. Parking and access are free.

Maps: For a free brochure and hiking guide, write to Smith River National Recreation Area at the address below. For a map, ask the U.S. Forest Service for Klamath National Forest. For a topographic map, ask the USGS for Devils Punchbowl.

Directions: From Crescent City, drive north on U.S. 101 for three miles to U.S. 199. Bear right (east) on U.S. 199 and drive 25 miles to Little Jones Creek Road. Turn right on Little Jones Creek Road/Jawbone Road (Forest Road 16) and drive south 9.6 miles to a fork with Forest Road 16N02. When the road forks, turn sharply left on Forest Road 16N02 and drive four miles to the trailhead, at the end of the road.

Contact: Smith River National Recreation Area, P.O. Box 228, Gasquet, CA 95543, 707/457-3131, www.fs.fed.us/r5—click on Forest Offices.

4 BUCK LAKE TRAIL (VIA DOE FLAT TRAIL)
6.2 mi / 3.0 hr   🏃2 ⛰️8

in the Siskiyou Wilderness east of Crescent City

Set in the heart of a wilderness forest at an elevation of 4,300 feet, Buck Lake is a little crystal lake surrounded by old-growth firs. After parking, the first 0.75 mile of this easy hike is on a closed forest service road. After that, a trail is routed through forest and then intersects with Buck Lake Trail. Turn right on Buck Lake Trail and hike 0.1 mile to the lake. There are plenty of deer and bear in the area, and the brook trout at the lake are abundant, though small. Traveling to the primitive campground at nearby Doe Flat, you'll cross through beautiful meadows and forest, including Douglas, white, and red firs, along with some maples. In the fall, the changing colors of the maples add a pretty touch to the trip. There is an excellent backpacker's campsite at Doe Flat. The first time we saw Buck Lake was a Memorial Day weekend, the opening day of trout season here, and there were so many rising brook trout that all the dimples on the lake surface looked like rain drops.

User Groups: Hikers, dogs, and horses. No mountain bikes. No wheelchair facilities.

Permits: No permits are required. A campfire permit (free) is required for overnight use. Parking and access are free.

Maps: For a free brochure and hiking guide, write to Smith River National Recreation Area at the address below. For a map, ask the U.S. Forest Service for Six Rivers and Klamath National Forest. For a topographic map, ask the USGS for Devils Punchbowl.

Directions: From Crescent City, drive north on U.S. 101 for three miles to U.S. 199. Bear right (east) on U.S. 199 and drive 25 miles to Little Jones Creek Road/Jawbone Road (Forest Road 16). Turn right on Little Jones Creek Road/Jawbone Road (Forest Road 16) and drive south 9.6 miles to a fork with Forest Road 16N02. When the road forks, turn sharply left on Forest Road 16N02 and drive four miles to the trailhead at the end of the road. Take Doe Flat trailhead.

Contact: Smith River National Recreation Area, P.O. Box 228, Gasquet, CA 95543, 707/457-3131, www.fs.fed.us/r5—click on Forest Offices.

5 DEVILS PUNCHBOWL (VIA DOE FLAT TRAIL)
12.2 mi / 1.5 days   🏃5 ⛰️10

in the Siskiyou Wilderness east of Crescent City

BEST (

You'll be wondering if you're afflicted with a hex or a charm when you take the trip to Devils Punchbowl, set at an elevation of 4,800 feet. The hex? The trail includes a climb of 1,500 feet in two miles that'll have you wheezing like a donkey low on hay. The charm? The first view of Devils Punchbowl is not only drop-dead gorgeous but is a sight you will never forget. It's small but pristine, set in a mountain granite bowl, framed by an imposing back wall—a shrine.

After parking, the first 0.75 mile is easy, a downhill glide on a closed forest service road. After that, a trail is routed through forest and then intersects with Buck Lake Trail (Buck Lake is only 0.1 mile off to the right). Turn left, staying on Doe Flat Trail, and you will quickly reach Doe Flat and its campsite. Continue past Doe Flat and a short way along Doe Creek. Just after the trail passes a little dirt mound, look for a right turn across Doe Creek. The turn is signed Devils Punchbowl, but the sign is occasionally stolen, so be alert for the trail on the right side of Doe Creek.

From here, you start the first of several switch-backs up Bear Mountain—a long, forbidding butt-kicker. When you finally top the ridge, the route crosses Devils Creek and leaves the forest behind, crossing bare granite domes. The trail is marked by small stacks of rocks, known as trail ducks. You pass a smaller lake, cross a rise, and then the beautiful, gemlike lake awaits. This place is something of a legend but is visited only by those willing to pay the price of the terrible climb to reach it.

Special note: The entire region surrounding Devils Punchbowl consists of sheets of bare granite. The few campsites here are merely small, flat sleeping spaces on rock. There is no firewood available, so bring a backpacking stove for cooking. Bring sealable plastic bags to carry out waste.

User Groups: Hikers and dogs. No horses or mountain bikes. No wheelchair facilities.

Permits: No permits are required. A camp-fire permit (free) is required for overnight use. Parking and access are free.

Maps: For a free brochure and hiking guide, write to Smith River National Recreation Area at the address below. For a map, ask the U.S. Forest Service for Six Rivers and Klamath National Forest. For a topographic map, ask the USGS for Devils Punchbowl.

Directions: From Crescent City, drive north on U.S. 101 for three miles to U.S. 199. Bear right (east) on U.S. 199 and drive 25 miles to Little Jones Creek Road/Jawbone Road (Forest Road 16). Turn right on Little Jones Creek Road (Forest Road 16) and drive south 9.6 miles. When the road forks, turn sharply left on Forest Road 16N02 and drive five miles to the trailhead, at the end of the road.

Contact: Smith River National Recreation Area, P.O. Box 228, Gasquet, CA 95543, 707/457-3131, www.fs.fed.us/r5—click on Forest Offices; Klamath National Forest, Happy Camp Ranger District, P.O. Box 377, 63822 Highway 96, Happy Camp, CA 96039-0377, 530/493-2243, www.fs.fed.us/r5—click on Forest Offices.

6 WILDERNESS FALLS
18.0 mi / 2.0 days   👫 3   ⛰ 10

in the Siskiyou Wilderness east of Crescent City

Wilderness Falls is one of the great secrets of northwestern California. It's a true hidden jewel, dramatic and pure, and not only un-touched, but largely unseen. This bubbling tower of water, created by Clear Creek, crashes down about 35 feet into a boulder then pounds its way down into a foaming pool that's 100 feet across.

The recommended route is to start on Clear Creek National Recreation Trail out of Youngs Valley (see *Youngs Valley Trail* in this chapter). Follow Clear Creek Trail for about nine miles to the waterfall. The trail features a 600-foot descent to the stream, then a gentle descent the rest of the way. There is an excellent campsite about a quarter of a mile upstream from the falls. It's an easy hike to the waterfall, but the trip back is up all the way and is best started very early in the morning, when the tempera-ture is the coolest.

Wilderness Falls can also be accessed out of Doe Flat (see *Doe Flat Trail* in this chapter), but in late May and June, this route includes a wet, cold, and slippery ford of Clear Creek. In summer, it is a much easier crossing.

User Groups: Hikers, dogs, and horses. No mountain bikes. No wheelchair facilities.

Permits: A campfire permit (free) is required for overnight use. Parking and access are free.

Maps: For a map, ask the U.S. Forest Service for Six Rivers and Klamath National Forest. For a topographic map, ask the USGS for Devils Punchbowl.

Directions: From Crescent City, drive north on U.S. 101 for three miles to U.S. 199. Bear right (east) on U.S. 199 and drive 32 miles to Forest Road 18N07. Turn right and drive five miles to Forest Road 18N07. Continue on Forest Road 18N07 for 10 miles (twisty) toward Sanger Lake. Just before Sanger Lake, bear right on Forest Road 4803 (signed Youngs Valley Trail) and drive one mile to the trailhead, at the end of the road.

Contact: Klamath National Forest, Happy Camp Ranger District, P.O. Box 377, 63822 Highway 96, Happy Camp, CA 96039-0377, 530/493-2243, www.fs.fed.us/r5—click on Forest Offices; Smith River National Recreation Area, P.O. Box 228, Gasquet, CA 95543, 707/457-3131, www.fs.fed.us/r5—click on Forest Offices.

7 ISLAND LAKE TRAIL
12.0 mi / 2.0 days

in Smith River National Recreation Area east of Crescent City

Island Lake is a mountain bowl framed by the back wall of Jedediah Mountain, a wild, primitive area where threatened spotted owls are more common than hikers. The trailhead is at the Bear Basin area. The hike starts with a walk on a portion of trail that is routed down to the South Fork Smith River, where you'll enter the untouched Siskiyou Wilderness. Enjoy the stream; the hike that follows can have some begging for the memory. The trail intersects with the old route and then rises along a mountain spine, climbing up, up, and up for what seems like an endless three miles. It finally tops a ridge and turns around a bend, where little Island Lake comes into view. A great sense of relief will wash over you.

There are two excellent camps at the lake, set in trees near the lake's shore. The trout are eager to bite, but most are very small, dinker-sized brook trout. A great afternoon side trip is to hike the rim around the lake, which is most easily done in a counterclockwise direction to the top of Jedediah Mountain—a perfect picnic site and a great lookout.

If you hiked to Island Lake in years prior to 2003, you will note that the trailhead has been moved a few miles, lengthening the distance to the lake from four miles to six miles. The purpose of this trailhead change is to keep vehicles away from the wilderness, because a fungus that is most commonly introduced from tires on vehicles threatens Port Orford cedars.

User Groups: Hikers, dogs, and horses. No mountain bikes. No wheelchair facilities.

Permits: A campfire permit is required. Parking and access are free.

Maps: For a free brochure and hiking guide, write to Smith River National Recreation Area at the address below. For a map, ask the U.S. Forest Service for Six Rivers and Klamath National Forest. For a topographic map, ask the USGS for Devils Punchbowl.

Directions: From Crescent City, drive north on U.S. 101 for three miles to U.S. 199. Bear right (east) on U.S. 199 and drive 25 miles to Little Jones Creek Road/Jawbone Road (Forest Road 16). Turn right and drive eight miles to Forest Road 16N02. Turn left and drive 2.5 miles to Forest Road 16N10. Turn right. The trailhead is located on your immediate right.

Contact: Smith River National Recreation Area, P.O. Box 228, Gasquet, CA 95543, 707/457-3131, www.fs.fed.us/r5—click on Forest Offices; Klamath National Forest, Happy Camp Ranger District, P.O. Box 377, 63822 Highway 96, Happy Camp, CA 96039-0377, 530/493-2243, www.fs.fed.us/r5—click on Forest Offices.

8 SEIAD VALLEY TO OREGON BORDER (PCT)
36.0 mi one-way / 3.0 days

in Klamath National Forest from Seiad Valley to the Siskiyou Mountains

Not many people hike this section of the Pacific Crest Trail (PCT), the northernmost segment in California. But it's a great chunk of trail, whether for a day hike or for the whole duration—all the way to Wards Fork Gap, on the edge of the Rogue Wilderness, in southern

Oregon. The ambitious few will head up from the trailhead to the junction of the Boundary National Recreation Trail, a seven-mile trip one-way. The first five miles are a steep climb out of the Klamath River Valley, rising to Upper Devils Peak, which has an elevation of 6,040 feet. This features sensational views to the south of Mount Shasta.

This hike marks the final steps of the 1,700-mile Pacific Crest Trail in California, an epic journey for all, but always classic, even if only sections are enjoyed. If you decide to attempt the south-to-north route, see the *Grider Creek to Seiad Valley (PCT)* hike in this chapter.

User Groups: Hikers, dogs, and horses. No mountain bikes. No wheelchair facilities.

Permits: No permits are required. Parking and access are free.

Maps: A trail information sheet can be obtained by contacting the Happy Camp Ranger District at the address below. For a map, ask the U.S. Forest Service for Klamath National Forest. For a topographic map, ask the USGS for Seiad Valley.

Directions: From Yreka, take I-5 north to Highway 96. Turn west on Highway 96 and drive approximately 50 miles to Seiad Valley. Continue another mile west on Highway 96 to the trailhead, on the north (right) side. Parking is minimal; park across the highway.

Contact: Klamath National Forest, Happy Camp Ranger District, P.O. Box 377, 63822 Highway 96, Happy Camp, CA 96039-0377, 530/493-2243, www.fs.fed.us/r5—click on Forest Offices.

❾ GRIDER CREEK TO SEIAD VALLEY (PCT)
7.0 mi one-way / 1.0 day

In Klamath National Forest, southeast of Happy Camp to the Grider Creek Trailhead

Most hikers use this trailhead to head south into the Marble Mountain Wilderness, not north. For PCT hikers heading south to

north, the trail is seven miles one-way, with an additional five miles of road to Seiad Valley on Highway 96. This is an excellent place for PCT hikers to pick up a food stash and dump garbage. You could walk the road, but most try to hitch a ride. The trail here follows Grider Creek, an easy descent northward as the stream pours toward the Klamath River. The only downer is that the last three miles are on a dirt Forest Service road, but for PCT hikers, it's a sign that the next restaurant is not far off. The area features magnificent stands of virgin timber—a mixed conifer forest of cedar, pine, and fir. A good Forest Service campground (Grider Creek Camp) is available about three miles before reaching Seiad Valley.

To pick up the next trail heading for the Oregon border, see the *Seiad Valley to Oregon Border (PCT)* hike in this chapter. If you are hiking this trail in reverse, see the *Etna Summit to Grider Creek (PCT)* hike in this chapter to continue south.

User Groups: Hikers, dogs, and horses. No mountain bikes. No wheelchair facilities.

Permits: A campfire permit (free) is required. Parking and access are free.

Maps: A trail information sheet can be obtained by contacting the Happy Camp Ranger District at the address below. For a map, ask the U.S. Forest Service for Klamath National Forest. For a topographic map, ask the USGS for Seiad Valley.

Directions: From Yreka, take I-5 north to Highway 96. Turn west on Highway 96 and drive approximately 40 miles to Walker Creek/Grider Creek Road (Forest Road 46N64), located one mile before Seiad Valley. Turn left on Walker Creek Road and drive about 50 feet (staying to the left as it runs adjacent to the Klamath River) to Grider Creek Road. Turn right and drive two miles to the trailhead.

Contact: Klamath National Forest, Happy Camp Ranger District, P.O. Box 377, 63822 Highway 96, Happy Camp, CA 96039-0377, 530/493-2243, www.fs.fed.us/r5—click on Forest Offices.

🔟 HAYPRESS MEADOWS TRAILHEAD

29.0 mi / 3.0 days   🚶3   ⛺8

In the Marble Mountain Wilderness near Somes Bar

BEST (

The Cuddihy Lakes basin is one of the prettiest sections of the Marble Mountain Wilderness. It also is home to one of the largest concentrations of bears anywhere in California. This is a great trip, leading out to One Mile Lake and the Cuddihy Lakes. This area is perfect for backpacking, with beauty, lookouts, and good trail access.

Park at the trailhead (at 4,500 feet), then begin the first two miles of trail, up and across a fir-covered slope of a small peak (a little butt-kicker of a climb). Then the trail descends into Haypress Meadows, a major junction. Turn right and head up Sandy Ridge, which is a long, steady climb. Plan to top the ridge and then camp at Monument Lake, Meteor Lake, One Mile Lake, or Cuddihy Lakes. The view from Sandy Ridge is a sweeping lookout of the Marble Mountains to the east and the Siskiyous to the west, with mountaintop glimpses of Mount Shasta and the Marble Rim.

User Groups: Hikers, dogs, and horses. No mountain bikes. No wheelchair facilities.

Permits: A campfire permit (free) is required for overnight use. Parking and access are free.

Maps: A trail information sheet can be obtained by contacting the Ukonom Ranger District at the address below. For a map, ask the U.S. Forest Service for Klamath National Forest or Marble Mountain Wilderness. For a topographic map, ask the USGS for Somes Bar.

Directions: From Willow Creek, at the junction of Highways 299 and 96, take Highway 96 north (twisty at first) for 42 miles to Orleans. Continue eight miles to Somes Bar and Salmon River Road. Turn right on Salmon River Road (Highway 93) and drive 100 feet to a sign that says Camp 3/Haypress Trailhead

and Forest Road 15N17 (Offield Mountain Road). Turn left and drive 14.6 miles to Forest Road 15N17E. Turn left and drive 1.5 miles to the access road for Haypress trailhead. Turn left and drive one mile to the trailhead.

Contact: Klamath National Forest, Orleans Ranger District, P.O. Box 410, Orleans, CA 95556-0410, 530/627-3291, www.fs.fed.us/r5—click on Forest Offices.

🔢 SPIRIT LAKE TRAIL

34.0 mi / 4.0 days   🚶3   ⛺10

In the Marble Mountain Wilderness near Somes Bar

BEST (

We've hiked to hundreds and hundreds of mountain lakes, and Spirit Lake is one of the prettiest we've ever seen. It sits at the bottom of a mountain bowl encircled by old-growth trees, with a few campsites set at the side of the lake. The Karuk tribe considers this a sacred place. The abundance of wildlife can be remarkable. The far side of the lake is a major deer migration route, an osprey makes regular trips to pluck trout out of the lake for dinner, and the fishing is quite good, especially early in the summer.

Spirit Lake can be the feature destination for a week-long backpack loop, beginning on Haypress Meadows Trail and leading up to Sandy Ridge and then out to the lake, about 17 miles one-way. Most hikers will stop for the night at One Mile or the Cuddihy Lakes on the way out, and that is why those two areas get so much use. Spirit Lake is best visited during the first week of June, when the nights are still cold, the people are few, and the area abounds with fish and deer.

User Groups: Hikers, dogs, and horses. No mountain bikes. No wheelchair facilities.

Permits: A campfire permit (free) is required for overnight use. Parking and access are free.

Maps: A trail information sheet can be obtained by contacting the Ukonom Ranger

SHASTA HIKING

District at the address below. For a map, ask the U.S. Forest Service for Klamath National Forest or Marble Mountain Wilderness. For a topographic map, ask the USGS for Somes Bar.

Directions: From Willow Creek, at the junction of Highways 299 and 96, take Highway 96 north (twisty at first) for 42 miles to Orleans. Continue eight miles to Somes Bar and Salmon River Road. Turn right on Salmon River Road (Highway 93) and drive 100 feet to a sign that says Camp 3/Haypress Trailhead and Forest Road 15N17 (Offield Mountain Road). Turn left and drive 14.6 miles to Forest Road 15N17E. Turn left and drive 1.5 miles to the access road for Haypress trailhead. Turn left and drive one mile to the trailhead.

Contact: Klamath National Forest, Orleans Ranger District, P.O. Box 410, Orleans, CA 95556-0410, 530/627-3291, www.fs.fed .us/r5—click on Forest Offices.

12 KELSEY CREEK TRAIL
18.0 mi / 2.0 days   🏃3 ⛰9

in the Marble Mountain Wilderness west of Yreka

This section of the Kelsey Creek Trail offers many miles of beautiful streamside travel, with Paradise Lake basin as the intended destination for most hikers on this route. The trailhead for this section is set near the confluence of Kelsey Creek and the Scott River, and from there, the trail follows Kelsey Creek upstream. Wildflowers are abundant in the meadows. After four miles and two creek crossings, you'll reach Maple Falls, one of the few waterfalls in the region. The trail continues up the canyon, finally rising to intersect with the Pacific Crest Trail, just below Red Rock. From this junction, hikers have many options. The closest lake is secluded Bear Lake, a pretty spot but, alas, with some tules and mosquitoes. To reach it from the junction requires a short but steep drop into the basin to the immediate west.

User Groups: Hikers, dogs, and horses. No mountain bikes. No wheelchair facilities.

Permits: A campfire permit (free) is required for overnight use. Parking and access are free.

Maps: A trail information sheet can be obtained by contacting the Scott River Ranger District at the address below. For a map, ask the U.S. Forest Service for Klamath National Forest or Marble Mountain Wilderness. For topographic maps, ask the USGS for Scott Bar and Grider Valley.

Directions: From Redding, take I-5 to Yreka and the exit for Highway 3/Fort Jones. Take that exit to the stop sign, turn left, and drive a short distance to the lighted intersection. Turn left on Highway 3 and drive 16.5 miles to Fort Jones and Scott River Road. Turn right on Scott River Road and drive 16.8 miles to the Scott River Bridge. Cross it and then turn left immediately, following the road for 0.3 mile. Bear right on another dirt road (do not continue to a second bridge) and drive 0.25 mile to the trailhead.

Contact: Klamath National Forest, Salmon River & Scott River Ranger Districts, 11263 North Highway 3, Fort Jones, CA 96032-9702, 530/468-5351, www.fs.fed.us/r5—click on Forest Offices.

13 PARADISE LAKE TRAIL
4.0 mi / 2.75 hr   🏃3 ⛰8

in the Marble Mountain Wilderness west of Yreka

Paradise Lake, set at an elevation of 5,920 feet, is the easiest lake to reach of the 79 lakes in the Marble Mountain Wilderness. The pretty hike is short enough for a day trip, and it has good lakeside campgrounds if you want to turn your trip into an overnighter. There are also some excellent side trips, including climbing Kings Castle (see the following hike), which tops the mountain rim on the back side of the lake.

From the trailhead (at 4,880 feet), the route

quickly enters the designated wilderness, then climbs for nearly two miles (steeply in some areas) and switches back and forth through an old, untouched forest. It then emerges from the trees and rises to a saddle. On the other side is Paradise Lake. It is nestled in a mountain pocket, emerald green and peaceful. Paradise Lake is a mostly shallow lake with few trout, but it does have one deep area. Because the hike to the lake takes only two hours, there are usually campers here all summer long.

User Groups: Hikers, dogs, and horses. No mountain bikes. No wheelchair facilities.

Permits: No permits are required. A campfire permit (free) is required for overnight use. Parking and access are free.

Maps: A trail information sheet can be obtained by contacting the Scott River Ranger District at the address below. For a map, ask the U.S. Forest Service for Klamath National Forest or Marble Mountain Wilderness. For topographic maps, ask the USGS for Scott Bar and Marble Mountain.

Directions: From Redding, take I-5 to Yreka and the exit for Highway 3/Fort Jones. Take that exit to the stop sign, turn left, and drive a short distance to the lighted intersection. Turn left on Highway 3 and drive 16.5 miles to Fort Jones. Turn right on Scott River Road and drive 16.8 miles to the turnoff for Indian Scotty Campground. Cross the concrete bridge, bear left on Forest Road 44N45, and drive about five miles. Turn right on an unmarked forest road and drive six miles (signed Paradise Lake) to the trailhead, near the wilderness border.

Contact: Klamath National Forest, Salmon River & Scott River Ranger Districts, 11263 North Highway 3, Fort Jones, CA 96032-9702, 530/468-5351, www.fs.fed.us/r5—click on Forest Offices.

▌14 KINGS CASTLE TRAIL
5.5 mi / 5.0 hr   ⛹4 ⛰10

in the Marble Mountain Wilderness west of Yreka

Kings Castle is the imposing perch that sits on the back side of Paradise Lake. From the lake, a half-mile climb tops out at the summit at 7,405 feet. It's a great hike with unforgettable views. You look down at little Paradise Lake as well as far beyond to Northern California's most famous mountain peaks. From the trailhead of Paradise Lake Trail (see previous detailed hike), you make the 1,040-foot climb up to Paradise Lake. From the foot of Paradise Lake, bear to the left and cross the lake's inlet, on the left side. Here you will pick up the route. It climbs up out of the basin to a ridge (great views start here). The trail bears to the left up the back side of the rock monolith. You then gain the peak of Kings Castle by climbing a series of switchbacks up the back side. It is a special trip every step of the way. It's a climb of 2,525 feet from the trailhead. Although not a maintained trail, the route is worn well enough to follow. On the first trip here, this guy didn't see the trail and instead scrambled up the face, bushwhacking it—a difficult ascent, steep all the way, and scrambling up the face. On the top, he was congratulating himself for being such an intrepid mountaineer, when right then, these two Girl Scouts came bounding up to the summit, easy and happy. "How'd you get here?" he asked. "We just took the trail," one answered. "Trail? What trail?" Guess who the misled guy was: Yep, you guessed it.

User Groups: Hikers only. No dogs, horses, or mountain bikes. No wheelchair facilities.

Permits: No permits are required. A campfire permit (free) is required for overnight use. Parking and access are free.

Maps: A trail information sheet can be obtained by contacting the Scott River Ranger District at the address below. For a map, ask the U.S. Forest Service for Klamath National

SHASTA HIKING

Forest or Marble Mountain Wilderness. For topographic maps, ask the USGS for Scott Bar and Marble Mountain.

Directions: From Redding, take I-5 to Yreka and the exit for Highway 3/Fort Jones. Take that exit to the stop sign, turn left, and drive a short distance to the lighted intersection. Turn left on Highway 3 and drive 16.5 miles to Fort Jones. Turn right on Scott River Road and drive 16.8 miles to the turnoff for Indian Scotty Campground. Cross the concrete bridge, bear left on forest road 44N45, and drive about five miles. Turn right on an unmarked forest road and drive six miles (signed Paradise Lake) to the trailhead near the wilderness border. Hike 1.9 miles to Paradise Lake; bear right and continue another 0.5 mile to Kings Castle.

Contact: Klamath National Forest, Salmon River & Scott River Ranger Districts, 11263 North Highway 3, Fort Jones, CA 96032-9702, 530/468-5351, www.fs.fed.us/r5—click on Forest Offices.

15 MARBLE MOUNTAIN RIM
16.0 mi / 2.0 days   🏃3 ⛰9

In the Marble Mountain Wilderness west of Yreka

Marble isn't usually thought of as a precious stone, but it's gemlike for hikers on this trail. With Marble Valley nearby, climbing the Marble Mountain Rim can be a perfect weekend trip and is easily extended into a longer one. The trailhead at Lovers Camp is probably the most popular in the entire wilderness, especially for packers going by horse into Marble Mountain Wilderness (corrals are available at the trailhead). The route heads up Canyon Creek, a moderate climb, then intersects the Pacific Crest Trail at Marble Valley. This area is very scenic, with lots of deer and wildflowers. Turn left, and the trail crosses the flank of Marble Mountain itself. Once you've arrived, a side trip to the Marble Rim is

mandatory. The views are stunning, sweeping in both directions, with steep drop-offs adding to the quiet drama. The rock itself is unlike anything else in Northern California—a mix of black, red, and tan marble, something you'll never forget.

User Groups: Hikers only. No dogs, horses, or mountain bikes. No wheelchair facilities.

Permits: A campfire permit (free) is required for overnight use. Parking and access are free.

Maps: A trail information sheet can be obtained by contacting the Scott River Ranger District at the address below. For a map, ask the U.S. Forest Service for Klamath National Forest or Marble Mountain Wilderness. For topographic maps, ask the USGS for Scott Bar and Marble Mountain.

Directions: From Redding, take I-5 to Yreka and the exit for Highway 3/Fort Jones. Take that exit to the stop sign, turn left, and drive a short distance to the lighted intersection. Turn left on Highway 3 and drive 16.5 miles to Fort Jones. Turn right on Scott River Road and drive 16.8 miles to the turnoff for Indian Scotty Campground. Cross the concrete bridge, bear left on Forest Road 44N45, and drive 5.4 miles to Forest Road 43N45. Turn left and drive 1.7 miles to Lovers Camp. Bear right and drive 0.1 mile to the trailhead.

Contact: Klamath National Forest, Salmon River & Scott River Ranger Districts, 11263 North Highway 3, Fort Jones, CA 96032-9702, 530/468-5351, www.fs.fed.us/r5—click on Forest Offices.

16 SKY HIGH LAKES
14.0 mi / 2.0 days   🏃3 ⛰8

In the Marble Mountain Wilderness west of Yreka

The Sky High Lakes make for a great overnighter, a seven-mile hike each day, or an inspired one-day in-and-outer. The trip starts at the Canyon Creek trailhead near Lovers

Camp. For this trip, take Canyon Creek Trail for about a mile up to a fork, and continue straight (do not turn left and cross Canyon Creek). From here the trail continues to climb, skirting below Marble Mountain, and eventually to Lower Sky High Lake. This is your destination, set below a monster of a rock, Peak 6817. Upper Sky High Lake provides a side jaunt. Note that the trail continues to climb up to the rim and hooks up with the Pacific Crest Trail, making an 18-mile loop trip possible.

User Groups: Hikers, dogs, and horses. No mountain bikes. No wheelchair facilities.

Permits: A campfire permit is required only for hikers planning to camp in the wilderness. Parking and access are free.

Maps: A trail information sheet can be obtained by contacting the Scott River Ranger District at the address below. For a map, ask the U.S. Forest Service for Klamath National Forest or Marble Mountain Wilderness. For a topographic map, ask the USGS for Marble Mountain.

Directions: From Redding, take I-5 to Yreka and the exit for Highway 3/Fort Jones. Take that exit to the stop sign, turn left, and drive a short distance to the lighted intersection. Turn left on Highway 3 and drive 16.5 miles to Fort Jones. Turn right on Scott River Road and drive 16.8 miles to the turnoff for Indian Scotty Campground. Cross the concrete bridge, bear left on Forest Road 44N45, and drive 5.4 miles to Forest Road 43N45. Turn left and drive 1.7 miles to Lovers Camp. Bear right and drive 0.1 mile to the Canyon Creek trailhead.

Contact: Klamath National Forest, Salmon River & Scott River Ranger Districts, 11263 North Highway 3, Fort Jones, CA 96032-9702, 530/468-5351, www.fs.fed.us/r5—click on Forest Offices.

🔢17 SHACKLEFORD CREEK TRAIL
13.0 mi / 2.0 days

in the Marble Mountain Wilderness west of Yreka

Campbell, Cliff, and Summit Lakes are three pretty lakes in the Marble Mountain Wilderness. It is only 5.5 miles to Campbell Lake, reachable via the Shackleford Trail, which makes this a popular destination all summer long. The trail is routed up Shackleford Creek to a basin set just below the Pacific Crest Trail. Here you'll find the series of small mountain lakes.

Note that ambitious trekkers traveling off-trail, cross-country style, can create routes to little Gem, Jewel, and Angel Lakes. Trekking is not for everybody, however, which is why this trip rates a 4. If you want to extend the trip into a loop, you can hike up to the rim of the Pacific Crest Trail, then turn right and go three miles to the Sky High Lakes.

User Groups: Hikers, dogs, and horses. No mountain bikes. No wheelchair facilities.

Permits: A campfire permit is required only for hikers planning to camp in the wilderness. Parking and access are free.

Maps: A trail information sheet can be obtained by contacting the Scott River Ranger District at the address below. For a map, ask the U.S. Forest Service for Klamath National Forest or Marble Mountain Wilderness. For a topographic map, ask the USGS for Boulder Peak.

Directions: From Redding, take I-5 to Yreka and the exit for Highway 3/Fort Jones. Take that exit to the stop sign, turn left, and drive a short distance to the lighted intersection. Turn left on Highway 3 and drive 16.5 miles to Fort Jones and Scott River Road. Turn right on Scott River Road and drive seven miles to Quartz Valley Road. Turn left on Quartz Valley Road and drive about four miles to the sign for Shackleford trailhead and Forest Road 43N21. Turn right and drive 6.5 miles to the trailhead, at the end of the road.

Contact: Klamath National Forest, Salmon River & Scott River Ranger Districts, 11263 North Highway 3, Fort Jones, CA 96032-9702, 530/468-5351, www.fs.fed.us/r5—click on Forest Offices.

18 MULE BRIDGE TRAILHEAD
28.0 mi / 4.0 days
🚶5 ⛺8

In the Marble Mountain Wilderness west of Etna

The trailhead at Mule Bridge is set alongside the Salmon River, and once you've tightened your backpack, get ready for a long climb up the river drainage. The trail follows the Salmon River all the way up to its headwaters, gaining about 3,500 feet in the process. Plan on climbing for 14 or 15 miles along the river until you start reaching the higher country, where there are many lakeside camps. The trail forks eight miles from the trailhead. The right-hand fork leads to Shelly Meadows and the Pacific Crest Trail.

The main trail continues north for access to Upper Abbotts Camp and many lakes in the upper drainage. This trail ties in with Little North Fork Trail near Hancock Lake. The prettiest glacial-formed lakes in this region are Lake of the Island (12-mile hike), Abbott Lake (13-mile hike), and Lake Ethel (14-mile hike). Even more remote lakes are Wooley Lake, Milne Lake, and Osprey Lake. All of these are hard to reach and require cross-country travel. Several other lakes are in the region, allowing this trek to be extended by several days.

User Groups: Hikers, dogs, and horses. No mountain bikes. No wheelchair facilities.

Permits: A campfire permit (free) is required for campfires and stoves. Parking and access are free.

Maps: A trail information sheet can be obtained by contacting the Salmon Ranger District at the address below. For a map, ask the U.S. Forest Service for Klamath National Forest or Marble Mountain Wilderness. For a topographic map, ask the USGS for Sawyers Bar.

Directions: From Redding, take I-5 to Yreka and the exit for Highway 3/Fort Jones. Take that exit to the stop sign, turn left, and drive a short distance to the lighted intersection. Turn left on Highway 3 and drive southwest 28 miles to Etna. Turn west on Etna-Somes Bar Road (which is Main Street in town) and drive 21 miles to Idlewild Campground. As you enter the campground, take the left fork in the road and continue two miles to the trailhead.

Contact: Klamath National Forest, Salmon River & Scott River Ranger Districts, 11263 North Highway 3, Fort Jones, CA 96032-9702, 530/468-5351, www.fs.fed.us/r5—click on Forest Offices.

19 LITTLE NORTH FORK TRAILHEAD
16.0 mi / 2-3.0 days
🚶4 ⛺7

In the Marble Mountain Wilderness near Sawyers Bar

Your destination options from this trailhead? There are many: Chimney Rock, Clear Lake, Lily Lake, and Chimney Rock Lake. This trail provides an excellent trip—as long as you don't mind the long grind of a climb to reach the lakes. Like a lot of trails on the edge of the wilderness, this one starts with a long haul out of a river canyon. From the Little North Fork trailhead, start by climbing out toward Chimney Rock, grunting out a rise of about 4,000 feet as you leave the river lowlands and reach the Marble Mountain Wilderness. It's about an eight-mile trip to Clear Lake, a good first day's destination. Although you can simply return the next day, most people will take several days to venture deeper into the wilderness, with 13 lakes and 20 miles of stream in the Upper Abbotts Camp and English Peak areas.

User Groups: Hikers, dogs, and horses. No mountain bikes. No wheelchair facilities.

Permits: A campfire permit (free) is required for campfires and stove. Parking and access are free.

Maps: A trail information sheet can be obtained by contacting the Salmon Ranger District at the address below. For a map, ask the U.S. Forest Service for Klamath National Forest or Marble Mountain Wilderness. For a topographic map, ask the USGS for Sawyers Bar.

Directions: From Redding, take I-5 to Yreka and the exit for Highway 3/Fort Jones. Take that exit to the stop sign, turn left, and drive a short distance to the lighted intersection. Turn left on Highway 3 and drive southwest 28 miles to Etna at Sawyers Bar Road. Turn west on Sawyers Bar Road and drive about 25 miles to Sawyers Bar. Continue west on the same road for four miles to Little North Fork Road (Forest Road 40N51). Turn right (north) and drive two miles to the trailhead, at the end of the road.

Contact: Klamath National Forest, Salmon River & Scott River Ranger Districts, 11263 North Highway 3, Fort Jones, CA 96032-9702, 530/468-5351, www.fs.fed.us/r5—click on Forest Offices.

20 HORSE TRAIL RIDGE NATIONAL RECREATION TRAIL

13.0 mi one-way / 2.0 days 3 ◣5

In Six Rivers National Forest on the western edge of the Trinity Alps Wilderness east of Hoopa

This is one of the lesser-known national recreation trails in the western United States, but it has many excellent features, and, alas, a few negative ones as well. The six-mile trip to Mill Creek Lakes is set in the least-explored western sector of the Trinity Alps. Although some of the region has been burned severely by wildfire, the Mill Creek Lakes area remains untouched by fire, like an island of green, and makes for a good overnighter.

From the trailhead (at 4,800 feet), the grades are gradual, with relatively easy elevation climbs and descents. A majority of the forest along the trail was burned in the 1999 Megram fire. While there are many continuous stretches of burned areas, there are also pockets of greenery that the fire missed and ground-level vegetation is making a good comeback. In all, the fire affects 10 miles of this route.

Special note: Do not drink the water available here without first treating it with the best filtration system you can afford.

User Groups: Hikers, dogs, and horses. No mountain bikes. No wheelchair facilities.

Permits: A wilderness permit is required for hikers planning on camping. Parking and access are free.

Maps: For a map, ask the U.S. Forest Service for Six Rivers National Forest. For topographic maps, ask the USGS for Tish Tang Point and Trinity Mountain.

Directions: From the Arcata area, take Highway 299 east to Willow Creek and Highway 96. Turn north on Highway 96 and drive about 12 miles into Hoopa Valley to Big Hill Road. Turn right (east) on Big Hill Road and drive 11 miles to the Six Rivers National Forest border (the road becomes Forest Road 8N01). Continue for 4.5 miles (the road becomes Forest Road 10N02) to the Redcap Trailhead (once off Hoopa reservation land, stay on the chip-seal road).

Contact: Six Rivers National Forest, Lower Trinity Ranger District, P.O. Box 68, Willow Creek, CA 95573, 530/629-2118, www.fs .fed.us/r5—click on Forest Offices.

21 LITTLE SOUTH FORK LAKE TRAIL

13.0 mi / 2.0 days 🚶5 ⛰10

in the Trinity Alps Wilderness near Cecilville

You have to be a little bit crazy to try this trip, and that's why we signed up. This is one of the most difficult lakes to reach in California. Yet Little South Fork Lake has two idyllic campsites, excellent swimming, and large trout. This route is largely off trail and requires skirting around a big waterfall, but there's no better way in—we've tried three different routes. If you want an easy, clearly marked trail, this is not the hike for you.

From the South Fork trailhead, the trip starts out easy enough. Start by hiking four miles along the Salmon River until reaching the Little South Fork Creek. Turn up the trail upstream along Little South Fork Creek. The trail quickly becomes faint and starts to resemble a game trail—this is where so many people give up. The trail eventually dead-ends into Little South Fork Creek. (A faint route on the other side of the creek, the north side, climbs through brush and up the canyon, and should be avoided.) From here, there is no trail available; the best route, though still steep and very difficult, is to lateral across the slope on the right side of the stream. It is 1.25 miles upstream to a beautiful, pristine waterfall. Pal Michael Furniss named it Crystal Falls.

To get around the waterfall, loop back and circle it to the right; if you go to the left (which we've tried), you'll add several dreadful hours to the trip scrambling on all fours straight up the slope. Remember that there is no trail and no marked route; this is a cross-country scramble and very slow going. It's another 1.25 miles to the lake, which can take hours of hiking up and across the wooded slope until you emerge from the forest onto granite plates. Ahead is the lake, beautifully set in a rock bowl framed by a high back wall. There are excellent campsites at each end of the lake.

We hiked into this lake once from Caribou Lakes by climbing the Sawtooth Ridge and dropping down into the basin—the entire route, also off trail, but that creates a potentially hazardous proposition, with some rock climbing and descents with packs. On another trip from Caribou Lakes, we dropped down into Little South Fork Canyon, losing thousands of feet in altitude and in the process getting caught in a brush field like bugs in a spider web. Neither of these other two routes is recommended. In fact, the suggested route is not recommended either. One ranger said we were crazy to include it in the book. He was right, of course.

User Groups: Hikers only. Dogs are permitted but strongly advised against. No horses or mountain bikes. No wheelchair facilities.

Permits: A free wilderness permit is required for hikers planning to camp.

Maps: For a map, ask the U.S. Forest Service for Klamath National Forest or Trinity Alps Wilderness. For a topographic map, ask the USGS for Thompson Peak.

Directions: From Redding, drive north on I-5 for 70 miles. Just past Weed, take the Edgewood exit. At the stop sign, turn left and drive through the underpass to another stop sign. Turn right on Old Highway 99 and drive about six miles to Gazelle. Turn left on Gazelle-Callahan Road and drive 27 miles to Callahan. From Callahan on Highway 3, turn west on Cecilville Road and drive 28 miles to Caribou Road/County Road 1E003 (across from East Fork Campground). Turn left (south) on Caribou Road and drive 3.5 miles to a fork. Bear left at the fork and drive 2.5 miles to the South Fork trailhead.

Contact: Klamath National Forest, Salmon River & Scott River Ranger Districts, 11263 North Highway 3, Fort Jones, CA 96032-9702, 530/468-5351, www.fs.fed.us/r5—click on Forest Offices.

22 GRIZZLY LAKE

12.0 mi / 2.0 days or
38.0 mi / 5.0 days   👥5 ⛰10

in the Trinity Alps Wilderness north of
Junction City

BEST (

This is a butt-kicker climb to Grizzly Lake, the signature lake in the Trinity Alps. The lake is gorgeous (and we'll get to that), the trek is just plain hard (we'll get to that, too), but the surprise is that despite the extreme difficulty there always seem to be folks here in the summer. You only seem to get it to yourself in the fall, when the nights are cold.

Grizzly Lake is set below awesome Thompson Peak (8,863 feet), with one of the most beautiful wilderness waterfalls anywhere, 80-foot Grizzly Falls, set at the lake's cliff outfall. The lake is so pristine that you can spend hours just looking at it.

There are two ways to get in. Take your pick: From the China Creek trailhead, a butt-kicking six-mile climb with a 5,000-foot elevation gain (with a 1,500-foot canyon descent included on the way); or from the Hobo Gulch trailhead, a moderate grade over the course of 19 miles to make the lake.

Given a choice, most people take the short, butt-kicker route, then cuss at themselves on the way in for doing so. There is almost nothing rewarding about it, and most complete the trip with head down, trying to think about something else. Before you race off to this destination, think long and hard if you really are ready to pay a terrible physical toll to get there. Surprisingly, many do this regardless of the price, and the place gets fairly heavy use.

Or, on the other hand, you could take the longer but more gradual climb from the Hobo Gulch trailhead, set deep in the national forest along Backbone Ridge. On this route, Grizzly Lake is 19 miles away. There's also some forest fire damage along the route. So instead of camping along lakes, hikers camp along pretty streams and flats, taking days to reach the promised land at Grizzly Lake. The trail from Hobo Gulch starts by heading straight north about five miles along the North Fork Trinity River to Rattlesnake Camp, climbing very gently. Cross Rattlesnake Creek, and continue another three miles past the old Morrison Cabin (from the mining days) and on to Pfeiffer Flat. Here the North Fork Trinity is joined by Grizzly Creek, an attractive backpacking destination. From Pfeiffer Flat, the trail follows Grizzly Creek, rising high toward the Trinity Sawtooth Ridge and requiring an uphill pull to beautiful Grizzly Meadows and then to Grizzly Lake; the final mile is a scramble over a clear hiking route amid rock.

For rock climbers, climbing the lake bowl in a clockwise direction makes for an exciting scramble to Thompson Peak and a perch just below the rock summit; to reach the tip-top of the mountain requires a technical climb.

User Groups: Hikers, dogs, and horses. No mountain bikes. No wheelchair facilities.

Permits: A wilderness permit is required for hikers planning to camp.

Maps: For a map, ask the U.S. Forest Service for Shasta-Trinity National Forest or Trinity Alps Wilderness. For a topographic map, ask the USGS for Thurston Peaks.

Directions: To reach the China Creek trailhead from Redding, drive north on I-5 for 70 miles. Just past Weed, take the Edgewood exit. At the stop sign, turn left and drive through the underpass to another stop sign. Turn right on Old Highway 99 and drive about six miles to Gazelle. Turn left on Gazelle-Callahan Road and drive 27 miles to Callahan and Cecilville Road. Turn west on Cecilville Road and drive 27 miles to Forest Road 37N24. Turn south and drive 3.8 miles to Forest Road 37N07 (it's well signed). Take Forest 37N07 and drive six miles to the trailhead.

To reach the Hobo Gulch trailhead from Weaverville, drive 13 miles west on Highway 299 to Helena and East Fork Road. Turn north on East Fork Road (County Road 421) and drive 3.9 miles to Hobo Gulch Road. Turn left on Hobo Gulch Road (Forest Road 34N07Y) and drive 12 miles to the Hobo Gulch trailhead, located at Hobo Gulch Campground, at the end of the road.

Contact: Shasta-Trinity National Forest, Weaverville Ranger Station, P.O. Box 1190, 210 Main Street, Weaverville, CA 96093, 530/623-2121, www.fs.fed.us/r5—click on Forest Offices.

23 TREE OF HEAVEN TRAIL
3.5 mi / 2.0 hr   🏃1 ⛰7

on the Klamath River in Klamath National Forest northwest of Yreka

The trail out of the Tree of Heaven Campground provides one of the few streamside trails anywhere along the Klamath River. Heading downstream along the Klamath, it's a level path routed through heavy vegetation and at times provides direct river access. The fall is an excellent time for berry picking. The trail ends at a good fishing access spot, but the fishing is poor during the prime camping/hiking/vacation season. Salmon start arriving in September; steelhead in November and December. The Tree of Heaven River access is also a good take-out point for rafters and drift boaters making the all-day run down from Iron Canyon Dam.

User Groups: Hikers, dogs, horses, and mountain bikes. No wheelchair facilities.

Permits: No permits are required. Parking and access are free.

Maps: For a map, ask the U.S. Forest Service for Klamath National Forest. For a topographic map, ask the USGS for Badger Mountain.

Directions: From Yreka, drive north on I-5 for 10 miles to the Highway 96 exit. Turn west on Highway 96 and drive about five miles. Look for the Tree of Heaven Campground, on the left. The trailhead is located at the west end of the campground.

Contact: Klamath National Forest, Salmon River & Scott River Ranger Districts, 11263 North Highway 3, Fort Jones, CA 96032-

9702, 530/468-5351, www.fs.fed.us/r5—click on Forest Offices.

24 JUANITA LAKE TRAIL
1.75 mi / 1.0 hr   🏃1 ⛰7

in Klamath National Forest east of Yreka

Not many people know about Juanita Lake, including many Siskiyou County residents, but once they find out, on their first visit, they often will take this easy loop trail around the lake to get a feel for the place. The lake is set in a mixed conifer forest, though few trees here are large. Wildlife in the area includes osprey and bald eagles. In the last hour of light during summer, both osprey and eagles occasionally make a fishing trip to the lake. Juanita Lake is a small lake that provides lakeside camping and fishing for brook trout—it's stocked with 2,000 per year. The small fishing piers are wheelchair accessible.

A good side trip is driving on the forest road up to Ball Mountain, about two miles southwest of the lake, for great views of Mount Shasta from the 7,786-foot summit.

User Groups: Hikers and leashed dogs. No mountain bikes or horses. The fishing piers are wheelchair accessible.

Permits: No permits are required. Parking and access are free.

Maps: For a map, ask the U.S. Forest Service for Klamath National Forest. For a topographic map, ask the USGS for Panther Rock.

Directions: From Redding, take I-5 north about 60 miles to the exit for Central Weed/Klamath Falls (Highway 97). Take that exit to the stop sign, turn right and drive 0.5 mile to the intersection with Highway 97. Bear right (north) on Highway 97 and drive 35 miles to Ball Mountain Road. Turn left and drive two miles to a signed turnoff for Juanita Lake. Turn right and drive about three miles to the lake (it's well signed). The trailhead is near the boat dock at the campground.

Contact: Klamath National Forest, Goosenest

Ranger District, 37805 Highway 97, Macdoel, CA 96058, 530/398-4391, fax 530/398-4599, www.fs.fed.us/r5—click on Forest Offices.

25 DEER MOUNTAIN
4.0 mi / 2.25 hr

in Klamath National Forest north of Mount Shasta

Deer Mountain is the second in a line of small peaks set on the north side of Mount Shasta that extend all the way to the Medicine Lake wildlands. North from Shasta, the first peak is the Whaleback, at an elevation of 8,528 feet, and the second is Deer Mountain, at 7,006 feet. Starting elevation at the parking area is 6,200 feet, and from here you climb 800 feet through forest consisting of various pines and firs to gain the summit. This route gets very little use, even though it's easy to reach and the destination is a mountaintop. Most out-of-towners visiting this area are attracted to the trails on Mount Shasta instead, and most locals just plain overlook it. These slopes get heavy use by hunters, usually from late September through late October.

User Groups: Hikers, dogs, horses, and mountain bikes. No wheelchair facilities.

Permits: No permits are required. Parking and access are free.

Maps: For a map, ask the U.S. Forest Service for Klamath National Forest. For a topographic map, ask the USGS for Whaleback.

Directions: From Redding, take I-5 north about 60 miles to the exit for Central Weed/Klamath Falls (Highway 97). Take that exit to the stop sign, turn right and drive 0.5 mile to the intersection with Highway 97. Bear right (north) on Highway 97 and drive about 15 miles to Deer Mountain Road/Forest Road 19 (Forest Road 42N12). Turn right and drive four miles to Deer Mountain Snowmobile Park and Forest Road 44N23. Turn left on Forest Road 44N23 and drive about two miles. There is no designated trailhead; park

off the road and hike cross-country to the top of the mountain. Forest Road 43N69 loops around the base of the mountain; you may also hike from anywhere along that road.

Contact: Klamath National Forest, Goosenest Ranger District, 37805 Highway 97, Macdoel, CA 96058, 530/398-4391, fax 530/398-4599, www.fs.fed.us/r5—click on Forest Offices.

26 THE WHALEBACK
3.0 mi / 2.5 hr

in Klamath National Forest north of Mount Shasta

After you pass Mount Shasta on I-5, driving north, look off to your right and you'll see a large, humplike mountain that sits directly north of Shasta. It looks like a huge volcanic bump that was born when Shasta was active. That's because it is. This is the Whaleback, 8,528 feet high. It provides a hike with a payoff view at the top, and a surprise: a large crater. The Whaleback Summit is actually a volcanic cinder cone with a collapsed center. This interesting geology, along with the unsurpassed view of Mount Shasta to the south, makes this a first-rate hike. Yet almost nobody tries it, most likely because they don't realize how near you can drive to the top, or because there is no formal trail. After parking at the gate, you just hike cross-country style up to the rim; it's steep all the way. The 1.5-mile hike is a scramble only in a few places. In the process, you'll climb 1,100 feet, from a starting elevation of 7,400 feet, to Whaleback Rim.

User Groups: Hikers, dogs, horses, and mountain bikes. No wheelchair facilities.

Permits: No permits are required. Parking and access are free.

Maps: For a map, ask the U.S. Forest Service for Klamath National Forest. For a topographic map, ask the USGS for Whaleback.

Directions: From Redding, take I-5 north about 60 miles to the exit for Central Weed/Klamath Falls (Highway 97). Take that exit to the stop sign, turn right and drive 0.5 mile to the intersection with Highway 97. Bear right (north) on Highway 97 and drive 15 miles to Deer Mountain Road. Turn right on Deer Mountain Road and drive four miles to Deer Mountain Snowmobile Park. Drive east on Deer Mountain Road/Forest Road 19 (Forest Road 42N12) for three miles to Forest Road 42N24. Turn right on Forest Road 42N24 and drive three miles to a gate. Park and hike in. There is no designated trail; you must hike cross-country from the road. The peak is about 1.5 miles from the gate.

Contact: Klamath National Forest, Goosenest Ranger District, 37805 Highway 97, Macdoel, CA 96058, 530/398-4391, fax 530/398-4599, www.fs.fed.us/r5—click on Forest Offices.

27 WHITNEY FALLS TRAILHEAD

3.4 mi / 2.5 hr

on the northwest slope of Mount Shasta

Mount Shasta, at 14,162 feet, is the most prominent landmark in Northern California, and it's well known for its outstanding summit routes on its southern slopes. What is less known, however, is that there are four trailheads set on Shasta's northern and eastern foothills that grant hikers choice day walks and mountaineers a starting point for difficult climbs over glaciers to the top. Those four forgotten trailheads are at Whitney Falls, North Gate, Brewer Creek, and Clear Creek.

The Whitney Falls trailhead is at about 5,600 feet, and from it, the trail heads uphill (for the most part, something of a nightmare). This trailhead and first mile were buried under a flow of mud and debris from a flash flood. Although interesting to geologists, it requires hikers to negotiate rocks, boulders, logs, and deep erosion channels. Look for the faint trail on the right side of the flow. Follow this trail uphill until you pass through a small gorge, then look for the trail heading out of the

drainage. The trail spans 1.6 miles to a fork at 6,400 feet, and for day hikers the best bet is turning right and climbing partially up the treeless slope for a fantastic lookout and picnic site. Here you'll discover hidden Whitney Falls, a 250-foot waterfall, with its thin, silvery wisp tumbling through a narrow chute in a dramatic ashen gorge. It takes perfect timing to see this waterfall at anything more than a trickle. The view to the north of Shasta Valley is outstanding, highlighted by the series of hummocks, which are actually chunks of Shasta's former summit that were carried here like miniature hilltops in a massive lava flow after Shasta's last eruption, 600 years ago.

Special notes: If you turn left at the fork instead, you'll venture through forest, then up through another gutted stream drainage. The trail ends, and mountaineers will have to pass Coquette Falls, and then near the peak at the Bolam Glacier, in order to make the summit. Safety gear and expert climbing skills are required. Also note that this trailhead was long called the Bolam Creek trailhead. That was changed in 2002. A new Bolam Creek Trail and route up the north flank of Shasta is planned when funds and manpower become available.

User Groups: Hikers only. No dogs, horses, or mountain bikes. No wheelchair facilities.

Permits: Parking and access are free. A free wilderness permit is required for both day use and overnight use; $30 summit permit required for hikers climbing over 10,000 feet in elevation. All climbers are required to pack out waste and must bring a pack-out bag.

Maps: For a map, ask the U.S. Forest Service for Shasta-Trinity National Forest or Mount Shasta Wilderness. For a topographic map, ask the USGS for Mount Shasta.

Directions: From I-5, drive to the Central Weed/Klamath Falls (Highway 97) exit. Take that exit and drive through Weed to Highway 97. Turn right and drive 11 miles to Bolam Road (Forest Road 43N21), which is usually unsigned. (If you reach County Road A12 on the left, you have gone 0.25 mile too far.) Drive on Bolam Road for four miles toward the mountain (Mount Shasta), crossing the railroad tracks and continuing to the trailhead, at the end of the road. A high-clearance vehicle is required.

Contact: Shasta-Trinity National Forest, Mount Shasta Ranger District, 204 West Alma, Mount Shasta, CA 96067, 530/926-4511, www.fs.fed.us/r5—click on Forest Offices; Fifth Season Climbing Report, 530/926-5555; Mount Shasta Avalanche and Climbing Hotline, 530/926-9613 or www.shastaavalanche .com; Shasta Mountain Guides, 530/926-9613 or www.shastaguides.com.

28 NORTH GATE TRAILHEAD
4.0 mi / 2.75 hr 🥾3 ⛰8

on the north slope of Mount Shasta

The North Gate trailhead, set at about 7,000 feet, is one of Mount Shasta's most obscure and least-used trails. It sits on the north flank of Shasta, just below a mountain mound called North Gate. The route skirts this mound, following a small stream uphill for 1.6 miles; then farther along, the trail deteriorates and disappears as it nears tree line at 8,400 feet. From here, most day hikers will climb another 400 feet to the source of the creek, a small spring, and have lunch while enjoying the view to the north.

Special note: Mountain climbers who use this route to climb to the Shasta Summit will discover the going is quite easy at first after leaving tree line. The trip then becomes very steep, difficult, and dangerous, whether via Bolam or Hotlum Glacier. This route is only for experienced mountain climbers who are aware of the extreme risks of crossing steep, sheer glaciers.

User Groups: Hikers only. No dogs, horses, or mountain bikes. No wheelchair facilities.

Permits: Parking and access are free. A free wilderness permit is required for both day use and overnight use; $30 summit permit required for hikers climbing over 10,000 feet

in elevation. All climbers are required to pack out waste and must bring a pack-out bag.

Maps: For a map, ask the U.S. Forest Service for Shasta-Trinity National Forest or Mount Shasta Wilderness. For a topographic map, ask the USGS for Mount Shasta.

Directions: From I-5, drive to the Central Weed/Klamath Falls (Highway 97) exit. Take that exit and drive through Weed to Highway 97. Turn right and drive 13.5 miles to Military Pass Road (Forest Road 19). Turn right and drive 4.5 miles to a fork with Forest Road 42N16 (Andesite Logging Road). Bear right and drive four miles to the parking area, at the end of the road.

Contact: Shasta-Trinity National Forest, Mount Shasta Ranger District, 204 West Alma, Mount Shasta, CA 96067, 530/926-4511, www.fs.fed.us/r5—click on Forest Offices; Fifth Season Climbing Report, 530/926-5555; Mount Shasta Avalanche and Climbing Hotline, 530/926-9613 or www.shastaavalanche .com; Shasta Mountain Guides, 530/926-9613 or www.shastaguides.com.

29 BLACK BUTTE TRAIL
5.0 mi / 3.5 hr 🥾4 ⛰8

in Shasta-Trinity National Forest between I-5 and Mount Shasta

Anybody who has cruised I-5 north to Oregon and gawked in astonishment at Mount Shasta has inevitably seen Black Butte right alongside the highway. That's right, it's that barren cinder cone set between the highway and Mount Shasta, and it can pique a traveler's curiosity. The trail is routed right to the top and can answer all of your questions. But you may not like all of the answers. Over the course of 2.5 miles, you'll climb 1,845 feet—much of it steep, most of it rocky, and in the summer, all of it hot and dry. Shade is nonexistent. There are only two rewards. One is claiming the summit, at 6,325 feet, where you'll find the foundation of an old U.S. Forest Service lookout and great 360-degree views; the other is that the hike is an excellent warm-up for people who are planning to climb Mount Shasta. (That is, providing you don't need a week to recover.)

User Groups: Hikers and dogs. No horses or mountain bikes. No wheelchair facilities.

Permits: No permits are required.

Maps: A trail information sheet is available by contacting the Mount Shasta Ranger District at the address below. For a map, ask the U.S. Forest Service for Shasta-Trinity National Forest. For a topographic map, ask the USGS for Mount Shasta city.

Directions: From Redding, take I-5 north to the exit for Central Mount Shasta. Take that exit to the stop sign. Turn right and drive one mile east on Lake Street, and then bear left on Washington Drive (it merges, and then Washington Drive becomes Everitt Memorial Highway). Continue on Washington/Everitt Memorial Highway (past the high school) for about two miles, and look for the sign for Spring Hill Plantation (on the right) and Forest Road 41N18 (on the left). Turn left on Forest Road 41N18/Ash Flat (a gravel road), drive about 200 yards, and bear right, continuing on Forest Road 41N18 for 2.5 miles. After the road crosses under the overhead power line, turn left on Forest Road 41N18A (Black Butte Road) and drive 0.75 mile to the trailhead. Parking is very limited; be sure to park off the road.

Contact: Shasta-Trinity National Forest, Mount Shasta Ranger District, 204 West Alma, Mount Shasta, CA 96067, 530/926-4511, www.fs.fed.us/r5—click on Forest Offices.

30 SAND FLAT TRAILHEAD
3.4 mi / 2.75 hr   👣 3 ⛰ 8

on the southern slope of Mount Shasta

The hike from Sand Flat to Horse Camp, a distance of 1.7 miles, will give you a good taste of the Mount Shasta experience, and you're likely to savor the flavors. Many who make this day hike are compelled to return to climb all the way to the top.

Sand Flat provides a good shaded parking area to start from, at a 6,800-foot elevation. The trail immediately takes off uphill—gradually at first, but then it becomes quite steep. At 7,360 feet, it intersects with Bunny Flat Trail and then continues rising through the forest. Along the way are amazing examples of how avalanches have knocked down entire sections of forest. When you reach Horse Camp, at 7,800 feet, nearing timberline, you'll find many rewards. The first is springwater flowing continuously out of a piped fountain near the Sierra Hut; it's perhaps the best-tasting water in the world. The second is the foreboding view of Red Bank, which forms the mountain rim above Horse Camp. The third is the opportunity to hike up a short way above tree line for the sweeping views to the south of Castle Crags and Lake Siskiyou. After taking the first steps on Summit Trail, you'll likely yearn to keep going all the way to the very top of this magic mountain. If you wish to hike Summit Trail, see the following hike out of Bunny Flat trailhead.

User Groups: Hikers only. No dogs, horses, or mountain bikes. No wheelchair facilities.

Permits: Parking and access are free. A free wilderness permit is required for both day use and overnight use; a $30 summit permit is required for hikers climbing over 10,000 feet in elevation. All climbers are required to pack out waste and must bring a pack-out bag.

Maps: For a map, ask the U.S. Forest Service for Shasta-Trinity National Forest or Mount Shasta Wilderness. For a topographic map, ask the USGS for Mount Shasta.

Directions: From Redding, take I-5 north to the exit for Central Mount Shasta. Take that exit to the stop sign. Turn right and drive one mile east on Lake Street, and then bear left on Washington Drive (it merges, and then Washington Drive becomes Everitt Memorial Highway). Continue on Washington/Everitt Memorial Highway (past the high school) for eight miles to Sand Flat Loop (Forest Road

41N60). Turn left and drive a short distance to the trailhead.

Contact: Shasta-Trinity National Forest, Mount Shasta Ranger District, 204 West Alma, Mount Shasta, CA 96067, 530/926-4511, www.fs.fed.us/r5—click on Forest Offices; Fifth Season Climbing Report, 530/926-5555; Mount Shasta Avalanche and Climbing Hotline, 530/926-9613 or www .shastaavalanche.com; Shasta Mountain Guides, 530/926-9613 or www.shasta guides.com.

31 SHASTA SUMMIT TRAIL

14 mi / 1.5 days   👣5 ⛰10

on the southern slope of Mount Shasta in the Shasta-Trinity National Forest

BEST (

The hike to the top of Mount Shasta is a great challenge, an ascent of 7,000 feet over ice, snow, and rock while trying to suck what little oxygen you can out of the thin air. It may be the greatest adventure in the West that most people have an honest chance of achieving. The primary dangers are from tumbling boulders and bad weather (which stops half the people who try the climb), including high winds on top in May and June. Yet most hikers in good condition who start the trip very early and have the proper equipment can summit, especially from mid-July through August, when the weather is benign. Early? You should depart from Bunny Flat by 3 A.M., or hike in a day early, set up a base camp at Horse Camp (at tree line), and start no later than 4 A.M. Equipment? A daypack with warm clothes, a windbreaker, two canteens of water, food, and an ice ax and crampons are mandatory. Refill your canteen wherever you find a rivulet of water (it's occasionally possible at Red Bank); rangers recommend using a water filter.

It's an absolute must to make an early start. In the hot summer months, towering cumulus clouds sometimes form on Mount Shasta during the afternoon, and by then you'll want to be making the trip down. If towering cumulonimbus begin forming by noon, intense thunderstorms are possible by mid-afternoon.

The trip starts out of Bunny Flat at 6,900 feet, leads through a forest of Shasta red firs, climbs to where the trail intersects with the route out of Sand Flat, then turns right and rises to Horse Camp, at an elevation of 7,800 feet and a distance of 1.8 miles. It is a must to fill your canteens here. After filling your canteens at the spring, start hiking Summit Trail. Make your first steps across a series of large stones called Olberman's Causeway. From here, the trail quickly rises above timberline, gaining 1,000 feet per mile for six miles, and after a short time, it becomes a faint path. Often this is where the snow and ice start, and you must stop and strap your crampons onto your boots. The walking is easy with crampons. The trail climbs up Avalanche Gulch, and some people stop to make trail camps at a flat spot called Helen Lake, at 10,440 feet. Hikers not acclimated to high altitudes may begin experiencing some dizziness, but there's no relief in sight. At this point, the hike gets steeper (about a 35-degree slope), and some give up before reaching Red Bank—a huge, red, volcanic outcrop at about 12,500 feet. At Red Bank you'll need your ice ax in order to pull your way through a narrow and steep rock/ice chute, where a slip is certain without crampons.

When you emerge atop Red Bank, you are nearly 13,000 feet high, at the foot of a glacier field and Misery Hill, named so because it's a long, slow climb—through snow in spring and scree in summer. It's a myth that a lot of people actually mistake it for the peak—if you were that off base, you'd never make it this far. Once atop Misery Hill, you'll see the true Shasta Summit, a massive pinnacle of lava that seems to jut straight up into the air. Cross a sun-cupped glacier field to reach the pinnacle and there you will see the trail routed up to the top. With a final push, follow the trail, grabbing rocks to help pull you up and sucking the thin air, and with a few last steps, you'll be on top, at 14,162 feet. On clear days you can see hundreds of miles in all directions, and the sky is a deeper cobalt blue than you ever imagined. On top, you'll sign your name in a logbook in an old rusted metal box, then take in the grand wonders surrounding you. It's a remarkable trip, one that can inspire some people to keep their bodies in good enough shape to make the trip every year.

All hikers must pack out their waste. Special waste pack-out bags are available at no charge at the trailhead and at the Mount Shasta Ranger Station in Mount Shasta.

The biggest danger and largest number of injuries on Mount Shasta come not from falling, but from being hit by tumbling boulders. In fact, our former research assistant, Robyn Brewer, was struck in the foot by a boulder in her first attempt at climbing Shasta. She was hit so hard that it knocked her hiking boot off, breaking her foot and requiring an emergency helicopter airlift out for medical treatment. Always keep a good distance between you and your hiking partners, don't hike in a vertical line, and if a rock comes bouncing down, always shout, "Rock! Rock!" Some guides recommend wearing helmets. By the way, Robyn returned to Mount Shasta the following two years and made it to the top on both trips.

The mountain is best hiked when it still has a good coating of snow and ice, which provide excellent footing with crampons. When the snow and ice melt off in late fall, tromping through the small volcanic rocks is like slogging in mushy sand.

Drink lots of water. In high altitudes, dehydration is a common problem and can result in early exhaustion and extreme vulnerability to mountain sickness.

User Groups: Hikers only. No dogs, horses, or mountain bikes. No wheelchair facilities.

Permits: Parking and access are free. A free wilderness permit is required for both day use and overnight use; a $30 summit permit required for hikers climbing over 10,000 feet in

elevation. All climbers are required to pack out waste and must bring a pack-out bag.

Maps: For a map, ask the U.S. Forest Service for Shasta-Trinity National Forest or Mount Shasta Wilderness. For a topographic map, ask the USGS for Mount Shasta.

Directions: From Redding, take I-5 north to the exit for Central Mount Shasta. Take that exit to the stop sign. Turn right and drive one mile east on Lake Street, and then bear left on Washington Drive (it merges, and then Washington Drive becomes Everitt Memorial Highway). Continue on Washington/Everitt Memorial Highway (past the high school) for 10 miles to Bunny Flat. As you drive in, the trailhead is on the left.

Contact: Shasta-Trinity National Forest, Mount Shasta Ranger District, 204 West Alma, Mount Shasta, CA 96067, 530/926-4511, www.fs.fed.us/r5—click on Forest Offices; Fifth Season Climbing Report, 530/926-5555; Mount Shasta Avalanche and Climbing Hotline, 530/926-9613 or www.shastaavalanche.com; Shasta Mountain Guides, 530/926-9613 or www.shastaguides.com.

32 GRAY BUTTE

2.8 mi / 1.75 hr   🏃2 △10

from Panther Meadows on the southern slope of Mount Shasta in Mount Shasta Wilderness

BEST (

Panther Meadows is considered a sacred Native American site. Even those who are unaware of it seem to realize intuitively that this is a special place and find themselves walking softly and talking quietly when visiting. The trail is easy to reach, located just off to the right of the wide, paved, two-lane Everitt Memorial Highway. This hike is a short one, from Panther Meadows to Gray Butte and back.

From the parking area, the trail starts by heading east past meadow and forest, and after 0.6 mile, it turns right and begins a steady climb for 0.8 mile to Gray Butte. To reach the top (at 8,119 feet), it is a scramble over sharp-edged volcanic rock. But it is well worth it: There is a perfect lookout to the south, with Castle Crags, Mount Lassen, and the drop-off in the Sacramento Valley all prominent.

The northeast flank of Gray Butte is a sculpted volcanic valley that is called The Gate. Some mountain visitors consider this to be the mountain's sacred portal to the spiritual dimension. Gray Butte can also be reached easily from the Squaw Valley trailhead, which is located another mile up the access road; look for the signed trailhead and the small parking area on the right.

User Groups: Hikers only. Dogs are allowed at Gray Butte, but not beyond. No horses or mountain bikes. No wheelchair facilities.

Permits: Parking and access are free. A free wilderness permit is required for both day use and overnight use; $30 summit permit required for hikers climbing over 10,000 feet in elevation. All climbers are required to pack out waste and must bring a pack-out bag.

Maps: For a map, ask the U.S. Forest Service for Shasta-Trinity National Forest or Mount Shasta Wilderness. For a topographic map, ask the USGS for Mount Shasta.

Directions: From Redding, take I-5 north to the exit for Central Mount Shasta. Take that exit to the stop sign. Turn right and drive one mile east on Lake Street, and then bear left on Washington Drive (it merges, and then Washington Drive becomes Everitt Memorial Highway.) Continue on Washington/Everitt Memorial Highway (past the high school) for 13 miles (past Bunny Flat) to the trailhead on the right.

Contact: Shasta-Trinity National Forest, Mount Shasta Ranger District, 204 West Alma, Mount Shasta, CA 96067, 530/926-4511, www.fs.fed.us/r5—click on Forest Offices; Fifth Season Climbing Report, 530/926-5555; Mount Shasta Avalanche and Climbing Hotline, 530/926-9613 or www.shastaavalanche.com; Shasta Mountain Guides, 530/926-9613 or www.shastaguides.com.

33 OLD SKI BOWL TRAILHEAD

2.5 mi / 2.0 hr

on the southern slope of Mount Shasta

One of the great hikes on Mount Shasta is climbing from the Old Ski Bowl lodge site up to Green Butte. At 7,800 feet and set just above timberline, it's the highest drive-to trailhead on Mount Shasta. That means the entire route crosses a volcanic slope, with great views every step of the way and leading to a unique destination as well. Green Butte, a huge rock outcrop set at 9,193 feet, is a perfect perch.

At the parking area, there's a clear route (though it's unsigned) that leads up toward Green Butte, which is also clearly obvious just a mile away. But while the trip is short, it's very steep, with a 1,300-foot elevation gain. Along the way, a great bonus is a natural spring set about halfway up the butte; be sure to find it and fill your canteen with this sweet-tasting springwater. Although Green Butte is the destination of most visitors here, the hiking route continues to 9,600 feet before disintegrating in the lava rubble and snow. The Old Ski Bowl is one of the legendary spots on Shasta. It was here that a developer desecrated Shasta wildlands by building a ski area above tree line. Well, nature gives, and nature takes back. With no trees to hold snow in place, the old mountain wiped out the ski lifts with an avalanche. Ironically, in the mid-1990s, a new ski area was proposed at the same spot. The week before the decision was made, another avalanche pounded through, clearing a giant swath of trees and wiping out an area right where the lodge had been proposed. Now again, the Shasta Wilderness is untouched by the hand of mankind, rising like a diamond in a field of coal.

User Groups: Hikers only. Dogs are permitted in Old Ski Bowl, but not beyond into Mount Shasta Wilderness. No horses or mountain bikes. No wheelchair facilities.

Permits: Parking and access are free. A free

wilderness permit is required for both day use and overnight use; $30 summit permit required for hikers climbing over 10,000 feet in elevation. All climbers are required to pack out waste and must bring a pack-out bag.

Maps: For a map, ask the U.S. Forest Service for Shasta-Trinity National Forest or Mount Shasta Wilderness. For a topographic map, ask the USGS for Mount Shasta.

Directions: From Redding, take I-5 north to the exit for Central Mount Shasta. Take that exit to the stop sign. Turn right and drive one mile east on Lake Street, and then bear left on Washington Drive (it merges, and then Washington Drive becomes Everitt Memorial Highway). Continue on Washington/Everitt Memorial Highway (past the high school) for 13.5 (past Bunny Flat) to parking and the trailhead.

Contact: Shasta-Trinity National Forest, Mount Shasta Ranger District, 204 West Alma, Mount Shasta, CA 96067, 530/926-4511, www.fs.fed.us/r5—click on Forest Offices; Fifth Season Climbing Report, 530/926-5555; Mount Shasta Avalanche and Climbing Hotline, 530/926-9613 or www.shastaavalanche.com; Shasta Mountain Guides, 530/926-9613 or www.shastaguides.com.

34 BREWER CREEK TRAILHEAD

4.2 mi / 3.0 hr 3 9

on the northeast slope of Mount Shasta

It's so quiet here that you can practically hear the wildflowers bloom. We've hiked the north slope of Shasta out of the Brewer Creek trailhead several times and have never seen another person. The trip is a perfect day hike. The trailhead is set near Brewer Creek (at 7,200 feet), hence the name. After a short walk through a section of forest that was selectively logged many years ago, you'll enter the Shasta Wilderness and be surrounded by old-growth firs, many scraggly from enduring harsh winters and the short growing season.

Here the trail climbs more. It's a steady climb up through forest, with gradual switchbacks as it goes. When you near tree line, at 7,700 feet, the trail turns to the left and begins to lateral across the mountain. It's 2.1 miles to timberline from the trailhead, and most people hike to this point, then turn back. However, you can add an easy mile or two by climbing a wide, volcanic slope with good footing all the way, and rising to 9,500 feet. This is a great spot for a picnic, providing nice views to the north and also perhaps inspiring dreams of the day you'll next climb all the way to the top of Shasta.

Special note: Mountaineers who try to climb Shasta from this trailhead have only one good route from the point where the trail meets tree line, which is to head to the right up and over Hotlum Glacier. This route is extremely difficult, very steep, and dangerous.

User Groups: Hikers only. No dogs, horses, or mountain bikes. No wheelchair facilities.

Permits: Parking and access are free. A free wilderness permit is required for both day use and overnight use; $30 summit permit required for hikers climbing over 10,000 feet in elevation. All climbers are required to pack out waste and must bring a pack-out bag.

Maps: For a map, ask the U.S. Forest Service for Shasta-Trinity National Forest or Mount Shasta Wilderness. For a topographic map, ask the USGS for Mount Shasta.

Directions: From Redding, take I-5 north for 47 miles to the Highway 89/McCloud-Reno exit. Bear right on Highway 89 and drive nine miles to McCloud, then continue for another 2.8 miles to Pilgrim Creek Road. Turn left on Pilgrim Creek Road (Forest Road 13) and drive 7.1 miles to Forest Road 19 (Sugar Pine Butte Road). Turn left and drive 0.9 mile to Forest Road 42N02. Turn left and drive two miles to Forest Road 42N10. Turn left and drive two miles to the trailhead parking area.

Contact: Shasta-Trinity National Forest, Mount Shasta Ranger District, 204 West Alma, Mount Shasta, CA 96067, 530/926-4511, www.fs.fed.us/r5—click on Forest

Offices; McCloud Ranger District, 530/964-2184. A 24-hour climbing report is available by calling 530/926-5555.

35 MUD CREEK FALLS

2.0 mi / 1.5 hr 🚶3 ⛺8

on the southeast slope of Mount Shasta

A short walk on the remote southeast flank of Mount Shasta can provide entry to a land of enchantment. It features deep canyons, views of glaciers and Mount Shasta's prettiest waterfall. The drive in is circuitous but well signed, and it's a surprise to ever find other cars parked at the trailhead. The hike starts on an old overgrown jeep road. It slowly emerges from a sparse forest of Shasta red fir and then climbs to the eastern edge of the dramatic Mud Creek Canyon, at about 7,000 feet in elevation. From here, most hikers climb on for another 15 minutes, arriving at an overlook viewpoint of the waterfall at the bottom of the canyon. The waterfall, best viewed with binoculars, is perhaps 125 feet high. It's wide, and silver, but distant. This area is rich in natural history—the canyon was carved by a glacier and is still fed with water from the towering, fractured Konwakiton Glacier, which runs the color of volcanic silt.

User Groups: Hikers only. No dogs, horses, or mountain bikes. No wheelchair facilities.

Permits: Parking and access are free. A free wilderness permit is required for both day use and overnight use; $30 summit permit required for hikers climbing over 10,000 feet in elevation. All climbers are required to pack out waste and must bring a pack-out bag.

Maps: For a map, ask the U.S. Forest Service for Shasta-Trinity National Forest or Mount Shasta Wilderness. For a topographic map, ask the USGS for Mount Shasta.

Directions: From Redding, take I-5 north for 47 miles to the Highway 89/McCloud-Reno exit. Bear right on Highway 89 and drive nine miles to McCloud, then continue for another 2.8 miles to Pilgrim Creek Road. Turn left on Pilgrim Creek Road (Forest Road 13) and drive five miles (paved) to Forest Road 41N15 (Widow Springs Road). Turn left and drive about five miles to Forest Road 31 (McKenzie Butte). Cross this road and drive straight on Forest Road 41N61 (Cold Creek Road), a dirt and gravel road, for about a mile. Turn left on Forest Road 41N25Y (Clear Creek Road) and drive about three miles to the parking area for the Clear Creek trailhead. The road is well signed.

Contact: Shasta-Trinity National Forest, Mount Shasta Ranger District, 204 West Alma, Mount Shasta, CA 96067, 530/926-4511, www.fs.fed.us/r5—click on Forest Offices; McCloud Ranger District, 530/964-2184. A 24-hour climbing report is available by calling 530/926-5555 or 530/926-9613.

36 ETNA SUMMIT TO GRIDER CREEK (PCT)

49.0 mi one-way / 4.0 days 🚶3 ⛺10

from Etna Summit north into the Marble Mountain Wilderness west of Etna

The Etna Summit is one of the major access points for the Pacific Crest Trail in Northern California. There is a good, safe parking area (with a nice view), and at an elevation of 5,492 feet, you don't have to start your hike with a wicked climb that is demanded at so many other wilderness trailheads. From Etna Summit, the trail starts by crossing rugged, dry, and often hot terrain that is best dealt with in the morning. You'll reach Shelly Lake about eight miles in. Note that there is no water available along this route until Shelly Lake. The campground at Shelly Meadows is a good first-night stopover. From there, an excellent second-day destination is the Marble Valley, about another 10 miles north, with camping in the nearby Sky High Lakes Basin. The next 20 miles of trail cross through and out of the Marble Mountains.

SHASTA HIKING

You'll pass Marble Mountain (a side trip to Marble Rim is mandatory), Paradise Lake (many visitors will make camp here), and Kings Castle. Most of the trail here is above tree line, with outstanding lookouts at several points, including a great vista from Marble Rim. Moving onward, the trail follows Big Ridge to Buckhorn Mountain (6,908 feet), continues past Huckleberry Mountain (6,303 feet), and then drops down to the headwaters of Grider Creek, the next major trailhead-access point. As you head north, the trail becomes less and less traveled.

To pick up the next trail heading north, see the *Grider Creek to Seiad Valley (PCT)* hike in this chapter. If you are walking this trail in reverse, see the *Cecilville Road to Russian Wilderness (PCT)* hike in this chapter to continue south.

User Groups: Hikers, dogs, and horses. No mountain bikes. No wheelchair facilities.

Permits: Campfire permits (free) are required for campfires and stoves. Parking and access are free.

Maps: A trail information sheet can be obtained by contacting the Salmon River Ranger District at the address below. For a map, ask the U.S. Forest Service for Klamath National Forest or Marble Mountain Wilderness. For a topographic map, ask the USGS for Eaton Peak.

Directions: From Redding, take I-5 to Yreka and the exit for Highway 3/Fort Jones. Take that exit to the stop sign, turn left, and drive a short distance to the lighted intersection. Turn left on Highway 3 and drive 28 miles to Etna. Turn west on Etna-Somes Bar Road (called Main Street in town) and drive 10.5 miles to Etna Summit. The parking area is along the road.

Contact: Klamath National Forest, Salmon River & Scott River Ranger Districts, 11263 North Highway 3, Fort Jones, CA 96032-9702, 530/468-5351, www.fs.fed.us/r5—click on Forest Offices.

37 TAYLOR LAKE TRAIL
1.0 mi / 0.5 hr 🏃1 ⛰7

from Etna Summit into the Russian Wilderness west of Etna

BEST (

Taylor Lake is proof that wilderness-like lakes can be accessible by wheelchair. The trail is made of hard-packed dirt and is wheelchair accessible, though wheelchairs with wide wheels are recommended. For those with boots instead of wheels, it's about a 10-minute walk to Taylor Lake, a long, narrow lake set on the northern end of the Russian Wilderness. Trout fishing is often very good here, and the walk is short enough for hikers to bring along a small raft or float tube. The only downer here is that the Forest Service occasionally permits cows to graze, and they stomp the grass at the far end of the lake—and sometimes even walk in the shallows. Although cows are still permitted, the Forest Service has rerouted the trail so that hikers won't be walking amid them at the meadow.

For a side-trip option, the Pacific Crest Trail runs east just above the lake. There is a very steep cut-off trail that climbs from the lake up to the PCT.

User Groups: Hikers, wheelchairs, dogs, and horses. No mountain bikes.

Permits: No permits are required for day use. A campfire permit (free) is required for campfires and stoves. Parking and access are free.

Maps: A trail information sheet can be obtained by contacting the Salmon Ranger District at the address below. For a map, ask the U.S. Forest Service for Klamath National Forest or Marble Mountain Wilderness. For a topographic map, ask the USGS for Eaton Peak.

Directions: From Redding, take I-5 to Yreka and the exit for Highway 3/Fort Jones. Take that exit to the stop sign, turn left, and drive a short distance to the lighted intersection. Turn left on Highway 3 and drive 28 miles southwest to Etna. Turn west on Etna-Somes Bar Road (called Main Street in town) and drive

10.25 miles just past Etna Summit to Forest Road 41N18 (a signed access road). Turn left and continue to the trailhead.

Contact: Klamath National Forest, Salmon River & Scott River Ranger Districts, 11263 North Highway 3, Fort Jones, CA 96032-9702, 530/468-5351, www.fs.fed.us/r5—click on Forest Offices.

38 STATUE LAKE

6.0 mi / 4.0 hr

in the Russian Wilderness west of Etna

Statue Lake earned its name from the unique granite sculptures that frame the back wall of the lake. When you first arrive at the small lake, it's a gorgeous yet solemn sight, one of nature's mountain temples. No place else looks like this. Some of the granite outcrops look like fingers sculpted with a giant chisel. There is a small primitive campsite on a granite overlook, from which you can often see small brook trout rising to feed in the lake.

After parking at the Music Creek trailhead, start the trip by hiking up a moderate grade and climbing about a mile to the Pacific Crest Trail. Turn right and hike on the PCT for about 1.5 miles, an easy walk in the forest. When you reach a small spring creek, stop and fill your canteens, then leave the trail and head uphill. It's about a 30-minute, cross-country hike to the lake, and the last 10 minutes is over a large field of boulders.

User Groups: Hikers only. Dogs are permitted but not advised because of the route crossing a boulder field. No horses or mountain bikes. No wheelchair facilities.

Permits: No permits are required for day use. A campfire permit (free) is required for campfires and stoves. Parking and access are free.

Maps: A trail information sheet can be obtained by contacting the Salmon Ranger District at the address below. For a map, ask the U.S. Forest Service for Klamath National Forest or Marble Mountain Wilderness.

For a topographic map, ask the USGS for Sawyers Bar.

Directions: From Redding, take I-5 to Yreka and the exit for Highway 3/Fort Jones. Take that exit to the stop sign, turn left, and drive a short distance to the lighted intersection. Turn left on Highway 3 and drive 28 miles southwest to Etna. Turn west on Etna-Somes Bar Road (called Main Street in town), drive over Etna Summit, and continue down the other side to Forest Road 40N54 (just before the Salmon River Bridge). Turn left on Forest Road 40N54 and drive eight miles to the Music Creek trailhead. (A sign that says Pacific Crest Trail is usually posted. The sign for Music Creek trailhead is repeatedly stolen.)

Contact: Klamath National Forest, Salmon River & Scott River Ranger Districts, 11263 North Highway 3, Fort Jones, CA 96032-9702, 530/468-5351, www.fs.fed.us/r5—click on Forest Offices.

39 TRAIL CREEK TRAIL

7.0 mi / 2.0 days

in the Russian Wilderness west of Callahan

Trail Creek Trail is no longer an official trail. (Apparently no one but us tried hiking it.) The Forest Service has decommissioned it, which means no trail maintenance is performed. It is now more of a route, one leading into the Russian Wilderness. The Trail Creek Trail (or route) starts out as more of an old jeep road, involving a steep climb and drop, and then a short cross-country jaunt. (When you finish, you could always write the book, *My Life as a Jeep*.) From Trail Creek Campground to the PCT, you are unlikely to see anybody but your companions, and that's a plus. This is also a good route with dogs, because you won't see a soul.

For most hikers, the trailhead for the Pacific Crest Trail off the Cecilville-Callahan Road is by far preferable. This provides a much easier route into the southern portion of the Russian

Wilderness, but it will add 10 miles to your round-trip. That's the attraction of starting here instead.

The trailhead is located a short distance up a gravel road across from Trail Creek Campground, which is on Cecilville-Callahan Road. For the first 1.5 miles, the trail ventures steeply up on an old fire lane. It continues to climb, and as you near the crest, you'll junction with the Pacific Crest Trail. Turn left on the PCT, and then just five minutes later, turn at a signed junction to Syphon Lake. This is a good first night's camp. Russian or Waterdog Lakes are good second-day destinations.

Once you hit the high country, the lakes are very beautiful, especially Russian Lake, which is excellent for swimming. Because the wilderness here is small, it does not take many people hiking in to take up the campsites. Expect occasional cow sightings in midsummer near Syphon Lake. The Russian Wilderness is a place so pristine and so small that it just can't handle many visitors. If you go, walk softly, and treat the fragile area with care.

User Groups: Hikers, dogs, and horses. Mountain bikes allowed only outside of the wilderness border. No wheelchair facilities.

Permits: A wilderness permit is required for hikers planning to camp. Parking and access are free.

Maps: For a map, ask the U.S. Forest Service for Klamath National Forest. For topographic maps, ask the USGS for Deadman Peak and Eaton Peak.

Directions: From Redding, drive north on I-5 for 70 miles. Just past Weed, take the Edgewood exit. At the stop sign, turn left and drive through the underpass to another stop sign. Turn right on Old Highway 99 and drive six miles to Gazelle. Turn left at Gazelle on Gazelle-Callahan Road and drive about 20 miles to Callahan. From Callahan on Highway 3, turn west on County Road 402 (Cecilville Road) and drive 17 miles to Trail Creek Campground. The trail heads north from a gravel road located across from the campground.

Contact: Klamath National Forest, Salmon River & Scott River Ranger Districts, 11263 North Highway 3, Fort Jones, CA 96032-9702, 530/468-5351, www.fs.fed.us/r5—click on Forest Offices.

40 CECILVILLE ROAD TO RUSSIAN WILDERNESS (PCT)

3.0 mi one-way / 1.0 day   👥3   🔺7

from Cecilville Road west of Callahan to the southern border of the Russian Wilderness

This section of the trail is rarely used—it's estimated that less than 1,000 people a year hike here. Most hikers use this as a jump-off spot to the Russian Wilderness. This involves a long, steady climb up to the southern border of the Russian Wilderness. A good destination to the south is the short hike to Hidden Lake or South Fork Lakes.

Those venturing onward along the PCT enter a complex habitat web that includes the headwaters of the Scott, Salmon, and Trinity Rivers, along with the beautiful scenery that such diversity creates.

Either way, you start from the bottom of the canyon at the North Fork Scott River, so you'll face a climb no matter what your destination.

To pick up the next trail heading north (actually, in this case, heading west), see the *Etna Summit to Grider Creek (PCT)* hike in this chapter. If you are walking this trail in reverse, see the *Scott Mountain to Cecilville Road (PCT)* hike in this chapter to continue east.

User Groups: Hikers, dogs, and horses. No mountain bikes. No wheelchair facilities.

Permits: No permits are required for this section. Parking and access are free.

Maps: For topographic maps, ask the USGS for Deadman Peak and Eaton Peak.

Directions: From Redding, drive north on I-5 for 70 miles. Just past Weed, take the Edgewood exit. At the stop sign, turn left and drive through the underpass to another stop sign.

Turn right on Old Highway 99 and drive six miles to Gazelle. Turn left at Gazelle on Gazelle-Callahan Road and drive about 20 miles to Callahan. From Callahan, turn west on Cecilville Road (County Road 402, narrow at times) and drive 11.5 miles to the Cecilville Summit. Parking is limited here; a larger parking area is located just past Cecilville Summit at the Carter Meadows trailhead (it will add 0.25 mile to your hike).

Contact: Klamath National Forest, Salmon River & Scott River Ranger Districts, 11263 North Highway 3, Fort Jones, CA 96032-9702, 530/468-5351, www.fs.fed.us/r5—click on Forest Offices.

41 TRAIL GULCH
4.5 mi / 3.25 hr   👣3   ⛰8

in the Trinity Alps Wilderness west of Callahan

The Trail Gulch Trail rises along Trail Gulch Creek, steeply at times, but in just 2.25 miles, you'll arrive at Trail Gulch Lake. That makes it close enough to go in and out in a day, or better yet, you can make it a good weekend overnighter without tremendous strain. It is set northeast of Deadman Peak (7,741 feet) in the Trinity Alps Wilderness. This round, pretty lake is stocked by airplane every year with small trout (a nice bonus). Another bonus is how simple it is to extend your trip either to other mountain lakes or deep into the Trinity Alps Wilderness. Long Gulch Lake is just another three miles from Trail Gulch Lake, making it a good side trip.

Note: If you choose to extend into the Trinity Alps, the trail is routed along North Fork Coffee Creek to Kickapoo Waterfall, about nine miles from Trail Gulch Lake. This trip is crowded on summer weekends. Experienced hikers may note that on many maps, Trail Gulch Lake is misidentified as Long Gulch Lake, and vice versa.

User Groups: Hikers, dogs, and horses. No mountain bikes. No wheelchair facilities.

Permits: A wilderness permit is required for hikers planning to camp. Parking and access are free.

Maps: For a map, ask the U.S. Forest Service for Klamath National Forest or Trinity Alps Wilderness. For topographic maps, ask the USGS for Deadman Peak and Billys Peak.

Directions: From Redding, drive north on I-5 for 70 miles. Just past Weed, take the Edgewood exit. At the stop sign, turn left and drive through the underpass to another stop sign. Turn right on Old Highway 99 and drive about six miles to Gazelle. Turn left on Gazelle-Callahan Road and drive about 20 miles to Callahan. From Callahan, turn west on County Road 402 (Cecilville Road) and drive 11 miles. Turn left on Forest Road 39N08 and drive 1.5 miles to the trailhead.

Contact: Klamath National Forest, Salmon River & Scott River Ranger Districts, 11263 North Highway 3, Fort Jones, CA 96032-9702, 530/468-5351, www.fs.fed.us/r5—click on Forest Offices.

42 SCOTT MOUNTAIN TO CECILVILLE ROAD (PCT)
18.0 mi one-way / 2.0 days   👣4   ⛰10

from Highway 3 at Scott Mountain Campground to Cecilville Road near the northern border of the Trinity Alps Wilderness

What makes this section of the PCT appealing is that there are a number of wilderness lakes along the way that can be reached by side-trip hikes. From the camp at Scott Mountain, the trail is routed west for five miles, where the first of a series of lakes is within 0.5 mile of the trail. They include Upper Boulder, East Boulder, Mid Boulder, and Telephone Lakes—all quite pretty and accessible from the main trail. After hiking past Eagle Peak, set at 7,789 feet, you'll pass additional short cutoffs that are routed to West Boulder, Mavis, and Fox Creek Lakes. Hikers often camp at one of these lakes before the steep drop down to the South Fork

Scott River and heading north into the Russian Wilderness.

To pick up the next trail heading north (actually, in this case, heading west), see the *Cecilville Road to Russian Wilderness (PCT)* hike in this chapter. If you are walking this trail in reverse, see the *Mumbo Basin to Scott Mountain (PCT)* hike in this chapter to continue south.

User Groups: Hikers, dogs, and horses. No mountain bikes. No wheelchair facilities.

Permits: A wilderness permit is required for camping in the Trinity Alps Wilderness. Contact the Weaverville Ranger District at the address below for information.

Maps: For topographic maps, ask the USGS for Scott Mountain, Tangle Blue Lake, Billys Peak, and Deadman Peak.

Directions: From Callahan, drive south on Highway 3 about seven miles to the trailhead, at Scott Mountain Campground.

Contact: Shasta-Trinity National Forest, Weaverville Ranger Station, P.O. Box 1190, 210 Main Street, Weaverville, CA 96093, 530/623-2121, www.fs.fed.us/r5—click on Forest Offices.

43 KANGAROO LAKE TRAILHEAD

3.0 mi / 2.25 hr   👫 3   ⛰ 9

in Klamath National Forest east of Callahan

BEST (

Kangaroo Lake is one of the most easily reached pristine mountain lakes, with a campground, wheelchair-accessible fishing, and a great trailhead located out of the campground. The remote, but paved Rail Creek Road leads to a parking area set adjacent to the walk-in campground and trailhead for the short walk to the lake.

From the lake, a spur trail rises steeply to the Pacific Crest Trail. Turn left and the PCT rises steeply to the rim overlooking the lake. A nearby scramble to Cory Peak, at 7,737 feet, provides a 360-degree view. This is a great picnic site. All of Northern California's prominent mountain peaks are in view here, and immediately below you, to the west, is Kangaroo Lake, like a large sapphire. The lake covers only 21 acres but often produces large brook trout, most of them 12- to 14-inchers. Backpackers can extend this trip eastward four miles on the Pacific Crest Trail past Robbers Meadow to Bull Lake, a small lake in a relatively sparse setting. In an unsolved conflict, most hikers call this the Kangaroo Lake trailhead, while some Forest Service rangers refer to it as the Fen trailhead.

User Groups: Hikers, dogs, horses, and mountain bikes. Fishing is wheelchair accessible.

Permits: No permits are required. Parking and access are free.

Maps: A trail guide can be obtained by contacting Klamath National Forest at the address below. For a map, ask the U.S. Forest Service for Klamath National Forest. For a topographic map, ask the USGS for Scott Mountain.

Directions: From Redding, drive north on I-5 for 70 miles. Just past Weed, take the Edgewood exit. At the stop sign, turn left and drive through the underpass to another stop sign. Turn right on Old Highway 99 and drive about six miles to Gazelle. Turn left on Gazelle-Callahan Road and drive over the summit. Continue down the other side of the mountain about five miles to Rail Creek Road. Turn left on Rail Creek Road and drive seven miles to where the road dead-ends, at the parking area for Kangaroo Lake. The trail starts to the right of the campground.

Contact: Klamath National Forest, Salmon River & Scott River Ranger Districts, 11263 North Highway 3, Fort Jones, CA 96032-9702, 530/468-5351, www.fs.fed.us/r5—click on Forest Offices.

44 DEADFALL LAKES- MOUNT EDDY TRAIL

5.0 mi / 3.0 hr   🚶2 ⛰10
or
11 mi / 5 hr   🚶4 ⛰10

at Parks Creek Trailhead in Shasta-Trinity National Forest west of Mount Shasta

BEST (

This is one of the best all-around mountain hikes in California. You can do it easy, the 2.5-mile nearly flat walk to Middle Deadfall Lake. Or you can do it hard, an 11-mile round-trip with a climb of 2,200 feet to the 9,025-foot summit. Either way, this hike is a 10.

The sight of Middle Deadfall Lake is always a happy shock to newcomers. Here, tucked away on the west side of Mount Eddy, are three wilderness lakes, the prize being Middle Deadfall. At 25 acres, it's far larger than one might expect—and far prettier, too. Because the parking area and trailhead are at the ridgeline, the hike to this lake is much easier than to other wilderness lakes, often flat or with a very slight grade, making it an excellent day hike.

Start the trip by taking the Pacific Crest trailhead at the south end of the parking lot. The trail is routed through a mixed conifer forest, with views of the Trinity Alps off to the west and with a very gentle rising grade most of the way. As you near the lake, you'll cross a shallow stream (protruding rocks will keep you dry) and come to a junction (the Pacific Crest Trail bears to the right; the Mount Eddy Summit Trail turns to the left). Continue straight ahead (many people walk past a winter-snow survey marker) up a short rise, and then suddenly below you is Middle Deadfall Lake, at 7,300 feet—one of the highlights along the Pacific Crest Trail. The best and most secluded campsite here is around the back side of the lake. There are two other lakes nearby: tiny and rarely visited Upper Deadfall, at 7,800 feet, and even smaller Lower Deadfall, at 7,150 feet, which covers five acres and is overlooked in the shadow of its nearby big brother.

From Middle Deadfall, the summit climb is irresistible to most. Facing the ridge, you can pick the trail back up to your left. The climb becomes steeper, climbing 900 feet past the two small Upper Deadfall Lakes and then up to the ridge overlooking the Deadfall Lakes Basin. The long distance views to the west are breathtaking, and the ridge-top makes for a natural rest stop to soak them up. From here the trail bears to the left (north), rising above tree line, and then climbs another 900 feet in less than a mile, with seven switchbacks routed up a barren slope. In the process, there is no hint of a view of Mount Shasta. Then, suddenly, just as you gain the top of Mount Eddy, the entire western exposure of Mount Shasta comes into view, a stunning moment with an additional 125 miles of scenic points stretching into the distance. Looking down to the east, you can see how the giant Shasta rises 11,000 feet from the 3,000-foot elevations of the valley below. We put a new notebook and pen in a Ziploc bag in a can here so hikers can sign in.

There is one continuing problem on this route. On a regular basis, mountain bikers illegally ride the Pacific Crest Trail here (which overlaps this route for three miles) between the trailhead above Gumboot Lake, to the north, and the Parks Creek trailhead, to the south. Bikes are banned from the entire length of the PCT, of course.

User Groups: Hikers, dogs, and horses. No mountain bikes. No wheelchair facilities.

Permits: A campfire permit (free) is required for overnight use. Parking and access are free.

Maps: For a map, ask the U.S. Forest Service for Shasta-Trinity National Forest. For a topographic map, ask the USGS for Mount Eddy.

Directions: From Redding, drive north on I-5 for 70 miles. Just past Weed, take the Edgewood exit. At the stop sign, turn left and drive through the underpass to another stop sign. Turn right on Old Highway 99 and drive 0.5 mile to Stewart Springs Road. Turn left on Stewart Springs Road and drive to the road's end, at Stewart Springs Resort. Bear right on

SHASTA HIKING

Forest Road 17 (Parks Creek Road) and drive nine miles to the Deadfall Lakes parking area, at the summit. The trailhead is at the south side of the parking area. Take the Pacific Crest Trail, heading south.

Contact: Shasta-Trinity National Forest, Mount Shasta Ranger District, 204 West Alma, Mount Shasta, CA 96067, 530/926-4511, www.fs .fed.us/r5—click on Forest Offices.

45 TOAD LAKE TRAIL
1.5 mi / 2.0 days

in Shasta-Trinity National Forest west of Mount Shasta

BEST (

You might be wondering why a 1.5-mile round-trip hike, with a difficulty rating of only one, is projected as a two-day trip. The reason is the drive to the trailhead. It's an endless, twisting road that winds its way up the Middle Fork drainage of the Sacramento River, rising up along the west flank of Mount Eddy. No one should go up and back in a day. (And keep your tongue in your mouth, because the ride is so jarring that you might bite off the end of it when you hit a big pothole.) But once parked, you'll immediately notice the perfect calm, and then, with a 15-minute walk to the lake (at 6,950 feet), you'll be furnished with a picture-perfect lakeside campsite.

The lake covers 23 acres, provides excellent swimming, fair fishing for small trout, and great side trips. The best is the one-mile hike from Toad Lake to Porcupine Lake, an idyllic spot for a picnic or a walk along the shore. To get there from Toad Lake, take the trail that's routed behind the lake up to the Pacific Crest Trail, and then walk south for 0.25 mile on the PCT to the Porcupine Lake cutoff, on the right.

User Groups: Hikers, dogs, and horses. No mountain bikes allowed on the Pacific Crest Trail. No wheelchair facilities.

Permits: No permits are required. Parking and access are free.

Maps: For a map, ask the U.S. Forest Service for Shasta-Trinity National Forest. For a topographic map, ask the USGS for Mount Eddy.

Directions: From Redding, take I-5 north to the exit for Central Mount Shasta. Take that exit to the stop sign. At the stop sign, turn left and drive 0.5 mile to Old Stage Road. Turn left on Old Stage Road and drive 0.25 mile to a fork with W. A. Barr Road. Stay to the right at the fork and drive two miles, cross Box Canyon Dam at Lake Siskiyou, and continue around the lake on W. A. Barr Road (which becomes Forest Road 26/South Fork Road). Continue four miles past the Lake Siskiyou Camp resort, cross an unnamed concrete bridge, and look for a dirt road on the right (signed Toad Lake/Morgan Meadows). Turn right and drive 0.2 mile to the first fork, bear left, and drive 11 miles to the lake trailhead parking area. The road is very rough and twisting, and for the last 0.5 mile, a high-clearance, four-wheel-drive vehicle is recommended. It is a 0.5-mile walk from the parking area to the lake.

Contact: Shasta-Trinity National Forest, Mount Shasta Ranger District, 204 West Alma, Mount Shasta, CA 96067, 530/926-4511, www.fs.fed.us/r5—click on Forest Offices.

46 SISSON-CALLAHAN
14.0 mi one-way / 2.0 days

in Shasta-Trinity National Forest near Lake Siskiyou west of Mount Shasta

The Sisson-Callahan Trail is something of a legend in the Mount Shasta area, yet almost nobody makes this trek. Long ago, it was a well-traveled route up the east flank of Mount Eddy, over the top (through a saddle below the summit) and down to Deadfall Lakes. But with a much easier route long available from the Deadfall Lakes trailhead, this trail is passed over.

SHASTA HIKING

This route is long, steep, and hot, climbing 5,000 feet over the course of nine miles to the top of Mount Eddy (at 9,025 feet), then down nearly 2,000 feet in two miles to Deadfall Lakes for the nearest campsite. In addition, the great scenic beauty doesn't start until you've climbed several thousand feet, and by then you'll care more about how much water is left in your canteen than about the incredible sweeping view of Mount Shasta to the east. Alas, you'll then face killer switchbacks to reach the Eddy Ridge. As you reach the Eddy crest, look close and you will find an old sign for a former route for the Pacific Crest Trail; it might be 50 or 60 years old. From here it is mandatory to hike the switchbacks up to the Mount Eddy Summit. After that, it's a 1,750-foot descent to Middle Deadfall Lake, where you make camp. Your hiking reward comes the next morning, when after lounging around at Lower Deadfall Lake, you walk out three nearly level miles to the Park Creek/PCT trailhead, then catch your shuttle ride back to Mount Shasta. All in all, this is a genuine butt-kicker of a trail. Unless you want to do a hike that no one else does, a much better route to the Deadfall Lakes and Mount Eddy is from the Parks Creek trailhead, listed in this chapter as *Deadfall Lakes–Mount Eddy Trail*.

User Groups: Hikers, dogs, and horses. No mountain bikes. No wheelchair facilities.

Permits: No permits are required. Parking and access are free.

Maps: For a map, ask the U.S. Forest Service for Shasta-Trinity National Forest. For topographic maps, ask the USGS for Mount Shasta city and Mount Eddy.

Directions: From Redding, take I-5 north to the exit for Central Mount Shasta city. Take that exit to the stop sign. Turn left and drive 0.5 mile to Old Stage Road. Turn left on Old Stage Road and drive 0.25 mile to a fork with W. A. Barr Road. Stay to the right at the fork and drive two miles to North Shore Road (if you cross the dam at Lake Siskiyou, you have gone too far). Turn right on North Shore (which becomes Forest Road 40N27/Deer Creek Road) and drive four miles, across the bridge on Deer Creek to the next major junction, Forest Road 40N27C. Turn left on Forest Road 40N27C and park along the edge of the road before the ford on the North Fork Sacramento. (The water here is sometimes deeper than it looks; don't be tempted to drive it.) The Sisson-Callahan Trail (which first appears as a road) starts on the other side of the ford, on an old logging skid road that goes to the right. Within 0.5 mile, it turns into a trail.

Contact: Shasta-Trinity National Forest, Mount Shasta Ranger District, 204 West Alma, Mount Shasta, CA 96067, 530/926-4511, www.fs.fed.us/r5—click on Forest Offices.

47 HEART LAKE TRAIL
3.0 mi / 2.25 hr   2   10

at Castle Lake in Shasta-Trinity National Forest west of Mount Shasta

The tale of Castle Lake, set at an elevation of 5,450 feet, is that the water is like none other in the world, which has led some people to jump into the lake for complete renewal. In scientific reality, the water is so pure, containing few nutrients of any kind, that UC Davis has a water-sampling station here in an ongoing comparison study with Lake Tahoe.

The trailhead is on the left side of the lake, just across the outlet stream. From here, the trail rises up along the slope just left of the lake. Below to your right is Castle Lake, a pretty sight that's set in a rock bowl with a high back wall. The trail rises up to a saddle at 5,900 feet. At the saddle, bear uphill to the right on the faint trail. It's an easy scramble up over a lip at 6,050 feet, where little Heart Lake is tucked away. Because the lake is small, the water warms up by midsummer, making it great for wading or a quick dip (but it's too small to really swim). In addition, if you scramble up the back wall of the little lake, you'll get a breathtaking view of Mount

Shasta. Also note that the best drive-to spot anywhere for photographs of Mount Shasta is on Castle Lake Road at a turnout about one mile downhill from the Castle Lake parking area.

User Groups: Hikers and dogs. Not suitable for horses or mountain bikes. No wheelchair facilities.

Permits: No permits are required. Parking and access is free.

Maps: For a map, ask the U.S. Forest Service for Shasta-Trinity National Forest or Castle Crags Wilderness. For a topographic map, ask the USGS for Mount Shasta city.

Directions: From Redding, take I-5 north to the exit for Central Mount Shasta city. Take that exit to the stop sign. Turn left and drive 0.5 mile to Old Stage Road. Turn left on Old Stage Road and drive 0.25 mile to a fork with W. A. Barr Road. Stay to the right at the fork and drive two miles, cross Box Canyon Dam at Lake Siskiyou, and continue 0.5 mile to Castle Lake Road. Turn left and drive 7.5 miles to the parking area at the end of the road, at Castle Lake. The trailhead begins on the eastern end of the parking lot.

Contact: Shasta-Trinity National Forest, Mount Shasta Ranger District, 204 West Alma, Mount Shasta, CA 96067, 530/926-4511, www.fs.fed.us/r5—click on Forest Offices.

48 MIDDLE FALLS TRAIL
0.5-2.0 mi / 0.5-1.0 hr 🏃1 ⛰10

at Fowler's Camp in Shasta-Trinity National Forest east of McCloud

Middle Falls, on the McCloud River, is one of the prettiest waterfalls in Northern California. It is a wide and tall cascade of water that pours over a 50-foot cliff into a deep pool in a rock bowl. This easy hike is a 10- to 15-minute walk on a paved trail that starts at Lower Falls and skirts the left side of the McCloud River. You'll round a bend, probably hearing the waterfall before you see it, and then suddenly, there it is, this wide sheet of falling water. It's something like a miniature Niagara Falls. On summer weekends, teenagers climb to the rim above the falls, then plunge 50 feet into the pool like human missiles. It's a dangerous venture that we don't recommend.

From the base of the plunge pool, you can extend your walk by hiking up a series of switchbacks that tops out at the volcanic rim encircling the pool. From here, you may continue to hike upstream to Upper Falls, a narrow, staircase-type waterfall. It is also possible to drive to a parking area near the brink of the falls, reducing the hike to about 50 yards. A restroom is available at this parking area.

The one frustrating element is that some visitors litter at this spot, or worse, they discard their cigarette butts on the trail. We try to reverse this offensive practice by packing out any trash that we see.

User Groups: Hikers and dogs. No horses or mountain bikes. The paved path from Lower Falls to Middle Falls is wheelchair accessible.

Permits: No permits are required. Parking and access are free.

Maps: For a map, ask the U.S. Forest Service for Shasta-Trinity National Forest. For a topographic map, ask the USGS for McCloud.

Directions: From Redding, take I-5 north for 47 miles to the Highway 89/McCloud-Reno exit. Bear right on Highway 89 and drive nine miles to McCloud. Continue southeast on Highway 89 for five miles to the sign for Fowler's Campground and Forest Road 39N28. Turn right and drive one mile to a fork. Bear left at the fork for Fowler's Campground, drive through the campground to the restroom, and park. The trailhead is across the road from the restroom.

Contact: Shasta-Trinity National Forest, McCloud Ranger District, P.O. Box 1620, 2019 Forest Road, McCloud, CA 96057, 530/964-2184, www.fs.fed.us/r5—click on Forest Offices.

SHASTA HIKING

49 CARIBOU LAKES TRAIL

18.0 mi / 2.0 days

in the Trinity Alps Wilderness northwest of Trinity Lake

The Caribou Lakes Basin provides the classic Trinity Alps scene: three high mountain lakes, beautiful and serene, with the back wall of the Sawtooth Ridge casting a monumental backdrop on one side, and on the other side, a drop-off and great views of a series of mountain peaks and ridgelines. Sunsets are absolutely remarkable when viewed from here. The centerpiece is Caribou Lake, the largest lake in the Trinity Alps Wilderness. Because it's a nine-mile hike to the Caribou Lakes Basin, this makes a good first-day destination for backpackers exploring this section of the Trinity Alps Wilderness.

The trail starts at the bottom of the Salmon River, however, and like all trails that start at the bottom of canyons, it means you begin the trip with a terrible climb that never seems to end, especially on hot summer afternoons. Plan on drinking a full canteen of water, and be certain not to miss the natural spring located near the crest, just off to the right. (Look for the spur-like footpath to it.) After reaching the crest, the trail travels counterclockwise around the mountain, several hours en route, and then drops into the Caribou Lakes Basin. Ignore your urge to stop at the first lake, because the best campsites, swimming, and views are from Caribou Lake, the last and largest lake you'll reach in this circuit. Because this is a popular destination, fishing is often poor. The lake is stocked, but these fish are very smart from the relatively large number of people making a cast over the course of a summer.

User Groups: Hikers and dogs. Horses are permitted but not recommended. No mountain bikes. No wheelchair facilities.

Permits: A wilderness permit is required for camping.

Maps: For a map, ask the U.S. Forest Service for Klamath National Forest or Trinity Alps Wilderness. For a topographic map, ask the USGS for Caribou Lakes.

Directions: From Weaverville, take Highway 3 north past Trinity Lake and continue to Coffee Creek Road/County Road 104 (located near the Coffee Creek Ranger Station). Turn left and drive 17 miles to the trailhead at the end of the road, at Big Flat Campground.

Contact: Shasta-Trinity National Forest, Weaverville Ranger Station, P.O. Box 1190, 210 Main Street, Weaverville, CA 96093, 530/623-2121, www.fs.fed.us/r5—click on Forest Offices; Klamath National Forest, Salmon River & Scott River Ranger Districts, 11263 North Highway 3, Fort Jones, CA 96032-9702, 530/468-5351, www.fs.fed.us/r5—click on Forest Offices.

50 UNION LAKE TRAIL

12.0 mi / 2.0 days

in the Trinity Alps Wilderness northwest of Trinity Lake

Union Lake sits in a granite basin below Red Rock Mountain. The hike in and out is a good weekend affair, but most visitors are backpackers who are using the camp at the lake as a first-day destination for a multiday trip. Of the trailheads on Coffee Creek Road, this one is often overlooked. The trail starts near an old sawmill along Coffee Creek, heads south (to the left), and in less than a mile starts the climb adjacent to Union Creek (on your right). Like most hikes that start at a streambed, you pay for your pleasure, going up, not down. After about two miles, the trail crosses Union Creek and continues on for a few miles, now with the stream on the left. You'll pass a trail junction for Bullards Basin, and about 0.5 mile later, turn right on the cutoff trail to Union Lake.

User Groups: Hikers, dogs, and horses. No mountain bikes. No wheelchair facilities.

Permits: A wilderness permit is required for hikers planning to camp.

Maps: For a map, ask the U.S. Forest Service for Shasta-Trinity National Forest or Trinity Alps Wilderness. For a topographic map, ask the USGS for Caribou Lakes.

Directions: From Weaverville, take Highway 3 north past Trinity Lake and continue to Coffee Creek Road/County Road 104 (located near the Coffee Creek Ranger Station). Turn left and drive about 10 miles to the trailhead, on the left.

Contact: Shasta-Trinity National Forest, Weaverville Ranger Station, P.O. Box 1190, 210 Main Street, Weaverville, CA 96093, 530/623-2121, www.fs.fed.us/r5—click on Forest Offices.

51 BIG BEAR LAKE TRAIL
8.0 mi / 2.0 days   🏃3 ⛰8

in the Trinity Alps Wilderness south of Callahan

The four-mile hike up to Big Bear Lake, a large, beautiful lake by wilderness standards, can make for a weekend backpack trip. If there's a negative to this trip, it's this: The trail ends at the lake, so if the lakeside campsites are already taken when you arrive, you're out of luck for a quality place to camp. The trailhead is easy to reach, located just off Highway 3 north of Trinity Lake. The route is simple but not easy. It follows Bear Creek for the entire route, with one stream crossing, but climbing all the way. Once you reach the lake, a bonus is the side trip to Little Bear Lake, which takes about a mile of scrambling cross-country to reach. The trail is steep, popular, and beautiful.

User Groups: Hikers and dogs. Horses are allowed but not recommended. No mountain bikes. No wheelchair facilities.

Permits: A wilderness permit is required for hikers planning to camp in the wilderness.

Maps: For a map, ask the U.S. Forest Service for Shasta-Trinity National Forest. For a topographic map, ask the USGS for Tangle Blue Lake.

Directions: From Redding, take I-5 to Yreka and the exit for Highway 3/Fort Jones. Take that exit to the stop sign, turn left, and drive a short distance to the lighted intersection. Turn left on Highway 3 and drive about 40 miles to Callahan. Continue south on Highway 3 for about 13 miles to Bear Creek Loop Road. Turn right and drive a short distance (on an unpaved road) to the signed trailhead (located near the Bear Creek road crossing).

Contact: Shasta-Trinity National Forest, Weaverville Ranger Station, P.O. Box 1190, 210 Main Street, Weaverville, CA 96093, 530/623-2121, www.fs.fed.us/r5—click on Forest Offices.

52 MUMBO BASIN TO SCOTT MOUNTAIN (PCT)
35.0 mi one-way / 4.0 days   🏃3 ⛰10

in Shasta-Trinity National Forest from Gumboot trailhead to Scott Mountain

The PCT starts at a popular trailhead but quickly jumps northward into remote, beautiful country. The first highlight, only a mile up the trail, is the view below, to the left of secluded Picayune Lake. The trail then heads on, passing little yet pristine Porcupine Lake. A short spur trail provides access to this must-see spot. Back on the PCT, the trail heads over the rim and down to Deadfall Lakes, an excellent camping spot. From the ridge, an irresistible side trip is the 4-mile (one-way) trek to the top of Mount Eddy (at 9,025 feet), with its incomparable view of Mount Shasta. From Deadfall Lakes, the trail continues down to the Parks Creek Trailhead and crosses a paved road. It then eventually descends and curves around the headwaters of the Trinity River, then climbs back up Chilcoot Pass and Bull Lake. From here, it's a 10-mile pull to the Scott Mountain Summit trailhead (see the *Cecilville Road to Russian Wilderness (PCT)* hike in this chapter).

If you are walking this trail in reverse, see

the *Castle Crags to Mumbo Basin (PCT)* hike in this chapter to continue south.

User Groups: Hikers, dogs, and horses. No mountain bikes. No wheelchair facilities.

Permits: No permits are required. Parking and access are free.

Maps: For topographic maps, ask the USGS for Mumbo Basin, South China Mountain, and Scott Mountain.

Directions: From Redding, take I-5 north to the exit for Central Mount Shasta city. Take that exit to the stop sign. Turn left and drive 0.5 mile to Old Stage Road. Turn left on Old Stage Road and drive 0.25 mile to a fork with W. A. Barr Road. Stay to the right at the fork and drive two miles, cross Box Canyon Dam at Lake Siskiyou, and continue around the lake on W. A. Barr Road (which becomes Forest Road 26/South Fork Road). Continue four miles past the Lake Siskiyou Camp resort and continue up the canyon for 12.5 miles to Gumboot Lake Road. Bear right, staying on Forest Road 26, and continue 2.5 miles to the ridge and the parking area and trailhead.

Contact: Shasta-Trinity National Forest, Mount Shasta Ranger District, 204 West Alma, Mount Shasta, CA 96067, 530/926-4511, www.fs.fed.us/r5—click on Forest Offices.

53 GUMBOOT LAKE TRAILHEAD

1.5 mi / 1.5 hr

in Shasta-Trinity National Forest west of Mount Shasta

This is an off-trail trek for people who like to scramble to ridges for views. If you must always have a trail to hike on, well, this trip is not for you. But if you don't mind a little cross-country scramble to a mountain rim then a short cutoff to a peak, with spectacular views of Gumboot Lake and Mount Shasta beyond, then sign up for this hike.

The trip starts at Gumboot Lake (6,050

elevation), which is pretty and has good trout fishing. You circle the lake on the right side, where there's a good trail. At the back of the lake, break off to the right of the trail and start climbing the slope, heading up toward the ridge that circles the back of the lake. A little less than halfway to the top, you'll pass Little Gumboot Lake and after that, you will scramble your way to the ridge, where you'll intersect with the Pacific Crest Trail. Head to the left for a short distance, then again break off the trail, this time to the left, heading on the mountain spine toward the peak that towers over Gumboot Lake, with Mount Shasta as the backdrop off to the east. This peak is your destination. The world may not be perfect, but from this lookout, it comes close.

User Groups: Hikers and dogs only. No horses or mountain bikes. No wheelchair facilities.

Permits: No permits are required. Parking and access are free.

Maps: For a map, ask the U.S. Forest Service for Shasta-Trinity National Forest. For a topographic map, ask the USGS for Mumbo Basin.

Directions: From I-5 at Mount Shasta city, take the Central Mount Shasta exit. At the stop sign, turn west and drive 0.5 mile to Old Stage Road. Turn left on Old Stage Road and drive 0.25 mile to a fork with W. A. Barr Road. Stay to the right at the fork and drive two miles, cross Box Canyon Dam at Lake Siskiyou, and continue around the lake on W. A. Barr Road (which becomes Forest Road 26/South Fork Road). Continue four miles past the Lake Siskiyou Camp resort and continue up the canyon to Gumboot Lake Road (Forest Road 40N37). Bear left on Gumboot Lake Road and drive 0.5 mile to the parking area near the shore of the lake.

Contact: Shasta-Trinity National Forest, Mount Shasta Ranger District, 204 West Alma, Mount Shasta, CA 96067, 530/926-4511, www.fs.fed.us/r5—click on Forest Offices.

54 TAMARACK LAKE TRAILHEAD

5.0 mi / 4.0 hr   🥾5 ⛰10

in Shasta-Trinity National Forest southwest of Mount Shasta

This is sacred country for some hikers, set high in the Trinity Divide at 5,900 feet. Tamarack is a beautiful alpine lake and a place of remarkable serenity. If you can pull yourself away from it, there's a rugged, cross-country route to the north that approaches the summit of Grey Rocks, a series of dark, craggy peaks. This route is steep and difficult, but the view of Castle Crags, Mount Shasta, the ridges of the Trinity Divide, and the Sacramento River Canyon will have you thanking a higher power for the privilege of breathing the air here.

User Groups: Hikers and dogs. Not suitable for horses or mountain bikes. No wheelchair facilities.

Permits: No permits are required.

Maps: For a map, ask the U.S. Forest Service for Shasta-Trinity National Forest. For a topographic map, ask the USGS for Chicken Hawk Hill.

Directions: From Redding, take I-5 north for about 50 miles to the exit for Castella/Castle Crags State Park. Take that exit to the stop sign, turn left and drive west on Castle Creek Road. Continue past the park (the road becomes Forest Road 25/Whalen Road) and continue 12.5 miles on to Forest Road 38N17 (Tamarack Road). Turn left on Forest Road 38N17 and drive about six miles to the trailhead. The end of this road is extremely rough, with the last mile passable only to four-wheel-drive vehicles with large tires and high clearance. For other vehicles, before this bad section of road, there is a primitive parking area on the right side.

Contact: Shasta-Trinity National Forest, Mount Shasta Ranger District, 204 West Alma, Mount Shasta, CA 96067, 530/926-4511, www.fs.fed.us/r5—click on Forest Offices.

55 ROOT CREEK TRAIL

2.3 mi / 1.75 hr   🥾1 ⛰7

in Castle Crags State Park south of Mount Shasta

Castle Crags State Park features a series of huge granite spires that tower over the Sacramento River Canyon, the kind of sight that can take your breath away the first time you see it from I-5. That sight inspires a lot of people to take one of the hikes at the park, and while most don't have the time, energy, or body conditioning to complete Castle Crags Trail, Root Creek Trail is a good second choice.

As you drive up the access road, look for the signed trailhead to the left, just as you arrive at the parking area. The elevation is 2,500 feet at the trailhead. Start at this trailhead, which is signed for Castle Crags Trail, and walk 0.25 mile to a trail junction. Turn right on Root Creek Trail. From here, the trail is routed through a thick, cool forest, an easy walk that most visitors overlook. It continues to Root Creek, a pretty, babbling stream. There's a hidden waterfall upstream from here that almost nobody knows about.

User Groups: Hikers only. No dogs, horses, or mountain bikes. No wheelchair facilities.

Permits: No permits are required. A state park entrance fee of $6 is charged for each vehicle.

Maps: A trail map can be obtained for a fee by contacting Castle Crags State Park at the address below. For a topographic map, ask the USGS for Dunsmuir.

Directions: From Redding, take I-5 north for about 50 miles to the exit for Castella/Castle Crags State Park. Take that exit to the stop sign, turn left and drive west on Castle Creek Road. Drive 0.25 mile to the park entrance, on the right. Turn right and drive to the kiosk. Just past the kiosk, bear right and drive two miles (past the campground) to the parking area for Vista Point. The signed trailhead is at the west edge of the parking area.

Contact: Castle Crags State Park, P.O. Box

80, Castella, CA 96017, 530/235-2684, www.parks.ca.gov—click on Find A Park.

56 CASTLE CRAGS TO MUMBO BASIN (PCT)
25.0 mi one-way / 2.0 days 🏃4 ⛰10

from Castle Crags State Park west into Shasta-Trinity National Forest

This is a key juncture for the PCT, where the trail climbs out of a river canyon and back to high ridgelines. It's in a classic region, the Trinity Divide, known for lakes sculpted in granite and sweeping views of Mount Shasta. From the start, the trail runs beneath the spires of Castle Crags, a setting that can astonish newcomers. From the Sacramento River at Castle Crags, at an elevation of 2,000 feet, the trail laterals up the north side of Castle Creek Canyon, rising just below the base of the awesome crags. It finally hits the rim at the back side of Castle Ridge. Then it follows the rim in a half circle to the west, to the Seven Lakes Basin and beyond to the Mumbo Basin and the Gumboot Lake trailhead. The final five miles of this segment pass by a dozen pristine mountain lakes, but most are well off the trail.

To continue north on the PCT, see the *Mumbo Basin to Scott Moutain (PCT)* hike in this chapter. If you are walking this trail in reverse, see the *Ash Camp to Castle Crags Wilderness (PCT)* hike in this chapter to continue south.

User Groups: Hikers only. No dogs, horses, or mountain bikes. No wheelchair facilities.

Permits: No permits are required. A state park entrance fee of $6 is charged for each vehicle.

Maps: A trail map can be obtained for a fee by contacting Castle Crags State Park at the address below. For topographic maps, ask the USGS for Dunsmuir, Seven Lakes Basin, and Mumbo Basin.

Directions: From Redding, take I-5 north for about 50 miles to the exit for Castella/Castle Crags State Park. Take that exit to the stop sign, turn left and drive west on Castle Creek Road. Drive 0.25 mile to the park entrance, on the right. Turn right and drive to the kiosk. Just past the kiosk is a special parking area for PCT hikers. For day hikers, continue by bearing right, and then drive two miles to the end of the road, where there is a parking area for Vista Point. From the Vista Point parking area, the signed trailhead is back down the road about 50 yards.

Contact: Castle Crags State Park, P.O. Box 80, Castella, CA 96017, 530/235-2684, www.parks.ca.gov—click on Find A Park.

57 CRAGS TRAIL TO CASTLE DOME
5.7 mi / 4.0 hr 🏃4 ⛰10

in Castle Crags State Park south of Mount Shasta

From Vista Point in Castle Crags State Park, hikers can gaze up at the fantastic crags and spot Castle Dome (at 4,966 feet), the leading spire on the crags' ridge. This high, rounded, missile-shaped piece of rock is your destination on Castle Crags Trail. If you're out of shape, be warned: This climb is a butt-kicker, gaining in elevation all the way.

As you drive up to the parking area, you will see the signed trailhead on your left just as you reach the parking area. The elevation is 2,500 feet. Start by taking Castle Crags Trail for 0.25 mile; when you reach a three-trail junction, continue on Castle Crags Trail. Here the trail launches off, rising through a thick forest. It climbs steeply at times before eventually turning to the right, emerging from the forest, and winding through the lower crags. Once above tree line, the views get better with each rising step. In spring, snow and ice fields are common this high. An excellent picnic spot is at Indian Springs (at 3,600 feet), and many hikers get no farther than this point. But the trail goes onward, always climbing, then getting quite steep before finally reaching a saddle at the foot of Castle Dome, where a few trees have somehow gained toeholds. When you set foot on this divine perch and gaze north at Mount Shasta, it will be a moment you'll prize forever.

It isn't quite pristine, unfortunately, because of highway noise emerging from the canyon, as well as the inevitable freight train. Regardless, the views and photographs are eye-popping, making it a must-do for those who rate their hikes based on the lookouts.

User Groups: Hikers only. No dogs, horses, or mountain bikes. No wheelchair facilities.

Permits: No permits are required. A state park entrance fee of $6 is charged for each vehicle.

Maps: A trail map can be obtained for a fee by contacting Castle Crags State Park at the address below. For a topographic map, ask the USGS for Dunsmuir.

Directions: From Redding, take I-5 north for about 50 miles to the exit for Castella/Castle Crags State Park. Take that exit to the stop sign, turn left and drive west on Castle Creek Road. Continue 0.25 mile to the park entrance, on the right. Turn right and drive to the kiosk. Just past the kiosk, bear right and drive two miles to its end, at the parking area for Vista Point. The signed trailhead is back down the road about 50 yards.

Contact: Castle Crags State Park, P.O. Box 80, Castella, CA 96017, 530/235-2684, www.parks.ca.gov—click on Find A Park.

58 ASH CAMP TO CASTLE CRAGS WILDERNESS (PCT)

30.0 mi one-way / 2.0 days 4 △10

from Ash Camp on the McCloud River west into Castle Crags State Park

Of the hundreds of rivers along the Pacific Crest Trail, it's the McCloud River that often seems most vibrant with life. This segment of the PCT starts right alongside the lush McCloud River at Ash Camp, set at about 3,000 feet. The trail is then routed downstream above the McCloud for 2.5 miles, one of the most prized sections of trail in this region. At Ah-Di-Na Camp, the trail starts to rise, eventually turning up Squaw Valley Creek and climbing steeply to top Girard Ridge (at 4,500 feet), a long, tiring, and dry climb. But when you top the ridge, Mount Shasta, Black Butte, and Castle Crags suddenly pop into view. After traversing the ridge for a few miles, the trail suddenly drops and cascades down to the Sacramento River Canyon. Your toes will be jamming into your boots as you head downhill. At the river you might stop to soak your feet before picking up and heading west into Castle Crags State Park.

To continue north on the PCT, see the *Castle Crags to Mumbo Basin (PCT)* hike in this chapter. If you are walking this trail in reverse, see the *McArthur-Burney Falls Memorial State Park to Ash Camp (PCT)* hike, in *Moon California Camping*, to continue south.

User Groups: Hikers, dogs, and horses. No mountain bikes. No wheelchair facilities.

Permits: Wilderness permits are required only in Castle Crags Wilderness.

Maps: For topographic maps, ask the USGS for Shoeinhorse Mountain, Yellowjacket Mountain, and Dunsmuir.

Directions: From Redding, take I-5 north for 47 miles to the Highway 89/McCloud-Reno exit. Bear right on Highway 89 and drive nine miles to McCloud and Squaw Valley Road. Turn right on Squaw Valley Road, and drive about five miles. (Squaw Valley Road becomes Forest Road 11/Hawkins Creek Road.) Continue on Forest Road 11, keeping right past the McCloud boat ramp, and continue over the McCloud Dam. Turn right (still Forest Road 11) and drive down the canyon for one mile. At the turnoff for Ash Camp, bear right and drive a short distance to the parking area.

Contact: Shasta-Trinity National Forest, McCloud Ranger District, 2019 Forest Road, P.O. Box 1620, McCloud, CA 96057,

530/964-2184, fax 530/964-2938, www.fs
.fed.us/r5—click on Forest Offices.

59 McCLOUD NATURE TRAIL
4.5 mi / 2.5 hr   🏃1 ⛺9

at Nature Conservancy on the McCloud River
south of McCloud

BEST (

Have you ever yearned for a place where old
trees are left standing, deer and bobcat roam
without fear, and a crystal-perfect river flows
free in an untouched canyon? The McCloud
River Preserve is such a place, and because
it's managed by the Nature Conservancy, it
will always remain that way. Although the
lower McCloud River is best known for its
fly-fishing for trout, there's an excellent hiking trail that runs alongside the river, spanning more than two miles from the parking
area on downstream. It's an easy yet beautiful
walk among woods and water, requiring a bit
of boulder hopping in a few spots. It's well
worth it to hike out to the end, where the
river plunges into a series of deep holes and
gorges. Note that an angler's trail also runs
upstream from Ah-Di-Na Campground, but
while pretty, this is not the feature walk here.
The trailhead for this hike is another one-mile
drive at road's end, at the Nature Conservancy
section of land.

User Groups: Hikers only. No dogs, horses, or
mountain bikes. No wheelchair facilities.

Permits: No permits are required. Parking
and access are free.

Maps: For a map, ask the U.S. Forest Service for Shasta-Trinity National Forest. For
a topographic map, ask the USGS for Lake
McCloud.

Directions: From Redding, take I-5 north for
47 miles to the Highway 89/McCloud-Reno
exit. Bear right on Highway 89 and drive nine
miles to McCloud at Squaw Valley Road. Turn
right on Squaw Valley Road and drive five
miles (the road becomes Forest Road 11). At
the McCloud boat ramp, bear right and drive

on Forest Road 11 to the end of Battle Creek
Cove and Forest Road 38N53/Ah-Di-Na Road
(a dirt road) on the right. Turn right and drive
four miles (past Ah-Di-Na Campground) to
the road's end, at Fisher Creek. The Nature
Conservancy boundary is 0.5 mile down the
trail.

Contact: Shasta-Trinity National Forest,
McCloud Ranger District, P.O. Box 1620,
2019 Forest Road, McCloud, CA 96057,
530/964-2184, www.fs.fed.us/r5—click on
Forest Offices.

60 NEW RIVER TRAILHEAD
18.0 mi / 2.0 days   🏃3 ⛺6

in the Trinity Alps Wilderness east of
Willow Creek

Most backpackers in the Trinity Alps Wilderness like high mountain lakes, but here is a
trail that features small streams and is set in
the relative vicinity of the Megram burn area
of 1999. The highlights are the headwaters
of the New River (a tributary to the Trinity River), the history of the area, and Mary
Blaine Meadow. Because this is a river trail,
not a lake trail, and because of the Megram
fire at the headwaters of the New River, it gets
very little use.

The trail starts right along the New River
and immediately begins by dropping to Bar-
row Creek. In about a mile, you'll reach the
historic and largely eroded site of the Megram Cabin, the first landmark along the
trail. After another mile, bear right at the
fork in the trail and hike along Slide Creek.
After two miles you'll arrive again at a fork,
and you should again stay to the right. The
trail passes Robbers Roost Mine, Emmons
Cabin, and the Old Denny Cabin site, all on
the way to Mary Blaine Meadow, a distance
of about nine miles from the trailhead. The
meadow is set below Mary Blaine Mountain,
and to the north, Dees Peak. The whole region is cut with small streams in crevices and

SHASTA HIKING

canyons. From the air, you can see how the fire burned a huge area but cut a mosaiclike swath, leaving patches of green amid blackened scars.

User Groups: Hikers, dogs, and horses. No mountain bikes. No wheelchair facilities.

Permits: A wilderness permit is required for hikers planning to camp.

Maps: For a map, ask the U.S. Forest Service for Shasta-Trinity National Forest or Trinity Alps Wilderness. For topographic maps, ask the USGS for Jim Jam Ridge, Dees Peak, and Trinity Mountain.

Directions: From Weaverville, take Highway 299 west about 35 miles to Denny Road. Turn north (right) on County Road 402 (Denny Road) and drive about 21 miles. Turn left on Forest Road 7N15 and drive four miles north to the trailhead parking area.

Contact: Shasta-Trinity National Forest, Weaverville Ranger Station, P.O. Box 1190, 210 Main Street, Weaverville, CA 96093, 530/623-2121, www.fs.fed.us/r5—click on Forest Offices.

🔢61 EAST FORK LOOP
20.0 mi / 3.0 days

in the Trinity Alps Wilderness east of Willow Creek

Where else can you hike 20 miles with a chance of not seeing anybody? The East Fork trailhead provides access to one of the more primitive, less-traveled regions of the Trinity Alps Wilderness. It's an area known for streams and forests in the lower reaches and bare limestone ridges in the higher reaches. The trip starts at East Fork trailhead, adjacent to the East Fork New River. It climbs along this watershed and, after two miles, turns before coming to Pony Creek. In the next six miles, which include sections that are quite steep, the trail climbs to Limestone Ridge, near little Rattlesnake Lake. At Limestone Ridge, turn right on New River Divide Trail

and head south for six miles, passing Cabin Peak at 6,870 feet and arriving at White Creek Lake.

To complete the loop, turn right on the trail at White Creek Lake and start the trip back, descending most of the way. The trail goes past Jakes Upper Camp and Jakes Lower Camp before linking up again with East Fork Trail for the jog back to the parking area. Note that some bypass this trip because of the fear of walking through burned areas from the Megram fire of 1999. The reality is the Megram fire was west of Slide Creek, and that East Fork is not in the fire area.

User Groups: Hikers, dogs, and horses. No mountain bikes. No wheelchair facilities.

Permits: A wilderness permit is required for hikers planning to camp.

Maps: For a map, ask the U.S. Forest Service for Shasta-Trinity National Forest or Trinity Alps Wilderness. For a topographic map, ask the USGS for Jim Jam Ridge.

Directions: From Weaverville, turn west on Highway 299 and drive about 35 miles to Denny Road. Turn north on County Road 402 (Denny Road) and drive 22 miles (the last four miles of the road become unpaved Forest Road 7N01) to the trailhead parking area.

Contact: Shasta-Trinity National Forest, Weaverville Ranger Station, P.O. Box 1190, 210 Main Street, Weaverville, CA 96093, 530/623-2121, www.fs.fed.us/r5—click on Forest Offices.

🔢62 BURNT RANCH FALLS
1.25 mi / 1.0 hr

in Shasta-Trinity National Forest on Highway 299 east of Willow Creek

Burnt Ranch Falls isn't a spectacular cascade of water like other, more famous waterfalls, but it is the center of a very pretty, easy-to-reach scene on the Trinity River. It's a relatively small but wide waterfall, comprised of about 10 feet of rock that creates a natural barrier for migrating salmon and steelhead during low-water conditions. Thus the highlight comes when river flows rise a bit in the fall, so that you can watch the spectacular sight of salmon and steelhead jumping and sailing through the air to get over and past the falls.

The trail is a short but steep 0.75-mile jaunt down from the Burnt Ranch Campground. When you arrive at the river, walk out a short way on the rocky spot to watch the fish jump. The setting, in an area along Highway 299, has a magnificent natural landscape. From the river, the Trinity Canyon walls look like they ascend into the sky. Unlike most waterfalls, Burnt Ranch Falls is a far less compelling scene at high water. During high, turbid flows, it becomes much more difficult to see fish jumping past the falls.

User Groups: Hikers and dogs. No horses or mountain bikes. No wheelchair facilities.

Permits: No permits are required.

Maps: For a map, ask the U.S. Forest Service for Shasta-Trinity National Forest. For a topographic map, ask the USGS for Ironed Mountain.

Directions: From Weaverville, drive west on Highway 299 to Burnt Ranch. From Burnt Ranch, continue 0.5 mile west on Highway 299 to the trailhead at Burnt Ranch Campground, on the right.

Contact: Shasta-Trinity National Forest, Weaverville Ranger Station, P.O. Box 1190, 210 Main Street, Weaverville, CA 96093, 530/623-2121, www.fs.fed.us/r5—click on Forest Offices.

63 NEW RIVER DIVIDE TRAIL
30.0 mi / 3.0 days   🚶3 ⛺7

in the Trinity Alps Wilderness north of Trinity River's Big Bar

The New River Divide Trail provides access to the Limestone Ridge of the Trinity Alps, taking a ridgeline route most of the way. This is an area known for having lookouts from mountain rims, the headwaters of many small feeder streams, and few people. The trip starts at the Green Mountain trailhead, at an elevation of 5,052 feet, and in the first three miles, the route skirts the southern flank of Brushy Mountain, past Panther Camp and Stove Camp, and along the eastern flank of Green Mountain. As the trail climbs toward the Limestone Ridge, you'll find yourself perched on a divide, where the streams on each side pour into different watersheds. Eventually the trail rises all the way to Cabin Peak (at 6,870 feet) and beyond to little Rattlesnake Lake, a one-way distance of about 15 miles. Note that the Megram fire of 1999 consumed a huge area of acreage at the headwaters of the New River, off to the northwest from this ridge route.

User Groups: Hikers, dogs, and horses. No mountain bikes. No wheelchair facilities.

Permits: A wilderness permit is required. Parking and access are free.

Maps: For a map, ask the U.S. Forest Service for Shasta-Trinity National Forest or Trinity Alps Wilderness. For a topographic map, ask the USGS for Del Loam.

Directions: From Weaverville, drive west on Highway 299 for 28 miles to French Creek Road (Forest Road 5913). Turn north (right) and drive seven miles (the road becomes Forest Road 5N04). Continue straight for four miles to the trailhead, at the Green Mountain parking area.

Contact: Shasta-Trinity National Forest, Big Bar Ranger Station, Star Route 1, Box 10, Big Bar, CA 96010, 530/623-6106, www.fs.fed .us/r5—click on Forest Offices.

64 CANYON CREEK LAKES TRAILHEAD
16.0 mi / 2.0 days   🚶2 ⛺10

in the Trinity Alps Wilderness north of Weaverville

This is the kind of place where wilderness lovers think they can find religion. But what they find, guaranteed, are tons of other people: Expect about 50 other hikers on weekdays and 200 to 300 on weekends. The destination is Canyon Creek Lakes, set high in a mountain canyon, framed by Sawtooth Mountain to the east and a series of high granite rims to the north. The route in is no mystery; it's a climb of 3,100 feet over the course of eight miles. The trail heads straight upstream along Bear Creek for about 0.25 mile, crossing Bear Creek before continuing along Canyon Creek. Four miles out, you'll reach the first of four waterfalls. The first is the smallest, then they get progressively taller, and all are gorgeous. After the last waterfall, walk 0.5 mile to reach Lower Canyon Creek Lake, seven miles out from the trailhead. From this place, which is now largely above tree line, cross Stonehouse Gulch to reach the first of two lakes. The trail skirts the left side of the first of the Canyon Creek Lakes, then in 0.5 mile, it arrives at the head of the larger one. They are like jewels set in the bottom of a gray, stark, high mountain canyon, and once you've seen them, you'll have their picture branded permanently in your mind. This has become a special weekend favorite for hikers from Eureka and Redding.

User Groups: Hikers, dogs, and horses. No mountain bikes. No wheelchair facilities.

Permits: A wilderness permit is required for hikers planning to camp.

Maps: For a map, ask the U.S. Forest Service for Shasta-Trinity National Forest or Trinity Alps Wilderness. For a topographic map, ask the USGS for Dedrick.

Directions: From Weaverville, drive west on Highway 299 for eight miles to Junction City and Canyon Creek Road. Turn north on Canyon Creek Road and drive 13 miles to the trailhead, at the end of the road (.75 mile past Ripstein Campground).

Contact: Shasta-Trinity National Forest, Weaverville Ranger Station, P.O. Box 1190, 210 Main Street, Weaverville, CA 96093, 530/623-2121, www.fs.fed.us/r5—click on Forest Offices.

65 SOUTH FORK NATIONAL RECREATION TRAIL

20.0 mi / 2.0 days   👫2 ⚠6

in Shasta-Trinity National Forest east of Ruth Lake on Highway 36

This remote trail is best known for following along the South Fork Trinity River, heading south toward the Yolla Bolly Wilderness. This is an early-season trail, accessible when so many other mountain routes are still snowbound. And because of that, mountain bikers and equestrians often share the trail on warm spring weekends. There are no lakes anywhere near the trail, and for the most part, the trail just meanders along, with that stream nearby providing a constant point of reference.

Even the trailhead, a short drive out of the Hell Gate Campground, is remote and obscure. Immediately, the trail picks up the stream, and in less than an hour, you might even feel as if you've discovered your own private little universe. The temperatures can really smoke out here in the summer, and the stream is your savior. How far might you go? For many, an hour in, an hour out is plenty. Hikers can keep going to St. Jacques Place, an abandoned camp about 10 miles farther one-way, or even another five miles to the trail's end at Double Cabin site, where you can leave a shuttle car and make this a one-way trip. Note that the trail crosses private property several times; stay on the trail, respect property rights, and help keep this trail open.

User Groups: Hikers and dogs. No horses or mountain bikes. No wheelchair facilities.

Permits: Campfire permits are required for overnight use. Parking and access are free.

Maps: For a map, ask the U.S. Forest Service for Shasta-Trinity National Forest. For a topographic map, ask the USGS for Forest Glen.

Directions: From Red Bluff, take Highway 36 (very twisty) west and drive 47 miles to Platina and continue to the junction with Highway 3. Continue west on Highway 36 for 10 miles to the Hell Gate Campground (on the left) and

Forest Road 1526. Turn left on Forest Road 1526 and drive to the trailhead.

Contact: Shasta-Trinity National Forest, Hayfork Ranger Station, P.O. Box 159, Hayfork, CA 96041, 530/628-5227, www.fs .fed.us/r5—click on Forest Offices.

66 BLACK ROCK LAKE TRAIL
4.5 mi / 3.0 hr   👣2 ⛰8

on the northern boundary of the Yolla Bolly Wilderness west of Red Bluff

This 2.25-mile hike from the Stuart Gap trailhead to Black Rock Lake is one of the best day hikes in the Yolla Bolly Wilderness. One of the highlights comes in mid- to late June, when the wildflower blooms are absolutely beautiful. From the trailhead at the northern tip of the wilderness, at 5,600 feet, start by hiking about a mile on the Pettyjohn Trail. It is set along the northwestern flank of North Yolla Bolly Mountain (7,863 feet) and is routed toward Pettyjohn Basin. When you reach the Black Rock Lake Trail, turn right on it and tromp another 1.25 miles to the lake. The trail contours through open stands of pine and fir and some small meadows. Small Black Rock Lake is set just below Black Rock Mountain (7,755 feet), is ideal for swimming, and is stocked with trout by air every other year.

There are many other excellent day hikes from this trailhead: Yolla Bolly Lake (stocked with trout every other year), Black Rock Mountain (great views), North Yolla Bolly Mountain (more sweeping vistas), and Cedar Basin (several creeks). Any of these make for classic days, remote and quiet. The trailhead can also be used as a jump-off spot for a hike straight south on Pettyjohn Trail into the wilderness interior. Note that this trail is usually impassable prior to Memorial Day.

User Groups: Hikers, dogs, and horses. No mountain bikes. No wheelchair facilities.

Permits: A campfire permit is required for hikers planning to camp.

Maps: For a map, ask the U.S. Forest Service for Shasta-Trinity National Forest or Yolla Bolly Wilderness. For a topographic map, ask the USGS for North Yolla Bolly.

Directions: From Red Bluff, take Highway 36 (very twisty) west and drive 47 miles to Platina. Continue west on Highway 36 for 11 miles to Forest Road 30 (Wildwood–Mad River Road). Turn left (south) and drive nine miles to Forest Road 35. Turn left (east) on Forest Road 35 and drive 10 miles to the intersection of several roads. Take the signed fork for Stuart Gap trailhead and drive 1.8 miles (unpaved) to the trailhead parking area. Hike on Pettyjohn Trail for one mile to reach Black Rock Lake Trail.

Contact: Shasta-Trinity National Forest, Yolla Bolly and Hayfork Ranger Station, Hayfork, 530/628-5227, www.fs.fed.us/r5—click on Forest Offices.

67 SWIFT CREEK TRAIL TO GRANITE LAKE
12.0 mi / 2.0 days   👣4 ⛰9

in the Trinity Alps Wilderness west of Trinity Center

When hikers scan wilderness maps, they often search for trails that are routed a short distance to a beautiful lake for a first night's camp. That's exactly what you get at Granite Lake, but although the trip in is only about six miles, it's anything but easy. From the trailhead, start by tracing the right side of Swift Creek. Don't be fooled. Just beyond the confluence of Swift and Granite Creeks, you must cross the stream to the left and then pick up Granite Lake Trail. This trail runs along the right side of Granite Creek for four miles and includes a very steep section in the final mile that will have you wondering why you ever thought this was going to be such a short, easy trip.

Two notes on the way in: 1. For the most

SHASTA HIKING

part, the creek is not accessible as a water source, so monitor your canteen level. 2. There is a series of tumbling, churning waterfalls on Swift Creek—that is, no great free falls, but lots of whitewater.

Finally you'll rise to Gibson Meadow and just beyond, Granite Lake, a gorgeous sight below Gibson Peak. For a natural mountain lake, it's a fair size, with good swimming during the day and trout fishing in the evening. This is a popular spot, so plan on company.

User Groups: Hikers, dogs, and horses. No mountain bikes. No wheelchair facilities.

Permits: A wilderness permit is required for hikers planning to camp.

Maps: For a map, ask the U.S. Forest Service for Shasta-Trinity National Forest or Trinity Alps Wilderness. For topographic maps, ask the USGS for Covington Mill and Trinity Center.

Directions: From Weaverville, take Highway 3 north for 28 miles to Trinity Center and Swift Creek Road. Turn left and drive 6.8 miles to the parking area, at the wilderness border.

Contact: Shasta-Trinity National Forest, Weaverville Ranger Station, P.O. Box 1190, 210 Main Street, Weaverville, CA 96093, 530/623-2121, www.fs.fed.us/r5—click on Forest Offices.

68 LONG CANYON TRAILHEAD
16.0 mi / 2.0 days

in the Trinity Alps Wilderness northwest of Trinity Lake

Your mission, should you choose to accept it, is the 6.5-mile largely uphill hike to the west side of Gibson Peak, where Deer Lake, Summit Lake, Luella Lake, Diamond Lake, and Siligo Peak can provide days of side-trip destinations. From the trailhead, the trip starts by tracing along the East Fork Stuart Fork, a feeder creek to Trinity Lake. After two miles you'll arrive at a fork in the trail. Take the

right fork (the left fork is routed to Bowerman Meadows and little Lake Anna), which climbs farther along the stream and then traces the southern flank of Gibson Peak. At times the trail is steep in this area, but finally you'll pass Gibson Peak, and Siligo Peak will come into view. The trail also intersects a loop trail that circles Siligo Peak and provides access to four high mountain lakes. Summit Lake is the favorite.

User Groups: Hikers, dogs, and horses. No mountain bikes. No wheelchair facilities.

Permits: A wilderness permit is required for hikers planning to camp.

Maps: For a map, ask the U.S. Forest Service for Shasta-Trinity National Forest or Trinity Alps Wilderness. For a topographic map, ask the USGS for Covington Mill.

Directions: From Weaverville, take Highway 3 north to Covington Mill and Forest Road 115. Turn left and drive for 2.5 miles to the trailhead.

Contact: Shasta-Trinity National Forest, Weaverville Ranger Station, P.O. Box 1190, 210 Main Street, Weaverville, CA 96093, 530/623-2121, www.fs.fed.us/r5—click on Forest Offices.

69 STUART FORK TRAILHEAD
28.0 mi / 4.0 days

in the Trinity Alps Wilderness northwest of Trinity Lake

Don't say we didn't warn you: This trail doesn't have a difficulty rating of five for nothing. The hike requires an endless climb—very steep at times, particularly as you near the Sawtooth Ridge—spanning nearly 14 miles to Emerald Lake. The first nine miles are easy, and it will have you thinking that this hike is a piece of cake—long, but easy. But surprise! The last five miles from Morris Meadows are the killer. But after arriving and resting up for a night, you'll find that ecstasy follows. Emerald Lake is one of three lakes set in line in a canyon below the Sawtooth Ridge; the others on this side of the ridge are Sapphire and Mirror. The surroundings are stark and prehistoric, and the lakes are gemlike, blue, and clear, with big rainbow trout and water that is perfect for refreshing swims. The trail continues a mile past Emerald Lake to Sapphire Lake, and from there, it's an off-trail scramble, often across big boulders, as you climb another mile to reach Mirror Lake. The entire scene is surreal.

Special note: On the way to Emerald Lake, you might notice a cutoff trail to the right. On your trail map, you'll notice that it crosses the Sawtooth Ridge and leads in to the acclaimed Caribou Lakes Basin. On the map it appears to be a short, easy trip, but in reality, it involves a terrible climb with more than 100 switchbacks. Don't say you weren't warned.

User Groups: Hikers, dogs, and horses. No mountain bikes. No wheelchair facilities.

Permits: A wilderness permit is required for hikers planning to camp.

Maps: For a map, ask the U.S. Forest Service for Shasta-Trinity National Forest or Trinity Alps Wilderness. For a topographic map, ask the USGS for Covington Mill.

Directions: From Weaverville, take Highway 3 north to Trinity Lake and Trinity Alps Road. Turn left on Trinity Alps Road and drive 2.5 miles to the trailhead at Bridge Camp.

Contact: Shasta-Trinity National Forest, Weaverville Ranger Station, P.O. Box 1190, 210 Main Street, Weaverville, CA 96093, 530/623-2121, www.fs.fed.us/r5—click on Forest Offices.

70 HIRZ BAY TRAIL
3.2 mi / 1.75 hr

on the McCloud arm of Shasta Lake
north of Redding

Most people discover this trail by accident, usually while camping at Hirz Bay Group Camp. That is because this trail, routed along

the west side of the beautiful McCloud arm of Shasta Lake, is a natural hike from that camp. The trail traces the shoreline of the lake, in and out along small coves and creek inlets. Straight across the lake are pretty views of the deep coves at Campbell Creek and Dekkas Creek, of unique limestone outcrops, and of Minnesota Mountain (at 4,293 feet).

User Groups: Hikers and leashed dogs. No mountain bikes or horses. No wheelchair facilities.

Permits: No permits are required. A parking fee of $6 per vehicle is charged if parking at the Hirz Bay boat launch.

Maps: For a map, ask the U.S. Forest Service for Shasta-Trinity National Forest. For a topographic map, ask the USGS for O'Brien.

Directions: From Redding, take I-5 north to Shasta Lake and the exit for Salt Creek/Gilman Road. Take that exit and drive east on Gilman Road/County Road 7H009 for 10 miles to the access road for Hirz Bay boat launch and campground. Turn right and drive to the parking area.

Contact: Shasta-Trinity National Forest, Shasta Lake Ranger District, 14225 Holiday Road, Redding, CA 96003, 530/275-1587; Shasta Lake Visitor Center, 530/275-1589, www.fs.fed.us/shastatrinity.

71 GREENS CREEK BOAT-IN TRAIL
1.0-12.0 mi / 0.5-7.0 hr

on the McCloud arm of Shasta Lake
north of Redding

Let's get a few things straight from the start: 1) almost no one hikes this entire trail, 2) almost no one hikes part of this trail, and 3) almost no one even knows about this trail. Why? Because even with two million people estimated to visit Shasta Lake every year, the only way to access this trail is from an obscure, boat-in campsite at Greens Creek, on the east side of the McCloud arm of the lake. At the back of the cove at Greens Creek, you'll find a small U.S. Forest Service billboard posted with recreation guide sheets, and behind it are the campground and trailhead.

There are many fascinating side trips on the steep climb up toward a saddle between Town Mountain, at 4,325 feet, and Horse Mountain, at 4,025 feet. The trail enters an oak and madrone forest that is interspersed with limestone formations. The latter are worth exploring, and if you spend enough time hiking and investigating, you may find some small caves, a highlight of the trip. Most people are inspired to hike just high enough to get a good clear view of the lake below, but not much farther.

User Groups: Hikers and leashed dogs. No horses or mountain bikes. No wheelchair facilities.

Permits: No permits are required. A parking fee of $6 per vehicle is charged.

Maps: For a map, ask the U.S. Forest Service for Shasta-Trinity National Forest. For a topographic map, ask the USGS for O'Brien.

Directions: Load your boat and, from Redding, drive on I-5 north to Shasta Lake and the exit for Salt Creek/Gilman Road. Take that exit and drive east on Gilman Road/County Road 7H009 for 10 miles to the access road for Hirz Bay boat launch. Launch your boat, drive out in the McCloud arm of Shasta Lake toward the Shasta Caverns. Turn left at Greens Creek Cove and land your boat at Greens Creek Boat-In Campground.

Other nearby boat ramps are located to the south, at Lakeview Marina Resort (off Shasta Caverns Road) and at Bailey Cove.

Contact: Shasta-Trinity National Forest, Shasta Lake Ranger District, 14225 Holiday Road, Redding, CA 96003, 530/275-1587; Shasta Lake Visitor Center, 530/275-1589; www.fs.fed.us/shastatrinity.

72 BAILEY COVE LOOP TRAIL

2.8 mi / 1.5 hr   🏃2 △8

on the McCloud arm of Shasta Lake
north of Redding

This hike is best done in May and June, when the lake is full and at its highest levels. In late summer or fall, when the levels are down, you'll be looking out at a lot of red dirt. A favorite part of Shasta Lake is the McCloud arm, where the mountain canyon features limestone formations and the lake's clear, emerald waters. This trail provides a great view of these phenomena, as well as a close-to-the-water loop hike on one of the lake's peninsulas.

From the trailhead, start by hiking on the left fork, which travels out along Bailey Cove. As you continue, the loop trail heads in a clockwise direction, first along the McCloud arm of the lake, then back to the parking area along John's Creek Inlet. When you reach the mouth of Bailey Cove, stop and enjoy the view. Directly across the lake are the limestone formations, featuring North Gray Rocks (at 3,114 feet) and topped by Horse Mountain (at 4,025 feet). The famous Shasta Caverns are located just below North Gray Rocks. And hey, watch out for the poison oak just off the trail.

User Groups: Hikers and leashed dogs. No mountain bikes or horses. No wheelchair facilities.

Permits: No permits are required. A parking fee of $6 per vehicle is charged.

Maps: For a map, ask the U.S. Forest Service for Shasta-Trinity National Forest. For a topographic map, ask the USGS for O'Brien.

Directions: From Redding, take I-5 north to Shasta Lake and the exit for O'Brien/Shasta Caverns. Take that exit and turn east on Shasta Caverns Road and drive 0.1 mile to the sign for Bailey Cove Boat Ramp. Bear right at the sign and drive 0.5 mile to the day-use parking area.

Contact: Shasta-Trinity National Forest, Shasta Lake Ranger District, 14225 Holiday Road, Redding, CA 96003, 530/275-1587;

Shasta Lake Visitor Center, 530/275-1589, www.fs.fed.us/shastatrinity.

73 WATERS GULCH OVERLOOK

3.8 mi / 2.0 hr

at Packers Bay on Shasta Lake
north of Redding

Shasta Lake is so big—the biggest reservoir in California—that it can be difficult to know where to start in your mission to explore it. A good answer is right here on the Waters Gulch Loop. It connects to the Overlook Trail, a cutoff of 0.8 mile that climbs atop a small mountain and furnishes a view of the main lake. The trailhead is at Packers Bay, which is easily accessible off I-5. From the trailhead at the parking area, walk down the road and start hiking the trail from the Packer's Bay boat-ramp parking lots, and then finish back at the trailhead parking areas. This provides the best loop hike. Highlights of this trip include a route that extends onto one of the lake's peninsulas; Waters Gulch; a cove on the main Sacramento River arm of the lake; and several lookout points. Although there are many drive-to areas with lake views, you can get a little seclusion here as well.

User Groups: Hikers and leashed dogs. No horses or mountain bikes. No wheelchair facilities.

Permits: No permits are required. Parking and access are free.

Maps: For a map, ask the U.S. Forest Service for Shasta-Trinity National Forest. For a topographic map, ask the USGS for O'Brien.

Directions: From Redding, take I-5 north to Shasta Lake and the exit for Packers Bay. Take the exit and drive southwest on Packers Bay Road for one mile to the trailhead, on the right (.25 mile before the boat ramp).

Contact: Shasta-Trinity National Forest, Shasta Lake Ranger District, 14225 Holiday

Road, Redding, CA 96003, 530/275-1587; Shasta Lake Visitor Center, 530/275-1589, www.fs.fed.us/shastatrinity.

74 BOULDER CREEK FALLS

6.4 mi / 3.5 hr

at Whiskeytown Lake National
Recreation Area west of Redding

The pay-off on this hike is Boulder Creek Falls, an 81-foot waterfall with a 28-foot cataract. This view is great, a full-front direct-on view of the narrow falls and the wider cataract and plunge pool. From the trailhead, the start is unimpressive, on a logging road that is wide and exposed for a mile. When you reach the creek, the landscape gets a lot prettier—a mix of pine, fir and oak. From here, you will follow along the creek upstream and cross it three times. After the third crossing, look for a fork a bit up the trail. Take the right fork, keep on for another crossing, and then look for the signed spur trail for the water (3 miles total). This short spur leads to several faint paths, where others have tried to find the best vantage point. Ignore these paths and walk up the steps on the left, leading to a rock perch for the best view of the main falls. Although you can hike on to Mill Creek Road, the best route back is to return the way you came in.

User Groups: Hikers, mountain bikes, dogs, and horse. No wheelchair facilities.

Permits: A parking fee of $5 per vehicle is charged.

Maps: For a detailed trail map, contact Whiskeytown National Recreation Area at the address below. For a topographic map, ask the USGS for Igo.

Directions: From Redding, turn west on Highway 299 and drive 10 miles to the Whiskeytown Visitors Center on the left. Continue west on 299 for seven miles to Carr Powerhouse Road. Turn left and drive 0.5 mile to Carr Powerhouse Road and South Shore Road.

Continue straight on South Shore Road for 2.7 miles to the trailhead.

Contact: Whiskeytown National Recreation Area, P.O. Box 188, 14412 J. F. Kennedy Memorial Drive, Whiskeytown, CA 96095, 530/246-1225, www.nps.gov/whis.

75 DAVIS GULCH TRAIL
3.3 mi one-way / 3.5 hr   🏃1 ⛰7

at Whiskeytown Lake National
Recreation Area west of Redding

The Davis Gulch Trail is Whiskeytown Lake's easiest hike. This meandering route along the southwest end of the lake starts out at 1,414 feet (at an information billboard along an access road) and winds its way down to the Brandy Creek Picnic Area, at 1,240 feet. It is a moderate descent on a wide, flat footpath surrounded mostly by oak and manzanita. Along the way, there are many good views of Whiskeytown Lake. The trail spans 3.3 miles and dead-ends. With two vehicles, it is possible to make it a one-way hike with a shuttle and then (better yet) hike the whole route downhill.

User Groups: Hikers and dogs. No horses or mountain bikes. No wheelchair facilities.

Permits: A parking fee of $5 per vehicle is charged.

Maps: For a detailed trail map, contact Whiskeytown National Recreation Area at the address below. For a topographic map, ask the USGS for Igo.

Directions: From Redding, turn west on Highway 299 and drive 10 miles to the Whiskeytown Visitors Center on the left. Turn left at the visitors center and drive on J. F. Kennedy Memorial Drive for three miles to the Davis Gulch trailhead, on the right. To reach the Brandy Creek Picnic Area (and end of the trail), continue three more miles on J. F. Kennedy Memorial Drive.

Contact: Whiskeytown National Recreation

Area, P.O. Box 188, 14412 J. F. Kennedy Memorial Drive, Whiskeytown, CA 96095, 530/246-1225, www.nps.gov/whis.

76 WHISKEYTOWN FALLS
3.4 mi / 2.5 hr   🏃3 ⛰9

at Whiskeytown Lake National Recreation
Area west of Redding

This trail to Whiskeytown Falls features a stunning route next to the falls where a staircase has been cut into rock, with a piped hand rail for safety. Hold on tight and enjoy a series of waterfall lookouts called "Photographer's Ledge" and, up near the top, "Artist's Ledge." The waterfall is estimated at 220 feet tall, top to bottom.

From the parking area, the hike starts on the James K. Carr Trail and leads down an old logging road to Crystal Creek. You cross a bridge, and then start the climb. At one spot, known as Cougar Rock, you will see some unique granite boulders that look like they've been stacked up. Look for the signed trailhead up a ways to the right and continue as the trail keeps climbing up through pretty, shaded Steep Ravine. It's aptly named, so be prepared and ignore the logging spurs off to the sides. In fall, the leaves come alive in golds and yellows. Eventually, the old logging road trail levels out, and after the viewpoint at Wintu View, you'll arrive at a picnic area where bikes and horses must be left. The final piece of trail runs along the creek for 0.25 mile and leads to the base of the falls.

Here, it only gets better. Climb the stone staircase to the left for the best views of the Whiskeytown Falls.

This "secret" waterfall was "unknown" for many years, was "discovered" in 2004, and "revealed to the public" in 2005. The truth is a small number of people have known about it for more than 50 years, but didn't tell anybody.

SHASTA HIKING

I've seen this "hidden" waterfall, and about 15 others, from my airplane for many years.

User Groups: Hikers, mountain bikes, and horses are permitted up to picnic area. Hikers only allowed after this point. No dogs. No wheelchair facilities.

Permits: A parking fee of $5 per vehicle is charged.

Maps: For a detailed trail map, contact Whiskeytown National Recreation Area at the address below. For a topographic map, ask the USGS for Igo.

Directions: From Redding, turn west on Highway 299 and drive 10 miles to the Whiskeytown Visitors Center on the left. Continue west on 299 for eight miles to Crystal Creek Road. Turn left and drive 2.75 miles to reach Mill Creek Trailhead. Look here for the signed James K. Carr trailhead for Whiskeytown Falls.

Contact: Whiskeytown National Recreation Area, P.O. Box 188, 14412 J. F. Kennedy Memorial Drive, Whiskeytown, CA 96095, 530/246-1225, www.nps.gov/whis.

77 BRANDY CREEK FALLS
3.0 mi / 2.0 hr   3   9

at Whiskeytown Lake National Recreation Area west of Redding

Brandy Creek Falls is a cascade chute with a series of pool-and-drops that pour into a big pool. It is spectacular at high water, a cataract where all the waterfall pools are connected into a massive whitewater flow. At low water, it splits into two thin cascades with a series of small drops. This is not a Yosemite-like freefall and the trailhead is still fairly obscure.

From the trailhead, you'll cross a creek in 0.5 mile. There is a large debris field of logs and boulders in the creek, the result of the 1977 flood. Continue on and in another 0.25 mile, you will reach a junction with the Rich Gulch Trail. Though you pass this by and

continue ahead, note that the trail narrows here and is accessible only for hikers. From here to the falls, the trail enters the Brandy Creek Canyon with fern grottoes and cliff-like dropoffs. It can be slippery, but the route heads right along the cascade. As you forge on, you will find steps cut in rock that will lead you past five pools and falls that run about 50 feet. Very special stuff.

User Groups: Hikers only. No mountain bikes, dogs, or horses. No wheelchair facilities.

Permits: A parking fee of $5 per vehicle is charged.

Maps: For a detailed trail map, contact Whiskeytown National Recreation Area at the address below. For a topographic map, ask the USGS for Igo.

Directions: From Redding, turn west on Highway 299 and drive 10 miles to the Whiskeytown Visitors Center on the left. Turn left at the visitors center, and continue south on Kennedy Memorial Drive to a fork. Bear right at the fork, cross over the dam, and continue past the Brandy Creek area to Shasta Bally Road. Turn left and drive 2.5 miles on the dirt road to a junction. Turn left and drive 0.75 miles to a small parking area. The signed trailhead is 150 feet up the road.

Contact: Whiskeytown National Recreation Area, P.O. Box 188, 14412 J. F. Kennedy Memorial Drive, Whiskeytown, CA 96095, 530/246-1225, www.nps.gov/whis.

78 SYD CABIN RIDGE TRAIL
8.0 mi / 2.0 days   3   7

on the eastern boundary of the Yolla Bolly Wilderness west of Red Bluff

Not many people hike into the Yolla Bolly Wilderness, set up a camp, then hike back out the next day. But here is a chance to do exactly that. The trailhead is at the Tomhead Saddle, located just west of Tomhead Mountain, at an elevation of 6,757 feet. From here, hike past

Tomhead Spring on Syd Cabin Ridge Trail, then drop down into Hawk Camp. Set just below the confluence of three feeder streams, Hawk Camp is a spot to overnight. On the way back, expect a steady climb with no water between Tomhead Spring and Hawk Camp. If you plan on extending your trip for several days into the wilderness, a network of trails intersects just beyond Hawk Camp, but note that a stream crossing is required.

User Groups: Hikers, dogs, and horses. No mountain bikes. No wheelchair facilities.

Permits: A campfire permit is required for hikers planning to camp.

Maps: For a map, ask the U.S. Forest Service for Shasta-Trinity National Forest or Yolla Bolly Wilderness. For a topographic map, ask the USGS for North Yolla Bolly.

Directions: From Red Bluff, turn west on Highway 36 (twisty) and drive about 13 miles to Cannon Road. Turn left (south) on Cannon Road and go approximately five miles to Pettyjohn Road. Turn right (west) on Pettyjohn Road and drive to Forest Road 27N06. Turn left (south) on Forest Road 27N06 and continue three miles to the parking area at Tomhead Saddle Campground. From Highway 36, this route is a dirt road all the way in. A high-clearance vehicle is recommended. It can also be slippery when wet.

Contact: Shasta-Trinity National Forest, Yolla Bolly and Hayfork Ranger Station, Hayfork, 530/628-5227, www.fs.fed.us/r5—click on Forest Offices.

LASSEN HIKING

© ANN MARIE BROWN

BEST HIKES

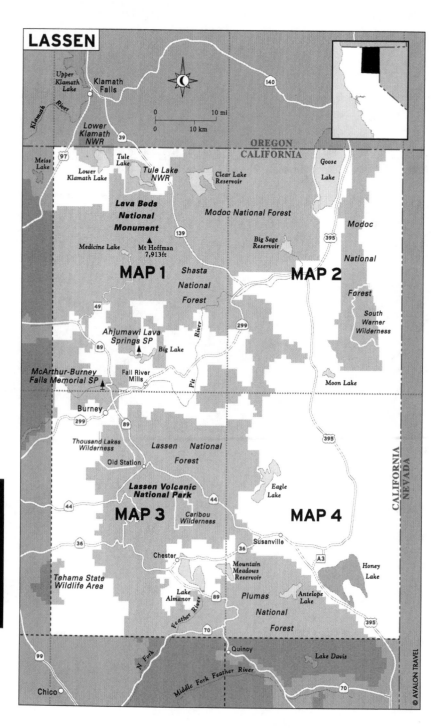

LASSEN HIKING

© AVALON TRAVEL

Map 1

Hikes 1-11

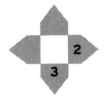

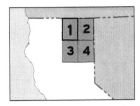

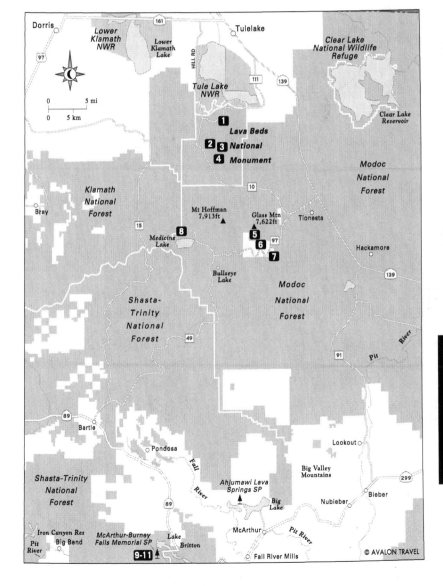

Map 2

Hikes 12-21

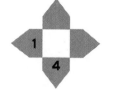

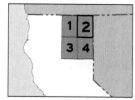

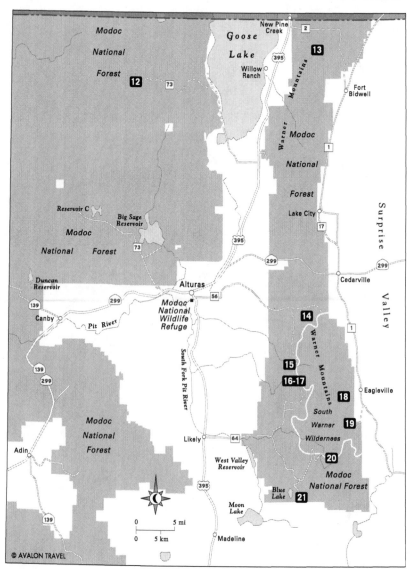

LASSEN HIKING

© AVALON TRAVEL

Map 3

Hikes 22-54

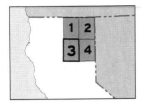

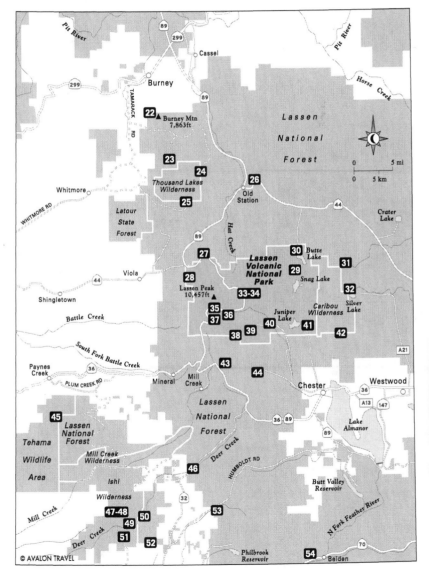

Map 4

Hike 55

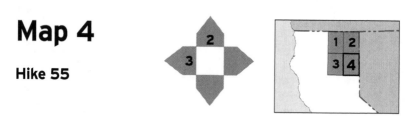

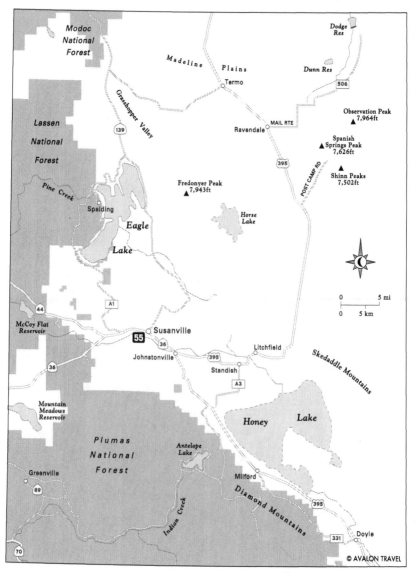

© AVALON TRAVEL

1 CAPTAIN JACK'S STRONGHOLD

1.7 mi / 1.5 hr   👫1 🏔7

in Lava Beds National Monument south of Klamath Wildlife Refuge

BEST (

Captain Jack's Stronghold provides a history lesson and an introduction to the Lava Beds National Monument. It's an easy walk on a clear trail amid a volcanic plateau, with a few trenches, dips, and rocks. From this trailhead, there are actually two loop trails available, including a shorter route that is just 0.5 mile long. The general terrain is level, with a trailhead elevation of 4,047 feet and a high point of 4,080 feet.

Captain Jack was a Modoc warrior who fought U.S. troops attempting to relocate Native Americans off their lands and onto a reservation. His hiding place was betrayed by his own troops, and in 1873, Captain Jack was finally captured and hanged, and this site was later named for him.

Note that during the winter, this is an outstanding area to see mule deer. Many of the famous photographs of big bucks in California were taken in this area. The wildlife viewing is best at the onset of winter, after the first inch or two of snow has fallen. In addition, a good nearby side trip is Tule Lake, a favorite wintering area for waterfowl and bald eagles.

User Groups: Hikers only. No dogs, horses, or mountain bikes. No wheelchair access.

Permits: No permits are required. A park entrance fee of $10, good for seven days, is charged per vehicle.

Maps: A free brochure is available by contacting Lava Beds National Monument at the address below. For a topographic map, ask the USGS for Captain Jack's Stronghold.

Directions: From Redding, take I-5 north for 68 miles to the exit for Central Weed/Highway 97–Klamath Falls. Take that exit to the stop sign, turn right and drive one mile through town to the junction with Highway 97. Bear right on Highway 97 and drive 54 miles to Highway 161. Turn right (east) on Highway 161 and drive 20 miles to Hill Road. Turn right (south), drive 18 miles to the visitors center, and look for the main road of the Lava Beds National Monument (it's unnamed). Turn north and drive 13 miles on the main monument road to the Captain Jack's Stronghold access road. Turn right and drive to the trailhead.

Contact: Lava Beds National Monument, 1 Indian Well Headquarters, Tulelake, CA 96134, 530/667-2282, www.nps.gov/labe.

2 WHITNEY BUTTE TRAIL

6.8 mi / 4.0 hr   👫2 🏔8

in Lava Beds National Monument south of Klamath Wildlife Refuge

The Whitney Butte Trail is one of three wilderness trails in Lava Beds National Monument, and for many, it's the best of the lot. From the trailhead at Merrill Cave, set at 4,880 feet, the trail goes west for 3.4 miles, skirting the northern flank of Whitney Butte (5,004 feet) and ending at the edge of the Callahan Lava Flow, on the park's southwest boundary. Be sure to climb Whitney Butte. This area bears a resemblance to the surface of the moon, and skilled photographers who know how to use sunlight to their advantage can take black-and-white pictures that can fool most people into thinking they are looking at a lunar surface. Most people arrive just to see the Merrill Ice Cave (which is actually a lava tube) at the beginning of the hike. If you plan to explore the cave, bring plenty of flashlight power, a hard hat, and kneepads.

User Groups: Hikers and horses. No dogs or mountain bikes. No wheelchair facilities.

Permits: No permits are required. A park entrance fee of $10, good for seven days, is charged per vehicle.

Maps: A free brochure is available by contacting Lava Beds National Monument at the address below. For a topographic map, ask the USGS for Schonchin Butte.

Directions: From Redding, take I-5 north for 68 miles to the exit for Central Weed/Highway 97–Klamath Falls. Take that exit to the stop sign, turn right and drive one mile through town to the junction with Highway 97. Bear right on Highway 97 and drive 54 miles to Highway 161. Turn right (east) on Highway 161 and drive 20 miles to Hill Road. Turn right (south), drive 18 miles to the visitors center, and look for the main road of the Lava Beds National Monument (it's unnamed). Turn north and drive two miles north on the monument main road to the turnoff for Merrill Ice Cave. Turn left and drive 0.75 mile to parking lot and trailhead, at the end of the road.

Contact: Lava Beds National Monument, 1 Indian Well Headquarters, Tulelake, CA 96134, 530/667-2282, www.nps.gov/labe.

3 THOMAS WRIGHT TRAIL
2.2 mi / 1.0 hr 🥾1 ⛰7

in Lava Beds National Monument
south of Tulelake Wildlife Refuge

After just 0.25 mile on this trail, hikers reach the awesome Black Crater. In the world of volcanic geology, this is a spatter cone. It feels as if you are looking into the bowels of the earth. In time, as you continue on, you might even get the sense that ghosts are shadowing your footsteps. That is because some say this area is haunted by the ghosts of Modoc Indians, who fought troops in several violent battles for custody of the land. Though the Modoc warriors eventually lost that war, some say they actually won in the long run, since their spirits haunt modern-day visitors. At the end of the trail are interpretive signs that explain the Thomas Wright battlefield site. For an excellent side trip from here, continue off trail, clambering up to the Hardin Butte, a 130-foot climb, for a view. The butte sits on the western edge of the huge Schonchin Lava Flow.

User Groups: Hikers only. No dogs, horses, or mountain bikes. No wheelchair facilities.

Permits: No permits are required. A park entrance fee of $10, good for seven days, is charged per vehicle.

Maps: A free brochure is available by contacting Lava Beds National Monument at the address below. For a topographic map, ask the USGS for Captain Jack's Stronghold.

Directions: From Redding, take I-5 north for 68 miles to the exit for Central Weed/Highway 97–Klamath Falls. Take that exit to the stop sign, turn right and drive one mile through town to the junction with Highway 97. Bear right on Highway 97 and drive 54 miles to Highway 161. Turn right (east) on Highway 161 and drive 20 miles to Hill Road. Turn right (south) and drive five miles to the trailhead on the left (the visitors center is another five miles south).

Contact: Lava Beds National Monument, 1 Indian Well Headquarters, Tulelake, CA 96134, 530/667-2282, www.nps.gov/labe.

4 SCHONCHIN BUTTE TRAIL
1.8 mi / 1.0 hr 🥾3 ⛰8

in Lava Beds National Monument
south of Tulelake Wildlife Refuge

This is a short hike, but for many, it's a butt-kicker. A portion of it is quite steep—enough to get most folks wheezing like old steam locomotives. The trail climbs 600 feet, from a trailhead elevation of 4,700 feet to the lookout at 5,300 feet. There are benches along the trail in case you need to catch your breath. Schonchin Butte has an old fire lookout, and the views are spectacular, of course, especially of the Schonchin Lava Flow to the northeast. Because of the proximity to the visitors center, as well as the short distance involved, many visitors make the tromp to the top. After completing this trip, always explore some of the caves in the matrix of underground lava tubes. You need a hard hat and flashlight to do it (available for a fee at the visitors center). For extensive caving, always wear kneepads. There are more than 700 caves in a five-mile radius, including 15 with signed entrances on the Cave Loop.

User Groups: Hikers only. No dogs, horses, or mountain bikes. No wheelchair facilities.

Permits: No permits are required. A park entrance fee of $10, good for seven days, is charged per vehicle.

Maps: A free brochure is available by contacting Lava Beds National Monument at the address below. For a topographic map, ask the USGS for Schonchin Butte.

Directions: From Redding, take I-5 north for 68 miles to the exit for Central Weed/Highway 97–Klamath Falls. Take that exit to the stop sign, turn right and drive one mile through town to the junction with Highway 97. Bear right on Highway 97 and drive 54 miles to Highway 161. Turn right (east) on Highway 161 and drive 20 miles to Hill Road. Turn right (south), drive 18 miles to the visitors center, and look for the main road of the Lava Beds National Monument (it's unnamed). Turn north and drive 2.3 miles to the turnoff for Schonchin Butte. Turn right at the sign for Schonchin Butte and drive about one mile on a gravel road to the trailhead.

Contact: Lava Beds National Monument, 1 Indian Well Headquarters, Tulelake, CA 96134, 530/667-2282, www.nps.gov/labe.

⑤ MEDICINE LAKE LOOP
0.5–4.5 mi / 0.5–2.5 hr

in Modoc National Forest northeast of Mount Shasta

When you stand on the shore of Medicine Lake, it might be difficult to believe that this was once the center of a volcano. The old caldera is now filled with water and circled by conifers, and the lake is clear and crisp. Set at 6,700 feet, it's a unique and popular destination for camping, boating, and fishing. At some point in their stay, most campers will take a morning or afternoon to walk around the lake. Although there is no specific trail,

the route is clear enough. There is a sense of timelessness here. Although its geology is comparable to Crater Lake in Oregon, Medicine Lake is neither as deep nor as blue. But a bonus here is the good shore fishing for large brook trout, often in the 12- to 14-inch class, buoyed by the largest stocks of trout of any lake in the region (30,000 per year). There are also many excellent nearby side trips—including ice caves (along the access road on the way in); a great mountaintop lookout from Little Mount Hoffman, just west of the lake; and nearby little Bullseye and Blanche Lakes.

User Groups: Hikers, dogs, horses, and mountain bikes. There are wheelchair facilities at the beach and the boat ramp.

Permits: No permits are required. Parking and access are free unless you're camping.

Maps: A free brochure on the Medicine Lake Highlands is available by contacting the Doublehead Ranger District at the address below. For a map, ask the U.S. Forest Service for Modoc National Forest. For a topographic map, ask the USGS for Medicine Lake.

Directions: From Redding, take I-5 north for 57 miles to the exit for Highway 89/McCloud. Bear right on Highway 89 and drive 28 miles east to Bartle. Just past Bartle, turn left (northeast) on Powder Hill Road (Forest Road 49), and drive 31 miles (it becomes Medicine Lake Road) to the campground and lake access road. Turn left and drive 0.25 mile to the lake.

Contact: Modoc National Forest, Doublehead Ranger District, P.O. Box 369, Tulelake, CA 96134, 530/667-2246, www.fs.fed.us/r5—click on Forest Offices.

⑥ GLASS MOUNTAIN
2.5 mi / 1.5 hr

in Modoc National Forest east of Medicine Lake

Glass Mountain, a glass flow that covers 4,210 acres, is one of the most unusual settings in the Medicine Lake Highlands. It was created when glassy dacite and rhyolitic obsidian flowed from the same volcanic vent without mixing, creating a present-day phenomenon that exhibits no modification from weather, erosion, or vegetation. There are no designated trails on Glass Mountain, so visitors just wander about, inspecting the geologic curiosities as they go. Take care to stay clear of the obsidian, which is quite slippery and can have arrowhead-sharp edges. Don't walk on it, and don't handle it. Be sure to stay on the gray-colored dacite instead. Got it? Stay on the gray stuff. Stay off the black stuff.

User Groups: Hikers and dogs. The terrain is not suitable for horses or mountain bikes. No wheelchair facilities.

Permits: No permits are required. Parking and access are free.

Maps: A free brochure on the Medicine Lake Highlands is available by contacting the Doublehead Ranger District at the address below. For a map, ask the U.S. Forest Service for Modoc National Forest. For a topographic map, ask the USGS for Medicine Lake.

Directions: From Redding, take I-5 north for 57 miles to the exit for Highway 89/McCloud. Bear right on Highway 89 and drive 28 miles to Bartle. Just past Bartle, turn left (northeast) on Powder Hill Road (Forest Road 49) and drive about 29 miles (it becomes Medicine Lake Road) to County Road 97. Turn right on County Road 97 and drive about six miles to Forest Road 43N99. Turn north on Forest Road 43N99 and drive to the southern border of Glass Mountain.

Contact: Modoc National Forest, Doublehead Ranger District, P.O. Box 369, Tulelake, CA 96134, 530/667-2246, www.fs.fed.us/r5—click on Forest Offices.

◼ BURNT LAVA FLOW
2.5 mi / 1.5 hr

in Modoc National Forest south of Medicine Lake

When you walk across the Burnt Lava Flow, a land of "rocks that float and mountains of glass," it may seem as if you're exploring some prehistoric area that resembles the moon. But get this: The lava formation is only about 200 years old, the youngest flow in the Medicine Lake Highlands. It's located south of Glass Mountain and covers some 8,760 acres, with little islands of forest amid the bare, jet-black lava flow. When we took an aerial survey of the area, the Burnt Lava Flow was one of the most fascinating portions of the entire region. On foot, it's even stranger. There is no trail, so pick any direction—most visitors go from tree island to tree island. There are a few weird spots where the ground can be like quicksand when dry and like wet concrete when wet. Just walk around those spots, staying on the hard, black lava flow.

User Groups: Hikers and dogs. The terrain is not suitable for mountain bikes or horses. No wheelchair facilities.

Permits: No permits are required. Parking and access are free.

Maps: For a map, ask the U.S. Forest Service for Modoc National Forest. For a topographic map, ask the USGS for Porcupine Butte.

Directions: From Redding, take I-5 north for 57 miles to the exit for Highway 89/McCloud. Bear right on Highway 89 and drive 28 miles to Bartle. Just past Bartle, turn left on Powder Hill Road (Forest Road 49) and drive 24 miles (the road becomes Medicine Lake Road) to Forest Road 42N25. Turn right and drive (the road becomes Forest Road 56) to the Burnt Lava Flow Geologic Area.

Contact: Modoc National Forest, Doublehead Ranger District, P.O. Box 369, Tulelake, CA 96134, 530/667-2246, www.fs.fed.us/r5—click on Forest Offices.

8 MEDICINE LAKE LAVA FLOW
2.0 mi / 2.0 hr

in Modoc National Forest north of
Medicine Lake

The Medicine Lake Lava Flow covers 570 acres but has no designated trails. You can explore in any direction you wish, investigating the ancient, stony-gray dacite, which runs 50 to 150 feet deep. This is part of the Medicine Lake Highlands, located just a mile north of Medicine Lake, where there are "rocks that float and mountains of glass" (a poetic description from Forest Service geologists). Before the first lunar landing, many originally believed this area to resemble the surface of the moon. That is why this area was selected by the Manned Spacecraft Center in 1965 for study by astronauts preparing for the first manned trip to the moon. Most people will just poke around for an hour or two, take a few pictures, and leave, saying they've never seen anything like it.

User Groups: Hikers and dogs. The terrain is not suitable for mountain bikes or horses. No wheelchair facilities.

Permits: No permits are required. Parking and access are free.

Maps: A free brochure on the Medicine Lake Highlands is available by contacting the Doublehead Ranger District at the address below. For a map, ask the U.S. Forest Service for Modoc National Forest. For a topographic map, ask the USGS for Medicine Lake.

Directions: From Redding, take I-5 north for 57 miles to the exit for Highway 89/McCloud. Bear right on Highway 89 and drive 28 miles to Bartle. Just past Bartle, turn left (northeast) on Powder Hill Road (Forest Road 49) and drive 31 miles (it becomes Medicine Lake Road) to the Medicine Lake turnoff. Continue ahead (do not turn) for 2.5 miles, and look for the glass flow, on the left side of the road. Park and go for it.

Contact: Modoc National Forest, Doublehead Ranger District, P.O. Box 369, Tulelake, CA 96134, 530/667-2246, www.fs.fed.us/r5—click on Forest Offices.

9 BURNEY FALLS LOOP TRAIL
1.2 mi / 0.5 hr

in McArthur-Burney Falls Memorial State Park north of Burney

BEST

Visitors from across the West are attracted to this state park by the chance to see spectacular Burney Falls. At 129 feet high, the waterfall plunges over a cliff in two pieces, split at the rim by a small bluff, where two trees have managed toeholds (although the river flows over the top of them during high water from the spring snowmelt). Underground lava tubes also transport water to the site; water seems to ooze right from the surrounding moss. From the park entrance station, it's a 100-foot walk to the rocky falls overlook, a perfect place for photographs of the waterfall. This spot also marks the start of Burney Falls Loop Trail, an easy 1.2-mile loop around the waterfall and back. There is a 200-foot drop at the start of the trail, where you skirt the plunge pool of the waterfall. Then the trail is routed downstream along Burney Creek and crosses a wood bridge. Then hike upstream back to the waterfall for more fantastic views. The trail climbs up past the brink of the falls and continues upstream along Burney Creek. It then crosses another bridge and loops back to the Falls Overlook. It's a self-guided nature trail, but rather than having to carry a brochure with you, you can just read the small signs that explain the featured sites. To celebrate the expedition, the next destination is the park's snack bar, where visitors often go for an ice-cream cone. All in all, this is an easy, fun, beautiful, and memorable walk.

User Groups: Hikers only. No dogs, horses, or mountain bikes. There is paved wheelchair access at the falls overlook point, at the beginning of the trail.

Permits: No permits are required. A state park day-use fee of $6 is charged for each vehicle.

Maps: A trail guide is available for a fee at the

LASSEN HIKING

state park at the address below. For a topographic map, ask the USGS for Burney Falls. **Directions:** From Redding, take Highway 299 east for 50 miles to Burney and continue five miles to the junction with Highway 89. Turn left (north) and drive 5.8 miles to the state park entrance on the left. At the entrance station, continue straight for a short distance and park in the main lot on the right. The trailhead is across the road at the falls overlook. **Contact:** McArthur-Burney Falls Memorial State Park, 24898 Highway 89, Burney, CA 96013, 530/335-2777, www.parks.ca.gov—click on Find A Park.

10 RIM TRAIL
3.0 mi / 1.75 hr   👣2 ⛰8

at Lake Britton in McArthur-Burney Falls Memorial State Park north of Burney

The Rim Trail provides an ideal hike for campers at Burney Falls State Park. The trail starts at the campground and is routed to the rim of Lake Britton, a distance of 1.5 miles. It's an easy walk, and pretty too, heading first through forest, then emerging with a good lookout of the lake. The total elevation gain and loss is less than 250 feet. An easy side trip takes you down to the beach. The lake, set in a gorge, seems to have special qualities, sometimes shimmering with effervescence. The fishing is good, too—especially for crappie, but bass, bluegill, and trout are plentiful as well.
User Groups: Hikers only. No dogs, horses, or mountain bikes. No wheelchair facilities.
Permits: No permits are required. A state park day-use fee of $6 is charged for each vehicle.
Maps: A trail guide is available for a fee at the state park at the address below. For a topographic map, ask the USGS for Burney Falls.
Directions: From Redding, take Highway 299 east for 50 miles to Burney and continue five miles to the junction with Highway 89. Turn left (north) and drive 5.8 miles to the state park entrance on the left. At the entrance sta-

tion, continue straight for a short distance and park in the main lot on the right. The trailhead is across the road at the falls overlook.
Contact: McArthur-Burney Falls Memorial State Park, 24898 Highway 89, Burney, CA 96013, 530/335-2777, www.parks.ca.gov—click on Find A Park.

11 McARTHUR-BURNEY FALLS MEMORIAL STATE PARK TO ASH CAMP (PCT)
52.0 mi one-way / 4.0 days   👣5 ⛰5

from McArthur-Burney Falls Memorial State Park west into Ash Camp in Shasta-Trinity National Forest

It may be difficult to leave the woods, waters, and aura of Burney Falls, but off you go, facing dry country and some of Northern California's least-used portions of the Pacific Crest Trail. Typically the only hikers who complete this section are the ones hiking the entire route from Mexico to Canada; they're virtually forced to endure it, often at great hardship.

From Burney Falls, the PCT heads west, touching the Pit River arm of Lake Britton, and then continues forward into Lassen Volcanic National Park, crossing into Shasta-Trinity National Forest and up to Grizzly Peak. Much of this route is across dry, hot, exposed slopes, where the trail has deteriorated in many spots due to the encroachment of brush and the zero trail maintenance by the U.S. Forest Service. Knowing you're smack between the lush beauty of Burney Falls (behind you) and the McCloud River (ahead of you) can make dealing with the present brush-infested landscape a frustrating encounter. Always fill your canteens with water wherever you find it, and don't hesitate to make a camp if, late in the day, you find even a small flat spot with water nearby. In extremely dry years it's possible to travel this entire stretch without finding any water.

After the hot, beastly climb near Grizzly Peak,

most hikers will want to make a lightning-fast descent to the Eden of the McCloud River at Ash Camp. But hold your horses. As long as you've come this far, make the short side trip up to Grizzly Peak, and while you're looking at the incredible view of Mount Shasta and the McCloud flats, congratulate yourself for completing such a terrible hike. Considering the PCT is the feature national recreation trail in America, this stretch is an embarrassment to the U.S. Forest Service and an abomination to hikers.

To continue north on the PCT, see the *Ash Camp to Castle Crags Wilderness (PCT)* hike in the *Shasta* chapter. If you are walking this trail in reverse, see the *McArthur-Burney Falls Memorial State Park (PCT)* hike in this chapter to continue south.

User Groups: Hikers, dogs (except in the state park boundaries), and horses. No mountain bikes. No wheelchair facilities.

Permits: A campfire permit (free) is required. A fee of $6 is charged per vehicle at the state park.

Maps: For USGS topographic maps, ask for Burney Falls, Skunk Ridge, and Grizzly Peak.

Directions: From Redding, take Highway 299 east for 50 miles to Burney and continue five miles to the junction with Highway 89. Turn left (north) and drive 5.8 miles to the state park entrance on the left. At the entrance station, continue straight for a short distance and park in the main lot on the right.

Contact: McArthur-Burney Falls Memorial State Park, 24898 Highway 89, Burney, CA 96013, 530/335-2777, www.parks.ca.gov—click on Find A Park.

12 JANES RESERVOIR
1.0 mi / 0.75 hr 🥾1 ⛰7

in Modoc National Forest north of Alturas

A dirt road leads from the southwest corner of Janes Reservoir to Huffman Butte, about a two-mile drive. If your car can't handle the road, you can hike it. The best strategy is to

park at the base of the butte and make the easy climb to the top of it. The reward is a nice view of the lake and the surrounding stark terrain.

This is sagebrush country, the high-plateau land of Modoc County. You're likely to see cattle, possibly wild mustangs, and—with the number of wetlands in the area—lots of waterfowl, particularly Canada geese. However, you're unlikely to see people. Even though it's very remote for a drive-to area, a bonus is that there are a number of side trips possible to other lakes. The best are the Alphabet Lakes (Reservoir C has the best trout fishing) and Big Sage Reservoir, on Crowder Flat Road.

User Groups: Hikers, dogs, horses, and mountain bikes. No wheelchair facilities.

Permits: No permits are required. Parking and access are free.

Maps: For a map, ask the U.S. Forest Service for Modoc National Forest. For a topographic map, ask the USGS for South Mountain.

Directions: From Redding, take Highway 299 east for 144 miles (17 miles past Canby) to Crowder Flat Road. Turn left on Crowder Flat Road and continue about 30 miles to the reservoir.

Contact: Modoc National Forest, Devil's Garden Ranger District, 800 West 12th Street, Alturas, CA 96101, 530/233-5811, www.fs.fed.us/r5—click on Forest Offices.

13 HI GRADE NATIONAL RECREATION TRAIL
1.1 mi / 0.5 hr 🥾2 ⛰7

in Modoc National Forest east of Goose Lake

The Hi Grade National Recreation Trail is actually 5.5 miles long, but only 1.1 miles are specifically designed for hiking. The remainder of this trail is designated for four-wheel-drive use, one of the only national four-wheel-drive trails in the state. Of course, you can still hike all of it, but it's better to use four-wheeling to get out there, then hike the final mile to get way out there. As you go, watch for signs of old, abandoned mining operations, because gold was discovered here. They never found enough to cause any outpouring of gold miners, though, and the result is a sparsely populated county, with this area being abandoned completely. The surrounding habitat is a mix of high desert and timber, although the trees tend to be small.

A good side trip from the nearby Buck Creek Ranger Station is to Fandango Pass, where there are nice views to the east of Surprise Valley and the Nevada Mountains. This is where a group of immigrants arrived, topped the ridge, looked west, saw Goose Lake, and shouted, "Aha! The Pacific Ocean! We have arrived!" So they started dancing the fandango. That's how the mountain pass got its name. (As lore has it, Native Americans killed them).

User Groups: Hikers, dogs, horses, and mountain bikes. No wheelchair facilities.

Permits: No permits are required. Parking and access are free.

Maps: For a map, ask the U.S. Forest Service for Modoc National Forest. For topographic maps, ask the USGS for Mount Bidwell and Willow Ranch.

Directions: From Redding, take Highway 299 east for 146 miles to Alturas and the junction with U.S. 395. Turn north on U.S. 395 and drive about 35 miles to Forest Road 9. Turn right on Forest Road 9 and drive 4.5 miles to Buck Creek Ranger Station. At the Buck Creek Ranger Station, turn left on Forest Road 47N72 and drive about six miles to the trailhead. Four-wheel-drive vehicles are required.

Contact: Modoc National Forest, Warner Mountain Ranger District, P.O. Box 220, Cedarville, CA 96104, 530/279-6116, www.fs.fed.us/r5—click on Forest Offices.

14 PEPPERDINE TRAILHEAD
12.0 mi / 2.0 days 🚶3 ⛰9

on the northern boundary of the
South Warner Wilderness east of Alturas

The six-mile trip on Summit Trail to Patterson Lake is the most popular hike in the South Warner Wilderness. That still doesn't mean you'll run into other people or horses, because the Warners are a remote, lonely place rarely visited by hikers from the Bay Area, Sacramento, or Los Angeles. Patterson Lake is set in a rock basin at 9,000 feet, just below Warren Peak (9,718 feet), the highest lake in the wilderness and the highlight destination for most visitors. The Pepperdine trailhead (at 6,900 feet) is located just beyond Porter Reservoir, where a primitive campground and a horse corral are available. The hike is a sustained climb, gaining 2,100 feet, passing to the right of Squaw Peak (8,646 feet) and then tiny Cottonwood Lake. From Squaw Peak, looking east, you'll feel as if you're looking across hundreds of miles of a stark, uninhabited landscape.

User Groups: Hikers, dogs, and horses. No mountain bikes. No wheelchair facilities.

Permits: A campfire permit (free) is required. Parking and access are free.

Maps: For a map, ask the U.S. Forest Service for Modoc National Forest or South Warner Wilderness. For a topographic map, ask the USGS for Warren Peak.

Directions: From U.S. 395 at the south end of Alturas, turn east on County Road 56 and drive 13 miles to the Modoc National Forest boundary and Parker Creek Road. Turn left and drive six miles on Parker Creek Road, to the sign for Pepperdine Campground. Turn right and drive to the trailhead.

Contact: Modoc National Forest, Warner Mountain Ranger District, P.O. Box 220, Cedarville, CA 96104, 530/279-6116, www.fs.fed.us/r5—click on Forest Offices.

LASSEN HIKING

15 PINE CREEK TRAILHEAD
4.0 mi / 3.0 hr   🚶3 ⛰8

on the northwestern boundary of the
South Warner Wilderness east of Alturas

This is one of the great short hikes anywhere. The Pine Creek Trail is a magnificent traipse into the beautiful South Warner
Wilderness.

The trail starts along the south fork of Pine
Creek, about 6,800 feet in elevation, then
heads straight east into the wilderness, climbing the lush western slopes. In the course of
two miles, the trail rises 1,000 feet to the Pine
Creek Basin. Along the trail are several small
lakes, the largest being the two set right along
the trail as you enter the basin. Above you is a
stark, volcanic-faced rim with few trees, where
the headwaters of eight small creeks start from
springs, pour down the mountain, join, and
then flow into several small lakes. To lengthen
the hike, go on to Patterson Lake, a gorgeous
mountain lake surrounded by towering rock
walls; the round-trip is 11 miles.

Modoc County is the least-populated and
least-known region of California, with only
10,000 residents sprinkled across a huge area.
Yet there are many outstanding adventures
available here.

User Groups: Hikers, dogs, and horses. No
mountain bikes. No wheelchair facilities.

Permits: No permits are required. Parking
and access are free.

Maps: For a map, ask the U.S. Forest Service
for Modoc National Forest or South Warner
Wilderness. For a topographic map, ask the
USGS for Eagle Peak.

Directions: On U.S. 395 at the south end of
Alturas, turn east on County Road 56 and
drive 13 miles to the Modoc National Forest boundary and West Warner Road. Turn
right (south) on West Warner Road and go
about 10 miles to the sign for the Pine Creek
trailhead. Turn left (east) and head 1.75 miles
to the parking area. The road is unpaved for
the last 12 miles.

Contact: Modoc National Forest, Warner
Mountain Ranger District, P.O. Box 220,
Cedarville, CA 96104, 530/279-6116, www
.fs.fed.us/r5—click on Forest Offices.

16 SOUP SPRING TRAILHEAD
3.0 mi / 2.0 hr   🚶2 ⛰8

on the western boundary of the
South Warner Wilderness east of Alturas

Mill Creek is a small, pristine trout stream
that brings the lonely Warner Mountains to
life. It's a short hike to get here, up a hill and
then down, heading into a valley. On this valley floor, you'll find Mill Creek, only a 1.5-
mile walk out of the Soup Spring trailhead.
Mill Creek is a great spot for a picnic lunch
or a high-finesse fishing trip. The trout are
extremely sensitive, so anything clumsy—like
letting your shadow hit the water or clanking
your boots on the shore—will spook them
off the bite. The trout are small, dark, and
chunky, unlike any seen elsewhere.

Some hikers use Slide Creek Trail as a way
of climbing up near the Warner Rim and to
the intersection with the Summit Trail, the
feature hike in the South Warner Wilderness.
That makes sense, as there is a primitive campground and corral at the trailhead; then it's
a four-mile romp uphill to the Summit Trail
junction. It includes a 1,000-foot climb on the
way, with the trail routed up the Slide Creek
Canyon over the last two miles.

User Groups: Hikers, dogs, and horses. No
mountain bikes. No wheelchair facilities.

Permits: No permits are required. Parking
and access are free.

Maps: For a map, ask the U.S. Forest Service
for Modoc National Forest or South Warner
Wilderness. For a topographic map, ask the
USGS for Eagle Peak.

Directions: From Alturas, take U.S. 395 south
for 18.5 miles to Likely and Jess Valley Road
(County Road 64). Turn east on Jess Valley
Road and drive nine miles to West Warner

Road (Forest Road 5). Turn left on West Warner Road (Forest Road 5) and drive 4.5 miles to Soup Loop Road (Forest Road 40N24). Turn right and drive six miles (a gravel road) to the campground parking lot, on the right.

Contact: Modoc National Forest, Warner Mountain Ranger District, P.O. Box 220, Cedarville, CA 96104, 530/279-6116, www .fs.fed.us/r5—click on Forest Offices.

17 MILL CREEK FALLS TRAILHEAD
0.5 mi / 0.5 hr 🏃‍♂️1 ⛰️9

on the southwestern boundary of the South Warner Wilderness east of Alturas

The short, easy walk from the Mill Creek Falls trailhead to Clear Lake leads to one of the prettiest spots in Modoc County. It's 0.5 mile to Mill Creek Falls and another 0.5 mile to Clear Lake. At the fork, bear left for the waterfalls, or bear right for the lake. Most hikers will take in both. The trail skirts along the perimeter of a pretty lake set at 6,000 feet. Of the lakes and streams in the Warners, it's Clear Lake that has the largest fish, with brown and rainbow trout ranging to more than 10 pounds. There just aren't many of them. Backpackers can head onward from Clear Lake on Poison Flat Trail, but expect a very steep howler of a climb before intersecting with Mill Creek Trail.

User Groups: Hikers, dogs, and horses. Some wheelchair-accessible facilities are available at the nearby campground, but there is no wheelchair access on this trail. No mountain bikes.

Permits: No permits are required. Parking and access are free.

Maps: For a map, ask the U.S. Forest Service for Modoc National Forest or South Warner Wilderness. For a topographic map, ask the USGS for Eagle Peak.

Directions: From Alturas, take U.S. 395 south for 18.5 miles to Likely and Jess Valley Road

(County Road 64). Turn east on Jess Valley Road and drive nine miles to a fork. At the fork, bear left on Forest Road 5 and drive 2.5 miles to Forest Road 40N46. Turn right and drive two miles to the trailhead.

Contact: Modoc National Forest, Warner Mountain Ranger District, P.O. Box 220, Cedarville, CA 96104, 530/279-6116, www .fs.fed.us/r5—click on Forest Offices.

18 EMERSON TRAILHEAD
7.0 mi / 2.0 days 🏃‍♂️5 ⛰️9

on the eastern boundary of the South Warner Wilderness east of Alturas

Don't be yelpin' about the dreadful climb up to North Emerson Lake, because we're warning you right here, loud and clear, that it qualifies as a first-class butt-kicker. If you choose to go anyway, well, you asked for it. The trail climbs 2,000 feet in 3.5 miles, but much of that is in a hellish 0.5-mile stretch that'll have you howling for relief. Your reward is little North Emerson Lake at 7,800 feet, a wonderland in a rock bowl with a high sheer back wall.

The Emerson trailhead, the most remote of those providing access to the Warners, is located on the east side of the mountain rim, near stark, dry country. A primitive campground is available at the trailhead. Out of camp, take North Emerson Trail. And while you're at it, get yourself in the right frame of mind to cheerfully accept that you'll be getting your butt kicked. But rest assured that North Emerson Lake is worth every step. You also get incredible long-distance views across the desert to the east.

User Groups: Hikers, dogs, and horses. No mountain bikes. No wheelchair facilities.

Permits: A campfire permit (free) is required. Parking and access are free.

Maps: For a map, ask the U.S. Forest Service for Modoc National Forest or South Warner

Wilderness. For a topographic map, ask the USGS for Emerson Peak.

Directions: From Alturas, take Highway 299 east for 22 miles to Cedarville and County Road 1. Turn right (south) on County Road 1 and go about 16 miles to Eagleville and continue another 1.5 miles south on County Road 1 to Emerson Road. Turn right on Emerson Road and go three miles to the trailhead. Emerson Road is very steep and is slippery when wet or icy.

Contact: Modoc National Forest, Warner Mountain Ranger District, P.O. Box 220, Cedarville, CA 96104, 530/279-6116, www .fs.fed.us/r5—click on Forest Offices.

19 EAST CREEK LOOP

15.0 mi / 2.0 days

on the southern boundary of the
South Warner Wilderness east of Alturas

The East Creek Loop is a favorite loop hike in the Warner Mountains. It can be completed in a weekend, not including driving time, and provides a capsule look at the amazing contrasts of the Warners. The hike includes small, seemingly untouched streams, as well as high, barren mountain rims.

To start this trip, take the East Creek Trail, elevation 7,100 feet. It is routed 5.5 miles north into the wilderness. Just before the junction with Poison Flat Trail, a spring is located on the left side of the trail. Don't miss it—you'll need the water for the upcoming climb. Turn right at the junction with Poison Flat Trail to make the 800-foot climb above tree line, and turn right again on Summit Trail. The loop is completed by taking Summit Trail back south, crossing high, stark country—most of it more than 8,000 feet in elevation. In the last two miles, the trail drops sharply, descending 1,000 feet on the way to Patterson Campground, which marks the end of the loop trail. Reaching the parking area at the East Creek trailhead requires a 0.5-mile walk on the forest road.

User Groups: Hikers, dogs, and horses. No mountain bikes. No wheelchair facilities.

Permits: A campfire permit (free) is required. Parking and access are free.

Maps: For a map, ask the U.S. Forest Service for Modoc National Forest or South Warner Wilderness. For a topographic map, ask the USGS for Emerson Peak.

Directions: From Alturas, take U.S. 395 south for 18.5 miles to Likely and Jess Valley Road (County Road 64). Turn east on Jess Valley Road and drive nine miles to South Warner Road (Forest Road 64). Turn right and drive southeast (heading toward Patterson Campground) to the access road for East Creek Trail. Turn left and drive a short distance to the parking area.

Contact: Modoc National Forest, Warner Mountain Ranger District, P.O. Box 220, Cedarville, CA 96104, 530/279-6116, www .fs.fed.us/r5—click on Forest Offices.

20 SUMMIT LOOP

45.0 mi / 4.0 days

on the southern boundary of the
South Warner Wilderness east of Alturas

The Summit Loop is the backpacking trek that most hikers yearn to take someday. If you are one of the lucky few to get here, you'll find this hike traverses both sides of the Warner ridge, providing an intimate look at a diverse place. The west side of the Warner Mountains is a habitat filled with small pine trees, meadows, and the headwaters of many small streams. The east side, however, is stark and rugged, with great long-distance lookouts to the east across high desert and miles of sagebrush and juniper.

Start the trip at the Patterson Camp trailhead (at 7,200 feet). From here the trail climbs quickly, rising to 8,200 feet in two miles,

LASSEN HIKING

accessing high, barren country. Great views abound from here as hikers head north. Then, to reach the north end of the wilderness, take the turn at Owl Creek Trail and hike to Linderman Lake, set at the foot of Devils Knob (8,776 feet). Continue past Squaw Peak (8,646 feet). To return in a loop, make the hairpin left turn at Summit Trail and walk back on the mostly lush western slopes of the Warners. Highlights on the return loop segment include Patterson Lake, 9,000 feet, the headwaters of Mill Creek and North Fork East Creek, and many beautiful and fragile meadows. The trail ends at the East Creek parking area, a 0.5-mile walk from the Patterson Camp trailhead.

Savor every moment of this trip—it's one of the greatest little-known hikes anywhere in the United States. The Warner Mountains have a mystique about them, a charm cultivated by the thoughts of hikers who dream of an area where the landscape is remote and untouched, and the trails are empty. However, only rarely do they get around to it. For most, the Warners are just too remote and too far away, and the trip requires too much time.

User Groups: Hikers, dogs, and horses. No mountain bikes. No wheelchair facilities.

Permits: A campfire permit (free) is required. Parking and access are free.

Maps: For a map, ask the U.S. Forest Service for Modoc National Forest or South Warner Wilderness. For a topographic map, ask the USGS for Emerson Peak.

Directions: From Alturas, take U.S. 395 south for 18.5 miles to Likely and Jess Valley Road (County Road 64). Turn east on Jess Valley Road and drive nine miles to South Warner Road (Forest Road 64). Turn right and drive 16 miles to Patterson Campground. The trailhead is at the camp.

Contact: Modoc National Forest, Warner Mountain Ranger District, P.O. Box 220, Cedarville, CA 96104, 530/279-6116, www .fs.fed.us/r5—click on Forest Offices.

21 BLUE LAKE LOOP NATIONAL RECREATION TRAIL
2.0 mi / 1.25 hr

at Blue Lake in Modoc National Forest southeast of Alturas

Blue Lake, shaped like an egg and rimmed with trees, is one of the prettiest lakes you can reach by driving. That makes the easy two-mile loop hike around the lake on Blue Lake Loop National Recreation Trail very special. With a campground at the lake, this trail makes a good side trip for overnight visitors. In addition, a fishing pier and wheelchair-accessible restroom are available. A bonus is that there are some huge trout in this lake—brown trout in the 10-pound class—and they provide quite a treasure hunt amid good numbers of foot-long rainbow trout.

User Groups: Hikers and dogs. The fishing pier and restroom are wheelchair accessible. No horses or mountain bikes.

Permits: No permits are required. Parking and access are free.

Maps: For a map, ask the U.S. Forest Service for Modoc National Forest. For a topographic map, ask the USGS for Jess Valley.

Directions: From Alturas, take U.S. 395 south for 18.5 miles to Likely and Jess Valley Road (County Road 64). Turn east on Jess Valley Road (County Road 64) and drive nine miles to a fork. When the road forks, bear right on Blue Lake Road (Forest Road 64) and drive seven miles to Forest Road 39N30 (signed for Blue Lake). Turn right and drive to the parking area.

Contact: Modoc National Forest, Warner Mountain Ranger District, P.O. Box 220, Cedarville, CA 96104, 530/279-6116, www .fs.fed.us/r5—click on Forest Offices.

LASSEN HIKING

22 BURNEY MOUNTAIN SUMMIT

0.25-8.0 mi / 0.25-3.0 hr

in Lassen National Forest south of Burney

The view is just so good from the top of Burney Mountain (elevation 7,863 feet) that the trip had to be included in this book. If you drive to the summit, the "hike" consists of just moseying around and gazing off in all directions. There is a fire lookout on top of the mountain. Occasionally, tours are available. Burney Mountain often gets lost in the shadow of its big brothers, Mount Lassen and Mount Shasta, but of the three, the view just might be best from Burney. That's because a view of Lassen or Shasta offers impressive panoramas that just can't be duplicated.

If you show up in the winter or after 6 P.M., when the access road is gated, or if you simply want the exercise, it's a four-mile hike up the road to the top of the mountain.

User Groups: Hikers, dogs, horses, and mountain bikes. No wheelchair facilities.

Permits: No permits are required. Parking and access are free.

Maps: For a map, ask the U.S. Forest Service for Lassen National Forest. For topographic maps, ask the USGS for Burney Mountain West and Burney Mountain East.

Directions: From Redding, take Highway 299 east for 50 miles to Burney and continue five more miles east to Highway 89. Turn south (right) on Highway 89 and drive 10.5 miles to Forest Road 26/Forest Road 34N19 (signed). Turn right on Forest Road 26 and drive 10 miles to Forest Road 34N23. Turn right and drive seven miles to the mountain summit. Note that the summit access road is blocked by a gate at 6 P.M. each day and throughout winter. You can park at the gate and hike to the top.

Contact: Lassen National Forest, Hat Creek Ranger District, 43225 East Highway 299, P.O. Box 220, Falls River Mills, CA 96028, 530/336-5521, www.fs.fed.us/r5—click on Forest Offices.

23 CYPRESS TRAILHEAD

6.0 mi / 1.0 day

on the north boundary of the Thousand Lakes Wilderness north of Lassen Volcanic National Park

The Cypress trailhead at 5,400 feet is the number-one starting point for the Thousand Lakes Wilderness, with many small lakes sprinkled about in a radius of just two miles. The primary destination is Lake Eiler, a round-trip of six miles, though it is 9.9 miles if you also hike around the lake and return to the trailhead. It is the largest lake in this region, set just below Eiler Butte. But a network of trails here connects to other lakes, so an option is to keep on going for an overnighter. From the south side of Eiler Lake, the trail loops deeper into the wilderness in a clockwise arc. It passes near several other lakes, including Box and Barrett Lakes. Both of these provide good fishing for small trout.

This wilderness is not called "Thousand Lakes" because there are a lot of lakes. After heavy rains or snowmelt, there are thousands of little pockets of water-breeding mosquitoes here in spring. And *that* is how it was named.

User Groups: Hikers, dogs, and horses. No mountain bikes. No wheelchair facilities.

Permits: No permits are required. Parking and access are free.

Maps: For a map, ask the U.S. Forest Service for Lassen National Forest. A wilderness trail map is available for a fee from the Hat Creek Ranger District. For topographic maps, ask the USGS for Thousand Lakes Valley and Jacks Backbone.

Directions: From Redding, take Highway 299 east for 50 miles to Burney and continue east five miles to Highway 89. Turn right (south) on Highway 89 and drive 10.5 miles to Forest Road 26 (Forest Road 34N19). Turn west on Forest Road 26 (Forest Road 34N19) and drive 8.5 miles to Forest Road 34N60. Turn left and drive 2.5 miles to the parking area.

LASSEN HIKING

Contact: Lassen National Forest, Hat Creek Ranger District, 43225 East Highway 299, P.O. Box 220, Falls River Mills, CA 96028, 530/336-5521, www.fs.fed.us/r5—click on Forest Offices.

24 TAMARACK TRAILHEAD
6.0 mi / 3.5 hr   🏃3 ⛰8

on the east boundary of the Thousand Lakes Wilderness north of Lassen Volcanic National Park

From the Tamarack trailhead, your first destination is Lake Eiler, a three-mile hike. Have a picnic, swim, or fish, and then return. If you are setting out on a multiday backpacking trek, then go onward to several other wilderness lakes.

The trail is then routed into the northwestern interior of the Thousand Lakes Wilderness. After two miles, you'll reach a fork in the trail; turn left (south) to reach Barrett Lake in just another mile of hiking.

Note that there is a complex trail network in this area with many junctions, creating a situation in which backpackers can invent their own multiday route. From Barrett Lake, other attractive destinations include Durbin Lake, 0.5 mile to the south, and Everett and Magee Lakes, another (very challenging) 2.7 miles away.

Also note that Tamarack is an alternative trailhead to Lake Eiler; the other is the previously listed Cypress trailhead. The difference is that this trailhead gets far less use, because the last 1.5 miles of the access road are very rough; a high-clearance, four-wheel-drive truck is required to make it in.

User Groups: Hikers, dogs, and horses. No mountain bikes. No wheelchair facilities.

Permits: No permits are required. Parking and access are free.

Maps: For a map, ask the U.S. Forest Service for Lassen National Forest. A wilderness trail map is available for a fee from the Hat Creek

Ranger District. For topographic maps, ask the USGS for Thousand Lakes Valley and Jacks Backbone.

Directions: From Redding, take Highway 299 east for 50 miles to Burney and continue east five miles to Highway 89. Turn right (south) on Highway 89 and drive about 14 miles to Forest Road 33N25. Turn west on Forest Road 33N25 and drive five miles to Forest Road 33N23Y. Turn right and head to the parking area at the end of the road. The last 1.5 miles are very rough; four-wheel-drive, high-clearance trucks are recommended.

Contact: Lassen National Forest, Hat Creek Ranger District, 43225 East Highway 299, P.O. Box 220, Falls River Mills, CA 96028, 530/336-5521, www.fs.fed.us/r5—click on Forest Offices.

25 BUNCHGRASS TRAILHEAD
8.0 mi / 2.0 days   🏃2 ⛰7

on the south boundary of the Thousand Lakes Wilderness north of Lassen Volcanic National Park

This trailhead is obscure and difficult to reach, and because of that, few visitors choose it as a jump-off spot for their treks. The destination is Durbin Lake, a four-mile hike one-way, making an easy weekend backpack trip. The trailhead elevation is 5,680 feet, and from here, it's a fair walk in, up, and down. If you're not in shape, you'll know it well before you reach the lake. You'll come to Hall Butte (at 7,187 feet) and then Durbin Lake.

A side-trip option is to climb Hall Butte. This is best done by breaking off the trail at three miles in, along the western side of Hall Butte. It is a 0.5-mile tromp to the top with no trail. In the fall this area gets traffic from deer hunters.

User Groups: Hikers, dogs, and horses. No mountain bikes. No wheelchair facilities.

Permits: A campfire permit (free) is required. Parking and access are free.

Maps: For a map, ask the U.S. Forest Service for Lassen National Forest. A wilderness trail map is available for a fee from the Hat Creek Ranger District. For topographic maps, ask the USGS for Thousand Lakes Valley and Jacks Backbone.

Directions: From Redding, take Highway 299 east for 50 miles to Burney and continue east five miles to Highway 89. Turn right (south) on Highway 89 and drive 31 miles to Forest Road 16 (Forest Road 33N16). Turn right on Forest Road 16 and drive seven miles to Forest Road 32N45. Turn right on Forest Road 32N45 and drive two miles to Forest Road 32N42Y (which is very steep). Turn left and head to the parking area, at the end of the road.

Contact: Lassen National Forest, Hat Creek Ranger District, 43225 East Highway 299, P.O. Box 220, Falls River Mills, CA 96028, 530/336-5521, www.fs.fed.us/r5—click on Forest Offices.

26 McARTHUR-BURNEY FALLS MEMORIAL STATE PARK (PCT)

40.0 mi one-way / 3.0 days

from the Highway 44 parking area north to McArthur-Burney Falls Memorial State Park

This section of the PCT includes the infamous 27-mile section without water. Unless you are through-hiking the entire PCT, there is no reason to suffer this ignominy. Yet this 40-mile section also features Hat Creek, Baum Lake, Crystal Lake, and spectacular Burney Falls.

From the trailhead at Highway 44, the trail passes through the wooded watershed of Hat Creek to a long, shadeless section that will have you counting the drops of water in your canteen. This is the Hat Creek Rim section of the PCT, the roughest section of the entire route from Mexico to Canada, with no

water available for 27 miles of trail. A single drop of water will be valued more than a $10,000 bill. A lot of PCT hikers cheat this section by leaving the trail for the highway, and some will even hitch a ride in the backs of pick-up trucks.

After departing from Hat Creek, the PCT heads past Baum and Crystal Lakes. You cross Highway 299, and from there, it's an eight-mile romp to Burney Falls State Park and its breathtaking 129-foot waterfall. It is a portrait of serenity along with nearby Lake Britton.

To continue north on the PCT, see the *McArthur-Burney Falls Memorial State Park to Ash Camp (PCT)* hike in this chapter. If you are walking this trail in reverse, see the *Lassen Volcanic National Park to Highway 44 (PCT)* hike in this chapter to continue south.

User Groups: Hikers, dogs (except in the state park boundaries), and horses. No mountain bikes. No wheelchair facilities.

Permits: A campfire permit (free) is required. A state park entrance fee of $6 is charged per vehicle.

Maps: For topographic maps, ask the USGS for Cassel, Dana, Old Station, Murken Bench, Hogback Ridge, and Burney Falls.

Directions: From Redding, take Highway 44 east for 60 miles to Highway 89/44. Turn left (north) on Highway 89/44 and drive 13 miles to Old Station and continue a short distance to Highway 44. Turn right (east) on Highway 44 and drive 0.25 mile beyond the Old Station Post Office to Forest Road 32N20. Turn right on Forest Road 32N20. The trail crosses the road about 0.5 mile from the junction of Highway 44 and Forest Road 32N20. If you have horses and need to park a horse trailer, use Mud Lake trailhead, located three miles from the junction of Highway 89 and Highway 44.

Contact: Lassen National Forest, Hat Creek Ranger District, 43225 East Highway 299, P.O. Box 220, Falls River Mills, CA 96028, 530/336-5521, www.fs.fed.us/r5—click on Forest Offices.

27 NOBLES EMIGRANT TRAIL
2.0-10.0 mi / 1.0 hr-1.0 day 🚶1 ⛰8

from the Manzanita Lake Trailhead in Lassen Volcanic National Park east of Red Bluff

The most difficult part of this hike is the first two steps. Why? Because the trailhead is set near the northern park entrance amid a number of small roads and a maintenance area, and despite a trail sign, many visitors can't find it and give up. It's worth the search, because it's a great day hike for campers staying at Manzanita Lake.

The trail, with its easy, moderate grade, passes first through an old forest with towering firs, cedars, and pines. About 2.5 miles in, you'll arrive at Lassen's strange Dwarf Forest. Not only will you be surrounded by stunted trees, but you also get views of Chaos Crags, a jumble of pinkish rocks constituting what's left of an old broken-down volcano. Many visitors hike to this point, then turn around and return to the campground. The trail follows part of a historical route that was originally an east–west portion of the California Trail, used by emigrants in the 1850s. There is no water available on the trail, so be sure to have at least one filled canteen per hiker. Because of the moderate slope, this trail is an ideal cross-country ski route in the winter months. Key note: No campfires are allowed in the park.

User Groups: Hikers and horses. No dogs or mountain bikes. No wheelchair facilities.

Permits: A wilderness permit (free) is required for hikers planning to camp in the backcountry. A park entrance fee of $10, good for seven days, is charged for each vehicle.

Maps: Trail maps are available for a fee from park visitors stations and at Lassen Loomis Museum Association. For a map, ask the U.S. Forest Service for Lassen National Forest. For a topographic map, ask the USGS for Manzanita Lake.

Directions: From Redding, take Highway 44 east for 46 miles to the junction with Highway 89. Turn right (south) on Highway 89 and drive one mile to the park entrance station. Continue on the main park road (Lassen Park Highway/Highway 89) for 0.5 mile to the turnoff for Manzanita Lake. The trailhead is across the road from Manzanita Lake, just past the Loomis Museum.

Contact: Lassen Volcanic National Park, P.O. Box 100, Mineral, CA 96063, 530/595-4444, www.nps.gov/lavo; Lassen Loomis Museum Association, P.O. Box 220, Mineral, CA 96063, 530/595-3399, www.lassenloomis.info.

28 MANZANITA LAKE TRAIL
1.6 mi / 1.0 hr 🚶1 ⛰8

at the northern entrance to Lassen Volcanic National Park on Highway 44

There's no prettier lake that you can reach by car in Lassen Park than Manzanita Lake. That is why many consider the campground here a perfect destination. With 179 sites, it's the largest camp in the park, and it's easy to reach, located just beyond the entrance station at the western boundary of the park. The trail simply traces the shoreline of this pretty lake at a 5,950-foot elevation and is easily accessible from either the parking area just beyond the entrance station or from the campground. A good side trip is across the road to Reflection Lake, a small and also very pretty lake, which adds about 0.5 mile to the trip. Note that the fishing at Manzanita Lake is catch-and-release only with the use of artificials—do not use bait, and do pinch down your barbs.

User Groups: Hikers only. No dogs, horses, or mountain bikes. No wheelchair facilities.

Permits: No permits are required. A $10 park entrance fee, good for seven days, is charged for each vehicle.

Maps: Trail maps are available for a fee from park visitors stations and at Lassen Loomis Museum Association. For a map, ask the U.S. Forest Service for Lassen National Forest. For a topographic map, ask the USGS for Manzanita Lake.

Directions: From Redding, take Highway 44 east for 46 miles to the junction with Highway 89. Turn right (south) on Highway 89 and drive one mile to the park entrance station. Continue on the main park road (Lassen Park Highway/Highway 89) for 0.5 mile, to the turnoff for Manzanita Lake Campground. Turn right and drive 0.5 mile to the day-use parking area.

Contact: Lassen Volcanic National Park, P.O. Box 100, Mineral, CA 96063, 530/595-4444, www.nps.gov/lavo; Lassen Loomis Museum Association, P.O. Box 220, Mineral, CA 96063, 530/595-3399, www.lassenloomis.info.

29 CINDER CONE TRAIL
4.0 mi / 3.0 hr   🏃3 ⛰8

from Butte Lake Trailhead in
Lassen Volcanic National Park

Huge chunks of Lassen Volcanic National Park are overlooked by visitors simply because access is not off the park's main roadway (Lassen Park Highway/Highway 89). Butte Lake and Cinder Cone Trail, set in the northeastern corner of the park, are such areas. When you arrive by car, you'll find large, attractive Butte Lake, quite a surprise for newcomers. The trailhead for Nobles Emigrant Trail/Cinder Cone Trail is set at an elevation of 6,100 feet, at the northwest corner of the lake. The trail starts out easy. It heads southwest through forest. But don't be fooled. After 1.5 miles, you'll reach the Cinder Cone cutoff, and there, everything suddenly changes. The last 0.5 mile rises to the top of the Cinder Cone, a short but very intense climb of 800 feet to the summit, at 6,907 feet. The views are unforgettable, especially south to the Painted Dunes and Fantastic Lava Beds. This is a classic volcanic landscape.

User Groups: Hikers only. No dogs, horses, or mountain bikes. No wheelchair facilities.

Permits: No permits are required. A park entrance fee of $10, good for seven days, is charged for each vehicle.

Maps: Trail maps are available for a fee from park visitors stations and at Lassen Loomis Museum Association. For a map, ask the U.S. Forest Service for Lassen National Forest. For a topographic map, ask the USGS for Prospect Peak.

Directions: From Redding, take Highway 44 east for 60 miles to Highway 89/44. Turn left (north) on Highway 89/44 and drive 13 miles to Old Station and continue a short distance to Highway 44. Turn right (east) on Highway 44 and drive 10 miles to Butte Lake Road (Forest Road 32N21). Turn right (south) on Butte Lake Road (Forest Road 32N21) and drive six miles to Butte Lake. The trailhead is located near the boat ramp.

Contact: Lassen Volcanic National Park, P.O. Box 100, Mineral, CA 96063, 530/595-4444, www.nps.gov/lavo; Lassen Loomis Museum Association, P.O. Box 220, Mineral, CA 96063, 530/595-3399, www.lassenloomis.info.

30 PROSPECT PEAK TRAIL
6.6 mi / 4.5 hr   🏃4 ⛰10

at Butte Lake in Lassen Volcanic National Park

Hiking to the top of most mountains requires a long, grinding climb. Gaining the summit of Prospect Peak is somewhat different. Long? No. Grinding? Yep. Your reward is some of the best views in Lassen Volcanic National Park and a trail that gets little use when compared to the others in the park.

The trailhead (Nobles Emigrant Trail), at 6,100 feet, is adjacent to Butte Lake. After less than 0.5 mile, you'll turn right at the junction with Prospect Peak Trail. The trail immediately starts to climb. Get used to it, because there's no respite for several hours. It climbs more than 2,200 feet over the course of just 3.3 miles. It finally tops the summit at 8,338 feet. From here, hikers can see most of the prominent peaks in the park. This includes Lassen Peak, Mount Hoffman, and Crater Butte, along with thousands and thousands of acres of national forest to the north. Since the snowmelt occurs earlier here than in the rest of the park, this trip makes a perfect hike in the early to mid-spring, when the air is still cool. If you wait until summer, you'll find this a dry, forsaken place.

User Groups: Hikers only. No dogs, horses, or mountain bikes. No wheelchair facilities.

Permits: No permits are required. A park entrance fee of $10, good for seven days, is charged for each vehicle.

Maps: Trail maps are available for a fee from park visitors stations and at Lassen Loomis Museum Association. For a map, ask the U.S. Forest Service for Lassen National Forest. For a topographic map, ask the USGS for Prospect Peak.

Directions: From Redding, take Highway 44 east for 60 miles to Highway 89/44. Turn left (north) on Highway 89/44 and drive 13 miles to Old Station and continue a short distance to Highway 44. Turn right (east) on Highway 44 and drive 10 miles to Forest Road 32N21. Turn right (south) on Forest Road 32N21 and drive seven miles to Butte Lake and the parking area near the boat ramp. Look for Nobles Emigrant trailhead (on the west side of the parking lot), and hike 0.5 mile to Prospect Peak Trail, on the right.

Contact: Lassen Volcanic National Park, P.O. Box 100, Mineral, CA 96063, 530/595-4444, www.nps.gov/lavo; Lassen Loomis Museum Association, P.O. Box 220, Mineral, CA 96063, 530/595-3399, www.lassenloomis.info.

31 CONE LAKE TRAILHEAD
4.0 mi / 2.5 hr   👫2 ⛰8

on the northern boundary of the Caribou Wilderness east of Lassen Volcanic National Park

The prize destination on this excellent day hike is Triangle Lake, a pretty spot set in the northern Caribou Wilderness near Black

Butte. The trailhead is located at tiny Cone Lake, just outside the wilderness. From here, you walk for nearly a mile before passing the wilderness boundary, which is clearly marked. At that point, you can sense the change in features, as the land becomes wild and untouched. Continue one mile south to Triangle Lake, which provides good fishing during the evening for pan-sized trout. If you want more, you can get more.

Here the trail forks. The right fork is routed right into Lassen Volcanic National Park, a distance of only 1.5 miles, from which you can access Widow Lake. A free wilderness permit is required from Lassen Volcanic National Park for overnight use. The left fork, on the other hand, leads to Twin Lakes over the course of just 0.5 mile.

User Groups: Hikers, dogs, and horses. No mountain bikes. No wheelchair facilities.

Permits: No permits are required for day use. Campfire permits are required for overnight use. Parking and access are free.

Maps: A trail map is available for a fee from the Almanor Ranger District. For a map, ask the U.S. Forest Service for Lassen National Forest or Caribou Wilderness. For a topographic map, ask the USGS for Bogard Buttes.

Directions: From Redding, take Highway 44 east for 60 miles to Highway 89/44. Turn left (north) on Highway 89/44 and drive 13 miles to Old Station and continue a short distance to Highway 44. Turn right (east) on Highway 44 and drive 30 miles to Bogard Work Station and nearby Forest Road 10. Turn right on Forest Road 10 and drive six miles to Forest Road 32N09. Turn right on Forest Road 32N09 and drive three miles to the Cone Lake trailhead. Note that the roads are unpaved from Highway 44 to the trailhead.

Contact: Lassen National Forest, Almanor Ranger District, P.O. Box 767, Chester, CA 96020, 530/258-2141, www.fs.fed.us/r5—click on Forest Offices.

32 CARIBOU LAKE TRAILHEAD

12.0 mi / 2.0 days   🚶3 ⛰9

on the eastern boundary of the Caribou Wilderness east of Lassen Volcanic National Park

The Caribou Lake trailhead provides a hiking trip that is a parade past mountain lakes. Rarely are so many wilderness lakes this close to a trailhead. The trip starts at Caribou Lake, heading west. In no time you pass all kinds of tiny lakes. The first one, Cowboy Lake, is only 0.25 mile down the trail. In another 15 minutes, you'll come to Jewel Lake. This procession of lakes never seems to stop. Eleanor Lake is next. Then, two miles in, turn left at the fork and you pass Black Lake, North and South Divide Lakes, and, farther on, Long Lake. This lake, six miles from the trailhead, should be your destination, since it makes a great two-day backpacking adventure. The Caribou Wilderness is quite small, just nine miles from top to bottom, and only five miles across, with elevations ranging from 5,000 to 7,000 feet. This trip will provide a visit to the best of it.

User Groups: Hikers, dogs, and horses (a horse corral is available at the trailhead). No mountain bikes. No wheelchair facilities.

Permits: A campfire permit (free) is required. Parking and access are free.

Maps: A trail map is available for a fee from the Almanor Ranger District. For a map, ask the U.S. Forest Service for Lassen National Forest or Caribou Wilderness. For a topographic map, ask the USGS for Red Cinder.

Directions: From Red Bluff, take Highway 36 east and drive 83 miles to Westwood (east of Lake Almanor) and County Road A21. Turn north on County Road A21 and go 14.1 miles to Silver Lake Road. Turn left on Silver Lake Road and drive five miles to a Y with Forest Road 10. Turn right on Forest Road 10 and drive 0.25 mile to a fork. Turn left and drive 0.25 mile to the trailhead.

Contact: Lassen National Forest, Almanor Ranger District, 900 East Highway 36, P.O. Box 767, Chester, CA 96020, 530/258-2141, www.fs.fed.us/r5—click on Forest Offices.

33 ECHO AND TWIN LAKES

8.0 mi / 5.5 hr   🚶2 ⛰10

in Lassen Volcanic National Park east of Red Bluff

BEST (

You get it all on this hike to Lower Twin Lake: beautiful lakes, forest, meadows, and wildflowers. The route provides testimony to the beauty of the Lassen Wilderness. The trailhead elevation is 7,000 feet. The trail starts on the north side of Summit Lake. Right off, the trail climbs 500 feet in the first mile. After this climb, the rest of the hike will be a breeze. You'll arrive at Echo Lake in just another mile and at Upper Twin and Lower Twin in the next two miles, dropping 500 feet on your way. It's all very pretty and is a great bonus for Summit Lake campers. It makes an outstanding day hike for campers staying at Summit Lake Campground or an easy overnighter for backpackers.

Special note: No campfires are permitted at any time in the wilderness at Lassen Volcanic National Park.

User Groups: Hikers and horses. No dogs or mountain bikes. No wheelchair facilities.

Permits: No permits are required. A park entrance fee of $10, good for seven days, is charged for each vehicle.

Maps: Trail maps are available for a fee at park visitors stations and at Lassen Loomis Museum Association. For a map, ask the U.S. Forest Service for Lassen National Forest. For a topographic map, ask the USGS for Reading Peak.

Directions: From Redding, take Highway 44 east for 46 miles to the junction with Highway 89. Turn right (south) on Highway 89 and drive one mile to the park entrance station. Continue on the main park road (Lassen Park Highway/Highway 89) for 12 miles to the turnoff for Summit Lake North Campground. Turn left and park in the day-use area near the lake. Look for the boardwalk that leads to a trail sign, then turn left and start your hike.

Contact: Lassen Volcanic National Park, P.O. Box 100, Mineral, CA 96063, 530/595-4444, www.nps.gov/lavo; Lassen Loomis Museum Association, P.O. Box 220, Mineral, CA 96063, 530/595-3399, www.lassenloomis.info.

34 SUMMIT LAKE LOOP
0.5 mi / 0.5 hr   🚶1 ⛰8

in Lassen Volcanic National Park east of Red Bluff

Summit Lake is a beautiful spot where deer visit almost every summer evening. Nearby campgrounds on both sides of the lake (north and south) are set in conifers, with a pretty meadow just south of the lake along Kings Creek. This hike is a simple walk around Summit Lake. It is best taken at dusk, when the changing evening colors reflect a variety of tints across the lake surface. Though no lakes in Lassen Volcanic National Park are stocked with trout and the fishing is terrible, you may still see a rising trout or two. The best place to see wildlife, especially deer, is in the meadow adjacent to Kings Creek, the lake's outlet stream. The elevation is 7,000 feet.

User Groups: Hikers and horses. No dogs or mountain bikes. No wheelchair facilities.

Permits: No permits are required. A park entrance fee of $10, good for seven days, is charged for each vehicle.

Maps: Trail maps are available for a fee at park visitors stations and at Lassen Loomis Museum Association. For a map, ask the U.S. Forest Service for Lassen National Forest. For a topographic map, ask the USGS for Reading Peak.

Directions: From Redding, take Highway 44 east for 46 miles to the junction with Highway 89. Turn right (south) on Highway 89 and drive one mile to the park entrance station. Continue on the main park road (Lassen Park Highway/Highway 89) for 12 miles to the turnoff for Summit Lake North Campground. Turn left and park in the day-use area near the lake.

Contact: Lassen Volcanic National Park, P.O. Box 100, Mineral, CA 96063, 530/595-4444, www.nps.gov/lavo; Lassen Loomis Museum Association, P.O. Box 220, Mineral, CA 96063, 530/595-3399, www.lassenloomis.info.

35 LASSEN PEAK TRAIL
5.0 mi / 4.0 hr   🚶4 ⛰10

in Lassen Volcanic National Park east of Red Bluff

BEST (

Lassen Peak crowns the horizon at 10,457 feet. It's a huge volcanic flume with hardened lava flows, craters, outcrops, and extraordinary views in all directions. The peak is a perfect example of a lava pinnacle plug dome. Exploring Lassen Peak has become a popular hike—perhaps the best introduction to mountain climbing a hiker could desire.

The trailhead (at 8,500 feet) is adjacent to a large parking area, set at the base of the summit along the main park road (Lassen Park Highway/Highway 89). Looking up from the parking lot, you can see most of the trail to the rim. The climb to the top is a 2.5-mile zigzag on a hard, flat trail, ascending just over 2,000 feet in the process. There are several spots with awesome vistas, looking down into sculpted bowls and to lakes both near and far.

On the rim, you get spectacular views without reaching the true plug-dome peak—Mount Shasta, 100 miles north, appears close enough to reach out and grab. To the east are hundreds of miles of forests and lakes, and to the west, the land drops off to several small volcanic cones and the northern Sacramento Valley. To crown the hike, continue on the trail north, which crosses a volcanic crag for 0.25 mile and then is routed on a path to the summit peak. Fantastic!

In summer, start early, preferably by 8 A.M. Bring a lunch and a canteen or two of water. In the morning, with the air still cool, it's about a two-hour walk to the top, with a 15 percent grade most of the way. This is an exceptional first climb for youngsters, providing for plenty of encouragement and rest stops.

Special note: Winds are common at Lassen Peak, especially on summer afternoons. Hikers should stash a windbreaker in their daypacks. In addition, if you see cumulus clouds starting to form on the rim, common on summer afternoons, don't go. Quick-forming thunderstorms with lightning are also common on hot afternoons. It's always a mistake to suddenly climb the summit without planning the trip. Stay at lower elevations if there's any chance of lightning activity.

User Groups: Hikers only. No dogs, horses, or mountain bikes. No wheelchair facilities.

Permits: No permits are required. A park entrance fee of $10, good for seven days, is charged for each vehicle.

Maps: Trail maps are available for a fee at park visitors stations and at Lassen Loomis Museum Association. For a map, ask the U.S. Forest Service for Lassen National Forest. For a topographic map, ask the USGS for Lassen Peak.

Directions: From Red Bluff, take Highway 36 east and drive 47 miles to the junction with Highway 89. Turn north (left) on Highway 89 and continue 4.5 miles to the park entrance. Continue seven miles on the main park road (Lassen Park Highway/Highway 89) to the parking area and store on the left. The trailhead is at the west end of the parking lot.

Contact: Lassen Volcanic National Park, P.O. Box 100, Mineral, CA 96063, 530/595-4444, www.nps.gov/lavo; Lassen Loomis Museum Association, P.O. Box 220, Mineral, CA 96063, 530/595-3399, www.lassenloomis.info.

36 SHADOW LAKE TRAIL
1.6 mi / 1.0 hr

in Lassen Volcanic National Park east of Red Bluff

A hike of less than a mile on this trail will take you past little Terrace Lake (7,800 feet) and then shortly after to Shadow Lake (7,600 feet). It's rare to reach such a pretty lake surrounded by wildlands in such a short distance. The trail involves a short, steep climb to Terrace Lake, and then a 0.25-mile junket to skirt the southeast shoreline of Shadow Lake (which is at least three times the size of Terrace Lake). The lakes are set just north of Reading Peak, 8,701 feet. The trailhead is at 8,000 feet, and because of the altitude, some hikers may experience shortness of breath when making the climb to the lakes. But if you're still feeling good, then by all means continue 0.75 mile to Cliff Lake (7,250 feet), a beautiful spot that's well worth the extra hour.

User Groups: Hikers only. No dogs, horses, or mountain bikes. No wheelchair facilities.

Permits: No permits are required. A park entrance fee of $10, good for seven days, is charged for each vehicle.

Maps: Trail maps are available for a fee at park visitors stations and at Lassen Loomis Museum Association. For a map, ask the U.S. Forest Service for Lassen National Forest. For a topographic map, ask the USGS for Reading Peak.

Directions: From Red Bluff, take Highway 36 east and drive 47 miles to the junction with Highway 89. Turn north (left) on Highway 89 and continue 4.5 miles to the park entrance. Continue nine miles on the main park road (Lassen Park Highway/Highway 89) to the parking area and trailhead, on the left (two miles past the parking area for Lassen Summit).

Contact: Lassen Volcanic National Park, P.O. Box 100, Mineral, CA 96063, 530/595-4444, www.nps.gov/lavo; Lassen Loomis Museum

Association, P.O. Box 220, Mineral, CA 96063, 530/595-3399, www.lassenloomis.info.

37 BUMPASS HELL TRAIL

3.0 mi / 2.0 hr   🏃2 ⛰10

in Lassen Volcanic National Park east of
Red Bluff

Bumpass Hell is like a walk into the land of perdition, complete with steam vents, boiling mud pots, and natural furnaces. It's all set amid volcanic rock and is prehistoric looking and a bit creepy, as if at any moment a T-Rex might charge around the bend and munch a few tourists. The trip to Bumpass Hell is the most popular hike in the park, and it makes sense, because it's not only the park's largest thermal area but also an excellent morning walk. The elevation at the trailhead is 8,200 feet.

The trail starts with a gradual 500-foot climb. You pass an excellent interpretive sign at an overlook that explains the origin and size of the gigantic Tehama Volcano. The trail continues in the first mile to a ridge overlooking the thermal area. You then descend 250 feet into the thermal basin. It sits in a pocket just below Bumpass Mountain (8,753 feet). Exhibits explain the area. There are usually large numbers of tourists at Bumpass Hell, but you can get beyond them by extending your trip to Cold Boiling Lake, another 1.5 miles (one-way), which includes two steep portions of trail.

Special note: For obvious reasons, it's important to stay on the trail or boardwalk near hydrothermal areas.

It is called "Bumpass" Hell because back in the old days, a guy named Bumpass slipped into the boiling water, scalded his feet, and in the ensuing newspaper report, the writer called the place "Bumpass's Hell," and the name stuck.

User Groups: Hikers only. No dogs, horses, or mountain bikes. No wheelchair facilities.

Permits: No permits are required. A park

entrance fee of $10, good for seven days, is charged for each vehicle.

Maps: Trail maps are available for a fee from park visitors stations and at Lassen Loomis Museum Association. For a topographic map, ask the USGS for Lassen Peak.

Directions: From Red Bluff, take Highway 36 east and drive 47 miles to the junction with Highway 89. Turn north (left) on Highway 89 and drive 4.5 miles to the park entrance. Continue six miles on the main park road (Lassen Park Highway/Highway 89) to the trailhead, on the right.

Contact: Lassen Volcanic National Park, P.O. Box 100, Mineral, CA 96063, 530/595-4444, www.nps.gov/lavo; Lassen Loomis Museum Association, P.O. Box 220, Mineral, CA 96063, 530/595-3399, www.lassenloomis.info.

38 DRAKE LAKE TRAIL

4.5 mi / 2.75 hr   🏃3 ⛰6

at Drakesbad in Lassen Volcanic National Park

Drake Lake is a somewhat swampy sub-alpine lake that brightens a largely dry hillside, where deer are often more plentiful than people. It is set in a remote forested pocket, very secluded, and just difficult enough of a climb that many take a pass on the trip. From the trailhead at Drakesbad, at about 5,650 feet, it's about an 800-foot climb over the course of two miles to Drake Lake (6,482 feet). Midway up the grade, the hike becomes steep and stays that way for nearly 45 minutes.

The lake is the payoff—emerald green and circled by firs. After you catch your breath, you may feel like jumping in and cooling off, particularly if it's a hot summer day. Well, we've got news for you: In early summer, the water is still ice cold, and just when you realize that, a battalion of mosquitoes will show up and start feasting on all your bare, sumptuous flesh. Then what? Jump in and freeze your buns? Stand there and get devoured? Heck no, you'll have your clothes back on in record time.

User Groups: Hikers only. Horses are allowed on a portion of the trail. No dogs or mountain bikes. No wheelchair facilities.

Permits: No permits are required. A park entrance fee of $10, good for seven days, is charged for each vehicle.

Maps: Trail maps are available for a fee from park visitors stations and at Lassen Loomis Museum Association. For a topographic map, ask the USGS for Reading Peak.

Directions: From Red Bluff, take Highway 36 east and drive 47 miles to the junction with Highway 89. Do not turn. Continue east on Highway 36 toward Lake Almanor and to Chester and Feather River Drive. Turn left on Feather River Drive and drive 0.75 mile. Bear left for Drakesbad and Warner Valley, and drive six miles to Warner Valley Road. Turn right and drive 11 miles to Warner Valley Campground. Continue for 0.5 mile to the trailhead, on the left. The last 3.5 miles is unpaved, and there is one steep hill that can be difficult for trailers or RVs.

Contact: Lassen Volcanic National Park, P.O. Box 100, Mineral, CA 96063, 530/595-4444, www.nps.gov/lavo; Lassen Loomis Museum Association, P.O. Box 220, Mineral, CA 96063, 530/595-3399, www.lassenloomis.info.

39 DEVILS KITCHEN TRAIL

4.4 mi / 2.5 hr

at Drakesbad in Lassen Volcanic National Park

Drakesbad is the undiscovered Lassen—beautiful, wild, and remote. It gets missed by nearly everybody because access is obscure and circuitous—on the way out of Chester en route to the Warner Valley Campground and nearby trailhead—rather than via Lassen's main park highway. There's no way to get here when entering from either of the main Lassen park entrances. But those who persevere will find a quiet paradise, along with this easy trip to Devils Kitchen, a unique geologic thermal area. The trail is an easy hike, heading west

above Hot Springs Creek. The elevation at the trailhead is 5,650 feet, with a gradual climb of 300 feet. After two miles it ventures into this barren pocket of steaming vents, boiling mud pots, and fumaroles. You'll immediately see why it was tagged Devils Kitchen. It is dangerous to walk off trail in this area.

User Groups: Hikers only. Horses are allowed on a portion of the trail. No dogs or mountain bikes. No wheelchair facilities.

Permits: No permits are required. A park entrance fee of $10, good for seven days, is charged for each vehicle.

Maps: Trail maps are available for a fee from park visitors stations and at Lassen Loomis Museum Association. For a topographic map, ask the USGS for Reading Peak.

Directions: From Red Bluff, take Highway 36 east and drive 47 miles to the junction with Highway 89. Do not turn. Continue east on Highway 36 toward Lake Almanor and to Chester and Feather River Drive. Turn left on Feather River Drive and drive 0.75 mile. Bear left for Drakesbad and Warner Valley, and drive six miles to Warner Valley Road. Turn right and drive 11 miles to Warner Valley Campground. Continue 0.5 mile to the trailhead, on the left. The last 3.5 miles are unpaved, and there is one steep hill that can be difficult for trailers or RVs.

Contact: Lassen Volcanic National Park, P.O. Box 100, Mineral, CA 96063, 530/595-4444, www.nps.gov/lavo; Lassen Loomis Museum Association, P.O. Box 220, Mineral, CA 96063, 530/595-3399, www.lassenloomis.info.

40 LASSEN VOLCANIC NATIONAL PARK TO HIGHWAY 44 (PCT)

32.0 mi one-way / 3.0 days

from Warner Valley Campground in Lassen Volcanic National Park

Every step on the Pacific Crest Trail in Lassen Volcanic National Park is a pleasure. Start at the wooded Warner Valley (at 5,680 feet), at Hot Springs Creek, and then head north into the park's most remote terrain. The trail is routed across Grassy Swale, past Swan Lake, and on to Lower Twin Lake (seven miles in), a pretty lake circled by conifers.

From here, the trail heads north through a strange but compelling volcanic area. It skirts the western flank of Fairfield Peak (7,272 feet) and then heads onward. It turns west past Soap Lake and Badger Flat, and continues out past the park's boundary. As you hike toward Highway 44, you'll be lateraling Badger Mountain (6,973 feet) to your right, with the Hat Creek drainage off to your immediate left. In this latter stretch of trail, you'll cross no major lakes or streams (plan your water well). You forge on through the national forest, which is mostly second-growth, crossing a few roads along the way. In the spring, wildflowers are exceptional near the Hat Creek area. Several primitive U.S. Forest Service campgrounds are located on the trail about 10 miles north of the border of Lassen Volcanic National Park. Note that no campfires are permitted at any time in the wilderness at Lassen Volcanic National Park.

To continue north on the PCT, see the *McArthur-Burney Falls Memorial State Park (PCT)* hike in this chapter. If you are walking this trail in reverse, see the *Domingo Springs to Lassen Volcanic National Park (PCT)* hike in this chapter to continue south.

User Groups: Hikers and horses. No dogs or mountain bikes are allowed in the Lassen Volcanic National Park section of the hike. No wheelchair facilities.

Permits: A wilderness permit (free) is required for hikers planning to camp in the Lassen Volcanic National Park backcountry and for equestrians. You may not camp with horses in the national park's backcountry, but a horse corral is available by reservation for overnighters at Summit Lake and Juniper Lake, and a small corral is located near the park's northern boundary for exclusive use by those on the Pacific Crest Trail. A park entrance fee

of $10, good for seven days, is charged for each vehicle.

Maps: For topographic maps, ask the USGS for Reading Peak, West Prospect Peak, and Old Station.

Directions: From Red Bluff, take Highway 36 east and drive 47 miles to the junction with Highway 89. Do not turn. Continue east on Highway 36 toward Lake Almanor and to Chester and Feather River Drive. Turn left (north) and drive 0.75 mile to Warner Valley Road (signed to Juniper Lake and Drakesbad). Turn left and drive six miles to Warner Valley Road. Turn right and drive 11 miles (on an improved dirt road) to the Warner Valley Campground and trailhead, on the right.

Contact: Lassen Volcanic National Park, P.O. Box 100, Mineral, CA 96063, 530/595-4444, www.nps.gov/lavo; Lassen National Forest, Hat Creek Ranger District, 43225 East Highway 299, Falls River Mills, CA 96028, 530/336-5521, www.fs.fed.us/r5—click on Forest Offices.

41 JUNIPER LAKE LOOP
7.5 mi / 4.0 hr   👣3 ⛰10

in Lassen Volcanic National Park north of Lake Almanor

The Juniper Lake Loop explores Lassen Volcanic National Park's least-known yet most beautiful backcountry. It features many lakes, many lookouts, and because there are pretty trail camps along the route, the chance to turn the trip into an overnighter. The adventure starts at the trailhead adjacent to the Juniper Lake Ranger Station, which requires a long bumpy ride out of Chester just to reach it. If you arrive late, a campground is available at the lake, at an elevation of 6,792 feet. At the north end of Juniper Lake, the trail heads straight north, and though it has plenty of ups and downs, along with a fairly level stretch through Cameron Meadow, it's mostly down, descending 800 feet to Snag Lake, at an elevation of 6,076 feet. The best advice is to turn south at Snag Lake and take the trail along Grassy Creek to Horseshoe Lake. This section is the prettiest of the hike.

On the second day, you'll skirt the south flank of Crater Butte (7,267 feet), head past Horseshoe Lake, and then continue on to the starting point. Alas, this trip is not flawless. The fishing is poor, mosquitoes are rampant in the early summer, and nights are very cold in the fall.

If you want to extend your trip, on the first day hike from Snag Lake out into the backcountry to Rainbow Lake; a mile later to Lower Twin Lake (6,537 feet); and another mile farther to Swan Lake (6,628 feet). Any of these can make for a good trail camp.

Note: From the north end of Juniper Lake, the 400-foot climb to Inspiration Point provides a lookout for the park's backcountry, but trees partially block the view. No campfires are permitted at Lassen Volcanic National Park. **User Groups:** Hikers and horses. No dogs or mountain bikes. No wheelchair facilities.

Permits: For overnight use, a wilderness permit (free) is required. A park entrance fee of $10, good for seven days, is charged for each vehicle.

Maps: Trail maps are available for a fee from park visitors stations and at Lassen Loomis Museum Association. For a topographic map, ask the USGS for Mount Harkness.

Directions: From Red Bluff, take Highway 36 east and drive 47 miles to the junction with Highway 89. Do not turn. Continue east on Highway 36 toward Lake Almanor and to Chester and Feather River Drive. Turn left on Feather River Drive and drive 0.75 mile to a Y. Bear right at the Y to Juniper Lake Road and drive 13 miles to the Snag Lake trailhead, near the ranger station. The access road is rough. Trailers and RVs are not recommended.

Contact: Lassen Volcanic National Park, P.O. Box 100, Mineral, CA 96063, 530/595-4444, www.nps.gov/lavo; Lassen Loomis Museum Association, P.O. Box 220, Mineral, CA 96063, 530/595-3399, www.lassenloomis.info.

42 HAY MEADOW TRAIL
6.0 mi / 2.0 days

on the southern boundary of the
Caribou Wilderness north of Lake Almanor

Hidden between South Caribou Peak and Black Cinder Rock is a little alpine pocket where dozens of small lakes are sprinkled about the southern Caribou Wilderness. It's a slice of paradise that some hikers call the Hidden Lakes. The trail out of Hay Meadow is a loop that crosses right through these lakes: Beauty, Long, Posey, and Evelyn.

After arriving at the trailhead at Hay Meadow, the trip starts easily enough, first crossing Hay Meadow. In another mile, you'll reach Beauty Lake, the first of the four lakes on this loop hike. They are all good for swimming, although a bit cold, and Beauty and Posey have the best trout fishing.

Although the trip can be made in a day, you likely won't feel like leaving, and planning an easy overnight backpacking trip is recommended. Another bonus of an overnight trip is that you can take the side trip up to Hidden Lakes, a series of several small but pretty waters, set just below South Caribou Mountain.

Note that although the Caribou Wilderness abuts Lassen Volcanic National Park, it's often overlooked in the big park's shadow. That's to your benefit, as long as you know about this trail. **User Groups:** Hikers, dogs, and horses (a horse corral is available at the trailhead). No mountain bikes. No wheelchair facilities.

Permits: A campfire permit (free) is required. Parking and access are free.

Maps: A trail map is available for a fee from the Almanor Ranger District. For a map, ask the U.S. Forest Service for Lassen National Forest or Caribou Wilderness. For a topographic map, ask the USGS for Red Cinder.

Directions: From Red Bluff, take Highway 36 east and drive 47 miles to the junction with Highway 89. Do not turn. Continue east on Highway 36 toward Lake Almanor and to

Chester. In Chester, continue east on Highway 36 for five miles to Forest Road 10. Turn north on Forest Road 10 and drive 9.5 miles to Forest Road 30N25. Turn left on Forest Road 30N25 and drive to the trailhead.

Contact: Lassen National Forest, Almanor Ranger District, P.O. Box 767, Chester, CA 96020, 530/258-2141, www.fs.fed.us/r5—click on Forest Offices.

43 SPENCER MEADOW TRAIL
10.0 mi / 1.0 day　　🏃3 ▲7

in Lassen National Forest just south of Lassen Volcanic National Park

Spencer Meadow is a pretty mountain meadow on the southern flank of Mount Conrad. Here explorers can discover an effervescent spring pouring forth, one source of Mill Creek and the creation of the headwaters of a Sacramento River tributary. Hiking access is easy; the trailhead is located at a parking area just off Highway 36.

Start the trip by taking the trail straight north toward Lassen on the Spencer Meadow Trail. Over the course of five miles, the trail passes a small spring (about halfway in, look for the faint spur trail on the left), then tiny Patricia Lake (on the right, hidden), and finally Spencer Meadow and Mill Creek Spring. Note that fishing at Mill Creek is restricted to catch-and-release and the use of artificials with single barbless hooks.

Special note: There is a trailhead closer to Spencer Meadow on Forest Road 29N40, but reaching it involves a long, rough drive.

User Groups: Hikers, dogs, horses, and mountain bikes. No wheelchair facilities.

Permits: No permits are required for day use. Campfire permits are required for overnight use. Parking and access are free.

Maps: A trail map is available for a fee from the Almanor Ranger District. For a map, ask the U.S. Forest Service for Lassen National Forest. For a topographic map, ask the USGS for Childs Meadows.

Directions: From Red Bluff, take Highway 36 east for 43 miles to Mineral, then continue east on Highway 36 for about seven miles to the trailhead parking area on the left.

Contact: Lassen National Forest, Almanor Ranger District, P.O. Box 767, Chester, CA 96020, 530/258-2141, www.fs.fed.us/r5—click on Forest Offices.

44 DOMINGO SPRINGS TO LASSEN VOLCANIC NATIONAL PARK (PCT)
11.0 mi one-way / 1.0 day　🏃2 ▲7

at the Domingo Springs Trailhead in Lassen National Forest west of Lake Almanor

From Domingo Springs, the Pacific Crest Trail runs straight north through Lassen National Forest. The Little North Fork of the North Fork Feather River is located 0.25 mile to the west and is a good side trip, both for swimming and for fishing for large brown trout. As you enter Lassen Volcanic National Park, you'll pass Little Willow Lake, and two miles later, you'll arrive at Boiling Springs Lake and the Warner Valley Campground. This is a good layover spot, and a side trip to Devils Kitchen is recommended.

To continue north on the PCT, see the *Lassen Volcanic National Park to Highway 44 (PCT)* hike in this chapter. If you are walking this trail in reverse, see the *Feather River to Humboldt Summit (PCT)* hike in this chapter to continue south.

User Groups: Hikers, dogs, and horses. No mountain bikes. No wheelchair facilities.

Permits: A campfire permit (free) is required. Parking and access are free.

Maps: For a map, ask the U.S. Forest Service for Lassen National Forest. For a topographic map, ask the USGS for Stover Mountain.

Directions: From Red Bluff, take Highway 36 east and drive 47 miles to the junction with Highway 89. Do not turn. Continue east on Highway 36 toward Lake Almanor and to Chester and Feather River Drive. Turn left (north) and drive 0.75 mile to Warner Valley Road (signed Juniper Lake and Drakesbad). Turn left and drive to Old Red Bluff Road (County Road 311) and go three miles to the parking area at Domingo Springs.

Contact: Lassen National Forest, Almanor Ranger District, P.O. Box 767, Chester, CA 96020, 530/258-2141, www.fs.fed.us/r5—click on Forest Offices.

45 McCLURE TRAIL
9.0 mi / 1.0 day 🚶2 ▲7

In the Tehama Wildlife Area east of Red Bluff

At first glance, the Tehama Wildlife Area might appear to be nothing more than rolling oak woodlands. But this is a habitat managed expressly for wildlife, and it includes a beautiful stream, abundant vegetation, and plenty of birds and animals.

This trail accesses the best of the wildlife area. From the McClure trailhead, hike down a steep canyon to Antelope Creek. The canyon is buffered by riparian vegetation. In late winter and spring, the canyon's adjoining hillsides come alive in green, and all wildlife seems to prosper. The stream is very pretty, and fishing is catch-and-release only with the use of artificials.

The area is huge, covering 44,862 acres, and is popular in the fall during hunting season for deer and wild pigs. Deer are rampant in late fall and migrate in after the hunting season is over. There are also lots of squirrels, hawks, and rattlesnakes. Low numbers of wild pigs roam the canyons but are never seen from trails. This area is also very popular with turkey hunters in season.

User Groups: Hikers and dogs. Mountain bikes and horses permitted but not recommended because of terrain. No wheelchair facilities.

Permits: A campfire permit (free) is required

for overnight use. Parking and access are free.

Maps: For a free map, contact the Tehama Wildlife Area at the address below. For a map, ask the U.S. Forest Service for Lassen National Forest. For a topographic map, ask the USGS for Dewitt Peak.

Directions: From Red Bluff, take Highway 36 east and drive 20 miles to Paynes Creek and Plum Creek Road. Turn right (south) on Plum Creek Road and go to Ishi Conservation Camp and continue about 2.5 miles south to High Trestle Road and follow it to Hogsback Road. Park across from the intersection of High Trestle and Hogsback Roads, and walk about 0.25 mile on the dirt road to the trailhead.

Access note: Access to the Tehama Wildlife Area is closed to the public from February to the first Saturday in April. Access is also restricted for a short period during deer season in late September. There are no closures on U.S. Forest Service trails.

Contact: Lassen National Forest, Almanor Ranger District, 900 East Highway 36, P.O. Box 767, Chester, CA 96020, 530/258-2141, www.fs.fed.us/r5—click on Forest Offices; Department of Fish and Game, Tehama Wildlife Area, P.O. Box 188, Paynes Creek, CA 96075, 530/597-2201; Department of Fish and Game, Region 1 Headquarters, 530/225-2300, www.dfg.ca.gov.

46 DEER CREEK TRAIL
1.0-8.0 mi / 1.0 day 🚶2 ▲9

In Lassen National Forest along Highway 32 west of Lake Almanor

BEST (

The Deer Creek Trail has all the ingredients to make it ideal for a trout angler, an explorer, or somebody just looking for a dunk on a hot day. The gorgeous stream runs right alongside the trail, with good access throughout and fish (often plenty of them) in the summer months.

From the parking area, look for the trail on the left side of the road. Start by hiking downstream. The trail is routed downstream along the river for about 10 miles. Rarely does anybody ever walk all the way to the end. Instead they take their time, perhaps fishing or swimming along the way.

In summer, Deer Creek is cold and clear, tumbling its way over rocks and into pools, with trout seemingly in every one. California Department of Fish and Game rules mandate catch-and-release fishing with artificials with a single barbless hook for most of the river. This trail has also become popular among mountain bikers. Most are courteous to hikers, and on a single-track trail, that's important. An interesting note is that the canyon rim is made up of a series of volcanic crags and basalt spires.

User Groups: Hikers, dogs, and horses. Mountain bikes aren't advised. No wheelchair facilities.

Permits: No permits are required. Parking and access are free.

Maps: A trail map is available for a fee from Almanor Ranger District. For a map, ask the U.S. Forest Service for Lassen National Forest. For a topographic map, ask the USGS for Onion Butte.

Directions: From Chico, take Highway 32 northeast for 40 miles (it becomes narrow and twisty). Just after crossing a small, red, metal bridge (locals call it the Red Bridge) that crosses Deer Creek, park on the right (south) side of the road, where there's a dirt pullout. The trailhead is just up from the bridge, on the left (north) side of the road.

Contact: Lassen National Forest, Almanor Ranger District, P.O. Box 767, Chester, CA 96020, 530/258-2141, www.fs.fed.us/r5—click on Forest Offices.

47 TABLE MOUNTAIN TRAIL
3.2 mi / 2.5 hr 🏃3 ⛰8

in the Ishi Wilderness east of Red Bluff

This trail may be short, but it's anything but sweet. Except, that is, from the top of Table Mountain, at 2,380 feet, where you're supplied with a sweeping view of the Sacramento Valley and the surrounding Land of Ishi. This is where Ishi, the last survivor of the Yahi Yana tribe, escaped from a band of white settlers who exterminated the rest of the Yahis. The Indians had lived here for 3,000 years before being killed off, another stellar moment in the history of the western frontier.

The trail starts from the northwest corner of the wilderness at the Table Mountain trailhead, and then goes 1.6 miles to the summit. It's very steep and challenging, and most hikers will be wheezing like worn-out donkeys before making the top. Because of the hot summers, it's absolutely critical either to start the trip very early in the morning or to time it so that it's done during cool weather. Bring plenty of water for your built-in radiator.

Special note: A wilderness trail map is strongly advised for those hiking in the Ishi Wilderness.

User Groups: Hikers, dogs, and horses. No mountain bikes. No wheelchair facilities.

Permits: A campfire permit is required for hikers planning to camp. Parking and access are free.

Maps: A trail map is available for a fee from Almanor Ranger District. For a map, ask the U.S. Forest Service for Lassen National Forest or Ishi Wilderness. For topographic maps, ask the USGS for Panther Spring and Butte Meadows.

Directions: From Red Bluff, take Highway 36 east and drive about 20 miles to Paynes Creek and then continue to Little Giant Mill Road. Turn right (south) on Little Giant Mill Road (Road 202) and drive about seven miles until you reach Ponderosa Way. Turn south at Ponderosa Way and drive about 10 miles

LASSEN HIKING

to Forest Road 28N57. Turn right (west) on Forest Road 28N57 and follow Peligreen Jeep Trail for six miles to the trailhead. The last five miles of road are suitable only for four-wheel-drive vehicles.

Contact: Lassen National Forest, Almanor Ranger District, P.O. Box 767, Chester, CA 96020, 530/258-2141, www.fs.fed.us/r5— click on Forest Offices.

48 RANCHERIA TRAIL
4.0 mi / 2.75 hr   🏃4 ⛰9

in the Ishi Wilderness east of Red Bluff

On a map, the Rancheria trailhead looks like the closest and easiest trailhead to reach into the Ishi Wilderness from Red Bluff. And the trail also appears short as well. But when you go there, a completely different picture comes into focus. First off, the trailhead access road is quite rough, impassable for most cars, and that's just a prelude to what lies ahead.

The trail starts by following an old jeep road, then leaves the road at a fence line off to the right. If it's hot, which is typical here most of the year, you'll already be reaching for your canteen. The trail then drops like a cannonball for 1,000 feet into the Mill Creek Canyon. This canyon is a surprising and awesome habitat with some of the prettiest areas of the Ishi Wilderness. The fishing is often good. Rules mandate catch-and-release with the use of artificials. Shadowing your trek and enjoyment of the Mill Creek Canyon is the knowledge that you have to climb back out of that canyon. To make it out before sunset, that climb will likely be during the hottest part of the day. By the time you reach the car, your butt will be thoroughly kicked.

Special note: A trail map is strongly advised for those hiking in the Ishi Wilderness.

User Groups: Hikers, dogs, and horses. No mountain bikes. No wheelchair facilities.

Permits: A campfire permit (free) is required for overnight use. Parking and access are free.

Maps: A trail map is available for a fee from Almanor Ranger District. For a map, ask the U.S. Forest Service for Lassen National Forest or Ishi Wilderness. For topographic maps, ask the USGS for Panther Spring and Butte Meadows.

Directions: From Red Bluff, take Highway 36 east and drive 20 miles to Paynes Creek and continue to Little Giant Mill Road. Turn right (south) on Little Giant Mill Road (Road 202) and drive seven miles to Ponderosa Way. Turn south and drive about 10 miles to Forest Road 28N57. Turn right (west) and follow the Peligreen Jeep Trail for two miles to the Rancheria trailhead. The last two miles of road are suitable only for four-wheel-drive vehicles.

Contact: Lassen National Forest, Almanor Ranger District, P.O. Box 767, Chester, CA 96020, 530/258-2141, www.fs.fed.us/r5— click on Forest Offices.

49 LOWER MILL CREEK
13.0 mi / 1.0 day   🏃2 ⛰9

in the Ishi Wilderness east of Red Bluff

If you have time for only one trail in the Ishi Wilderness, Mill Creek Trail is the one to pick. That goes whether you want to invest just an hour or a full day, because any length of trip can be a joy here. The trail parallels Mill Creek for 6.5 miles to its headwaters, at Papes Place, with magnificent scenery and many good fishing and swimming holes along the way. This is a dramatic canyon, and as you stand along the stream, the walls can seem to ascend into heaven. It's a land shaped by thousands of years of wind and water.

Directly across from the trailhead, on Ponderosa Way, is another trailhead, this one for a route that follows Upper Mill Creek into Lassen National Forest. Although not as spectacular as Lower Mill Creek, it provides a good option for hiking, fishing, and swimming. Note that fishing is restricted to catch-and-release and the use of artificials.

LASSEN HIKING

Special note: A trail map is strongly advised for those hiking in the Ishi Wilderness.

User Groups: Hikers, dogs, and horses. No mountain bikes. No wheelchair facilities.

Permits: A campfire permit (free) is required for overnight use. Parking and access are free.

Maps: A trail map is available for a fee from Almanor Ranger District. For a map, ask the U.S. Forest Service for Lassen National Forest or Ishi Wilderness. For topographic maps, ask the USGS for Panther Spring and Butte Meadows.

Directions: From Red Bluff, take Highway 36 east and drive 20 miles to Paynes Creek, and continue to Little Giant Mill Road. Turn right (south) on Little Giant Mill Road (Road 202) and drive seven miles to Ponderosa Way. Turn south at Ponderosa Way and drive about 17 miles to the Mill Creek trailhead. The access road is a slow go.

Contact: Lassen National Forest, Almanor Ranger District, P.O. Box 767, Chester, CA 96020, 530/258-2141, www.fs.fed.us/r5—click on Forest Offices.

50 MOAK TRAIL
14.0 mi / 1.5 days   👣2 ⛰7

In the Ishi Wilderness east of Red Bluff

Hit it right in the spring, and Moak Trail could be the best overnight hike in California's foothill country. Hit it wrong in the summer, and you'll wonder what you did to deserve such a terrible fate. In the spring, the foothill country is loaded with wildflowers and tall, fresh grass, and the views of the Sacramento Valley are spectacular. The trail includes a poke-and-probe section over a lava-rock boulder field, and there are good trail camps at Deep Hole (2,800 feet) and Drennan. It's an excellent weekend trip, including a loop route by linking Moak Trail with Buena Vista Trail, most of it easy walking. Alas, if you try this trip in the summer or fall, you'll need to have your gray

matter examined at Red Bluff General. No wildflowers, no shade, 100-degree temperatures, and as for water, you're dreamin'.

Special note: A trail map is strongly advised for those hiking in the Ishi Wilderness.

User Groups: Hikers, dogs, and horses. No mountain bikes. No wheelchair facilities.

Permits: A campfire permit (free) is required for overnight use. Parking and access are free.

Maps: A trail map is available for a fee from Almanor Ranger District. For a map, ask the U.S. Forest Service for Lassen National Forest or Ishi Wilderness. For topographic maps, ask the USGS for Panther Spring and Butte Meadows.

Directions: From Red Bluff, take Highway 36 east and drive 20 miles to Paynes Creek, and continue to Little Giant Mill Road. Turn right (south) on Little Giant Mill Road (Road 202) and drive seven miles to Ponderosa Way. Turn south at Ponderosa Way and drive about 24 miles to the Moak trailhead.

Contact: Lassen National Forest, Almanor Ranger District, P.O. Box 767, Chester, CA 96020, 530/258-2141, www.fs.fed.us/r5—click on Forest Offices.

51 DEER CREEK TRAIL
14.0 mi / 1.5 days   👣2 ⛰9

In the Ishi Wilderness east of Red Bluff

BEST (

It's no accident that Deer Creek Trail is the most popular hike in the Ishi Wilderness. Not only are hikers rewarded with striking surroundings, but the hike is a pleasurable romp even if you cut the trip short to just an hour or two. That's because the trail runs midway up naked slopes, offering spectacular views of Deer Creek Canyon's basaltic cliffs and spires, and of the stream below.

The trailhead is at the southeast border of the wilderness. Right from the start, it's routed along the north shore of Deer Creek. Iron Mountain (at 3,274 feet) is located to the immediate north. The trail continues along the stream into the wilderness interior. It skirts past the northern edge of what is called the Graham Pinery, a dense island of ponderosa pine growing on a mountain terrace. A bonus is good bird-watching for hawks, eagles, and falcons at the rock cliffs, and looking for a large variety of wildlife, including rattlesnakes (here's your warning) and lots of squirrels and quail. Note that the stream is stocked with rainbow and brook trout near Potato Patch and Alder Creek Campgrounds. Below Potato Patch Campground, fishing is catch-and-release only with the use of artificials.

Special note: A trail map is strongly advised for those hiking in the Ishi Wilderness.

User Groups: Hikers, dogs, and horses. No mountain bikes. No wheelchair facilities.

Permits: A campfire permit (free) is required for overnight use. Parking and access are free.

Maps: A trail map is available for a fee from Almanor Ranger District. For a map, ask the U.S. Forest Service for Lassen National Forest or Ishi Wilderness. For topographic maps, ask the USGS for Panther Spring and Butte Meadows.

Directions: From Red Bluff, take Highway 36 east and drive 20 miles to Paynes Creek, and continue to Little Giant Mill Road. Turn right (south) on Little Giant Mill Road (Road 202) and drive seven miles to Ponderosa Way. Turn south at Ponderosa Way and drive about 26 miles to the Deer Creek trailhead.

Contact: Lassen National Forest, Almanor Ranger District, P.O. Box 767, Chester, CA 96020, 530/258-2141, www.fs.fed.us/r5 — click on Forest Offices.

52 DEVILS DEN TRAIL

9.0 mi / 1.0 day   👥4 ⛰8

in the Ishi Wilderness east of Red Bluff

The Devils Den trailhead is less than 0.5 mile from the Deer Creek trailhead, but that is where the similarities between the two end. This trail includes a rough climb that's beastly in summer. Always bring a water filtration pump to fill your canteen at Deer Creek. The main attractions here are: 1) nobody else is usually around; 2) the trail is routed through a series of habitat zones over the course of the first 3.5 miles, providing a number of striking contrasts; and 3) nobody else is usually around. Getting the drift, eh?

The trail starts easy. It is routed along Deer Creek for the first mile. Note that fishing here is restricted to catch-and-release and the use of artificials. Enjoy yourself, because what follows is not exactly a picnic. The trail turns left and climbs up Little Pine Creek all the way to the ridge top, with the last mile on an old, hot, and chunky abandoned road. Along the way, the vegetation changes from riparian along the creek to woodland on the slopes, then chaparral on the ridge. The Deer Creek Rim is spiked by small volcanic spires and formations that, in some cases, look like they are from another planet. In addition, an island of conifers, the Graham Pinery, is available for viewing with a 0.25-mile side trip.

Special note: A trail map is strongly advised for those hiking in the Ishi Wilderness.

User Groups: Hikers, dogs, and horses. No mountain bikes. No wheelchair facilities.

Permits: A campfire permit (free) is required for overnight use. Parking and access are free.

Maps: A trail map is available for a fee from Almanor Ranger District. For a map, ask the U.S. Forest Service for Lassen National Forest or Ishi Wilderness. For topographic maps, ask the USGS for Panther Spring and Butte Meadows.

Directions: From Red Bluff, take Highway 36 east and drive about 20 miles to Paynes Creek and then continue to Little Giant Mill Road. Turn right (south) on Little Giant Mill Road (Road 202) and drive seven miles to Ponderosa Way. Turn south at Ponderosa Way and drive 32.5 miles to the Devils Den trailhead (just south of the Deer Creek trailhead).

Contact: Lassen National Forest, Almanor Ranger District, P.O. Box 767, Chester, CA 96020, 530/258-2141, www.fs.fed.us/r5—click on Forest Offices.

53 HUMBOLDT SUMMIT TO DOMINGO SPRINGS (PCT)

28.0 mi one-way / 2.0 days   🏃3   ⛰6

at Humboldt Summit in Lassen National Forest southwest of Lake Almanor

The idea of back-to-back 14-mile days to get through this chunk of trail may not appeal to many hikers, especially while carrying full-weight expedition packs. But that's standard for most hikers on this stretch of PCT, with little here to tarry for and with Lassen Volcanic National Park beckoning ahead. The trail starts just below Humboldt Peak, at 7,087 feet, and heads north along the ridgeline. For the most part, the trail is routed past Butt Mountain (7,866 feet) and down to Soldier Meadows. A spring and stream make this a delightful stop before crossing Highway 36, forging onward another three miles to the Stove Springs Campground. The trail then skirts around the western flank of North Stover Mountain and drops down to Domingo Springs, where another campground is available.

To continue north on the PCT, see the *Domingo Springs to Lassen Volcanic National Park (PCT)* hike in this chapter. If you are walking this trail in reverse, see the *Feather River to Humboldt Summit (PCT)* hike in this chapter to continue south.

User Groups: Hikers, dogs, and horses. No mountain bikes. No wheelchair facilities.

Permits: A campfire permit (free) is required. Parking and access are free.

Maps: For a map, ask the U.S. Forest Service for Lassen National Forest. For topographic maps, ask the USGS for Humboldt Peak and Stover Mountain.

Directions: From Red Bluff, take Highway 36 east and drive 47 miles to the junction with Highway 89. Turn south on Highway 89 and drive four miles to County Road 308 (Humboldt Road). Turn right and drive 15 miles to the trailhead parking area.

Contact: Lassen National Forest, Almanor Ranger District, P.O. Box 767, Chester, CA 96020, 530/258-2141, www.fs.fed.us/r5—click on Forest Offices.

54 FEATHER RIVER TO HUMBOLDT SUMMIT (PCT)

26.0 mi one-way / 2.0 days   🏃4   ⛰6

at the Belden Trailhead on Highway 70 in Plumas National Forest

The trail is not only rough from Belden to Humboldt Summit, it's not particularly pretty either, especially compared to the nearby wilderness. The climb is a mighty dry slice of rattlesnake country. From the North Fork Feather River at Belden (elevation 2,310 feet), the PCT climbs 4,777 feet over the course of this two-day thumper to Humboldt Summit, at 7,087 feet. There are no lakes along this trail, only a few small water holes requiring short side trips. Instead, the prettiest sections are along streams, the first being Chips Creek, which runs adjacent to the trail for eight miles. Then later, there's a short crossing over the headwaters of Willow Creek. Some might prefer to take three days instead of two to hike this section, but with the stunning Lassen Volcanic National Park looming ahead, most hikers are willing to put in long days to get through this area.

To continue north on the PCT, see the *Humboldt Summit to Domingo Springs (PCT)* hike in this chapter. If you are walking this trail in reverse, see the *Bucks Summit to Feather River (PCT)* hike, in *Moon California Camping*, to continue south.

User Groups: Hikers, dogs, and horses. No mountain bikes. No wheelchair facilities.

Permits: A campfire permit (free) is required. Parking and access are free.

Maps: For a map, ask the U.S. Forest Service for Plumas National Forest. For topographic maps, ask the USGS for Belden and Humboldt Peak.

Directions: From Quincy, drive west on Highway 70 about 26 miles to the trailhead, at the roadside rest area at Belden.

Contact: Plumas National Forest, Mount Hough Ranger District, 39696 State Highway 70, Quincy, CA 95971, 530/283-0555, fax 530/283-1821, www.fs.fed.us/r5—click on Forest Offices.

55 BIZZ JOHNSON
1.0-25.0 mi one-way / 0.5 hour-3.0 days

west of Susanville

In the 1960s, when Shasta legend John Reginato heard that Southern Pacific was going to abandon a rail line between Westwood and Susanville, he urged that it be converted to a hiking trail. It took many years, but the idea eventually struck home, and the Bureau of Land Management worked with the U.S. Forest Service to develop and refine it.

The Bizz Johnson Trail can be ideal for day trips, with trailhead access spaced five to seven miles apart. People can hike or bike different portions of the trail. You don't have to complete the entire route, of course. The seven-mile stretch west of Susanville is the most popular stretch of the 25-mile route.

The trailhead is at 4,200 feet, and the high point of the route is at 5,600 feet at Westwood Junction. The trail traces the old Fernley and Lassen railroad line, a branch line of the South Pacific Railroad. It is routed in the Susan River Canyon along the Susan River for 15 miles, then from the Susanville Railroad Depot to the Mason Station trailhead five miles north of Westwood. The surface is a mixture of compacted dirt and small gravel. The trail features beautiful views in many areas and passes through two old railroad tunnels and 11 old railroad bridges. You won't cross any developed areas.

In the winter, it makes a great trip on cross-country skis or on a snowmobile (snowmobiling is allowed on the western half of the trail, from Mason Station to just beyond Westwood Junction).

The one negative: Like most rails-to-trails projects, it's way too wide.

The future: The trail could eventually be extended all the way to Alturas for a distance of 100 miles. That would be a premier bike trip.

User Groups: Hikers, dogs (must be leashed near Susanville), horses, and mountain bikes. Wheelchair-accessible from Susanville and Hobo Camp trailhead.

Permits: No permits are required. Parking and access are free.

Maps: For a free brochure, contact the Bureau of Land Management at the address below. For a map, ask the U.S. Forest Service for Lassen National Forest. For topographic maps, ask the USGS for Westwood East, Fredonyer Pass, and Susanville.

Directions: From Susanville, take Highway 36 to Weatherlow Street. Turn on Weatherlow (it becomes Richmond Road) and drive 0.5 mile to the Susanville Depot Visitor Center (open May–early October) and the trailhead, on the right.

Alternate trailhead: From Westwood, take Highway 36 to County Road A21. Turn north and drive three miles to a signed trailhead access road (dirt). Turn right and drive 0.4 mile to the trailhead, on the left.

Contact: Susanville Depot Visitor Center, 530/257-3252; Lassen National Forest, Eagle Lake Ranger District, 477-050 Eagle Lake Road, Susanville, CA 96130, 530/257-4188, www.fs.fed.us/r5—click on Forest Offices; Bureau of Land Management, Eagle Lake Field Office, 2950 Riverside Drive, Susanville, CA 96130, 530/257-0456, www.ca.blm .gov—click on Field Offices.

Index

Lassen Camping

Shasta Hiking

Lassen Hiking

A–D

K–N

O–Z

E–J